Policy and Politics in Sport, Physical Education and Leisure

Edited by

Scott Fleming

Margaret Talbot

Alan Tomlinson

First published in 1995 by
Leisure Studies Association

A catalogue record for this book
is available from the British Library.

ISBN: 0 906337 66 6

Layout design and typesetting by Myrene L. McFee
Reproduction by University of Brighton
Binding by Kensett Ltd., Hove

Contents

Policy and Politics in Sport, Physical Education and Leisure: Themes and Issues

In the 1980s and the 1990s the interconnections between sport, physical education and leisure became increasingly prominent and important in the professional and educational worlds. This has been in part due to the active involvement of academics and researchers in policy-making, and to the willingness of policy-makers and providers to draw upon the findings of researchers and to engage in open debate concerning the integrated development of policy across these different spheres. The growth and expansion of academic courses in physical education, the sport sciences and leisure studies have also contributed to this professional cross-fertilization. Where once students on particular degree-programmes proceeded through their studies in a tightly-knit group, with few study options (cultivating a rather cocooned group culture), students of all of these multi-disciplinary fields now mingle in modular schemes and programmes of study. Future professionals in sport, physical education and leisure now have the opportunity to study contextual, professional, managerial, developmental and policy issues alongside each other. This is to be welcomed, challenging as it is for previously over-specialised professionals and providers. Working together can also combat professional or vocational territorialism: knowledge of the National Curriculum in Physical Education can be shown to be relevant for the future sports development officer; familiarity with the implications of Compulsory Competitive Tendering for public sector leisure provision can be useful for university sport and physical education directors.

The involvement of academics in the policy-making process of key agencies has contributed to this reframing of professional boundaries or, as Murdoch (1993) has put it, to the "collapsing boundaries" necessary for the reformulation of the fields. In turn, professionals in other sectors, such as schools and political and administrative agencies, have demonstrated a refreshing flexibility in working through these issues. Talbot (1993) has shown, for instance, how the views of Ian Beer, the Head Teacher of Harrow public school, were affected by genuinely open debate on the nature of physical education and sport during the process of the making of the National Curriculum. In the same piece she also noted how understanding of the professional recreation management/sports policy context was gained by and proved beneficial to the academics involved in that process.

The notion of an integrated professional approach to physical education, sport and related leisure forms is far from new. The founder of the Chelsea College of Physical Education (now the Chelsea School in the Faculty of Education, Sport and Leisure, The University of Brighton) had such a vision. Dorette Wilkie, in a lecture delivered in 1900, offered her version of mind-body-feelings harmony in the developed physical educationist: the latter should have "a body as hard as steel" to "help bear up against our many difficulties"; "a mind as clear as crystal, to see and understand all that is good and noble and beautiful in the world, and also to distinguish the true from the false"; and, finally, "a heart as warm as sunshine, so that we may feel and sympathise with the ways and troubles of our fellow creatures" (Webb, 1977: p. 57). One of Miss Wilkie's successors, Audrey Bambra, proposed that the female physical educator should be trained in twelve aspects of the professional role: organiser; performer; coach; leader; observer; assessor; recorder; educator; missionary; student; author; teacher (Webb, 1977: p. 332). Many sport and leisure development job remits in the last decade and a half of the twentieth century aspired to such breadth and scope. Early professionals in the field aimed to provide all-round professionals (they would not have called them *generic professionals with transferable skills*, but in the argot of the contemporary educational industry, that is what they were). It is interesting to note that such visions emanated from the educational rather than from other professional spheres. Almost a century later, developmental policies for integrated provision have, similarly, been promoted by physical educationists.

Such comprehensive visions have been less noticeably expressed by professional politicians. Political manifestos for sport during the 1990s have shared some of the naivete of the *fin de siècle* progressive idealists, but with none of their well-roundedness. During the ill-fated "Back to Basics" drive of the Conservative Prime Minister John Major, Sports Minister Iain Sproat led the way in his Party's crusade for traditional (and mostly male) sporting values. The philosophy of sport of this administration was spelled out in an address to the Sportswriters' Association:

> When I talk about sport in schools I do not mean step aerobics, going for country walks and listening to lessons on the history of diets. These are all right in their way but they are not what I want. I want team games properly organized — competitive team games, preferably those sports we invented, such as soccer, rugby, hockey, cricket and netball. (quoted in *The Guardian*, 28 January 1994, cited in Holt and Tomlinson, 1994: p. 452).

Missing from this appeal to tradition was any rationale for the *value* of such team sports , whose worth is simply taken-for-granted. Britain's first-ever sports minister — with a pithily simple remit from Labour Prime Minister Harold Wilson in 1964: "I would like you to go to Education and look after schools and sport. You will be the first Minister for Sport, it will be very exciting" (Howell, 1990: p. 141) — was Denis Howell. A quarter of a century on, Howell commented on the value of team games:

> I know of no better way for youngsters to relate to each other in a happy situation than through playing games together. The need to win well and with generosity and to lose gracefully are among the most important attributes in life. (Howell, 1990: p. 377).

Howell echoed here the pedagogic values of participatory sport, his views having much in common with the claimed values of sport in the athleticist initiatives of the nineteenth-century public schools (Mangan, 1981). He also commented with sadness on the contract culture of the 1980s that had undermined the input of teachers to school sport, and fostered the selling by local education authorities of invaluable playing fields.

Clearly, then, the nature of physical education and school sport, and the connections between schooling and the wider sports culture, have been on the British political agenda for some considerable time — although at very different levels of visibility and public profile over the last 25 years. Political capital can also be gained from the promotion of leisure policies and initiatives. When the Department of National Heritage was established in 1992, in part a reward for David Mellor's prominent role in the Conservative Party's against-the-odds victory, it brought together the cultural spheres of arts, broadcasting, museums/galleries, sports and tourism — so that, as Peter Brooke, Mellor's successor, put it, "'we can all take full advantage of being part of the same family'" (Holt and Tomlinson, 1994: p. 446). From Brooke's political perspective, leisure had importance as the sphere of social life in which individual access to heritage, culture and sport could be extended, thus enhancing quality of life; and because of "'the importance of our fields of interest to economic regeneration'" (Brooke, 1993). Sport, physical education and leisure have been promoted as explicitly political initiatives, and the policy processes that have facilitated or blocked their development are worthy of close analytical scrutiny. How the professionalization of sport, physical education and leisure has impinged upon employment markets and specific sites of leisure consumption is also worthy of focused consideration, vital as such impacts are to the implementation or realisation of broader policy initiatives.

The application of frameworks for policy analysis, and the critical analysis of policy processes and texts, in the study of sport, physical education and leisure are not so well-established as more generalised analyses of the politics of public sector policy and provision for sport and recreation. In the latter area, studies by Coalter *et al.* (1986) and, with a broad historical sweep, by Henry (1993) have provided applications of critical policy perspectives from the highly influential work of the likes of

Dunleavy. More specific forms of policy analysis have been produced in the careful scholarship of Houlihan, on topics such as sports crowds (1990) and school sport (1992). In this work, Houlihan has provided careful analysis of particular aspects of the policy process, giving attention, for instance, to the nature of policy communities. There has been less attention in the leisure studies and related literature to the various stages of the policy process that have been identified in traditional frameworks for policy analysis.

Hogwood and Gunn (1984: p. 4) "analyse the policy process in terms of a number of stages through which an issue may pass". They identify nine such stages. The first is issue-search or agenda-setting, what they call *deciding to decide*. The second is issue filtration, *deciding how to decide*. These two stages are followed by *issue definition*. The middle three stages are preparatory: *forecasting*; *setting objectives and priorities;* and *options analysis*. The final three stages are concerned with the implementation of policy and the understanding of its effects. Policy implementation involves *monitoring and control*; *evaluation and review* is the penultimate stage; and the final stage involves *policy maintenance, succession, or termination*. Each of these stages — or indeed the absence of them and the reasons for such an absence in particular cases — could be the focus for detailed scrutiny and investigation by researchers. And of course we know that the policy process is usually messier than such a rational-sounding list of stages tends to imply, compromised and muddied as such a process is by the dynamics of power and the machinations of organisational actors. But a list such as Hogwood and Gunn's is a useful reminder of what a full or ideal process would be, and it can help sharpen the analyst's understanding of the realities and shortcomings of the policy process in detailed individual cases. In a work first published in 1922, two years after his death, Max Weber (1967) listed the ideal-typical characteristics of the bureaucracy in the same essay in which he commented upon the paradoxes of rationality: "bureaucratic organization", he commented, has advanced due to "its purely technical superiority over any other form of organization..." (p. 214), yet "bureaucratic administration always tends to be an administration of 'secret sessions': in so far as it can, it hides its knowledge and action from criticism" (Weber, 1967: p. 233). Similarly, a recognition of the pertinence of the Hogwood and Gunn framework or "stage classification" is no automatic refusal to recognise the contradictions and conflicts within the policy process. In this book, studies of different aspects of policy — governmental policy, local authority policy, professional bodies' policies, quangos' policies, agency and organisational policies — are analysed and reviewed in a critical and reflective light. The book has not been organised as a tribute to the perspicacity and all-embracing relevance of Hogwood and Gunn; far from it, for their title could be seen as being seriously misleading, in that much of their discussion comprises a reminder of the importance of stages of policy in some ideal world, rather than detached analysis of the real world. Nevertheless, as they themselves point out, it is interesting to consider why policy typically does not pass seamlessly though the stages in their list: many of the case-studies in this book identify flaws in the idealised policy process, and contradictions in the processes and dynamics at the heart of the particular policy stage.

The contributions to this volume were initially presented at the Annual Conference of the Leisure Studies Association in September 1995. Entitled *Leisure, Sport and Education — the Interfaces*, the conference was hosted by the Chelsea School Research Centre, Faculty of Education, Sport and Leisure, University of Brighton. It was designed "to explore the connections between leisure, sport and education, in the rhetoric of their development, and the professional and policy contexts through which they are promoted" (Tomlinson, 1995: p.1). The contributions have been reviewed and edited into this and two further volumes — ***Leisure Cultures: Values, Genders, Lifestyles*** edited by Graham McFee, Wilf Murphy and Garry Whannel; and ***Professional and Development Issues in Leisure, Sport and Education*** edited by Lesley Lawrence, Elizabeth Murdoch and Stan Parker.

In ***Policy and Politics in Sport, Physical Education and Leisure***, the chapters have been organised into four sections concerned with the following themes: *Policy Evaluation in Physical Education and Sport; The Politics of Participation and Provision— Target Groups; Policy Challenges—Sport Spaces and Sites of Consumption*; and *The Politics of Professionalism—Courses and Careers.*

In the first section of the book there are six chapters which examine critically different aspects of policy in the spheres of physical education and the curriculum, and local and national sports policy. **Margaret Talbot** subjects 'The Politics of Sport and Physical Education' to a wide-ranging critical overview, moving from the particularities of the British Government's sport policy (as expressed in the Department of National Heritage's policy statement, *Sport: Raising the Game*), to a comparison of the national sports systems of the United Kingdom and Canada. She provides a timely reminder to the constituencies of sport, physical education and leisure that professional debates, developments and discourses however implicit or explicit (often, around gender) are inextricably woven into the politics of policymaking: and that "the shared task for researchers, policy makers and practitioners is not to ignore dominant ideologies, but to put them into perspective and to understand how they are formed, shaped and maintained" (p. 21). **Sue Campbell**, formerly Chief Executive of the National Coaching Foundation before becoming Chief Executive of the Youth Sport Trust, reflects upon the accomplishments and continuing challenges of initiatives in coach education and development. She suggests that progress in coaching development could "move so much faster if policy and practice were more closely aligned" (p. 31), and if policymakers and researchers appreciated that "it takes people to turn the words into effective practice" (*ibid.*). Evans and Brennan write in complementary ways on the place— or marginality — of dance in the policy implementation process. **Graeme Evans** reviews the place of dance in education, concluding that dance is becoming available only on an increasingly selective basis, and that "dance equity, most notably for boys, young men and the physically least confident", will be "the loser in the long run" (p. 50). **Deirdre Brennan**'s chapter centres on a study of newly trained physical education specialists, and their attitudes towards the establishment of dance as compulsory within Northern Ireland's National Curriculum for Physical Education, observing that all her respondents recognised and supported the educative value of dance for both boys and girls, but that "it should come as no surprise that dance has not been welcomed in male PE circles" (p. 67).

Ian McDonald reviews the policy ideal of "sport for all" in the light of the realities of sports development in the local authority context in London. He asserts that the policy framework for sport which emerged in 1994-95 was as "significant as the formation of the executive GB Sports Council in 1972" (p. 72), and that this political agenda "fetters rather than facilitates the opportunities for all sections of the population to participate" (p. 90). **Udo Merkel** reports on the politics of sport and leisure in 1990s Germany, covering sport's importance as an expression of nation-building, and as a reflection of post-Cold War integration; and the place of the voluntary sector in the German sports system. He argues that the German government in the future should provide "a positive climate for the voluntary sector to survive the increasing commercialisation of and individualisation in sport and leisure" (p. 106). **Tan Ying** and **Ken Roberts** analyse contemporary sports policy in the People's Republic of China, in the light of startling levels of success at world level by elite Chinese athletes in the 1990s. The successes are interpreted positively, with the Olympic Strategy achieving wide impact, increasing mass participation and "boosting Chinese confidence" (p. 124). But imbalances are also identified: "Talented athletes will certainly become dollar millionaires. Commercialism may lead to more drug abuse and bribery" (p. 124).

The second section of the book includes seven chapters. **Peter Green** reports on a study of the active elderly in Hove, probing the reasons why those at whom provision is aimed often do not benefit. He proposes that policymakers in this sphere should acknowledge "the need for self-determination and empowerment among the elderly in choosing what they want to do and feel comfortable with" (p. 141).

A similar theme is considered in **John Handley**'s in-progress study of the setting-up of a sports and leisure club for people with learning disabilities. He shows that the aim of the initiative (to empower members) was undermined by organisational and staffing constraints and deficiencies: steering group members could create disharmony; leadership and coordination was limited in its aspirations; and volunteers, lacking "appropriate training and support ... were not equipped with the knowledge or skills that would enable them to facilitate the empowerment of disabled club members" (p. 155).

John Horne's comprehensive survey of local authority leisure policies in Scotland concentrates on their targeting of black and ethnic minority groups. He reminds providers that to deny that there is a significant problem is sometimes to allow the problem to grow: "without proactive monitoring and research ... the situation will not get any better" (p. 172). **Melanie Limb**, **Hugh Matthews**, **Peter Vujakovic** and **Martin Phillips** report qualitative data on the experience of the countryside of two groups of Northampton wheelchair users. Their conclusion is a reminder that too many experts claim to speak for particular target-groups but listen too little to the voices of the members of those groups: "there is a need for the symbol for wheelchair access to become more than a salve for the conscience of the able-bodied community" (p. 194).

The final three chapters in this section are concerned with the potential contribution of sport and leisure to the rehabilitative process for offenders, and the contribution of the probation service to such initiatives. **Fiona McCormack** comments upon a phase in the recurrent calls for the promotion of leisure provision and recreational opportunity as a way of generating alternatives to youth crime. Her chapter concentrates upon provider and management issues within these debates, and calls for attempts "to overcome society's long established attitude that leisure and recreation are rewards" (p. 209). **Geoff Nichols** reports on interim results from the evaluation of a project in West Yorkshire which offered a programme of sports opportunities to offenders on probation. He proposes a methodology for measuring the effects of participation in the project, in particular in terms of changes in self-identity: "The central concept in the understanding of the impact of the project ... has been the way in which a participant can be helped to change ... behaviour through adopting a revised self-identity" (p. 221). **Alex Twitchen**, in the final chapter in the section, documents the persisting belief in some influential circles in the character building potential of sport. Citing Foucault and other work on the sociology of the body, he warns against too optimistic a reading of sport's potential for, *on its own*, dealing with the problems of people on probation. He argues that the "development of a more disciplinary society in which the technologies of surveillance are sophisticated and highly developed" (p. 232) could well be facilitated by certain uses of sport in the rehabilitation of offenders.

The worthiness of models of leisure policy and provision is sometimes best illustrated in the peripheral role of such models in the leisure industry and in forms of leisure provision rooted in the private sector and the marketplace. But there is a place for policy-led interventions and politically-motivated involvement in such spheres. In the third section of the book, policy challenges thrown up in debates about sport, space and consumption are identified. **Simon Hudson** reflects upon some of the ambiguities of the "greening" of ski resorts. Emphasising the case-study of

Verbier in Switzerland, he concludes that there is still much consciousness-raising to be done within both ski resorts and the skiing public, particularly on the recognition of the urgent necessity for sustainable development: but "pioneers of the first 'green ski resort' will become model examples of how to marry economics, recreation and the environment" (p. 253). **David Hudson** and **Robert J. Boewadt** provide a marketing perspective on the factors that have influenced and are likely to continue to influence the place of soccer in the United States of America. Concentrating upon the planned introduction of Major League Soccer in April 1996, they note that "cultural, competitive and promotional barriers must be overcome if the game, on the professional level, is to be embraced by American sports fans and media sponsors" (p. 271). Their analysis suggests that pure market forces alone will not sustain a high level of impact of soccer. Policies are needed in certain areas to consolidate its impact, and to sustain such impact regardless of crude market forces. **Alistair Loadman** provides a case-study of the contestations and conflicts which have arisen in the debates and disputes over the relocation of the local professional football club in Southampton. The contested meanings of landuse and of any reorganisation of the urban landscape must, Loadman shows, be recognised in any decision-making process: "The defining features of *community* activities are that they spring from, and actively engage, people within that community, and this entails empowering local people to make decisions about what forms of sport will take place and how those activities will be administered" (p. 281). Loadman's study is a reminder of the importance of the politics of popular struggle in the policy-making process.

In the final section of the book six contributions address a variety of concerns and issues on the subjects of sport curricula in Higher Education/pre-vocational training, leisure education, and employment markets. In the focus upon *courses and careers* that emerges in these case-studies and preliminary reports, the institutional and organisational politics of professionalism become explicit. **Mike Lowe**'s paper reviews the anomalies in and ambiguities of available statistics on employment in the leisure industry, pointing out that no detailed or reliable study of employment in leisure has ever been undertaken. "Given the complexity in defining a leisure industry", he states, "a totally accurate picture of employment is highly improbable" (p. 294). He calls, nevertheless, for the Department of National Heritage, as "coordinator of the industry", to provide both a definition and a detailed analysis of the industry. **Dan Morgan**'s report upon an "initial investigation" into the nature of the employment of "educated personnel" in the leisure industry offers some tentative conclusions from a review of weekly job advertisements in the Institute of Leisure and Amenity Management's advertisements service: "It is becoming more imperative that graduates have some level of experience within the industry" (p. 311). **Sharon Todd** raises educational and industry issues concerning work experience on leisure and recreation degree courses in an evaluation of practice and student/graduate experience at Brunel University College.

Drawing upon a survey of both graduates and work placement employers, she shows "the importance of networking — 43% used contacts from work placement or personal contacts to find employment" (p. 321). **Chris Wolsey** presents preliminary findings from interviews with academics and practitioners which were undertaken for a Master's study. In terms of academia and the workworld of leisure, Wolsey calls for a "symbiotic, not mutually exclusive" relationship: "Educational excellence should not be viewed as a battle between academic rigour and vocational relevance ... Theory should inform practice and vice-versa, on a dynamic basis" (p. 345). **Hugh Mannerings**' contribution is a working paper exploring some effects of the over-production of leisure studies graduates. Based on questionnaires administered to Buckinghamshire College Leisure Management students (1993 and 1994), it shows that student "perceptions of the interface between Higher Education and employment in the leisure industry" (p. 354) emphasised a widely-felt lack of work experience. **Clare Brindley** draws upon a case-study of the development of leisure-related courses in Manchester Metropolitan University, arguing that suspicious, territorial defensiveness between academic/University sport and leisure departments and management departments should be opposed: the *Suits* of the business/management departments and the *Jocks* of the sport/leisure departments are urged to work together to strengthen the framework of leisure studies: "Leisure's valuable contribution to higher education must not be eroded by internal squabbles ... teamwork and cooperation is required to make the area of leisure a powerful discipline" (p. 363).

The volume comprises a mix of working-papers, preliminary reports, case-studies, full research reports and overviews. The balance between evidence and theory, between description and analysis, varies widely across the twenty-three contributions to the book. In some respects this embodies the theory-practice challenges of sport, physical education and leisure studies as, simultaneously, multi-disciplinary, academically robust, applied scientific, and vocationally and policy-orientated areas of study and work. Taken as whole, the volume is a clear indication that sport, physical education and leisure will only be partially understood, evaluated and developed without an informed grasp of the varied policy and political contexts in which they are situated.

Scott Fleming *(Cardiff Institute of Higher Education)*
Margaret Talbot *(Leeds Metropolitan University)*
Alan Tomlinson *(University of Brighton)*

November 1995

References

Brooke, P. (1993) London Seminar of DNH (Department of National Heritage), 18 June.

Coalter, F., Long, J. and Duffield, B. (1986) *Rationale for public sector investment in leisure.* London: The Sports Council and the Economic and Social Research Council.

Henry, I. (1993) *The politics of leisure policy.* London: Macmillan.

Hogwood, B. W. and Gunn, L. A. (1984) *Policy analysis for the real world.* Oxford: Oxford University Press.

Holt, R. and Tomlinson, A. (1994) 'Sport and leisure', in D. Kavanagh and A. Seldon (eds) *The Major effect.* London: Macmillan, pp. 444-458.

Houlihan, B. (1990) 'The politics of sports policy in Britain: The examples of football hooliganism and drug abuse', in A. Tomlinson (ed) *Sport in society: Policy, politics and culture.* LSA Publication No. 43. Eastbourne: Leisure Studies Association, pp. 27-49.

Houlihan, B. (1992) 'The politics of school sport', in J. Sugden and C. Knox (eds) *Leisure in the 1990s: Rolling back the welfare state.* LSA Publication No. 46. Eastbourne: Leisure Studies Association, pp. 59-79.

Howell, D. (1990) *Made in Birmingham: The memoirs of Denis Howell.* London: Queen Anne Press, a division of Macdonald & Co. (Publishers) Ltd.

Mangan, J.A. (1981) *Athleticism in the Victorian and Edwardian public school: The emergence and consolidation of an educational ideology.* Cambridge: Cambridge University Press.

Murdoch, E. (1993) 'Education, sport and leisure: Collapsing boundaries?', in G. McFee and A. Tomlinson (eds) *Education, sport and leisure: Connections and controversies.* Eastbourne: University of Brighton [Chelsea School Research Centre Topic Report 3], pp. 65-72.

Talbot, M. (1993) 'Physical education and the national curriculum: Some political issues', in G. McFee and A. Tomlinson (eds) *Education, sport and leisure: Connections and controversies.* Eastbourne: University of Brighton [Chelsea School Research Centre Topic Report 3], pp. 34-64.

Tomlinson, A. (1995) 'Introduction', *Delegate Booklet, Leisure Studies Association Annual Conference on 'Leisure, Sport and Education — the Interfaces'*, September, p. 1.

Webb, I. (1977) *The History of Chelsea College of Physical Education with special reference to curriculum development, 1898–1973.* Submitted for degree of DPhil, University of Leicester, May/December.

Weber, M. (1967) *From Max Weber: Essays in sociology* [Translated, edited and with an introduction by H.H. Gerth and C. Wright Mills], Sixth Impression. London, Routledge and Kegan Paul, Chapter VIII.

I

Policy Evaluation in Physical Education and Sport

The Politics of Sport and Physical Education

Margaret Talbot

Leeds Metropolitan University

Over the last decade, the role and position of the government in sport and physical education have changed dramatically, following the trend towards centralisation of power and rationalisation of administration earlier argued by Bilton *et al.* (1983):

> The state comes to be the only legitimate authority...; and its administration increasingly operates on set principles and procedures. The trend to rational administration by officials culminates in bureaucracy .... (Bilton *et al.*, 1983: p. 176)

In the UK, there has been a distinct shift away from the position in the 1960s that sport and physical education were a matter of individual choice and therefore not a proper area for government involvement: "God preserve us from a Ministry of Sport" was one newspaper headline, and all three major political parties maintained the same "hands-off" relationship. As I shall try to illustrate, there has been a trend towards more direct government influence, achieved through various kinds of leverage, on both physical education and sport. John Major's personal interest in sport, and his particular conceptions of it, shared by several members of the Cabinet, have had significant effects on the profile and visibility of sports and physical education policy:

> ... note how many decisions of this kind have reflected the values, whims, even prejudices, of successive prime ministers, secretaries of state, junior ministers and their political advisers. We now even have the imposition of compulsory games for the 14s-16s at the behest of a Prime Minister who happens to be a sporting enthusiast and a Chelsea supporter! (Kelly, 1994: p. 143)

Despite this, the myth of the apolitical nature of sport and physical education remains, with many of their representatives choosing to ignore or deny political process or influence, even proclaiming the apolitical nature of sport or education as a defining characteristic and a moral code. Yet many of these representatives have themselves played an important part in locating physical education and sport in the political sphere.

The results, whether intended or unintended, both of government-led ideology and decisions, and of the efforts of those in physical education and sport to secure more state resources, or to protect existing allocations, are that the basis and infrastructure of sport and physical education have markedly changed. I shall argue that in many cases those still trying to influence events appear unaware of, or choose to ignore those changes; and indeed, that leaders of some sport and physical education organisations, and agents of government themselves, frequently fail to understand the implications and the opportunities of these changes and innovations.

A current example is the Minister for Sport's decision to abolish Regional Councils for Sport and Recreation, and to cut the relationships between their proposed replacements, the Regional Sports Fora and the regional offices of the Sports Council. Arguably, the Regional Councils were a very cost-effective way (for the Sports Council at least) of accessing expertise and knowledge, and of ensuring community support for Council strategy. But the Minister's perception appeared to be that Regional Councils for Sport and Recreation, dominated by local authorities, actually diverted or corrupted the implementation of Sports Council national strategy in the regions. He was unaware, as were apparently his senior civil servants, that the regional strategies were constitutionally developed and owned by the Regional Councils — not the Sports Council — notwithstanding that they were often without doubt led by Sports Council strategy and policy. This means that in the current consultation exercise, the Minister is holding to his decision, while the members of the various regional councils are trying to second-guess the extent to which they can retain the best aspects of the old regional councils, in setting the parameters of the proposed regional fora. There is little evidence that either the staff of the Sports Council (regional or national) or the members of the regional councils have decided to use the situation to establish new power structures or relationships between the Sports Council and its partners. The Sports Council's own consultation document (Sports Council, 1995) reflects the intention, as far as possible, to maintain the status quo: indeed, the proposed membership of the regional fora reflects more the systems of provision of a decade ago, and certainly does not reflect the changes in either local government or higher and further education which have so fundamentally altered sports provision and patronage. This is a point to which I shall return later.

Sport and education (including physical education) have long claimed political neutrality and denied or ignored the influence of power. Even when the contexts in which they operate have demonstrably become inextricably linked with government policy, there remains disingenuous denial of the role of politics in sport and physical education. This disingenuousness extends further, to become the basis of a dichotomy — the expectation that government finance will be provided for investment and support, while maintaining the assumption that there is no accountability for this funding; that there should be no state interference in the affairs of sport and physical education; and that funding will be allocated or continue merely because sport and physical education are self-evidently "good" for society. Government disingenuousness similarly leads to a dichotomy, for example, where there is expectation that systems will fulfil new roles and duties, or respond to fundamental change, without the additional resources required. The Policy Statement on Sport (Department for National Heritage, 1995) is an example: it provides sport and physical education with leverage, but little real additional currency.

The meanings and uses of the term "politics" can contribute to the understanding of the way prevailing views are maintained or challenged, decisions are made, resources allocated, and structures changed as a result of ideological belief or rhetoric. The title of Harold Lasswell's book, *Politics: Who Gets What, When, How?*, is perhaps the most concise definition, but it does not illuminate the processes which are so crucial to those outcomes.

I am adopting the general position that "politics" can be present in all social interactions and relationships, in accepting the essential definition of politics as the *exercise of power* (Worsley, 1964), a central tenet of both Marxist and feminist theory and praxis (Stanley, 1991). Such a concept of politics broadens the definition beyond what politicians do, to include the *exercise of control, constraint and coercion*; at the same time, it does not deny the possibility of *agency*, the capacity of individuals or groups to influence events.

It is not unusual for members of professions or interest groups to deny that power structures have any influence on their lives, or to assume that their organisational leaders will take care of any political in-fighting on their behalf, or in some cases, will prevent them ever having to hear about tensions or struggles for survival or influence. Such views are not infrequently shared by those leaders themselves, some of whom appear to have particular views of their role in membership organisations. As one senior administrator of a National Governing Body (NGB) responded when asked how he managed the tensions between running the NGB more professionally and the requirement that a membership organisation should provide means for the membership to express their views: *"We're not here to consult our members — we're here to represent them"* (Abrams *et al.*,, 1995).

In other cases, it appears that the members themselves wish not to be involved, like the physical education teachers on a National Curriculum INSET course who accused me of being "overly political" (Talbot, 1993) because I had outlined some of the dangers of ignoring threats to the subject posed by Ministers' perceptions of physical education as school sport:

> Power to most people seems distant and detached from their lives, 'not my concern'. ... But the very fact that individuals are often unable to see questions of power as permeating their lives is interesting in itself and raises the very important question of why they should accept domination and the limitations imposed on their lives by others. (Bilton *et al.*, 1983: p. 172)

So the view that "politics" has no role in everyday life, especially in areas like sport, leisure and physical education, is commonly held. Such views may be further legitimised by the argument that these areas are supposed to be about self-chosen, self-regulated activity, which still is regarded as having no part to play in "serious" matters like the economy and the social system (despite it being offered at times of crisis as an anodyne solution to structural problems like youth unemployment and social unrest). This perspective denies that understanding the social construction of institutions and ideologies, *necessarily* means also refusing to see them as given, immutable and unchallengeable.

It also requires the attempt to understand how certain conceptions of sport and physical education come to dominate over others, how the proponents of different views are coerced, sanctioned or excluded from systems and structures of influence, and how (or whether) those members of professions and service clients are persuaded of the legitimacy of the power of others and accept a subordinate or compliant, uncritical role in the relationships and structures of the profession and the service. Dominant ideologies are promulgated, to persuade the majority (and, of course, the popular media) that the power processes and structures are in the best interests of both the service and its clients, despite evidence of resistance or conflict from the professionals. Michael Barber's work on the ways in which the National Curriculum has been constructed and reconstructed provides excellent examples of these processes:

> ...a Government which claims to have spent a decade rolling back the frontiers of the state is not only prescribing in detail what should be taught and how it should be assessed, it is also exercising its powers to intervene in response to short-term political considerations.
>
> PE, art and music came at the end, their place in the pecking order firmly established. (Barber, 1993: pp. 11 and 16)

Analysis of political or power processes must be located within social context and structures: yet the importance of context in physical education and sport is often denied, or at best selectivele recognised (the influence of economic trends is one immediate and obvious exception). Similarly, the importance and influence of key stakeholders or main movers should not be underestimated; individuals and groups can and do influence decisions and events.

Politics is often described as "*the art of the possible*" (usually attributed to R. A. Butler). John Evans and Dawn Penney (1993) have referred to the policy process as *"a relational activity"*. What has interested me over the last decade, is the number of examples of apparent failure to understand, or capacity to ignore as irrelevant, each others' social worlds and means of expression, by both government (including Ministers and civil servants) and professional and interest groups. One example is the evident gap between, on the one hand, Ministers' and government rhetoric about "putting school sport back at the heart of school life" (Major, 1995), and on the other, the actual resources and frameworks for sport in most state schools. Ministerial pronouncements are made apparently without the benefit of either knowledge or understanding of existing structures and delivery systems, or of their constraints and limitations. In some cases, Ministers appear unaware of the effects of their own or their government's policies and decisions on the delivery mechanisms on which they now depend for the delivery of new policies. During the construction of the National Curriculum for physical education, representations by the Department of Education and Science (DES) PE Working Group to Robert Atkins, the then Minister of Sport, about the adverse effects of the demise of the physical education advisory service, led him to declare that he would see to it that every local authority *would* have a PE adviser. He was apparently unaware (or chose to ignore) that this demise had been one of the effects of his own government's sustained withdrawal of resources from, and curtailment of power of, local government.

Similarly, protests and resistance by interest groups have frequently revealed their dangerous lack of knowledge of how to engage the interest of Ministers, and lack of understanding of the strength of prevailing ideologies and conceptions. During the BAALPE (British Association of Advisers and Lecturers in Physical Education) conference in July 1995, which coincided with the launch of the Government's Policy Statement on Sport "Raising the Game" (Department for National Heritage, 1995), I watched with some dismay as proponents of dance berated a (sympathetic) senior Department of Education and Employment civil servant on the negative effects the Statement would have on dance, ignoring his admirable attempts to help them to appreciate dance's privileged place in physical education, notwithstanding the powerful influence of Ministerial (including Prime Ministerial) views of elite, male team sport.

It is possible that these dichotomies, the disjunctures between ideology and policy on the one hand, and structure and practice on the other, are the basis for the many anomalies and contradictions which professionals working in physical education and sport have to manage. Both the National Curriculum, including physical education, and the National Governing Bodies of Sport — the voluntary sector of sport — have become contested areas. I intend to use aspects of these contests to illustrate the effectiveness of different groups in the "art of the possible" — and to explore why some dominant ideologies endure, and others change, even when protected and promulgated by people in structural positions of authority and power.

Some of these have been laid bare by critical review of the political processes of the construction and implementation of the National Curriculum, and their effects on service delivery and the teaching profession:

> ... the Government's ideological hostility to unions had blinded its ability to see the potential for consensus across the whole of the curriculum, assessment and reporting. (Barber, 1993: p. 21)

> ...we may note that 'entitlement' is part of the rhetoric of the National Curriculum. Again too, however, we must note that it has little meaning within a framework which is essentially competitive and whose main focus is economic, or indeed in a scheme which excuses the more privileged members of society, those in public schools and city technology colleges, from participating in this 'entitlement'. (Kelly, 1994: p. 118)

> MacGregor also said that he was considering making PE optional as he believed that this could be largely achieved in after-school activities. Again, he was falling prey to the notion that state schools could follow the independent example where sports were often provided outside normal school hours. Like too many Conservative ministers, MacGregor has little idea of what actually happens in the state schools for which they are responsible. (Tytler, 1993: p. 30)

Tony Mangan has shown the influence of formative conceptions of sport, restricted by ideologies of masculinity and physicality, constructed in Nineteenth Century public schools (Mangan, 1995). Competing or conflicting ideologies are reified and polarised by distinctive discourses in sport and physical education (Evans and Penney, 1992a; Talbot, 1993). But it is worth reflecting on the distinctions between the official discourses and rhetoric of sport and physical education, which illustrate a more fundamental distinction — that between the views of the , exemplified by the struggle for control of the National Curriculum:

> Each of the working groups offers a microcosm of struggles within the educational state over definition and control of subject knowledge. They indicate both the reworking of the policy process and the potential for dislocation and conflict within that process. (Ball, 1990: p. 198)

Ministerial incapacity to see the National Curriculum as anything but a series of "subjects", of which Ministers held particular views, effectively prevented adequate treatment of the permeation issues like outdoor education, equal opportunities and personal and social education. Subject dominance among the "professionals" on subject working groups also prevented their addressing the issues in the time available. Even when they did and the issues were included in the proposals, the later Statutory Orders omitted them (Evans and Penney, 1992b; Foster and Bathmaker, 1993). The aspects of equity issues in the National Curriculum which were publically contested tended to focus on the issues of heritage, definitions of culture and "national" identity, although almost all the public debates and the subject Working Group reports marginalised issues of ethnocentrism and racism. Gender and culture or race were rarely dealt with together and even the proposals for Modern Languages dealt only cursorily with these issues. Physical Education in this case was exceptional:

> The working groups generally failed in their deliberations to link these. Only the PE working group goes some way to making the connection:
>
> "Teachers should be sensitive to the biological and cultural effects of being female or male, on the behaviour considered 'appropriate' for girls and boys of different cultures." (PE para 30) (Foster and Bathmaker, 1993: p. 48)

Government circles appear profoundly distrustful of these areas of discourse, despite during the same period close Ministerial identification with an ethics and sport campaign. Language proved to be a more powerful barrier than the professionals could ever have supposed (Evans and Penney, 1992b). Physical education was no exception:

> There was little doubt that in the eyes of some Conservative politicians, PE exemplified all that was wrong with the curriculum and teaching in the state education system (see Evans, 1990). It was too egalitarian, too abstract, too impractical, and was failing to focus on the skills, team games and attitudes that purportedly had made Britain great. (Evans and Penney, 1992b: p. 14)

The story of how the dominance of the ideology of so-called "national" team games was resisted has already been at least partly told (Talbot, 1993). During the period between 1990 and 1992 when the Physical Education National Curriculum was being drawn up and transferred from proposal form to statutory orders, the physical education profession and its powerful allies in sport rallied effectively to contain games' place in the physical education national curriculum, in spite of the stated wishes of successive Ministers for Sport and Secretaries of State. But the subsequent review of the National Curriculum by Ron Dearing — ironically a significant rapprochement from the Government to the teacher unions — provided opportunities for the old team-game ideology to be re-established, and ultimately for games to dominate the time available for physical education in children's schooling. In the event, the Dearing Review's consultation exercise was not taken seriously enough by those in physical education, perhaps because of their success in the previous rounds. Unfortunately, physical education was at that time a profession whose ability to exercise vigilance was inhibited by internal disagreements and struggles for power, and was not taking an effective lead in influencing the responses to the Dearing consultation. For example, without challenge from the physical education profession, the NGBs of sport were given advice from the Central Council for Physical Recreation (CCPR) which was based on misunderstandings of some of the questions in the consultation document. One damaging result was that physical education was, in effect, prevented from benefitting from the INSET (In-Service Education for Teachers) funds which were to be available for IT development, because it was suggested that IT in PE would prevent children being involved in *activity*. Furthermore, in spite of the fact that the overwhelming majority of responses to the consultation rejected the notion of compulsory team games at key stage 4 (ages 14-16), supported by the Schools Curriculum and Assessment Authority (SCAA), the Dearing proposals embraced Ministerial whim by requiring that one of the two activities to be chosen during Key Stage 4 should be a "competitive game". SCAA at least were able to utilise the conceptual confusion in Ministerial and civil servant minds between "team" and "competitive", and thereby widen choice for that age group. In this, SCAA showed some political acumen, but these events do reflect both the strength of the adherence to the team game ideology in Government circles, and (I believe) fear of reprisal on the part of the SCAA officers. They must, after all, have seen what had happened successively to the Schools Council and the National Curriculum Council after they had been perceived by the Government as "going native" (Graham, 1993).

There are other stories to be told, for instance about the struggle to retain swimming in the Physical Education National Curriculum at Key Stage 2. This was a struggle in which physical educationists were supported by the Swim for Life Campaign which was not so much a sport group as a group concerned for children's safety and which very effectively used the marketing experience of its chair to marshall public and media opinion; and by the House of Commons All-Party Committee on School Sport. But possibly the main reason for success was the DES's collection of hard data which demonstrated that the proposal would not require significant new funding. The initial hostility shown by Kenneth Clarke as Secretary of State for Education had been largely based on his own lack of knowledge of the number of children already learning to swim in state primary schools (about 80%) and his assumption that the proposal would require significant new investment.

Another example of mis-match between structures and policy has been the physical education profession's failure to see and act upon the changes in the delivery and support services over the last decade or so. To some extent, this is a function of the inherent conservatism of professional groups, and of the unwillingness to revisit or to change aspects of work which have been hard won and have demanded significant investment of self and time, sometimes at considerable personal cost. An example is the need for the physical education profession to learn to accept that it no longer has a monopoly of supply of physical activities for young people. The

distinctive role for physical education, in various sectors of provision, needs to be reassessed and acted upon: this will require a major shift.

The physical education profession now has new patrons, sponsors and partners. The task is to analyse and respond to their expectations and objectives, and to be aware of their relationships with the profession. Physical education now has a major new sponsor and partner — the Sports Council — through the Junior National Sports Programme. The criteria by which the profession decides to work with new partners and to accept new relationships including accountability need to be carefully evaluated, in also formulating the profession's new mission and role. Most important, the implications of the changes in physical education's place in the new infrastructure need to be better understood so that the profession is able to outline its own objectives and goals. The extent to which the profession is able to do this, given the fragmented and contested nature of its organisation, is questionable. The awareness of the profession's leaders of the changing context and role for physical education is crucial.

Terry Johnson (1984) has argued that increasing professionalism and specialisation can be seen as a mixed blessing, and asks whether professionalism actually undermines the capacity of individuals to take responsibility for their own development. Johnson argues that, partly because of the diversity of professions, and partly because of the struggle of new occupational groups to achieve status and recognition, professionalism has tended to become an occupational ideal in a society whose technological and educational advances have eroded the mystique which traditionally supported the esoteric and exclusive nature of professional knowledge. This means that any enquiry into the relationship of professions' status and their access to knowledge needs to take account of the power relations through which access and control are achieved and maintained. One of the dangers of professions being able to maintain and control access and behaviour, is not only that they may find themselves unable themselves to change when circumstances demand, but also that they close doors to new ideas and constructive criticism — they cease to develop, and practise gatekeeping and other power practices which maintain the status quo. The more uncertain the status of the profession, the less likely that it will be willing and able to manage change. Professions whose status is uncertain attempt to widen the knowledge gap between themselves and their clients, sometimes also even their close colleagues in allied professions, in order to re-establish and reinforce their professionalism.

I believe that the ways in which physical education, sports studies and sports science have evolved are examples of these processes. The widening of the knowledge gap can take several forms, all of which can be identified in these areas: increasing specialisation and depth of enquiry; entering into cooperation or collusion with other, more established disciplines (or in some cases citing the conventions of more established disciplines), often resulting in a distancing from the original focus or intention; adopting or

acquiring new technologies in order to control means of access; lengthening the period of professional education and increasing the strictures surrounding the profession; and adopting more exclusive, usually self-defined, inflexible entry requirements, often on the pretext of "protecting standards" or "quality control". In such cases, centralism develops effectively at the expense of diversity and pluralism — and quality becomes defined *as* centralism. In such cases, it is difficult to question the processes, even though they may be seen by outsiders as merely means of maintaining self image and status.

Alison Dewar and Alan Ingham (1987) have analysed the effects of these processes in academic physical education and sport on students' conceptions of "useful knowledge":

> Our data reinforce the idea that professionalism can negate or at least undermine the culture of critical discourse as defined in humanistic intellectualist terms ... we would add that professionalism may drive a wedge between the two groups ... (the humanistic intellectuals and the technical intelligentsia) at least as far as students' perceptions of really useful knowledge are concerned. (Dewar and Ingham, 1987: p. 13)

> We in physical education have spent decades questing after authority. The quest is professionalist and the quest stifles critical evaluation, creative problem formation and crap detecting. (Dewar and Ingham, 1987: p. 11)

In the academic and research communities of sport and physical education, the conflict between those who recognise the influence and power, and those who seek to deny it, is exemplified, possibly reified, by the competing and conflicting ideologies of the "scientific" and "critical" approaches to the study of sport and physical education.

Sue (Campbell, 1995), Chief Executive of the Youth Sport Trust, denies being involved in "research". Yet her capacity to make sense of complex situations and to select effective strategies and priorities indicates a sophisticated use of *analysis* — analysis which sadly can be absent from some of the projects and publications which do follow some of the more accepted conventions of "research" and especially so-called empirical research. Her diffidence illustrates the distance between some research and its application — and possibly also the distance between conventionally defined "real" research which requires the production of empirical evidence but not always any awareness of context, and the quality thinking and analysis which underlies effective sports policy.

In physical education and sport, the ways in which knowledge is constructed and valued, and research funded, illustrate some of the tensions identified by Dewar and Ingham. The Leisure Studies Association showed, by its response to the 1992 Research Assessment Exercise of the Higher Education Funding Council, that it can be an effective lobbying organi-

sation: but it must now ensure that it does not follow the example of other academic interest groups in appropriate definition and exclusion. 'Gatekeeping' is a useful term to describe the setting of standards, decisions and monitoring of what counts as knowledge, and the identification of what is seen as innovatory, by particular groups. Liz Stanley (1984) has identified the contribution of gatekeepers in the processes of academic professional control. She argues that the notion of gatekeeping is more useful than that of social control, because gatekeepers often act (or say they act), with the best of motives, to protect what is seen to be correct and right, rather than as deliberate seekers or keepers of power. Alison Dewar (1991) goes further:

> Orthodox means of judging the value, worth and usefulness of knowledge tend to be defined as proper and correct because they are the ones that appear to provide clear, simple solutions to the questions being posed. These judgements are ones that define "good" work as that which has the appearance of providing politically and ideologically neutral descriptions of the "facts". The problem is that this is only possible because individuals who attempt to follow these criteria are in fact subverting their ideological and political agendas in the name of "good science". Individuals who do not do this, who declare themselves feminist and explicitly articulate an ideological position risk being labelled biased and reactionary. Why? Because breaking the silence in the hegemony of orthodox, masculinist sociology is to do "bad" or unreliable work. (Dewar, 1991: p. 16)

It would not matter that there are competing and conflicting ideologies of research, if it were not for the importance of sources of funding for research. While the Sports Council's research budget is very small in comparison with the research councils and the amount of money generated by the higher education funding councils' research assessment, it has become an important source of external funding (and the latter is now itself an indicator of success for Funding Council allocations). The particular definitions and models of research used by the Sports Council and its partners: the gatekeeping practices used to ensure conformity, not only to the models of research, but often the areas to be researched, and the ways in which Sports Council projects are managed and used, are important influences in the polarisation which has taken place in sports research between the "scientific" and "critical" approaches. This can be compounded by the tendency for government agencies like the Sports Council to look for confirmation of their conclusions and practices, rather than progress in understanding complex phenomena and processes:

> ... social science furnishes the State and its functionaries with information, and it is often employed in formulating and assessing State policies to satisfy social needs. Ideologically the State

> often invokes expedient analyses and the results of social science, whether by collaboration or appropriation, to legitimise State pursuits and to rationalise established relations of power and domination. (Goldberg, 1992: p. 52)

The effects of these processes and power structures on the allocation of funding to research on sport, over the last ten years and the next ten years, would be a fascinating study.

A rather different example of power processes is the relationship between the Sports Council and the NGBs of sport. It has been Sports Council policy for several years to encourage the NGBs to increase their efficiency and productivity by rationalising their structures and professionalising their personnel and services: grant-aid leverage and advocacy by Sports Council liaison officers have been the main means of this encouragement. On the face of it, this is a reasonable and overdue change; in some sports, the proliferation of governing bodies for the various disciplines or branches of the sport, or for the four home countries, had led to duplication of effort, wasted resources, and confusion in international communication and competition.

However, there are potential losses in this shift towards increasingly professional organisations representing the interests of the whole sport. Since British sport depends heavily on volunteers, their contributions and needs require consideration and protection. In sports where single sex or single discipline organisations have merged, the interests and voices of women or other less powerful groups have lost visibility and influence (Abrams, Long, Talbot and Welch, 1995). These changes in the National Governing Bodies of Sport are examples of more informal political processes, within a macro political climate driven by government policy and ideology.

The distinguishing characteristics of NGBs of sport have been identified through two major pieces of research undertaken for the Sports Council at Leeds Metropolitan University (Long, *et al.*, 1992; Abrams *et al.*, 1995). These characteristics can be summarised as: frequently inadequate staff size for separate strategic and operational management; limited capacity to respond to changes in context; "stakeholding" cultures emanating from the self-investment by voluntary officers, and resulting in inherent conservatism and resistance to change; lack of clear accountability structures and systems; tensions between voluntarism and business demands; poor communication; recurrent financial problems; ambivalence or confusion regarding autonomy and accountability; unwieldy committee and decision making cycles; lack of stability and high turnover of paid staff.

These NGB characteristics are illustrated by the concerns identified in a recent consultative document for British Athletics (Radford, 1995), and provide reasons for resistance to certain aspects of professionalisation: the most prevalent are fear of loss of influence and autonomy, by individuals or groups; and "*suspicion that market forces had replaced sporting and social values as the most important motivation force*" (Radford, 1995: p. 20). Increasingly, NGBs are having to provide more services with less resources, be more efficient in the way they carry out their business, improve the quality and the quantity of their provision, and update the skill base of the professional and voluntary work force. They are also having to plan more for the long term and strategically, and be more financially aware. This highlights the potential problems for sports organisations, especially in the context of the increased expectations held for non-statutory agencies.

The professionalisation of sports organisations appears to be characterised by several or all of the following elements:

- recognition and acknowledgement of the obligations related to public funding, and the development of mechanisms for monitoring performance and for accountability;
- an increase in entrepreneurial activities, i.e. in capitalising on the potential income from the sport or its players in order to underwrite core costs and/or development work, and to reduce single agency financial dependency (e.g. on Sports Council, commercial sponsors);
- use of business terms like "efficiency", "marketing", "corporate image";
- use of concepts and methods such as organisational "effectiveness", task performance and the use of performance indicators, usually using quantitative measures;
- acknowledgement of the value of technical knowledge or expertise, e.g. in coaching, sports science and medicine;.
- acknowledgement of the place of generic management skills or knowledge;
- loss of monopoly of power of those people with sport-specific knowledge or experience;
- use of IT in administration;
- move towards forward/strategic planning and management, corporate planning;
- SME (small and medium enterprise) characteristics in business planning;
- employment of paid staff, active recruitment into functional officer roles of members with professional or technical knowledge or expertise;
- centralised NGB location and bureaucracy.

There have been similar changes in Canadian National Sports Organisations (NSOs), sponsored and supported by Sport Canada's very clear policy for increasing the international success of Canadian sportsplayers (Task Force Report, 1988). The typology of NSOs *(kitchen table ' boardroom ' executive office)* developed by Trevor Slack and his co-workers (Hall, Cullen and Slack, 1989; Slack, 1985; Slack and Hinings, 1987; Slack and Thibault, 1988), is a useful framework, but direct application to Britain may not be appropriate, because the contexts of Canadian and British/ English sport are so different. Some of these distinctions between the British and Canadian contexts illustrate both intended and unintended outcomes of government policy where existing sports systems and organisations were either not understood or were not valued.

In both Canada and Britain, there has been widespread uncritical *acceptance of the dominant strategic planning approach to sports policy*, and limited visibility of any consideration of the potential losses and gains in processes related to strategic planning. Underlying the strategic planning model is the assumption of rationalism and business-related performance evaluation criteria which may be inapplicable or misleading when applied to sports voluntary organisations, and there is little critical examination of the values and assumptions implicit in such an approach. In Canada the intention has been explicitly to rationalise NSO structures and to improve Canada's international sport performance, with ethical and equity issues, including regional inequities within the Canadian sports system, apparently being seen as secondary and less important:

> Underlying both issues, indeed, is a further question which is not strategic at all, but rather a matter of values and social priorities. (Whitson and Macintosh, 1989: p. 437)

The characteristic of diversity of interests among sports organisations can be a strength which can be overlooked, particularly when considering rationalisation or other moves towards "efficiency". Whitson and Macintosh (1989) argued that in the new Canadian policy structures, where priorities have been so radically altered and where the coercive power of grant aid has been used by Sport Canada, those people in NSOs who might have disputed the change in values and priorities have effectively been marginalised, and many others have become alienated or have been lost to the sport system:

> ... in these new policy structures, the voices of most of those who might have raised critical questions about how the scope and direction of NSOs' redefined 'missions' have been effectively marginalised, and others have become alienated and dropped out. (p. 446)
>
> ... the politics of such bodies produces more diversity and more sensitivity to minority aspirations than decision structures that are constructed by the world views of senior professional staff and politicians. (p. 447)

Whitson and Macintosh went on to cite the Sports Council in the UK as "a model of an 'arm's length' body" (p. 447) successfully supporting both the 'elite sector' and 'sport for all'.

The Slack *et al.*, typology, developed primarily for Canadian amateur sports organisations, heavily dependent on state resources, assumes that three major aspects of bureaucratisation have taken place in parallel — centralisation, formalisation and professionalisation. These have much in common with the influence of UK government policy on both sport and physical education, although the voluntary sector of UK sport (and other leisure activities) is different from Canada's. Volunteers in UK sports organisations are not *necessarily* associated with lower level activity: increasingly UK NGBs are setting out to use the highly developed professional skills of voluntary officers, even recruiting them for specific functions and positions. There is also reason to question the acceptance of the notion that the employment of professional staff necessarily moves sports organisations from the "governing body" model towards the "National Sports Organisation (NSO)" model. While in Canadian NSOs, the tendency was for professional officers to be concerned solely with the development of elite sport, this has not been replicated in the UK, and conflicts with the significant levels of grant aid provided by the Sports Council to establish sports development officer posts in local authorities and NGBs, mainly to increase participation in sport (Collins, 1995).

Macintosh and Whitson's (1990) analysis of the effects of *macro* changes on National Sports Organisations (NSO) in Canada provides useful comparisons with the British context. They outline the ways in which federal government, through Sport Canada, and by separating the funding and ideologies of recreational and representative, competitive sport, has pressured NSOs away from a voluntarist, fiercely autonomous, devolved regional structure and culture, towards becoming more "professional", centralised and government-dependent organisations whose major function is to produce Canadian international competitors. One major cost, according to Macintosh and Whitson (1990), is "the routine subordination of equity concerns to the production of performance" (p. 103).

The potential parallels with UK sports governance, and the current shift of Sports Council responsibilities towards performance and excellence, and towards focusing on fewer strategically selected sports, are clear. But there are at present several distinctions between the sports worlds in Canada and the UK, which also help to explain why this macro shift has not yet been effected in this country, and would in any case take different forms:

1. In the UK, some NGBs themselves appear to be very aware of the potential loss of autonomy contingent upon dependence on Sports Council grant aid. There is evidence (Abrams *et al.*, 1995; Long *et al.*, 1992) that there is a continuous tension between accountability and autonomy (Talbot, 1990a), although some NGBs do perceive that they have a "right" to grant aid without accountability.

2. The Sports Council has tried, through grant-aid criteria and procedures, and through Liaison Officer intervention, to raise NGB awareness of the need to reduce their financial dependence on the

Sports Council, which anyway appears to be rather less than had been the case in Canada before Sport Canada's move to centralisation (Task Force Report, 1988). The effectiveness of this process has been limited by Sports Council officer caseloads and by endemic or chronic problems amongst many NGBs which prevent financial health and strategic planning (Abrams, Long, Talbot and Welch, 1995).

3. The Central Council of Physical Recreation has acted as group voice and coordinating forum, and as a buffer between the Sports Council and NGBs. There is no such powerful collective lobby in Canada, and attempts to create one have been greeted with suspicion, ironically especially by voluntary NSO officers (Macintosh and Whitson, 1990).
4. In Canada, the influence of government has been felt more directly by NSOs because they are the main conduit for elite athlete financial support; so far in the UK, there has not been direct governmental financial support for elite athletes, which has tended to emanate more from the voluntary sector, albeit supported by business (e.g. Sports Aid Foundation), and through local government support direct to local athletes.
5. The British Olympic Association has constituted a further element of autonomy from the state in the UK (as seen in its resistance to governmental pressure to join the boycott of the Moscow Olympics, in contrast to the situation of Canada's Olympic team). The BOA has thus acted as another buffer between the Sports Council and Olympic NGBs, and has acted as a means of maintaining diversity in provision of services to elite athletes.
6. The "semi-detached" relationship between the Sports Council and the National Coaching Foundation, with Sports Council funding being used by the National Coaching Foundation (NCF) to carry forward national innovation (e.g. National Vocational Qualifications [NVQs], coach education), has meant that the NCF has been able to work direct with NGBs, through outreach programmes, rather than through Sports Council structures or Liaison Officers. NGBs frequently do not recognise this work as funded by the Sports Council (Long, Talbot and Welch, 1992). Conversely, NCF has also been able to work directly with government representatives to develop specific programmes like Champion Coaching, which has further delineated its autonomy from the Sports Council.
7. The European emphasis on, and ideology of, "Sport For All", and the Sports Council's success in being associated with mass sports participation, has thus far provided resistance to a Canadian-style model of direct government involvement in and focus on high-performance sport. This has been supported by Sports Council stated ideology, such as itsuse of the "sports development continuum" (Sports Council, 1993), which makes clear the inter-dependence between grass roots and elite sport in sports policy and delivery. Macintosh and Whitson

(1990) observe that the urban unrest of the 1980s contributed to the maintenance of UK sports policy as including recreation ("recreation as welfare"). Whether this commitment will survive in the "new" UK and English Sports Councils remains to be seen.

8. The Canadian policy was fundamentally influenced by earlier criticism of "kitchen table" operation of NSOs (Task Force Report, 1988). The Sports Council has adopted rather different approaches to recognition of the same "problem", i.e. that NGBs need to be more efficiently run. There has been an overt valuing of volunteers in Sports Council policy, while at the same time recognising the role which paid officers with particular knowledge and expertise can play. UK NGBs have successfully recruited volunteers with professional and/or technical expertise to chair functional committees or deliver services. While this has been at times at variance with expectations of "democratic" procedures, it does mean that appointments of this kind can help to resist wholesale centralisation and professionalisation. Voluntarism remains a central part of UK government ideology and policy, and more importantly, of the sport culture in the UK, especially at local level. The Sports Council has underwritten this commitment to supporting volunteers in sport through financial and programme support for coach education, training officials and through "Running Sport", a sports administration training programme. It is possible also that the Sports Council has noted the substantial costs being met now by Sport Canada of centralised sports administration for NSOs: the costs of moving too fast, or too far, towards a wholly professional NGB system with a large increase in paid officers, have to be borne in mind. What is clear is that in the UK the recognition of the role and contributions of voluntary officers with professional and technical skills has led to an acceptance of *professionalism within voluntarism*, and an acceptance that "professional" does not necessarily equate to "paid" NGB officers and staff.

9. The motives for and effects of centralisation of resources and support are less strong in the UK than in Canada, simply because of the differences between the two countries in physical scale and distance. While relationships in the UK between NGB national and regional operations, and between UK and home country NGBs, are frequently problematic, this is not such an overwhelming problem in Canada as it is in one of the largest land-mass countries in the world.

10. The Sports Council has gone about "rationalisation" of NGBs rather differently from Sport Canada. Whether consciously or unconsciously, it has encouraged movement towards interim structures of federation and consortia within traditionally fragmented sports, recognising the vigorous defence and protection of autonomy of sports disciplines and home country NGBs.

11. Until 1994-5, the Sports Council had not explicitly prioritised high

performance sport above "Sports For All" development work, especially through grant aid. Again, this is a feature of Council operation which will be of interest as new policies take effect, particularly the extent to which the parallel influence of emphasis on young people ameliorates the effects of any shift towards performance sport.

12. The Canadian motive to use centralisation to emphasise "nationhood" (Macintosh and Whitson, 1990: p. 55) is absent, or at least very low profile in the UK, where distance is less of a problem and where multiculturalism and cultural inequities have taken different forms, over a much longer period than in Canada.

13. In the UK, internal political pressure has been brought to bear on NGBs from schools GBs, women's commissions, disciplinary specialist panels, regional interest groups etc, providing a check to the centralising (monolithic?) effects of rational forward planning, while at the same time providing examples of agency, the capacity of relatively limited groups to effect change or to protect interests (Chin and Benne, 1969; Talbot, 1990a).

14. There is continuing influence from the very large numbers of voluntary coaches in British sport, coordinated by the National Association of Sports Coaches, which resists centralised bureaucratic or "technocratic" influence in NGBs by voicing their own specific technical needs.

15. Other important differences in the historical differences between the Canadian and English relationships between NSOs and their funding partners, relate to the previous Canadian NSO resistance to high performance sport, compared with some English NSOs' reluctance to become involved in sports development (Talbot, 1992), and the Canadian focus on specific funding for technical programmes, compared with the English scenario in which some governing bodies have continued to be funded merely to keep them alive!

These distinctions between the structures and context of Canadian and British sport should provide the Sports Council with cause to consider the wider context for future national policy, despite Ministerial and governmental apparent conviction that centralisation and greater control are desirable and necessary. Despite the amount of literature relating to the influence of power in organisations and relationships between the government and professions, it is striking how little it appears to be used by sports policy makers.

It is also striking how *gender blind* most of this work is. There is, however, a growing body of literature providing critiques from the point of view of gender power relations and engendered structures and reward systems, and their role as barriers and catalysts in organisational change and progress towards gender equity (see for example Davidson and Burke, 1994; Hearn and Parkin, 1983; Itzin and Newman, 1995; Kanter, 1977; Mills and Tancred, 1992; Tancred-Sheriff and Campbell, 1992). These studies raise further questions about the same organisational issues relating to ethnicity, class, age and disability — other power relations which seem to be less visible and to have been less well theorised in this area, especially in relation to organisations in sport and physical education.

In the context of sports organisations, a range of distributional analyses have been completed, which clearly illustrate the inequities in opportunity and position between men and women (Beamish, 1985; Fasting, 1993; Fitness and Amateur Sport, 1982, 1986; Hall, 1987; Macintosh and Beamish, 1987; Talbot, 1988; Talbot, 1990b; White and Brackenridge, 1985). These inequities remain broadly similar in voluntary, governmental or commercial sports organisations, although they appear to be more marked in NGBs.

More recently, there have been more analytical approaches, including focus on the experiences of women in sports organisations, and the processes and practices of resistance and protection which stem from masculine hegemonies and serve to prevent women either obtaining positions or advancing through organisations. (See, for example, Bryson, 1987; Fasting and Sisjord, 1986; Macintosh and Beamish, 1987; Macintosh *et al.*, 1987; Macintosh and Whitson, 1990; Talbot, 1990b; White *et al.*,, 1990; Whitson and Macintosh, 1988, 1989.) Some studies have wider significance than to illustrate the effects of gender power relations and examples of entrenchment by reactionary males in NGBs. They also illustrate the pervasiveness and power of inequitable practices and attitudes in NGBs; Sports Council policy is still not influencing these organisations, despite more than a decade of equity policies and strategies. The hostile reactions in the Press and by the public, to Jim McKay's (1992) research on the experiences of Australian women in national sports organisations, also show the deep-seated nature of prejudice (Miranda, 1993; Sydney Morning Herald, 1993). They throw into sharp relief the unquestioned ways in which sports structures and ideologies are not merely defended, but are actually defined and perpetuated by masculine hegemonies and male definitions of sport.

To conclude, these examples of the influence of political processes on physical education and sport confirm the paramount need for understanding of *context*, for researchers, for policy makers and for practitioners. Context includes the dynamics of how decisions are made and the ways key players resist, accommodate, implement or drive change. There are also implications for the education and training of both future sports policy makers and sports scientists: appreciation and understanding of context must be prerequisites in courses of initial training and post-experience professional development.

The shared task for researchers, policy makers and practitioners is not to ignore dominant ideologies, but to put them into perspective and to understand how they are formed, shaped and maintained. The tendency in contemporary research and commentary has been to focus on the pervasiveness of ideologies and social systems, possibly because most academics feel that they are on the outside, looking in. But there are now sufficient links between researchers and people involved in the policy process for that focus to shift, towards understanding the influence of key players, of tracing the effects of individual and group agency and subversion. If some of these key players will share their experiences and their struggles with researchers, both should be in a better position to influence events.

References

Abrams, J., Long, J., Talbot, M. and Welch, M. (1995) *The impact of organisational change on Governing Bodies of Sport.* A research report to the Sports Council. Leeds: Leeds Metropolitan University.

Abrams, J. and Talbot, M. (1995) *Organisational change and Sports Governing Bodies: A review of the literature.* Carnegie National Sports Development Centre, Leeds Metropolitan University.

Ball, S. (1990) *Politics and policy making in education.* London: Routledge.

Barber, M. (1993) 'Teachers and the National Curriculum: Learning to love it?', in M. Barber and D. Graham (eds) *Sense, nonsense and the National Curriculum.* Brighton: The Falmer Press, pp. 10-25.

Beamish, R. (1985) 'Sport executives and voluntary associations: a review of the literature and introduction to some theoretical issues', *Sociology of Sport Journal*, Vol. 2, No. 3: pp. 218-232.

Bilton, T., Bonnett, K., Jones, P., Stanworth, M., Sheard, K. and Webster, A. (1983) *Introductory sociology.* London: Macmillan.

Bryson, L. (1987) 'Sport and the maintenance of masculine hegemony', *Women's Studies International Forum*, Vol. 10, No. 4: pp. 349-360.

Campbell, S. (1995) Keynote address to the Leisure Studies Association conference 'Leisure, Sport and Education: The Interfaces'. 12-14 September, University of Brighton (Eastbourne).

Chin, R. and Benne, K. D. (1969) 'General strategies for effecting change in human systems', in W. G. Bennis, K. D. Benne and R. Chin (eds) *The planning of change.* New York: Holt Rinehart and Winston.

Collins, M. (1995) *Sports development locally and nationally.* Reading: Institute of Leisure and Amenity Management.

Davidson, M. and Burke, R. J. (1994) *Women in management: Current research issues.* London: Paul Chapman Publishing.

Department for National Heritage (1995) *Sport: Raising the game.* Government Policy Statement on Sport. London: DNH.

Dewar, A. (1991) 'Incorporation or resistance? Towards an analysis of women's responses to sexual oppression in sport', *International Review for the Sociology of Sport, Vol.* 26, No. 1: pp. 15-24.

Dewar, A. and Ingham, A. (1987) 'Really useful knowledge: Professionalist interests, critical discourse, student responses', Paper presented at Congress 'Movement and Sport in Women's Life'. University of Jyvaskyla, Finland.

Evans, J. (1992a) Investigating the Education Reform Act: Qualitative methods and policy oriented research. Research Supplement, *British Journal of Physical Education*, Vol. 11 (Summer): pp. 2-7.

Evans, J. and Penney, D. (1992b) Making a National Curriculum Physical Education: A Study In The Politics of Knowledge. Unpublished report to the Economic and Social Research Council. Southampton: University of Southampton.

——— (1993) 'Playing by market rules: Physical Education in England and Wales after ERA', in G. McFee and A. Tomlinson (eds) *Education, sport and leisure: Connections and controversies*. Chelsea School Topic Report 3. Eastbourne: University of Brighton, pp. 17-33.

Fasting, K. (1993) *Women and sport. Monitoring progress towards equality: A European Survey*. Oslo: Norwegian Confederation of Sport, Women's Commission.

Fasting, K. and Sisjord, M.-K. (1986) 'Gender, verbal behaviour and power in sports organisations', *Scandinavian Journal of Sport Science*, Vol. 8, No. 2: pp. 81-85.

Fitness and Amateur Sport (1982) *Women in sport leadership: Summary of National Survey*. Ottawa: Fitness and Amateur Sport Women's Program.

_____ (1986) *Sport Canada Quadrennial Planning and Evaluation Guide 1988-92*. Ottawa: Fitness and Amateur Sport.

Foster, E. and Bathmaker, A.-M. (1993) 'Equal opportunities and the national curriculum', in M. Barber and D. Graham (eds) *Sense, nonsense and the national curriculum*. Brighton: The Falmer Press, pp. 43-54.

Goldberg, T. (1992) *Racist culture: The politics and philosophy of meaning*. Oxford: Blackwell.

Graham, D. (1993) 'Reflections on the first four years', in M. Barber and D. Graham (eds) *Sense, nonsense and the national curriculum*. Brighton: The Falmer Press, pp. 2-9.

Hall, M. A. (1987) 'Women Olympians in the Canadian sport bureaucracy', in T. Slack and C. R. Hinings (eds) *The organization and administration of sport*. London: Sport Dynamics, pp. 101-126.

Hall, M. A., Cullen, D. and Slack, T. (1989) 'Organizational elites recreating themselves: the gender structure of national sport organizations', *Quest*, Vol. 41, No. 1: pp. 28-45.

Hearn, J. and Parkin, P. W. (1983) 'Gender and organizations: A selective review and critique of a neglected area', *Organization Studies*, Vol. 4, No. 3: pp. 219-242.

Itzin, C. and Newman, J. (1995) *Gender, culture and organizational change*. London: Routledge.

Johnson, T. (1984) 'Professionalism: Occupation or ideology?', in S. Goodlad (ed) *Education for the professions. Quis custodiet?*. Guildford, Surrey: Society for Research into Higher Education/ National Foundation for Educational Research.

Kanter, R. M. (1977) *Men and women of the corporation*. New York: Basic Books.

Kelly, A. V. (1994) *The national curriculum: A critical review*. London: Paul Chapman Publishing.

Long, J., Talbot, M. and Welch, M. (1992) *The effectiveness of Sports Council services to Sports Governing Bodies*. Research report to the Sports Council. Leeds: Leeds Metropolitan University.

Macintosh, D. and Beamish, R. (1987) 'Female advancement in national level sport administration positions', paper presented at ICHPER/ CAHPER Conference Vancouver, British Columbia.

Macintosh, D., Beamish, R., Whitson, D., Greenhorn, D. and MacNeill, M. (1987) *Professional staff and policy making in National Sport Organisations*. Research Report presented to Social Sciences and Humanities Research Council of Canada. Kingston: Queen's University.

Macintosh, D. and Whitson, D. (1990) *The game planners: Transforming Canada's sport system*. Montreal and Kingston: McGill-Queen's University Press.

McKay, J. (1992) *Why so few? Women executives in Australian sport*. Queensland: Department of Anthropology and Sociology, University of Queensland.

Major, J. (1995) 'Prime Minister's Introduction', in *Raising the game*. Government Policy Statement on Sport. London: Department for National Heritage.

Mangan, J. A. (1995) 'Athleticism: Origins, diffusion, and legacy in the specific context of militarism, masculinity, and mythology', in G. McFee, W. Murphy and G. Whannel (eds) *Leisure cultures: Values, genders, lifestyles*. LSA Publication No. 54. Eastbourne: Leisure Studies Association, pp. 23-46.

Mills, A. J. and Tancred, P. (eds) (1992) *Gendering organizational analysis*. Newbury Park, California: Sage.

Miranda, C. (1993) 'Report fails to address its principal concern', *The Canberra Times*, 26 February.

Radford, P. (1995) Athletics 21: *Strategic planning for British athletics in the 21st century: A consultation document*. Birmingham: British Athletics.

Slack, T. (1985) 'The bureaucratization of a voluntary sport organization', *International Review for the Sociology of Sport*, Vol. 20, pp. 145-166.

Slack, T. and Hinings, B. (1987) 'Planning and organizational change: A conceptual framework for the analysis of amateur sport organizations', *Canadian Journal of Applied Sport Sciences*, No. 12, pp. 185-193.

Slack, T. and Thibault, L. (1988) 'Values and beliefs: Their role in structuring national sport organizations', *Arena Review*, Vol. 12, pp. 140-155.

Sports Council (1993) *Young people and sport: Policy and frameworks for action*. London: Sports Council.

——— (1995) *Consultation Paper: Regional networks for sport — a future option*. London: Sports Council.

Stanley, L. (1984) 'How the social science research process discriminates against women', in S. Acker and D. Warren-Piper (eds) *Is higher education fair to women?*. London: Nelson, pp. 189-209.

Sydney Morning Herald (1993) 'Masters', 14 November: p. 16.

Talbot, M. (1988) 'Their own worst enemy? Women and leisure provision', in E. Wimbush and M. Talbot (eds) *Relative freedoms: Women and leisure*. Milton Keynes: Open University Press pp. 161-176.

——— (1990a) 'What Price British Sport? All to Play For'. Professorial Inaugural Lecture, Leeds Polytechnic.

——— (1990b) 'Women and sports administration: Plus ça change...'. Paper presented at General Assembly of International Sports Federations, Monaco.

——— (1992) *Analysis of responses to the Sports Council Consultation Exercise on Young People and Sport*. Leeds: Carnegie National Sports Development Centre, Leeds Metropolitan University.

——— (1993) 'Physical education and the national curriculum: Some political issues', in G. McFee and A. Tomlinson (eds) *Education, sport and leisure: Connections and controversies*. Chelsea School Topic Report 3. Eastbourne: University of Brighton, pp. 34-64.

Tancred-Sherif, P., and Campbell, E. J. (1992) 'Room for women: A case study in the sociology of organizations', in A. J. Mills and P. Tancred (eds) (1992) *Gendering organizational analysis.* Newbury Park, California: Sage, pp. 31-45.

Task Force on National Sport Policy (1988) *Toward 2000: Building Canada's sport system. The Report of the Task Force on National Sport Policy.* Ottawa: Government of Canada, Fitness and Amateur Sport.

Tytler, D. (1993) 'Observations of an outsider', in M. Barber and D. Graham (eds) *Sense, nonsense and the national curriculum.* Brighton: The Falmer Press, pp. 26-33.

White, A. and Brackenridge, C. (1985) 'Who rules sport? Gender divisions in the power structure of British sports organisations from 1960', *International Review for Sociology of Sport,* Vol. 20, 1/2: pp. 95-107.

White, A., Mayglothling, R. and Carr, C. (1990) *The dedicated few: The social world of women coaches in Britain in the 1980s.* Chichester: West Sussex Institute of Higher Education.

Whitson, D. and Macintosh, D. (1988) 'The professionalization of Canadian amateur sport: Questions of power and purpose', *Arena Review,* Vol. 12: pp. 81-96.

——— (1989) 'Rational planning versus regional interests: The professionalization of Canadian amateur sport', *Canadian Public Policy,* Vol. XV, No. 4: pp. 436-449.

Worsley, P. (1964) 'The distribution of power in industrial societies', in P. Halmos (ed) *The Development of Industrial Societies, Sociological Review Monograph* No 8.

Theory and Practice On Track? A Review of Coaching Development

Sue Campbell

Youth Sport Trust

I have recently moved from my role as Chief Executive of the National Coaching Foundation (NCF) to become Chief Executive of the Youth Sport Trust. This has allowed me to reflect on a number of issues which relate directly to the theory-practice relationship. As always I hope to challenge traditional ways of thinking in an attempt to stimulate debate. I am going to suggest that we have become overly concerned with the formulation of policy documents and strategies. This has resulted in us focusing too little energy on creating effective change. Change can only really happen on the ground through innovation — it takes courage, enduring commitment and an ability to manage the tension around the cutting edge.

In order to help me present some of the principles I wish to share I am going to focus on two key areas:

- the evolution of coach education including the development of sport-based National Vocational Qualifications (S/NVQs) in coaching;
- the evolution of coach development including Champion Coaching.

To support my comments I am going to draw on a piece of research commissioned by the Sports Council and conducted by Whiteley International. [Whiteley International's study drew from 24 sports. Postal questionnaires were sent to 2,546 coaches, with a response rate of 58%. Of the respondents, 67% were over the age of 30 years and 42% had ten or more years active coaching experience. The majority (81%) were in the upper socio-economic categories ABC1. Two thirds of respondents coached on a completely voluntary basis; 24% were paid part-time and 9% were paid full time coaches.]

When I look back at those early years at the NCF I realise how naive we were in policy terms. We did not have a policy framework — just a simple framework for action. Practice informed policy and we responded to 'need' quickly. We were not constrained by an over-elaborate planning process and we could change direction as required. Our strategy was a combination of ideology and realism. It did not please everyone — that is not possible — but it began to draw people to it as they recognised the opportunity to "make things happen".

With the support of many people within Higher Education, the NCF created a network of coaching centres to deliver courses on its behalf. We had the audacity to publish some guidelines, invite applications and interview Institutions to select our initial partners. At the time (1986) there was no cash and no status in being involved, just a shared vision — and a belief that sports coaches needed to access the ever-increasing performance-related knowledge that was available. Coaches themselves were becoming much more aware that there was more to coaching than the techniques and tactics of their sport. So began a movement which has resulted in the NCF being recognised across the world for its coach education materials.

Without question, the status of coach education has grown considerably, to a point where it parallels many other professional training programmes. However, has the status of coaches changed at the same rate? My own feeling is that it has not; but I willreturn to that later.

One of the questions that began to plague me after a few years at the NCF was *Coaches may know more but are they better coaches?* Had theory really impacted on practice?

The evolution of our tutor training programme, based on the principles of adult learning, was the beginning of a new phase. Information, however good, was not enough. How could we help coaches apply what they knew; how could we effect coaching behaviour? It was at this time that government legislation created vocational qualifications. Full of jargon, paper, headaches, a real problem — or was it? The fundamental principles underpinning vocational training made a great deal of sense. They were based on the assessment of competence rather than on an examination of knowledge.

Moving the Governing Bodies forward to adopt vocational qualifications was not a simple task. However, a small team of facilitators was employed to work with the Governing Bodies to assist them in examining the content, structure and delivery of their training programmes. Many of them undertook a thorough examination of their assessment procedures. The traditional course which started on a Monday and finished on a Friday with a 'test' no longer met the requirements of vocational training. Profiling, action planning, assessment in the work place — these became topics of discussion and debate. For those sports which have battled their way through the system at considerable cost (in terms of time and finance) what has emerged is a much stronger process.

However, the whole exercise was, and still is, bedevilled by bureaucracy — paperwork in abundance and a totally inflexible approach to implementation. Like many other administrators, those at the National Council for Vocational Qualifications fail to recognise the difficulties of moving from the theory into practice. They are unable to sway from their pre-determined plan to accommodate evolutionary development. There are no compromises, only rules! The future of vocational qualifications in coaching, which I still believe to be worthwhile, will largely depend on whether or not the theoreticians can develop a more empathetic approach to the practitioners.

The interface between Higher Education and the various sectors of the sport and recreation industry (now united under an umbrella organisation called SPRITO — Sport and Recreation Industry Training Organisation) is very weak. This must be rectified if we are to provide a continuum of education and professional development opportunities.

Who is managing the interface between academic awards and vocational qualifications? Do General NVQs really have equal status to the more traditional qualifications? How do we ensure there is a fair comparison between vocational competence and academic merit? This is a huge challenge for all of us and I believe that it is an urgent agenda item for the both the industry and yourselves to address.

I will leave the last words on this theme to coaches themselves. The Whiteley survey showed that just over half (51%) of respondents indicated that they were aware of the development of S/NVQs. Over half of these (59%) felt that the impact was likely to be positive — that it would provide consistent standards/recognised path, more recognition outside sport, help personal development and provide the basis of a pay structure. Those respondents who felt that S/NVQs were more likely to have a negative impact cited as their concerns more bureaucracy, coaches leaving or being put-off becoming coaches, and expense. A significantly high proportion of respondents (40%) offered no comment or had no idea what the likely impact would be!

Coach development

Coach development has as its central pillar coach education, but it is also concerned with the recruitment, employment (including ethical frameworks) and deployment (placement) of coaches. In the *Coaching Matters* document produced for the Sports Council by a coaching review panel, there were a number of key areas identified for action at local and national level. While everyone agreed *what* needed doing, no one knew *how* to bring about the kind of changes required. As with all such documents, there were pages of recommendations imploring all agencies to take action. But, what such documents constantly fail to appreciate is that people do not necessarily have the skills or knowledge to bring about change in themselves, others or their organisations.

When Champion Coaching first began, it was at the request of the then Minister for Sport, Robert Atkins. He wanted to raise the profile of school sport. Many people felt it was doomed to failure — it could not be done.

As it moved forward mistakes were made, but all the time they were used to inform practice. Innovation, energy, optimism and an endless drive pushed it on through barriers and over new horizons. It began to take on two distinct parallel issues — player development and coach development. Local communities which came on board were challenged to find the right coaches with the right qualifications to work with the right children. As with all such schemes requiring partnership in action (rather than partnership on paper) there was a great deal of tension to manage. Sorting out the arguments — between local authorities and governing bodies; between clubs and schools; between teachers and coaches — presented a daily challenge.

In true British tradition there was lots of criticism — the blueprint was too inflexible, the children were not of the right standard, the governing bodies could not hold up their end of the deal, volunteers were under too much pressure and so it went on. The outcome, however, is that Champion Coaching has been the biggest single stimulus for change in coaching at local level that this country has ever witnessed. Many local authorities now have coaching strategies, but more importantly they have professional staff who understand and value the role that coaches play in sport.

Alongside this work, career pathways for coaches have gradually been emerging and the Whiteley International survey asked coaches themselves about this issue. A clear majority (71%) of respondents felt that there was a clearly defined career path in their main or chosen sports. However, whilst a high proportion of them (62%) had been actively encouraged by their governing body to advance their personal development/training, only 37% had been encouraged to follow a coaching 'career path'. With the continued emphasis on coaching through documents such as the government's recent publication *Raising the Game*, there is no doubt that this will continue to evolve.

A major issue for consideration as we see this emerging profession is the ethical framework within which coaches operate. The British Institute of Sports Coaches (before its merger with the National Coaching Foundation) published a code of practice. Once again though, the difficulty is not in the publication of such a document but rather the enforcing of its code. I believe that we will eventually need to move to some form of licensing for coaches where those who break the code have their license revoked. However, this should be done by the profession itself — coaching needs to become a self-regulating profession. That I believe will take a little longer.

Deploying coaches is also critical and there is no doubt that the management of coaches at local and national level has been poor. At national level directors of coaching have often worked 'outside the main stream'. This has resulted in conflict between coaches and administrators. There is no question that the coach and athlete form the dynamic hub of sport — *they are where it matters* . The rest of us are there to create and support a positive environment in which they can thrive. Too frequently, administration becomes an end in itself rather than a means to other ends. Theory becomes more prestigious than practice. At local level, coach apprenticeships are beginning to emerge where coaches are placed rather than simply 'fall' into coaching positions.

The reality of putting such initiatives on the ground is much tougher than writing the documentation that accompanies it. As those presently struggling with the new teacher training framework know well, apprenticeships require mentoring and mentors require training. The other difficulty is that we need quality role models for the apprentice to work alongside or we will see a spiralling down of standards rather than any improvement upwards.

Coaching development has therefore begun to take place at all levels of sport in the UK. However, turning theory into practice continues to present enormous challenges, Are we on track? Yes, I believe we are gradually moving forward but I think we could move so much faster if policy and practice were more closely aligned. While knowledge, logic and technical ability are critical, there must also be an important place for enthusiasm, empathy, charisma, belief and conviction. Those involved in research and policy formulation need to appreciate that no matter how sound the 'theory' or how comprehensive the strategy, it takes people to turn the words into effective practice — people with courage, determination and a willingness to take a risk.

Dance in Education and PE — Backward Steps or Sporting Chance?

Their Role and Relationship in Curriculum and Community Provision

Graeme Evans

University of North London

Introduction

The focus of this paper is on the position of Dance in Education, in both school, and youth and community settings. The evolution of dance, although separate to a greater or lesser extent, is also bound up with the development of physical education (PE) as an educative and recreational activity. The relationship between dance and physical exercise can be traced as far back as Athenian Greece, where the Gymnasium integrated music and dance with physical training and sport. The gymnasium was open to all men for physical training and games, but also housed a theatre space, the Palaestra, for music and dance, which was used by men and boys of all ages. The tutor 'Paidotribe' ('boy-rubber') provided physical training and gymnastics skills, which combined dance and wrestling in the preparation of young men to compete in athletic contests and games, as well as for general fitness and health (Kitto, 1951). Games and festivals combined musical contests with athletic competitions. The renaissance in Greek dance was also a feature of dance and the introduction of dance education earlier this century, with Ruby Ginner's school of Greek dancing (1914). Though by then male domination of institutional dance/education had been reversed, a position reinforced by the recent demise of dance within the curriculum and the effective feminising of dance in education.

Dance as a social and art form is also evident in Renaissance eras, where courtly dance imported from the Continent (France and Italy) may have laid the foundations of some of our more formal 'ballroom' dance varieties (others, of course, imported from Latin and Folk Dance influences). The early Nineteenth and Twentieth Centuries also saw the import of exciting dance production and choreography, with Diaghalev's company, Isadora Duncan and others, far removed from the image of PE and movement studies which gradually overtook the practice of 'dance', under the influence of physical education and training and the adoption of English Folk dance in the Education syllabus. As Henderson (1989b: p. 5) remarks: "As dance teachers we owe our place in the school curriculum to the PE specialists of the '40s". The separation of creative dance from physical training (e.g. gymnastics) is a particularly English phenomenon, perhaps reflected in our susceptibility to these imported influences, and which continues today (e.g. popularity of 'Salsa'). The prevalence of physical theatre on the Continent (and the integration of dance and drama), contrasts with our more literal and 'physically inhibited' drama tradition; whilst the recognition and cross-over between circus skills, gymnastics and creative dance has long been a feature of central and eastern European practice.

A social history of dance and its role in education is obviously beyond the scope of this paper. A useful concise summary to 1980 is offered in Brinson's seminal study of Dance in Education (1980: p. 192-203) and a chronological summary is attached in Appendix I to this paper. An official histography of such a cultural and social phenomenon is unlikely, however, to reflect the involvement of the wider community in dance, outside of the formal, institutional and professional spheres, concentrated in London in terms of education, training establishments, and in professional performance. Folk dance, ballroom dancing, ritual and festival dancing, youth dance (e.g. 'raves'), jazz dance, black dance, other 'ethnic' dance forms, associated with sub-cultures and other marginalised or 'hidden' cultures, encompass a larger participation than the minority classical ballet and contemporary dance forms, including dance taught in schools. Over 5 million people go social dancing each week in the UK (General Household Surveys, 1987 and 1991); and as a reminder of the sociocultural significance of dancing, Michael Argyle's recent survey of the 'Sources of Joy' for people in Britain today (1995, and see 1987) ranked Dancing as the most 'joyful' (Politics was lowest), with the next highest Voluntary work and Charity, followed by Music, Religion, Socialising and only then Sport. Another indicator is the active membership of the ballroom dance movement (from adult education classes to the televised competitions seen on 'Come Dancing'), which is estimated at over 2 million in the UK.

Dance as a form of cultural expression and creativity, and Movement as an aspect of physical exercise and training, are inextricably linked. But a tension between the two has been a feature of the modern day development of dance and dance in education. The last 20 to 30 years have seen the reassertion of dance as a separate discipline and educational subject at school and Higher education, and in professional training. Dance (not limited to ballet) as an art form has found encouragement in policy and promotional efforts of national and regional arts agencies, all with dance departments and specialist officers, supporting professional dance companies, including those working in education. At the same time, dance as a recreational and cultural activity found a latent audience in young people, outside the school curriculum, through youth dance initiatives and activities via youth clubs, community arts and local centres. This was recognised in 1980 with the establishment of the National Youth Dance Festival. Dance's maturation was recognised by the first honours degree awarded by the Council for National Academic Awards (CNAA) in 1976 and the subject's availability at 'A' level. The growth in education and training provision, as well as professional performance, supported the development of professional dance teachers. Prior to this, dance and movement studies had been within the realm of the PE teacher in secondary schools, and in primary were under the guidance of generalist teachers — some of whom had training in PE, by seldom in dance.

Basis of study

The starting point for this study takes the regressive step of subsuming the study of dance back into PE, as one of the changes brought about by the Education Reform Act (ERA, 1988) and the ensuing National Curriculum. The impact and rationale for this move are assessed, drawing on dance in education provision and inspection in several London Education Authorities. Any review of curriculum change and the implications for resourcing, participation and the wider relationship of schools with community and 'extra-curricula' provision, should not be seen in isolation from other fundamental changes brought in at the time of the 1988 ERA; namely, delegation of school management through Local Management of Schools (LMS), and in London, the winding-up of the Inner London Education Authority (ILEA) in 1989 (which ceased operating on 31st March 1990). Along with other urban education authorities, ILEA pioneered dance in education as part of a wider 'arts in education' cultural policy (Though it was somewhat belated and under the influence and 'model' of the ill-fated Greater London Council's cultural policies until its cessation three years earlier). This manifested itself in the appointment of the first Inspector for Dance, John Auty, in 1986, taking dance 'away' from the PE Inspectorate. This post was unfortunately short-lived, ceasing with ILEA's abolition, along with the Centre for Physical Training which had acted as host for the dance inspectorate, as well as advisory and in-service work in inner London — including the Dance into Schools programme.

Data on the impact and responses to dance's weakened position in the curriculum and the associated decline in youth and community provision and access to school resources, and based on commissioned surveys of five local education authorities (LEAS) carried out in the five years following the ILEA's abolition. Four LEAs were in former ILEA (inner London) boroughs, which had created new Education Departments to handle this imposed statutory responsibility; and one in outer London, which therefore had a degree of continuity and independence from ILEA's policy and management. Anecdotal and practitioner observation was also gained from the author's position as Director (and subsequently as a governor) of a community education centre between 1980 and 1986 — Inter-Action, based in north London. This centre established the Weekend Arts College (WAC), a youth arts education programme, and through the use of a 'replication model' (Brinson, 1980: p. 92; Robinson, 1982; Brinson, 1992: p. 334), attempted to emulate the successful performances of youth companies at successive National Youth Dance Festivals. Inter-Action had also pioneered 'Action Sports Space', a precursor to the Sports Council's national Action Sport programme. Both initiatives were designed to break down barriers between arts and sports and offer second chance education and training in sport and performing arts to young people (Evans, 1987).

Three south-east London boroughs of Greenwich, Southwark and Lewisham, the east London borough of Hackney, all in inner London, and the outer London (north) borough of Haringey, were the subject of surveys of arts and leisure in education. These surveys used structured questionnaires to determine resources (staff, physical, financial) and levels of activity in dance and other arts subjects. Semi-structured interviews were held with subject specific teachers, department heads and in some cases with head teachers. Interestingly, in some schools heads were unwilling for their staff to be interviewed without being present themselves.) Subject Advisory teachers and (where they existed) Inspectors for arts and PE subjects were also interviewed, as well as youth and community officers, and community arts and animateurs involved in dance in each borough.

As a useful comparative element to these local studies, the Arts Council recently commissioned a national study of school arts advisory and inspection services (Rogers, 1993a, 1995) and several studies on school provision of PE/Sport and Expressive Arts have been published in this year alone (RSA, 1995; SHA [Secondary Heads Association], 1995; and see Rogers, 1995 and Home, 1995). These independent studies are a measure of the concern over the wider impacts of the prescriptive National Curriculum and Local Management of Schools on physical education, training and creativity in education.

As a reflection of how dance and dance in education were perceived, both in their own right and as a cross-curricular subject and 'experience', the ILEA Dance Inspector's statement below (Auty, 1988a) is worth restating and provides a good example of the educational justification of the attempt to create circumstances in which dance can:

i) have greater, deeper and more meaningful value than a simple 'backsides on seats' policy (i. e. participation was key)

ii) bring the expertise of the professional educationalists together with that of the professional dancer/choreographer

iii) [demonstrate] job related new potential

iv) [show] those who dance as normal human beings, relaying;

v) [employ] the non-verbal/body language/movement/dance medium as being accessible regardless of race, sex, class or disability, and

vi) [demonstrate] how the barriers of culture, religion, attitudes etc. can be crossed without hurt

vii) thus giving a basis for self-esteem and valuing of others, which is a genuine platform for the development of equal opportunity.

The normality and accessibility of dance and its potential for breaking down barriers and self-empowerment were key concerns arising from the relegation of dance under the National Curriculum (and see Fleming, 1993 and Miller, 1993):

> The absence of a subject such as dance ... will hamper the delivery of non-Western culture in the curriculum, as many of its most expressive manifestations rely on a close integration of dance, drama and music. The confidence through deeper understanding and control of bodily movement that dance has brought to a wider section of pupils in the last decade should not be denied to any pupil. While helping to unlock some rigid gender demarcation in the curriculum, it has given an immense new opportunity for creative expression for young men and women. (Auty, 1988b: p. 3)

Curriculum development in dance during the 1980s has resulted in a model for dance teaching in which dance was seen as an art form: as a distinct domain of study with its own unique concepts and 'culture'. The aims and objectives that were set out in the HMI document 'Physical Education 5/16' (DES, 1989) presented a mixture of aims for dance, which sometimes suggested an arts model, but never fully described one which matched the achievements and progress in this area of the curriculum. This outmoded framework used objectives such as 'expression of feelings' which fit with the old model for dance education, where dance was the expressive aspect of PE. This conception of dance could directly affect the content, and methods of teaching and assessment in dance courses. Hence dance would be relegated to the now old-fashioned expressionism in the arts which dominated in the 1920s and 30s (Henderson, 1989b). Through the introduction of the National Curriculum dance has a much wider range of aesthetic purposes: eclectic, and more in touch with contemporary 'youth' culture. There was no reference in the DES document to ways in which the school dance experience might relate to the wider community and to contemporary and popular dance experience and multi-culturalism (Auty, 1988b; and see Willis, 1991 and 1992).

Political economy of dance as physical training and 'sport'

The evolution of dance as a limited aspect of physical education and training is evidenced in the chronology attached (Appendix 1) and in the relatively recent achievement of separate status in school and higher education (especially in comparison with the core curriculum subjects of art and music). Magaret Talbot's (1993) excellent insight into the development of the PE curriculum notes the tension, "contested terrain', between PE and dance specialists. She also locates dance within PE, which is itself marginalised within the National Curriculum structure: "The place of both physical education and the arts in the National Curriculum was effectively marginalised by their place in the order of subject development" (Talbot, 1993: p. 45). Noting drama's demise as a separate subject, subsumed into English/Literature, she adds: "dance was fortunate to have a designated place in the National Curriculum, even if it was under the umbrella of physical education!" (p. 37).

The loss of specialist dance teachers and the deminishing critical mass within expressive or performing arts departments of secondary schools, brought about by curriculum changes, effectively accelerated the decline of dance opportunity within curricular and extra-curricular activity. This decline had, however, been evident in London LEAs prior to the effects of the National Curriculum had been felt. This was a result of expenditure reduction and reallocation, in part in anticipation of ERA and LMS, and in some cases due to falling school rolls. A particular impact of LMS confirmed in the surveys below, was the effect of excluding amateur, youth and community organisations from school facilities by substantial increases in rates of hire by schools seeking to maximise income. LMS makesthe Sports Council's promotion of the 'dual-use' of facilities (Sports Council, 1993; DES, 1991) appear somewhat hollow in practice.

In 1990 the Secondary Heads Association (SHA) in collaboration with the Central Council for Physical Recreation (CCPR), carried out their second study of school sport and PE in three years. Between 1986/87 and 1989/90 the study suggested a decline in extra-curricular school sport (after-school, weekends), and also in the availability (and willingness) of specialist PE/sport teachers. The national decline in the number of PE teachers confirms this, failing from 41,800 in 1977 to 24,400 in 1992. In the second report — an 'Inquiry into the Provision of PE in Secondary Schools' — the provision of PE in general as well as swimming, outdoor pursuits and sports leadership were assessed. No mention was made of dance as part of the PE curriculum. Whilst noting that between 96 and 98% of state schools still had compulsory PE for 14 and 15 years old respectively, the amount of time devoted to PE for 14 year olds had also declined. The frequency of the top ten activities undertaken within the PE curriculum shows the stark position of dance, most notably (by its ab-

Table 1 **State Secondary Schools (most frequent activity — not necessarily the most time devoted)**

	1990 Survey (n= 1,580)			1994 Survey (n=3000)
	Mixed	**Boys**	**Girls**	**State 14+**
1.	Football	Cricket	Tennis	Athletics
2.	Athletics	Athletics	Netball	Football
3.	Hockey	Basketball	Athletics	Basketball
4.	Cricket	Cross country	Hockey	Hockey
5.	Netball	Football	Rounders Cricket	
6.	Basketball	Rugby	Gymnastics	Netball
7.	Badminton	Badminton	Badminton	Tennis
8.	Tennis	Tennis	Health fitness	Rounders
9.	Cross country	Swimming	**Dance**	Volleyball
10.	Rounders	Table tennis	Trampolining	Health and fitness

sence) in boys and mixed schools (SHA, 1990). The recent 1994 survey gives an update, based on undifferentiated post-14 provision (SHA, 1994) (see Table 1):

'Taught by women, enjoyed by girls'

The gender 'imbalance' in dance participation in schools appears to be self-fulfilling and likely to worsen as the effects of the National Curriculum, and the decline in dance expertise in schools accumulate. The relative popularity of dance in girl-only schools is also an indication of their attitude to PE and school sport as well as the traditional association of dance as a 'feminine' activity (McFee and Smith: p. 63 and see Flintoff 1991 and Scraton, 1992). The profile of dance Professionals cements this divide, with 80% of dancers and dance teachers female, although this bias reduces with dance entertainers and choreographers (55% and 61% respectively). As in sport, there is also a clear 'age-decay' in dance professionals: 84% of dancers are under 30 compared with only 40% of dance teachers. The career progression is evident in the phases of dance occupation, with choreographers mainly aged over 35 years and 48% over 45. Significantly however, only 10 to 15% of dance teachers actually teach in state schools or work for LEAs; over 40% work in private tuition or higher education (Jackson *et al.*, 1995). Notwithstanding this gender 'advantage', a glass ceiling is still seen to operate in professional dance: "British dance in the twentieth century has been mainly shaped by women, but few senior managers in the large dance companies are women — there is only one woman artistic director amongst the Arts Council's revenue clients and there are few opportunities for women choreographers.... And yet it is predominantly women who want to train as dancers, who make up the majority of the audience and who dominate the animateur movement and teaching" (Hoyle, 1991: p. 7).

The position of young men in dance education is also problematic, fuelled by this teaching and practitioner bias, the lack of role models and dance specialists (male or female), and curriculum time devoted to dance. As Hoyle (1991) points out, "It has been the youth dance movement (that has) done much to challenge the traditional image of male dancers, as have companies such as *Phoenix* and *The Featherstonehaughs*". Yet the youth and voluntary arts sector (including adult education) is now the twilight zone of local provision and the most vulnerable to expenditure cuts, since it is entirely discretionary in nature (Brinson 1992a). If participation is strongly supply-led (Morrison and West, 1986), availability at school is fundamental and likely to reinforce participation and gender divides. In a recent study of youth participation in the arts (700 young people aged 14 to 24 years), two thirds said that they would have welcomed more arts involvement in the past. Young men were more likely to mention drawing, sculpture, graphics and music; and young women were more likely to mention expressive arts such as dance and drama (Harland, Kinder and Hartley, 1995). One practical response is seen in an INSET course for male PE teachers held in Leeds and run by dancers from the London and Northern Contemporary Dance companies: "part of a national move to tackle their subject's advance into relatively unfamiliar fields" (Wainwright, 1995: p. 6). One male PE teacher described the typical reaction at his school: "Tell them [the boys] it's dance today, and up goes a groan, whereas if it's five-a-side football, they all shout Yessss!" (*op. cit.*). However the positive impact of this twenty-five year movement and reassertion of dance is now seen in the experience of the majority of professional dance schools who observed that the proportion of boys applying had risen in recent years: "due to greater awareness of dance in the UK" (Jackson *et al.*, 1995: p. 29). This trend, the result of 10 to 20 years development and recognition of dance in education, risks being reversed if the trends in school provision and participation, and the run-down of youth and community education continue.

Dance as a focus sport

The inheritance of Cecil Sharp's English Folk Dance movement (still preserved in Cecil Sharp House and archive in Primrose Hill, north London) had fallen to the Sports Council, who grant-aided this institution and retained a policy of support for this activity. Folk dance and ballroom dancing were the only 'art forms' included in the government's first major review of leisure participation, (Sillittoe, 1969). When the Sports Council in London was contacted in 1994 for details of this policy and the rationale for their support, this connection was denied — after several attempts and confirmation with the English Folk Dance Society, this policy was reluctantly confirmed by the Sports Council.

It had been reported earlier this year that during a visit to the Sports Council's same headquarters, Sports Minister Iain Sproat found among the racks of publications a leaflet on 'dancing'. This did not please him: "I've got nothing against dancing...", [that tell-tale introduction of the bigot], "...but that is for the Arts Council, not for the Sports Council. You can't tell me that you learn as much from stepping up and down on a wooden bench as you do from playing cricket" (*Time Out*, May 3–10: p. 13). The offending leaflet had been a pamphlet on how to find a safe exercise-to-music class.

These incidents confirm the stereotype of Sport's resistance to 'dance' as a form of physical exercise and cultural expression, at least at the national level. In the London sports region however, dance has been recognised and adopted as a priority 'focus sport'. This arose due its popularity and potential in attracting women, thereby meeting fitness externalities and specific equal opportunities policies, targeting girls and young women. Drawing on dance's role in black and Asian racial and cultural groups, and in youth culture generally, this focus on dance also sought to bring dance activity into sports centres, beyond the mechanical ritual of the aerobics class. This opportunity had been promoted by a joint initiative between the Arts and Sports Councils 'Getting it Together' (1987), which outlined the practical possibilities of hosting arts and sports activities in each other's facilities. This guidance was backed up with case studies and a Sports Council Technical Unit specification on the requirements for dance in sports halls (1986). This idea was largely overtaken by the financial imperatives arising from the Compulsory Competitive Tendering (CCT) of sports centres; reduction in local authority arts and leisure spending; and the Local Management of Schools — all of which mitigate against community use and other low cost use of arts, sports and school facilities (Evans, 1995). This national promotion also lacked specific capital funding for the upgrading and conversion of spaces for dance and drama, and also focused solely on the 'physical'. It ignored the training of staff and overlooked fundamentally differing cultures of arts centres, sports centres and educational institutions.

This cultural difference clearly manifested itself in the early period of the National Youth Dance Festivals, which brought together youth dance companies and educationalists (Dance and PE) over several days each year. Here for the first time young people engaged in developing dance within educational contexts but primarily for themselves. They came together from a range of educational and regional backgrounds: both school and community-based. An urban/rural divide was evident, with black students in the minority, but representing the 'inner city' schools and youth groups.

These young people were more assertive than the others, created their own choreography, used their own music and integrated other art forms and practices (e.g. gymnastics, drama) more easily. They also did not respect the rules — they worked out in the playground, exercised in the corridors and generally had a good time — this was not the way the PE 'dance' establishment was used to working/controlling. It took several years before there was acceptance of many of the most talented black dancer. Many at that time had not gone through classical ballet training, or even formal dance curriculum at school — was this evidence of cultural difference or institutional racism? — probably a bit of both. In the mid-1980s a young black drama student from FUSION/ Weekend Arts College was rejected after audition by the Drama Centre on the grounds that there were no black roles for women in Shakespeare! Today she is a successful actress, from film and TV to stage drama.

With hindsight it has been the multicultural youth dance groups and schools that gave the impetus and raised the profile of youth dance, perhaps most notably Harehills School, Leeds (which spawned the all-male black dance company Phoenix), and FUSION from the Weekend Arts College, North London. Before this point there were few, if any, contemporary black dancers or companies, outside of the USA. Today all regions of the UK support at least one youth dance project, either linked to funded (Arts Council/Regional Arts Board) dance agencies or community arts companies. These provide much of the remaining professional dance and access to dance in schools through touring, residencies and other dance-in-schools initiatives. As a measure of the demand and importance of ethnic and multicultural dance in schools, in the recent SHA survey of secondary schools in England and Wales (1995), half of the dance companies working in schools were Black or Asian. In the survey of London LEAs this figure was nearer to 80%. Many of these were first generation students from the dance degree and community dance courses originating in the late 1970s.

A more recent initiative between the London Sports and Arts agencies developed a resource base, named *The Space Directory*. Housed at the Data Place, part of the National Dance Agency, this Directory acted as a free telephone/postal database of dance and studio facilities throughout London, for those wishing to book and gain access to classes, rehearsal and performance facilities. This data bank also confirmed the lack of dedicated dance spaces, i.e. those that are suitably equipped, heated and with sprung floors (essential to prevent damage to joints), which the shared-use of other centres, including school facilities, generally lack. This initiative also recognised that the growth of youth dance, classes and companies lacked appropriate, cheap and safe spaces for dance, with dance activity carried out on hard floors, under-heated, and often led by enthusiastic but unqualified youth workers and teachers. The lack of appropriate facilities for dance in schools was confirmed by the LEA studies reported below, and by the recent SHA survey:

> Dance and Drama often without studios have to compete between themselves and frequently with PE as well as for the use of school halls, to say nothing of the demands of assemblies, school meals and special events. (1995: p. 20)

The provision of dance in education: London LEAs and national comparisons

As already mentioned the commissioned surveys of five LEAs in London looked at all art forms, including dance within PE, expressive/performing arts, as well as community and extra-curricula activity. Dance within the curriculum was assessed within secondary and where available, in junior/ infant schools. The data presented below therefore treat dance seperately from other art form areas and express school provision in percentage terms (i.e. the proportion of schools within each LEA providing curricula and extra-curricula dance). Comments from interviews and questionnaires regarding trends, concerns and the physical facilities available for dance were obtained from subject and LEA advisory teachers, youth officers and inspectors for PE/dance. Tables 2 and 3 (overleaf) show the proportion of dance active schools, and the decline in dance advisory support and expertise within LEAs.

As well as the reduction in specialist Advisers and Teachers and a lack of dance expertise, even amongst PE advisers (see Table 4 overleaf), the role of the Adviser had, in some cases, been privatised and/or transferred to advisory teaching roles with a combined brief for other arts subjects. Several such teachers regularly supplemented in-school teaching 2 or 3 days a week. Since the ERA (1988) one in three Advisory posts (over 50% of Advisory teachers) and over 40% of arts adviser posts have disappeared. London LEAs now have the lowest percentage of arts advisers and teachers: "Half the posts involving dance have gone. The brief for dance is, in most cases, absorbed within PE adviser or advisory teacher posts — only 8% of the posts were exclusively for dance" (Rogers, 1993b: p. 13).

Table 2 Borough Education Institutions with identified dance activity of a substantial Datum

Borough / LEA	Pri-mary	Secon-dary	Special Needs	FE	AEI	Youth and Com-munity	TOTAL
Green-wich	16 *(20%)*	11 *(68%)*			2	2	31
Hackney	8 *(12%)*	6 *(60%)*	2 *(40%)*	1 *(33%)*	1	—	18
Lewis-ham	9 *(10%)*	9 *(70%)*	—	1 *(100%)*	2	—	21
South-wark	12 *(10%)*	9 *(56%)*	—	1 *(25%)*	1	6	29
Haringey	n/a	7 *(70%)*	1 *(33%)*	1 *(100%)*		1	10

Table 3 Advisers and Advisory Teachers in Borough LEAs — pre and post ERA (1988)

Borough /LEA	Inspectors /Advisers for PE/Dance	Advisory Teachers for PE/Dance	All Advisors /Teachers pre-LMS	All Advisors /Teachers after LMS
Greenwich	1 p/t PE	none	n/a	13/5
Hackney	none	none	23	10
Lewisham	1 p/t PE	15/20	15/20	16/none
Southwark	1 art, music, PE, drama	none	16/8	10/10
Haringey	1 PE, Eng/drama	none	15	13/3
Inner London (12 LEAs)	5 f/t, 2 p/t	1 f/t, 1 p/t	236/48	129/24

Table 4 % LEAs with arts/PE subject Advisers (1994)

	Advisers	Advisory teachers
Counties	56%	38%
Mets	42%	19%
London	22%	22%

In Greenwich there had been an overall reduction of 20% in dance either though non-replacement of dance teachers, leading to a total loss of provision, or from dropping the subject at GCSE level in timetabling under the new National Curriculum: "the squeeze on the arts will come from the emphasis on science and technology in the National Curriculum, schools will be forced to give less time and resources to the arts" (Greenwich primary School teacher). In the borough of Hackney, despite what was perceived to be enhanced quality of dance provision in the borough following the establishment of Hackney Dance Development in 1988 and a dance festival and dance forum, education provision had also suffered from these same cutbacks in time and teaching resources. Dance development work had shifted to the voluntary and community arts sector. In Hackney there was a drop of 30% over the previous 2 years, largely at primary level where the lack of dance expertise was most acute.

Dance provision was assessed by phase and by whether it was compulsory and open to all pupils, or whether it was selective, and whether it was provided only as an extra-curricular activity. In the case of Hackney schools the proportion of schools offering dance was as shown in in Table 5.

Table 5 Proportion of schools in Hackney offering dance

Level:	All pupils	Some pupils/option	Extra-Curricula
Primary	25%	55%	5%
Secondary (years 1 to 3)	50%	15%	—
Secondary (years 4 to 5)	—	50%	—
Special Schools	—	33%	
Youth Centres/Clubs			70%

Very few schools had dedicated dance spaces, or multi-use spaces equipped for dance. Whilst some schools used local arts and community facilities, there was no usage or 'cross-over' into sports centres — though generally these were of more modern design and construction, and contained more sprung floors than elsewhere in the borough. The popularity of dance in youth clubs contrasted with this, suggesting compensation for the decline in dance opportunity within school. The significance of the informal setting should not, however, be understated. As North American research into childhood determinants of adult participation indicates (Morrison and West, 1986), irrespective of variables such as class and educational attainment, it was the experience in community and non-institutional settings, rather than the experience in school, that revealed the greatest positive influence on subsequent participation: "non- school related participation (i. e. Youth club, amateur, church and community groups) is a stronger influence ... than school-related performance" (Dobson and West, 1988: p. 108).

All the borough LEAs and schools surveyed revealed a patchwork of provision and uneven distribution of dance and other arts subject provision. The decline in provision, both curricular and after-school, is clear at 14 years, as the GCSE priorities take over. With LMS and perhaps post-Dearing changes, this seems to reinforce the tendency for secondary schools to specialise. Given schools freedom to 'recruit' across borough boundaries, this has led to the emergence of US-style magnet schools. These are able to dedicate more resources into a narrower curriculum area, by specialising in certain subject areas in pursuit of 'excellence', critical mass and economies of scale. This is beneficial for those schools and those subject specialisms, but less so for the balanced curriculum, or for equal opportunity across all schools in a borough:

> Provision is patchy and piecemeal. Schools put back a few random and uncoordinated Saturday morning sessions to compensate for the comprehensive service which no longer exists. The gulf is accentuated between those parents who value and want arts provision ... and those who don't. Parents must now pay for what was once an entitlement and some have more buying power than others (in Rogers, 1994a: p. 10).

The position of staff teaching dance and PE is also reflected in the LEA Advisory structure, where in several boroughs the Inspector for dance was responsible for PE and other 'arts' subjects. In Haringey LEA the Inspector (an ex- PE teacher) was responsible for PE, drama and dance, and this post would have been cut altogether had it not been for the lobbying from primary schools who saw the Advisory function as essential to their dance and movement capability. In the case of Haringey, as in other LEAs, the responsibility and facilities for dance were predominantly PE-oriented (see Table 6).

Table 6 Haringey — responsibility and facilities for dance

Secondary school	Staff responsible for dance	Facilities for dance
White Hart Lane	3 f/t PE	Gym
St Thomas More	—	—
Fortismere	1 f/t, 1 p/t PE, 1 'dancer'	Gym
Highgate Wood	6 f/t PE, 1 p/t PE	Hall
Gladesmore	6 p/t dance and drama	
St David and Katherine	4 f/t PE	Gym
Northumberland Park	2 f/t PE, 1 f/t, 1 p/t	1 studio, theatre
William Harvey	—	Schoolhall
Hornsey School for Girls	—	—
Langham School	1 f/t PE, visiting dancer	Gym, studio
(f/t = full time, p/t = part time, PE = PE teacher)		

The most active school in this borough, Fortismere, has a renowned local reputation in arts subjects and study. It is significantly based in the more 'well-heeled' (middle-class, owner occupied housing) parts of this otherwise multicultural borough and uses it arts profile to promote itself, particularly to young girls (or at least their parents). Approximately 30 students took dance within expressive arts at GCSE in 1994 (compared with drama [12] and music [30]), but even in this atypical case the school felt that the National Curriculum had been negative: "it is difficult to find time for dance" (Head of Expressive Arts). In most other schools in this borough dance was a marginal aspect of PE, employing PE teachers "who also do dance". In no case was dance offered at 'A' level. In the only all-girls school, where generally dance has a greater presence: "Dance is only taught in year 6-7 by the PE department for a few weeks a year: no exams or assessment". PE generally as a non-examined subject lacks the motivation of the core curriculum subjects, however it is also clear from these schools, confirmed by the national surveys and decline in Advisory expertise in dance, that the PE curriculum is not meeting the expectation of dance, by at best concentrating the study of dance into a one-off series of sessions. Hardly a sound educational approach, and unlikely to sustain students interest and development of the subject. This was felt amongst youth dance groups that had formed through school or on an extra- curricula basis. As well as the limitations on access to rehearsal facilities and staff expertise, there was no opportunity to develop dance within the PE curriculum, although in some cases cross-curricular inclusion of dance was evident in drama.

Dance/PE, leisure and work

A rationale for the National Curriculum and the prioritisation of core subjects at GCSE and beyond rests on the development of skills within an arguably liberal education. Underlying these changes has been the vocational nature of education and the needs of the labour market, the 'world of work'. The non-examined nature of PE within the curriculum and by inference, dance, suggests that this area of study is secondary in vocational and employment terms. Whilst I will not attempt to develop an argument for PE, sport and the arts as passports to employment, the misconception of the changing labour market and within this, leisure and cultural activities, becomes apparent in the light of the educational surveys above. This can be summarised in the position that at secondary school level, arts and sport 'sell' schools. The facilities, extra-curricula activities and images of active enjoyment and a dose of rational recreation, are increasingly used in school and college promotion. This is reinforced through local press coverage throughout the year, publicising school members' achievements, events, competitions etc. When it comes to the hard fact of school *work*, exams and performance, however, this focus disappears. Except for the small number of highly talented young people, PE and the arts are not sought by employers and do not produce jobs (head teachers would do well to look at the career paths, or lack of, for chemistty and physics students, and the graduate unemployment in core educational subjects). To conclude, a cursory look at the changing labour market in the UK is of interest. An assessment of professional employment in dance (and drama) is also provided in Jackson *et al.* (1994) and see Brinson (1992).

Despite the depth and length of the recession, the growth in unemployment and consequent social and economic impacts, not least in reduced spending, the arts and cultural industries as a whole (and some sectors in particular) have experienced growth, and are estimated to continue growing in terms of consumer expenditure and employment. Between 1980 and 1988 employment in the cultural and recreational services sector rose by 16% nationally; the broadly similar Literary, Artistic and Sports category experienced the fastest growth in 1980-1990 of 32%

(135,000 FTE jobs). The latest national Labour Market and Skills Trends (Department of Employment, 1994/5) confirms both the significance of the small and medium-sized firm (SME), the growth of part-time and flexible working, and continued growth in employment in service activities such as *cultural, leisure, recreation* and *tourism*. These are forecast to increase by half a million jobs in the 1990s, an average growth rate of 2.6% per annum, compared with 0.2% across the economy as a whole. The regional economy, within which the above education areas are based, is forecast to produce growth in Distribution (15%); Business Services (31%) and other Services (11%) between 1991–2006 (LPAC, 1993): "The challenge is to create a broader economic base, encouraging sectors with robust prospects such as communications, the media, tourism, hotels and catering, arts, culture, entertainment and distribution" (op. *cit.*). In the outer London borough surveyed, interviews with the Haringey Education Business Partnership, a joint LEA and government 'Compact' scheme, showed a complete lack of knowledge or understanding of the significance of the leisure industries. Their educational business schemes, which included placing experts in schools alongside teachers to deliver GCSE and GNVQ curricula (including pilots for Leisure and Tourism and Arts and Design GNVQs), were limited to business studies, health and manufacturing sectors — all declining sectors of the local (and regional economy), whilst leisure and cultural industries were one of the very few growth areas (Evans, 1994).

In contrast, a more holistic view of the educational needs of a changing economy was recently expressed by an unlikely source (*my emphasis*):

> Employers' expectations of their employees are changing as rapidly as the nature of work itself. *Most importantly, employers look for creativity*;
>
> To be world class we need to create a continually learning individual ... These needs cannot be satisfied by producing an output from the education system that can only handle maths, English and science;
>
> If organisations do not reward *creativity, in favour of conformity*, then they are unlikely to encourage intelligent responses and to produce those brilliant combinations of scientific and marketing thinking: their product development will remain routine.
>
> ... we need *creativity, new ideas artistic fantasy* to stimulate vision beyond what we expect.

These statements (NCA, 1993: p. 15) came not from an arts or PE educator, but from Ian Toombs, Deputy General Manager of NEC (UK) and member of the CBI's Education Committee. The physicality and creativity uniquely combined in the best dance experience arguably deserves at least equal recognition in these terms, as sport, art and music, both as a source of joy and self-confidence. The relationship between education, curriculum, and vocational training would seem to suggest that the National Curriculum and its implementation demands a radical review, especially in view of the peripheral status of PE and dance. The semantic problem caused by 'PE' and Sport/Games has brought the suggestion, 'sport education' (Alderson and Crutchley, 1990: p. 48-9) — but this too is particularly unhelpful for dance (and PE), as is the government's attention to competitive sport. There appears to be little real evidence that the core and optional subject balance of the National Curriculum actually meets the needs they purport to.

The weakened position of dance within PE and PE's marginal position within the curriculum, alongsidethe deterioration in access to staff and physical resources for youth and community dance, suggest a bleak future for the wider participation and experience of dance. Given the seeds laid by the youth, community and dance education movements, and the underlying popularity of dance in society, these curriculum and resource diversions in themselves are not likely to reverse these advances altogether. The growth in Further Education college BTEC performing arts and dance foundation courses, and the establishment of regional dance agencies, indicate continued demand and switching from schools, whilst dance within sports centre 'culture' and programming remains a lost opportunity. However the teaching and development of dance risks being only selectively available and effectively privatised, leaving dance equity, most notably for boys, young men and the physically least confident, the loser in the long run.

References

Alderson, J. And Crutchley, D. (1990) 'Physical Education and the National Curriculum', in N. Armstrong (ed) *New directions in physical education Vol. 1.* Rawdon: Human Kinetics Publishers, pp. 37-62.

Argyle, M. (1987) *The psychology of happiness.* London: Routledge.

——— (1995) *Sources of joy: A survey.* Oxford: Oxford University Press.

Arts Council of Great Britain and The Sports Council (1987) *Getting it together? Guidance on housing sports and arts activities in the same building,* March. London, pp. 26.

Auty, J. (1988a)'Dance in schools programme', Minute to T. Kittle, County Hall, 14th March. London: Inner London Education Authority (ILEA).

——— (1988b) 'Transfer planning — overview paper: Dance', September. London: ILEA.

Brinson, P. (1992b) *Into the 1990s.* London: Council for Dance Education and Training.

Brinson, P. (ed) (1980) *Dance education and training in Britain.* London: Calouste Gulbenkian, Foundation.

——— (1991) *Dance as education.* Brighton: Falmer Press.

——— (1992a) *Arts and communities: The report of the National Inquiry into Arts and the Community.* London: Community Development Foundation.

CCPR/SHA (1991) *An enquiry into the provision of physical education in Secondary schools.* Aylesbury: Central Council for Physical Sport and Recreation/Secondary Heads Association.

Department of Employment (1994) *Labour market and skills trends — 1994/95.* Nottingham: DE.

DES (1989) *Physical education from 5 to 16, 'Curriculum Matters 16'*, HMI Series. London: HMSO.

——— (1991) *A sporting double: School and community.* London: Department of Education and Science.

——— (1992) *Physical education in the national curriculum.* London: HMSO.

Dobson, L. C. and West, E. G. (1988) 'Performing arts subsidies and future generations', *Journal of Cultural Economics: Canadian Perspectives.* Akron, USA, pp. 108-114.

Evans G. L. (1987) *Weekend Arts College: A model Youth Arts Training Programme* (Department of Arts Policy and Management). London: City University.

——— (1994) *An economic strategy for the arts and cultural industries in Haringey.* Haringey/London Arts Board, (Centre for Leisure and Tourism Studies), London: University of North London.

——— (1995) 'Survey of Local Authority Leisure Service Budgets — 1995/96'. London: Association of Metropolitan and District Councils.

Evans, G. L and Shaw, P. (1989) *The Arts after ILEA, Conference Report.* London: London Association of Arts Centres/Greater London Arts.

Fleming, S. (1933) 'Ethnicity and the physical education curriculum: Towards an anti-racist approach', in G. McFee and A. Tomlinson (eds) *Education, sport and leisure: Connections and controversies.* (Chelsea School Research Centre Topic Report 3). Eastbourne: University of Brighton, pp. 109-123.

Flintoff, A. (1991) 'Dance, masculinity and teacher education', *British Journal of Physical Education* (Winter), Vol. 22, No. 4: pp. 31-35.

Glick, R. (1986) *The dance and mime animateur movement*. London: Arts Council.

Greater London Arts (1990) *Dance into the nineties*. London: GLA.

Harland, J., Kinder, K. and Hartley, K. (1995) *Arts in their view: A study of youth Participation in the arts*. Slough: National Foundation for Education Research (NFER).

Henderson, J. (1986) 'Dance in the secondary school curriculum', *The Arts in Schools* (December). London: School curriculum Development Committee, pp. 8-9.

Henderson J. (1989a) 'Dance in the curriculum', *The Arts in Schools* (July). London: SCDC, pp. 16-17.

——— (1989b) 'Dance within physical education?', Coventry: National Foundation for Arts Education (NFAE), *Newsletter* 2 (December), pp. 4-5.

Horn, J. (1995) 'A share of cultural capital', *Guardian Education*. London: 11th July.

Hoyle, S. (1991) 'Dance', *National Arts and Media Strategy Discussion Document No. 24*. London: Arts Council of Great Britain.

ILEA (1988a) *A step in time: Dance for ILEA*. London: Inner London Education Authority.

——— (1988b) *Physical education, sport and dance — overview*. London: Inner London Education Authority.

——— (1987) *My favourite subject: Report of the Working Party in Physical Education and School Sport*. London: Inner London Education Authority.

Jackson, C., Honey, S., Hillage, J. and Stock, J. (1994) *Careers and training in dance and drama*. Brighton: Institute of Manpower Studies.

Kitto, H. D. (1951) *The Greeks*. Harmondsworth: Penguin.

LPAC (1993) Advice on Strategic Guidance for London. London: London Planning Advisory Committee.

McFee, G. (1993) 'Education, art and the physical: The case of the academic study of dance — present and future', in G. McFee and A. Tomlinson (eds) *Education, sport and leisure: Connections and controversies* (Chelsea School Research Centre Topic Report 3). Eastbourne: University of Brighton, pp. 95-108.

McFee, G. and Tomlinson, A. (eds) (1993) *Education, sport and leisure: Connections and controversies* (Chelsea School Research Centre Topic Report 3). Eastbourne: University of Brighton.

McFee, G. and Smith, F. (1995) 'Let's hear it for the boys: Dance, gender and education', in A. Tomlinson (ed) *Gender, sport and leisure: Continuities and challenges* (Chelsea School Research Centre Topic Report No. 4). Eastbourne: University of Brighton, pp. 63-80.

Miller, B. (1993) 'Femininity, Physical Activity and the curriculum', in G. McFee and A. Tomlinson (eds) *Education, sport and leisure: Connections and controversies* (Chelsea School Research Centre Topic Report 3). Eastbourne: University of Brighton, pp. 124-133.

Milosevic, L. (ed) (1995) *Fairplay, gender and physical education.* (A collection of discussion documents, research papers and practical guidance). Leeds: Leeds City Department of Education.

Morrison, W. G. and West, E. G. (1986) 'Child exposure to the performing arts: The implications for adult demand', *Journal of Cultural Economics*, Vol. 10, No. 1: pp. 17-24 (Akron, Ohio).

NCA (1993) *National Campaign for the Arts Newsletter* (Autumn)

NDTA (1989) *Dance in the school curriculum.* London: National Dance . London: NCA.Teachers Association.

——— (1990) 'Dance and the Child International — Towards the Future', Dance Education in the 1990s. Bedford: National Dance Teachers Association.

Rae, P. (1989) *Young people dancing.* London: Arts Council of Great Britain.

Robinson, K. (ed) (1982) *The arts in schools.* London: Gulbenkian Foundation.

Rogers, R. (1993a) *Looking over the edge: The debate. Advisory structures for the arts in education.* London: Arts Council of Great Britain.

——— (1993b) *Looking over the edge: The survey. Local Education Authority advisory services and inspection services.* London: Arts Council of Great Britain.

——— (1995) *Guaranteeing an entitlement to the arts in schools.* (May) London: Royal Society for the Arts.

Scraton, S. (1995) *Shaping up to womanhood: Gender and physical education.* Milton Keynes: Open University Press.

SHA (1994) *Enquiry into the provision of physical education in schools.* Aylesbury: Secondary Heads Association.

——— (1995) *Whither the arts? The state of the expressive arts in secondary schools.* Leicester: Secondary Heads Association.

Sillitoe, K. K. (1969) *Planning for leisure.* HMSO, London.

Sports Council (1986) *Movement and dance.* TUS Data Sheet No. 54, (February). London: Sports Council.

——— (1993) *Young people and sport: Policy and frameworks for action.* London: Sports Council.

Talbot, M. (1993) 'Physical education and the national curriculum: Some political issues', Education, Sport and Leisure, in G. McFee and A. Tomlinson (eds) *Education, sport and leisure: Connections and controversies* (Chelsea School Research Centre Topic Report 3). Eastbourne: University of Brighton, pp. 34-64.

Tomlinson, A. (ed) (1995) *Gender, sport and leisure: Continuities and challenges* (Chelsea School Research Centre Topic Report No. 4). Eastbourne: University of Brighton.

Wainwright, M. (1995) 'Dance: The men's movement', *Guardian Education,* 25th April, p. 6.

Willis, P. (199 1) 'Towards a new cultural map', *National Arts and Media Strategy Discussion Document No. 18.* London: Arts Council of Great Britain.

——— (1992) *Moving culture.* London: Calouste Gulbenkian Foundation.

Appendix I

Dance in Education — Selected Key Dates

1809	J H d'Egville — beginnings of first professional theatre dance school at Kings Theatre, London
1849	Benhamin Lumley — organised another also at the Kings Theatre
1872	Loen Espinosa — trained at Paris Opera, opened school in London
1876	His son, Eduard founded British Normal School of dancing, first school to hold exams and give certificate
1878	Ideas of the Swedish gymnast Ling introduced
1880	Martina Bergman Osterberg — opens her Physical Training College
1896	Rhoda Anstey, pupil of above, opens Physical Training College at Halesowen
1877	Isadore Duncan — new ideas of dance -1927
1909	Diaghilev company founded, taught by Erico Cechetti — who opened studio in London in 1918
1909	Board of Education's Syllabus of Physical Training recommends English Folk dance (Cecil Sharp occasional Inspector)
1910	Margaret Morris opened her own school in London
1914	Ruby Ginner founded her own school of Revived Greek dancing
1912	Eurhythmics of Emile Jacques-Dalcroze introduced
1920	Marie Rambert founded Rambert School
1926	Nanette de Valois — Academy of Choreograpic Art
1920-	Madge Atkinson developed 'The Dance based on Natural Movement' — opened school in Manchester 1930s
Growth of private schools — 1914 Bush School: 1939 Bush Davies School	
mid 30s	Joan Goodrich — trained at Bedford College of P. E. Studies with Mary Wiginan, Leipzig
1930	Leslie Burrows, Lousie Soelbcrg, Joan Goodrich, Diana Jordan — study M Morris and M Wigman
1931	Viv Wells ballet school opens
1934	Kurt Joos brings his dance co. to Britain with Sigurd Leeder who had been a pupil of Laban
1937	Educational Dance Drama Co. — first company to go into schools

(cont.)

1943	Rudolf Laban and Lisa Ullman open 'Art of Movement School' in Manchester
1947	S Leeder — own school in London
1962	'Dance for Everyone' — first professional dance co. in schools
1964	'Ballet for All' — Royal Ballet Company educational outreach project
1970-76	London Contemporary Dance Residencies in schools
1976	First BA (Hons) degree (Laban Centre, Goldsmiths College) in Dance recognised by the CNAA
1980	3 Projects: Dance Artists in Education, funded by the Arts Council
1982	National Youth Dance Festival established annually (supported by the Gulbenkian Foundation)
1982	Dance in Education conference — organised by the Arts Council and DES
1986	First Inspector for Dance appointed by the ILEA (moves Dance away from PE Inspectorate)
1988	Education Reform Act — National Curriculum and LMS. Dance subsumed into PE (Drama into English)
1989	Abolition of the ILEA, Dance Inspectorate and Centre for Physical Education wound-up (not maintained by host borough, Westminster). Dance into Schools programme ceases
1995	Dearing Review of the National Curriculum published — return to greater decision-making at school level but time for school PE and arts subjects, especially dance and drama, still under threat

Conflict with Policy Implementation in Physical Education: the Case of Dance in the Northern Ireland Curriculum

Deirdre Brennan

University of Ulster

Introduction

This paper focuses on the problems, real and perceived, surrounding dance as a discrete element within the new Northern Ireland Curriculum. Despite an allegedly common curriculum the compulsory status of dance at key stages one, two and three for boys and girls is unique to Northern Irish schools. I will not spend time reviewing the historical development of dance in physical education (PE) or debating the ideological differences and conceptual classification of dance. These background elements have been well covered elsewhere in work completed by Stevens (1992), Talbot (1993), Flintoff (1991) Lipscomb (1986) and Glaister (1987). Instead it is my intention to establish first the educational context within which this innovation is set, then explore the commonplace, stereotypical attitudes that have given dance its gendered status. However, the bulk of this paper is centred on an investigation into the attitudes of experienced and newly trained physical educational specialists to the establishment of dance as a compulsory element on the National Curriculum for Physical Education (NCPE) for Northern Ireland.

The context

Education in Northern Ireland, a society deeply divided along sectarian lines, possesses a unique selective educational system that segregates specifically in terms of academic ability and generally in terms of religious affiliation and social class. Sugden and Bairner (1993) state that although format recruitment from one section of the community does not exist, there is a tradition of sectarian self-selection that receives unspoken approval by church leaders and so ensures that the school system remains segregated. Elements of the school curriculum have been used to promote the separate Catholic and Protestant traditions and physical education is no exception. Sugden and Bairner (1993) state that through a differential promotion of sports and games PE can be criticised for exacerbating rather than dissipating differences between the two cultures.

From the outside, one might also suspect that the teaching of national dance as part of the PE programme might pose some problems between the two distinct cultures in the province. Historically dance has had a very strong tradition in girls' physical education programmes around the world, and Northern Ireland is a good example of this. However, from the writer's own experience and knowledge in the field, dance is not used in the school context to reinforce Gaelic culture over Anglo culture. On the contrary, English dance and a range of dances from elsewhere in Europe and in Israel are very prevalent in dance programmes in schools. In the context of Northern Ireland, the Working Party for Physical Education (DENI, 1990) identified dance as an activity which (if successfully presented and delivered, and if having the suggested impact) would not only promote health and movement but also address a variety of social problems inherent in the school curriculum relating to religion, gender and class.

Dance and the gender equity debate in Physical Education

Research carried out by Stevens (1992), Flintoff (1991), Talbot (1993) and Glaister (1987) suggests that the rationales for the inclusion of dance in physical education have altered and have been widely debated over the years. In brief they identify arguments supporting dance in PE that include its ability to: provide health and fitness benefits; develop artistic qualities, promote an understanding and appreciation of different cultures; provide a non competitive means of developing physically, emotionally and aesthetically and protect the distinction of physical education from sport. Although few would debate the educational value of dance, counter-arguments have been voiced suggesting that dance is the 'odd activity out' in physical education, that its rightful place is in the arts and that it is not a priority in an already overcrowded PE curriculum. However, it is dance's association with femininity that is probably the greatest deterrent to its establishment in boys' PE programmes. Sherlock (1987) adds that the educational artistic and aesthetic objectives inherent in dance teaching were and still are eagerly embraced by female professionals. This respect does not appear to be characteristic of most male professionals. Subsequently dance teaching has remained a stronghold of female PE and as such is seen mostly as a female subject and concern.

Evans (1989) believes strongly that the games-dominated physical education curriculum in evidence before the Education Reform Act 1988 was guilty of perpetuating gendered behaviour. It is questionable whether the provision of a common curriculum will challenge gender myths without adequate organisational, curriculum, pedagogical and assessment support. Talbot (1993) warns that open access alone will do little to challenge traditional views and stereotyped conceptions. Findings by Lever (1978) suggest that early socialisation patterns ensure children are aware of gender appropriate behaviour before attending school. This is then further compounded by the promotion and delivery of sex segregated activities in physical education at secondary school. These teaching and presentation practices are to the detriment of boys, who receive an inadequate experience of cooperative and aesthetic activities, like dance; and girls who receive a poor experience of sport (Evans, 1984; Talbot, 1993; Scraton, 1986). Reasons for this partly reflect the conflict between values attributed to sport and dance, and values attributed to femininity and masculinity respectively — both of which are beyond the control of the physical educationalist.

As popular prejudice aligns dance with femininity (Talbot, 1993; Connell, 1989) dancing for boys is seen as inappropriate. This cultural assumption is farther magnified by the ascribed low status of activities associated with girls and women, which is unlike the greater social value achieved by activities associated with boys and men. Stevens (1992) supports this by adding that the question of dance being viewed as essentially a female activity is due to the traditional views of masculinity held in society, and also the traditional games and sports dominated physical education courses largely found in male specialist colleges. In Northern Ireland, although male physical educational specialists from provincial single sex and coeducational teacher training institutions study dance in a practical form when undergoing training, dance has not traditionally been taught to boys in schools in Northern Ireland.

Scraton (1986) argues strongly that physical education has the potential to redress the gender argument. This is supported by Whitson (1990) who adds that as the body is central to ideologies of masculinity, femininity and sexuality, PE is likely to play a significant role. Connell (1989) adds that as physicality and physical prowess are central features of masculinity, particular sports are the very context within which boys learn how to project and experience power and physical presence. Not surprisingly dance, a traditional feminine domain, is therefore perceived as an unsuitable medium for what Brittain (1989) termed masculine identity work, and as a result it has never been a prominent feature in boys' PE.

In stark contrast Loadman (1992) argues that as well as providing a vehicle for aesthetic and emotional expression dance also provides an equally valuable medium through which those physical attributes perceived as masculine and desirable can be readily achieved. Dance in its multitudinous forms can encapsulate strength, power and athleticism, qualities conceived as archetypically male.

Now that the NCPE for Northern Ireland is in place the realism of having to teach dance to all pupils in Northern Ireland has arrived. McFee and Tomlinson (1993) believe that conflict, contestation and struggle is commonplace in the process of policy application and that simply designing and offering an entitlement curriculum is no guarantee that this is what teachers can and will deliver or what pupils will receive. Policies are, they add, inevitably adapted, adopted, contested and resisted during the process of implementation. Evans (*et al.*, 1993) stated:

> Whether teachers go forward, make progress, retreat or stay will depend not only on the physical resources that they bring to the subject but also on many other aspects of the sociocultural and economic conditions and contexts in which they work. (p. 18)

Methodology

The aim of this study was to illuminate the attitudes of PE specialists to the establishment of dance as a discrete element in the NCPE for Northern Ireland. The research sample consisted of thirty five physical education teachers practising in schools in the North Down area (four single sex schools and ten coeducational institutions) and nineteen teachers recently graduated from the 1993/4 Initial Teacher Training Course at the University of Ulster at Jordanstown. Attitude questionnaires were distributed asking subjects to record what they perceived as the physical education teacher's job, their attitudes towards dance and their perceived fears about teaching dance. There was a 71% return rate from the practising teachers and an 80% return rate from the new graduate teachers. 82% of the practising teacher respondents were female. 56% of this total were from coeduational institutions where the questionnaires were distributed to both male and female staff. Semi-structured interviews targeting two male and two female physical education specialists were used in order to facilitate deeper investigation of issues raised in the questionnaires returned.

Results of the study: Teachers — the tools of policy implementation

The research revealed that over 96% of the respondents concurred with the 'health focus' prevalent in the Northern Ireland Physical Education document, by stating that their job revolved around the promotion of all-round body development and health and fitness. Only 20% of the experienced teachers, in comparison to 41% of the new graduates, believed they have a duty to strive for excellence in a particular sport. It is possible to surmise that the recently trained and inexperienced professionals are unaware of the difficulties of such a task in the present physical education climate in schools. However the two research groups converge again (72% and 82%) when they consider that it is part of their job to encourage competition with other schools. It is interesting however that only 24% of the practising respondents agreed that their job entailed providing children with the opportunity to experience a variety of activities. A further 76% chose not to respond to the job characteristic described as 'enabling pupils to gain enjoyment and an aesthetic appreciation of movement through purposeful, progressive physical activity'. Both of these non-response rates are disturbing given the philosophy of the national curriculum that supports a broad and balanced curriculum. However in stark contrast, all of the new graduates agreed that it was their job to offer a wide range of physical activities through which children could gain enjoyment and an aesthetic appreciation of movement. It is possible to assert that the recently trained professionals comprehend fully, and are firm believers in, the NCPE as their training has been centred around it.

This study also revealed that although 60% of the practitioner respondents were undecided about whether dance was a worthwhile use of PE time, 92% agreed that it *is* an aspect of PE. In comparison, some 76% of the new graduates were in agreement that it is a worthwhile activity with only 24% undecided. All responded positively to the statement 'dance is an aspect of physical education'. This finding supports the statement by Talbot (1993) that although dance is valued it is not a priority within the taught curriculum with present practitioners. In addition, finding time in an already overcrowded curriculum for dance was perceived as problematic. However with the strong positive response from the graduate teachers it may be possible that in the future greater value will be placed on dance in real terms — i.e. in terms the quality of the programme and time allocation. Indeed there was a strong belief that dance merited inclusion in the National Curriculum, and over half the subjects in both groups (56% and 64%) agreed that it is integral to the general school curriculum. Further insights into the recorded teacher attitudes show that they consider dance an activity that might be more effectively placed and presented in another subject area, for example English, Drama or Music. However, Flintoff (1990: p. 90) rejects this, stating that:

> ...it is time for the outmoded, stereotypical attitudes towards dance held among some PE people to be banished once and for all, and for the profession to welcome dance, within its remit, rather than suggesting that it go elsewhere. (quoted in Talbot, 1993: p. 37)

Although both groups responded with a powerful negative reaction to the statements 'dance is feminine' (over 90%) and 'male dancers are effeminate' (over 80%) this must be seen in light of the fact that 82% of the practitioner respondents to the questionnaire were female specialists from within the fourteen targeted PE departments. 56% of this total were from ten coeducational institutions where the questionnaires were distributed to both male and female staff. The lack of response from practising male specialists in this sample speaks volumes regarding their dismissiveness of dance. It supports Evans (1989) who states that it is the male PE teachers who are the least committed and even antipathetic towards dance.

This study revealed that a lack of training and subsequently knowledge both in terms of possible content and suitable music were ranked as the greatest perceived problems among practising teachers with 68% and 36% of the respondents placing them 1st and 2nd respectively. 50% of the subjects stated fear of lack of personal ability for teaching and demonstrating between 1st and 4th. Lack of teacher confidence was identified by Davidson (1993) as probably one of the most limiting factors on the introduction and presentation of dance to boys in schools.

As Talbot (1993: p. 37) identifies, some members of the PE profession urged that it was the aesthetic activities of dance and gymnastics that set physical education apart from sport, and it is these very activities that most professionals find difficulty in teaching. Many dance specialists and many PE teachers (fearful of their lack of ability) urge that dance as an art form will be destroyed by the 'non dancer' PE teacher. But over half the practitioner respondents (52%) and 94% of the new graduates seem to believe that, just as one does not have to be a professional footballer to teach or enjoy football, so one can enjoy and teach dance without being a professional dancer.

In the sample of new graduate teachers, lack of knowledge concerning content and music and lack of confidence in presentation skills were ranked between 5th and 8th. It is possible to surmise that on teaching practice these students derived some gratification from the lack of expertise and experience in teaching dance among practising professionals. As a result they feel confident based on their recent and relevant training in the area of dance teaching. It was also revealed that dance is still under-represented, especially in the boys' PE curriculum, despite the innovation of the new Northern Ireland curriculum. Old stereotypes associated with dance, which are claimed to be natural and are rarely questioned, are still prevalent in society and schools in Northern Ireland today, Few male professionals have shown that they are prepared to take the risks inherent in challenging such conventions.

In discussion with the 1994 cohort of new graduate teachers on return from their final teaching practice it became evident that, although dance had secured a place on the designated programmes of study for physical education, for boys it typically appears to be in name only. One student remarked that in his teaching practice school, an all male grammar school, the department had even gone as far as to design a unit of work for inspection purposes only. This rejection of dance is evident throughout the school population and community, including Head teachers, PE teachers, other staff and parents, and is based on the belief that the activity is effeminate and could damage the school image. Male PE staff noted how they were cajoled by other male members of staff about having to teach dance, about having to invest in a pair of dance tights for the new school year instead of a new track suit. The stated fear that achieved greatest ranking by the new graduates was the statement 'I do not feel parents would value dance for their boys'. This could possibly be explained in terms of their own physical education histories as, with one exception, all attended either Catholic or Protestant grammar schools, where the emphasis has been very much on competitive team games. It is possible that in retrospect they feel their parents would not have liked to have seen dance detract from their potential to perform and succeed as young school stars in their respective sports. They are simply products of the system.

The next greatest fear or difficulty discerned by the newly trained professionals was without exception a combination of the attitudes of established teachers and the stereotypical attitudes of pupils towards dance that generally tend to result in a poor pupil response to dance classes (Davidson, 1993). Again it is possible to surmise that the students were actually faced with these very problems when on teaching practice. In practically every case where dance was on the programme, the male students were used to deliver the key stage three compulsory dance module due to the reluctance of existing professionals in the department. Although this may have been a difficult baptism for the students, at least it was one in which their expertise and the knowledge and awareness of the departmental members could be improved and extended.

At present the difficulties are mainly arising where boys, particularly in single sex schools, are being introduced to dance for the very first time. However, the development and effective teaching of dance in the primary school at key stage one and two should eventually reduce the alienation boys feel from what often becomes a female orientated activity. Nevertheless, one must ask just how realistic it is to expect PE professionals of 20 years experience or more, but with no dance expertise, to teach dance to boys with no training?. Levels of participation in PE classes are often determined by the quality of the experience. PE teachers, particularly those in inner city schools, already face challenges getting children to participate in traditional physical activities and games. Indiscipline often stems from the lack of appropriateness of lesson content for the pupils. If dance is taught by someone with no interest, enthusiasm or knowledge, to pupils with even less interest, enthusiasm and knowledge, we should not be surprised if pupils display negative feelings and behaviour in class. This task is therefore understandably avoided in many inner city all-boys secondary schools on what the professionals consider to be sound educational arguments. This is not to say that there are no problems in the coeducational setting. Evans (1989) foresees problems even in the coeducational setting stating that boys need to gain confidence in their own movement ability before being set alongside girls who have experienced dance for a number of years. Flintoff (1991) believes that, in the context of coeducational PE, dance is often left to the committed female PE teacher to struggle alone with mixed classes characterised by hostile and indifferent boys, because few male PE teachers are willing to discard their prejudices to make dance teaching attractive and relevant.

Before the National Curriculum, in the sample surveyed in this study, 96% of dance was taught by females. Little seems to have changed except that even more female professionals are now burdened with the task. Further work and preparation by the female specialist is therefore added to her commitments. Lipscomb (1986) suggests that the preparation that has to go into a dance lesson is often the reason why these lessons have been excluded by the teacher. After all, she says, you can give a ball to 22 youngsters and they will play for hours, but children find it strange to move around the room to music. Only occasionally is there any 'pay-back' by a male specialist into a girls' PE programme. Flintoff (1991) supports this, adding that it is seldom that games such as rugby and football are taught in mixed settings. The potential of these activities, "flag carriers of " (Bryson, 1990), as a major context for masculine identity work is severely reduced in a mixed environment (Whitson, 1990). The short term solution of female specialists delivering dance does not contribute to the erosion of stereotypical notions that are heavily connected to dance in the educational setting. As one respondent replied:

> "The absence of a male role model and the substitution of a female one will probably only serve to further reinforce stereotypical and traditional notions of dance as a feminine activity."

This study also revealed that some male professionals have interpreted and presented the dance programme of study in a form that reflects circuits or fitness training to music. Scraton (1993) found similar cases in her study and her explanation was that when a traditional female activity such as dance is considered for boys there is seen to be a need to adapt it to 'masculinity'. Consequently, powerful stereotypical attitudes remain and little physical liberation is taking place. Scraton also found that even when teachers taught Modern Educational Dance (MED) to their boys they presented it through 'appropriate' themes, that is, themes requiring stronger more assertive movements. This interpretation of dance is carefully protecting the sexuality of boys with a reinforcement of masculine qualities and dignity.

Many male specialists in Northern Ireland are protesting about the inclusion of dance, but this must be seen in light of the complete educational innovation. The Sports Council for Northern Ireland (SCNI) report details that at key stage three in 1990/91 boys were offered only two of the required elements of the new curriculum — i.e. athletics and an invasion game. Consequently there are pressures on male specialists to implement all the changes inherent in the new reform. Dance, whilst the greatest, is only one, and has caused great anxiety. In stark contrast most elements of the key stage three curriculum were covered in at least 90% of the girls schools. This Sports Council survey appears to suggest that the range of content has always been far superior in female physical education. In many respects this should not come as any surprise as women have a longer and more distinguished history in Physical Education. Sherlock

(1987) states that women have led the educational field, displaying a commitment and concern for educational philosophy and an emphasis on the education of the child through the physical.

It's not what you do, it's the way that you do it!

The National Curriculum makes it quite clear that to present the programmes of study successfully, pedagogical practices need to be scrutinised and in some cases modified. Evans *et al.* (1993) add that it is the didactic style and practices that emphasise performance, technical learning and the teacher as the only resource for learning that may no longer be appropriate. A direct style of teaching is required for a national dance lesson as the music is prescribed and a menu of steps, holds and formations is written down for you. Not surprisingly this was ranked as both the most popular (92%) and easiest (56%) form of dance to teach by practising specialists. The type of dance taught most frequently by the new graduates was MED (82%) possibly because specialist teachers were looking for new fresh content and presentation ideas in light of the programme of study for dance contained within the new physical education curriculum. Contemporary or MED requires greater thought, preparation and a skilled use of a variety of teaching strategies. In stark contrast to their professional counterparts, the new professionals responded with an even split between national dance (47%) and MED (48%) as easiest to teach. One could assume this reflects their recent introduction to ideas, resources and presentation strategies for both types of dance as part of their training.

A didactic style of teaching is arguably associated more with male specialists in the profession who have been more devoted to a disciplined approach to performance measurement and results. Therefore they have been bombarded, in a very short period, with the need to restructure their programmes and their pedagogical practices and assumptions. The security of established patterns will not be swapped too readily for the fear of the unknown. Nevertheless, the reality is that all PE teachers are now legally responsible and accountable for the programmes they present and the methods they use to deliver them. The rejection of innovations inherent in the new reform cannot be explained in pedagogical terms alone. In the case of dance for boys in particular, the consideration of gender cuts across all other problem boundaries. Indeed it may even be possible to contend that it is the challenge to stereotypical norms that is the root of the lack of confidence displayed in pedagogical terms by physical educationalists with a responsibility for teaching dance.

Lipscomb (1986) alleges that some physical educationalists find dance difficult to accept because "many are still smarting from the days when they pretended to be trees..." (p. 65). It is encouraging to see, from the research reported here, that there are so many positive responses to dance from the new graduate teacher cohort. The level of confidence recorded by them reflects real hope for the future of dance in Northern Ireland schools.

Flintoff (1991) states that ultimately it is ideas that provide the dynamics for changing attitudes and eradicating prejudices. Students in Initial Teacher Training (ITT) need to be encouraged to challenge, to analyse and to evaluate rather than simply absorb and imitate. Teacher training courses have a responsibility to address issues of equity and equality of opportunity on their courses. However with the shift to a school based approach to training already in effect, it remains to be seen whether the quality of training will be upheld. At the University of Ulster at Jordanstown the Post Graduate Certificate in Education course for physical education students prides itself in focusing unashamedly on the aspects of PE that set it apart from sport. Recognising that the majority of its students, male and female, arrive with a strong games background, the aesthetic elements of gymnastics and dance are singled out for special study during the year. The assumption that females are innately good at dance and that males are innately poor is strongly contested in theory and in practice. The truth is that in many cases the female professional is no happier with the thought of having to teach dance than her male colleague. Most have originated from a games background and have had only minimal experience in dance at school when compared to other activities. What they do have on their side is the appropriateness of dance for their gender, an acceptance that dance is suitable to be taught by them and performed by their girls. Male professionals on the other hand, who have little or no dance experience, have the task of overcoming established and accepted societal norms of masculine behaviour that do not promote dance as an appropriate training ground for boys or men.

Conclusions

Depending on your perspective, the challenges contained within the NCPE for Northern Ireland can be viewed as either dangerous or promising. The impact of the latter perspectives will be dramatically different in terms of the action and direction that could be taken and the progress that could be made in physical education. Laws (1994) uses the analogy of 'circling the wagon' to meet a threat, as one alternative that is available, this is to stand still or reduce oneself to travelling in circles. A second alternative is to do nothing, out of indecision, or in the hope that the danger will pass, Zeigler (1986) describes this irresolution as 'decidophobia'. But to view these current issues as promising opportunities is to commit to action and set about the task of defining strategies to make the best of each opportunity to improve the field of PE. Results of this study suggest that physical education teachers in Northern Ireland are represented in each of the latter categories. Some male PE teachers have taken up the challenge and are teaching dance to boys in school. Others have anticipated difficulties and as a result have negotiated with their female counterparts to sit in or team teach in the dance modules so that they gain experience in content variety and presentation techniques. Others have not made the change, either because of lack of knowledge and lack of confidence, or because they do not agree to it. The variety of responses by PE professionals can be partly explained by differences in pre-service dance training, school ethos, parental attitude, pupil attitudes and perceptions, resources and teacher professionalism. One physical education specialist outlined contextual factors such as the attitude of the school to equal opportunities, the attitude of the head teacher to dance, the status of PE in the school and the commitment of the PE staff as the determining 'in-house' factors in the acceptance or rejection of dance in schools. It is the responsibility of the government and its educational authorities to see that external factors such as adequate ongoing resourcing and inservice training are offered where there is a need and demand for them.

The results also indicate that PE professionals need to confront their own beliefs and prejudices and examine how these are reflected in their teaching. As Flintoff (1991) suggests, professionals need to challenge the role of PE in the reinforcement and reproduction of hegemonic masculinity that is central to the maintenance of patriarchal power relations. But to achieve this, professionals in the field must first be prepared to admit that there is a problem. Physical education professionals need to recognise that girls and boys are both alike and different. Once these differences and similarities are identified teaching strategies should be used which assure equal treatment. Many committed professionals who are unhappy with the present inclusion of dance are fearful on legitimate grounds. They put much time and effort into the presentation of sound, effective and stimulating lessons and do not want to run the risk of discouraging or disillusioning pupils with a dance module that they feel unable to present effectively which therefore only serves to initiate feelings of negativity towards physical education.

Educational reform is often a slow and difficult process. All that can be reasonably expected of teachers of dance (male or female) to boys and girls is that they present equitable, purposeful and enjoyable lessons. A small contribution to the erosion of gender norms is all that is required. Education is a microcosm of society. Teachers alone cannot be expected to challenge or dismantle the sociocultural conditions that have generated the gender debate. In the case of Northern Ireland if dance is taught effectively it could act as a catalyst for reform. It is time for the obsolete notions of dance as a 'wet weather' alternative (Stevens, 1992) and 'dance is for girls only' to be eradicated. The successful implementation and presentation of the National Curriculum is almost entirely reliant on the degree of professionalism and competency displayed by practising teachers and newly qualified professionals. In the case of dance in boys' PE in Northern Ireland the level of professionalism is being severely tested.

Although all the respondents unequivocally recognised and supported educative value of dance for both genders it should come as no surprise that dance has not been welcomed in male PE circles. The prevailing political climate prescribing an emphasis on equal opportunities created the opportunity for serious consideration of dance as an activity for all within the PE curriculum. However the recently released Government policy statement on sport, 'Sport: Raising the Game' (DNH, 1995), details as one of its proposals a revised PE curriculum with an enhanced role for team games that should now be in effect in schools in England and Wales. It stipulates that a minimum of two hours per week should be devoted to team games in the PE curriculum, with a further fours hours to be devoted to games for all interested pupils after school. Schools will be accountable for their sporting provision and performance with 'Gold Star' and Sportsmark' awards available for those that achieve high standards. Ignoring the widespread implications that this initiative has for PE in general, if this innovation was to be implemented in Northern Ireland there would be widespread implications. As identified earlier by Sugden and Bairner (1993), by prioritising games in a region like Northern Ireland where you are what you play, and by delivering these games through a segregated educational system, there is a risk of legitimising programmes that will reinforce and further strengthen sectarian boundaries and divisions. The concept of a broad and balanced curriculum as evidenced in the NCPE, which addresses all abilities, interests and maturities is also in danger. A process of prioritisation will jeopardise the position of the more aesthetic activities such as dance and gymnastics, as weel as individual and partner activities in the PE curriculum. Jennifer Hargreaves (1995) proposes that this initiative is regressive and likely to accentuate gender conventions in ways that are as much, if not more of a limitation for boys as for girls. It could be that if this proposal is accepted and implemented the perceived fears of male physical educationalists in Northern Ireland of dance will finally be alleviated, but at what cost?

Equality of opportunity, which the NCPE for Northern Ireland provides for, is a sound and admirable step taken by the policy makers that has forced educators to be reflective of their practices and address the equity issue. Irrespective of the possible forthcoming changes, Northern Ireland can be proud of their ownership of a farsighted policy which has stimulated an extension and improvement of both the teaching and learning experiences within the subject of physical education.

References

Brittain, A. (1989) cited in Flintoff, A. (1991) 'Dance, masculinity and teacher education', *The British Journal of Physical Education* (Winter): pp. 31-35.

Bryson, L. (1990) 'Challenges to male hegemony in sport', in M.A. Messner and D. F. Sabo (1990) (eds) *Sport, men and the gender order: Critical feminist perspective*. Illinois: Human Kinetics, pp. 173-184.

Connell, R. W. (1989) 'Cool guys, swots and wimps', *Oxford Review of Education*, Vol. 15, No. 3: pp. 292-303.

Davidson, M. (1993) 'Dance in the post primary school', *Inform*, published by the Northern Ireland Curriculum Council: pp. 7-8.

Department of National Heritage (1995) *Sport: Raising the game*. London: Department of National Heritage.

DENI (1990) *Proposals for physical education in the Northern Ireland curriculum*. Belfast: HMSO.

Evans, J. (1984) 'Muscle, sweat and showers. Girls' conception of physical education and sport: a challenge for research and curriculum reform', *Physical Education Review*, Vol. 7, No. 1: pp. 12-18.

——— (1989) 'Swinging from the crossbar. Equality and opportunity in the Physical Education Curriculum', *British Journal of Physical Education*, Summer, pp. 84-87.

——— (1989) 'Responses to the Gender Equity Debate', *The Australian Council for Health Physical Education and Recreation National Journal* (March), pp. 8-11.

Evans, J., Penney, D. and Bryant, A. (1993) 'Playing by market rules: Physical Education in England and Wales after ERA', in G. McFee and A. Tomlinson (eds) *Education, sport and leisure: Connections and controversies*. Chelsea School Research Centre (CSRC). Eastbourne: University of Brighton, pp. 17-33.

Flintoff, A. (1990) 'Physical education, equal opportunities and the national curriculum', *Physical Education Review*, Vol. 13, No. 2: pp. 85-100.

——— (1991) 'Dance, masculinity and teacher education', *British Journal of Physical Education* (Winter): pp. 31-35.

Glaister, I. (1987) 'Dance education 1938–1958', *British Journal of Physical Education*, Vol. 18, Part 3: pp. 104-106.

Hargreaves, J. (1995) 'Gender, morality and the National Physical Education Curriculum', in L. Lawrence, E. Murdoch and S. R. Parker (eds) *Professional and development issues in leisure, sport and education*. LSA Publication No. 56. Eastbourne: Leisure Studies Association: pp. 23–40.

Laws, C. J. (1994) 'New dimensions for physical education teacher training in England and Wales', in F. I. Bell and G. H. Van Gyn (eds) *Access to active living*. Proceedings of the 10th Commonwealth and International Scientific Congress 10-14 August 1994, University of Victoria, Canada, pp. 157-162.

Lever, J. (1978) 'Sex differences in the complexity of childrens play and games', *American Sociological Review*, Vol. 43, August: pp. 471-483.

Lipscomb, B. (1986) 'The trouble with dance is its name', *Bulletin of Physical Education*, Vol. 22: pp. 65-68.

Loadman, A. (1992) 'Dance, masculinity and teacher education: A reply to Flintoff', *British Journal of Physical Education* (Summer): p. 39.

McFee, G. and Tomlinson, A. (1993) 'Curriculum, change and critique: Themes in the study of education, sport and leisure', in G. McFee and A. Tomlinson (eds) *Education, sport and leisure: Connections and controversies*. Eastbourne: CSRC, University of Brighton, pp. 3-14.

Report prepared for the Sports Council for Northern Ireland by the Northern Ireland Council for Educational Research. Physical Education and Games in Post-Primary Schools in 1991.

Scraton, S. (1986) 'Gender and girls physical education', *British Journal of Physical Education*, Vol. 17, No. 4: pp. 145-147.

Sherlock, J. (1987) 'Issues of masculinity and femininity in British physical education', *Women's Studies International Forum*, Vol. 10, No. 4: pp. 443-45.

Stevens, S. (1992) 'Dance in the national curriculum', in N. Armstrong (ed) *New directions in physical education, Vol. 2. Towards a National Curriculum*. Illinois: Human Kinetics Publishers.

Sugden, J. and Bairner, A. (1993) *Sport, sectarianism and society in a divided Ireland*. England: Leicester University Press.

Talbot, M. (1993) 'Physical education and the national curriculum: Some political issues', in G. McFee and A. Tomlinson (eds) *Education, sport and leisure: Connections and controversies*. Eastbourne: CSRC, University of Brighton, pp. 34-64.

Whitson, D. (1990) cited in Flintoff, A. (1991) 'Dance, masculinity and teacher education', *The British Journal of Physical Education* (Winter) (1991): pp. 31-35.

Zeigler, E. (1986) cited in Laws, C. J., *New dimensions for physical education teacher training in England and Wales. Access to active living.* 10th Commonwealth and International Scientific Congress Conference Proceedings. Canada. University of Victoria, p. 159.

Sport For All — 'RIP'. A Political Critique of the Relationship between National Sport Policy and Local Authority Sports Development in London

Ian McDonald

Roehampton Institute London

Introduction

This paper is a political critique of local authority sports development in London. To undertake such a study effectively it is necessary to locate the specific practices in London within the wider social and political context in order to tease out the relationships and linkages between the two. It is the dialectical relationship between the specific and the general, and between the empirical and the theoretical, that underpins this analysis and political critique.

Sports development as a concept, as a profession, and as practice, has changed significantly in the last decade. Mostly, this is presented in positive and evolutionary terms as a process of maturation. This paper takes issue with and rejects this representation. It is symptomatic of a dominant discourse in sports development which is a theoretical and lacking in critical analysis. An alternative analysis is presented here which attempts to interpret practice based on a theorised account of sports development. From a perspective sympathetic to *Sport for All*, the contention is that, *on the whole*, the change in sports development has been regressive. Two related arguments will be put, which in propositional form are:

(i) that the sports development profession is turning its back on the mass participation goals of *Sport for All*,

(ii) that the dominant forms of local authority sports development are, in London at least, more of a fetter than a facilitator in extending the opportunities for sport and recreational activities to all.

This analysis is premised on a rejection of essentialist readings of values inherent in sport as a form of physical activity and an insistence on the social and cultural specificity of attributed meanings. Identifying and interpreting the social significance and values underpinning the notion of 'sport' in sports development is fundamental to the construction of this political critique.

Therefore the first part of the paper attempts to disentangle the two dominant conceptions of sport that relate to sports development. The first is the 'sport' referred to in the Government's policy document *Sport: Raising the Game* (DNH, 1995) and the second is the 'sport' which derives from the concept of *Sport for All*. Their relationship with Sports Council policy and the sports development profession will then be discussed before the analysis of local authority sports development in London.

Raise the game, break the tape

Over the past year, a policy framework for the development of sport has emerged which is as significant as the formation of the executive GB Sports Council in 1972 and as dramatic as the Action Sport projects initiated in 1982.

The emergence of this policy framework can be seen in two stages. First there was the announcement on the 8th July, 1994, by the Conservative 'Minister for Sport'[1], Iain Sproat, that a newly formed English Sports Council will "withdraw from the promotion of mass participation, and informal recreation, and leisure pursuits, and from health promotion", instead shifting its focus to "services in support of excellence" (DNH, 1994: p. 4).

Secondly, the government published a major sports policy statement, *Sport; Raising the Game* in July, 1995. The substance of the document advocates putting traditional, competitive team sports back at the heart of school life, as the first step on the road to excellence and "breaking the tape in an Olympic final" (DNH, 1995: p. 1).

Significantly John Major is closely associated with the new policy of an achievement-oriented drive to 'raise the game' designed to deliver sporting success. A clue as to why this should be the case is given in his introduction to Sport; Raising the Game where he states that "Sport is a central part of Britain's National Heritage" (DNH, 1995: p. 2). Yet as Lincoln Allison (1994) noted in an article reflecting on Sproat's announcement:

> ...all governments in this age of competition, the performance principle and global sport, have become aware that sporting success and failure are seen as an index of national well-being. (p. 24)

And John Major has certainly witnessed and indeed suffered politically from the fall-out of English sporting failure. In the Ashes series of 1993 the English cricket team plummeted to a 4-1 defeat to an unfancied Australian side. In football that same summer, England failed to qualify for the World Cup finals. The tabloid press encapsulated the national mood by portraying the England manager Graham Taylor as a turnip, soon followed by the transformation of cricket captain Graham Gooch into a potato. Comparisons were made between the hapless Taylor and Gooch with the helpless Prime Minister who was presiding over an increasingly divided and unpopular Tory party. Sproat acknowledged the parallels drawn between the malaise of England's traditional national sports and the economic and social malaise of the country, by writing in the Daily Telegraph that:

> The best way to lay the foundation for national victories (in sport) in the future is to start again teaching games widely and well in our schools ... in that way we shall improve ...national morale.... (Sproat, 1994: p. 39)

The Conservative government agenda for sport participation is based on politically expedient and instrumental aims, where the focus is on extrinsic benefits, such as the restoration of national/patriotic pride. A yawning chasm separates this perspective from the social philosophy of *Sport for All.*

The promise of *Sport for All*

The European Sports Charter charges all governments, "to enable every individual to participate in sport..." (Council of Europe, undated). This 'charge' is based on a belief in the potential of sport to contribute to the quality of life of 'every individual'. For sport to relate to 'every individual' it has to be defined universally. As Coghlan notes:

> *Sport for All* was defined (by the Council of Europe in 1976) as something quite different from the original concept of sport, embracing not only sport proper but also, *and perhaps above all* (my emphasis) various forms of physical activity from spontaneous unorganised games to the minimum of physical exercises regularly performed. (1990: p. 117)

In other words the 'sport' in *Sport for All* is a loose term for such disparate activities as informal recreation, leisure pursuits, play, health promotion activities as well as formal organised sport. In terms of social policy, Ravenscroft (1992: p. 23) argues that up until the mid-1980s *Sport for All* had six major aims:

1) to increase participation and performance in sport;
2) to have sport treated as a social service;
3) to produce a range of social benefits, such as the maintenance of moral standards and improved social welfare;
4) to produce a range of psychological benefits, such as the enjoyment of leisure and the advancement of personality;

5) to produce certain physiological benefits, such as an improvement in the nation's health and fitness; and
6) to improve the quality of life of the nation.

Although in principle *Sport for All* incorporated both elite and mass sport, in practice, wider social and political policy concerns dictated that the emphasis was on increasing opportunities for participation in a wide range of activities, rather than developing performance. In general terms, this policy took the form of facility development in the 1970s and participation schemes in the 1980s, although from the mid-1980s the development of excellence was placed more firmly on the agenda. In the mid-1990s excellence is *a key* objective of Sports Council policy.

It follows therefore, that the government and the Sports Council favour an interpretation which identifies and prioritises organised competitive sport. However, this is not simply an issue of picking and choosing from the basket of *Sport for All*, but reflects a different conception of sport.

The aforementioned policy aims contained within *Sport for All* were not by themselves especially radical, but they opened the door to the construction of a conceptual logic in which the participation and consumption of specific sport practices could be. Whannel's examination of pleasure involved in the consumption of sport as a spectator can be usefully adapted to illustrate the radical and subversive potential of a genuine mass *Sport for All* movement. Drawing on Dyer's concept of *utopian sensibility*, Barthe's concept of *jouissance* and Bakhtin's concept of the *carnivalesque*, Whannel (1993: p. 341) argues that:

> ...because it is a form of performance rather than an artefact, the sport event, at its best, represents the temporary triumph of process over product, the moment when the spontaneous inspiration of performance escapes, fleetingly, the tendency of capitalist commodity production to transform all such processes into calculated packaged objects for consumption. Sport holds out the possibility of remaining playful, of grasping pleasure and of holding reality at bay.

Through direct participation, that is in taking control over the 'process', this heady mixture of the *carnivalesque*, *jouissance* and *utopian sensibility* offers a vision of sport which can transcend an alienated conception of the ascetic sporting body-as-machine, to a view of the aesthetic and empowering sporting body.

Sport in the 90s; New horizons ... new policy?

For the Government, the philosophy and aims of *Sport for All* are not the priority. As Sproat says:

> These are laudable aims, but secondary to the pursuit of high standards of sporting achievement. (DNH, 1994: p. 4)

But what about the Sports Council? After all, in Sport in the Nineties; New Horizons, its chairman, Peter Yarranton at least declares his support for "a genuine vision of sport for all" (Sports Council, 1993: p. 3). However, more recently the new chairman of the GB Sports Council, Rodney Walker (1995) declared his support for the Government's position:

> I am as one with the minister (Sproat), that a greater share certainly of the Sports Council's resources, indeed the resources of our principal partners, should now be devoted to those who want and have the potential to climb their way up the performance ladder, and to support sportsmen and women when they have reached the levels of excellence. (Walker, 1995)

As already argued there is a gulf separating the values underpinning the concept of 'sport' in *Sport for All* and the Government's current view of sport. By explicitly favouring the nurturing of performance, it appears that the Sports Council has finally severed support for *Sport for All*.

Some within the sports policy community would refute this. The London Region of the Sports Council for example, in its June 1995 Sportsnews leaflet, claims that it, "has a broad portfolio of activity underpinned for over 20 years by the slogan, *Sport for All*". It then explains why the current focus on youth and excellence represents a continuation rather than a departure from this policy:

> The new focus of the Sports Council's work on Young People and the development of excellence is not an abandonment of sport for all, as all the Council's programmes are underpinned by a commitment to "equity".

This is a weak defense. First, "equity" can, presumably, only have relevance for those falling within the Sports Council's designated priority areas; the young and/or those aspiring towards excellence. The likely tendency will be for all the other traditional target groups, such as women, black and ethnic minorities and the disabled, to benefit from this commitment to "equity" only insofar as they are young and/or aspiring towards excellence.

Secondly, the concept of "equity" is ambiguous. Unlike equality, that seemingly old fashioned practice that used to underpin the Sports Council's work, the vogue, slick and professional sounding concept of "equity", does not necessarily demand positive action and intervention to prevent discrimination. This point is made with reference to women by Hargreaves (1994: p. 214) who argues that "equity":

> ...*assumes* [my emphasis] that all groups of women will be given comparable time, access to facilities, representation in planning and provision, and resources and funding.

"Equity" is a legalistic term which places a premium on fairness and justice within the Sports Council's structures and practices so that they are not actively discriminating against disadvantaged groups. Taking action to prevent discrimination on the one hand, and creating structures to avoid actively discriminating on the other, may seem a pedantic distinction, but in reality it may reflect a subtle if unintended shift by the Sports Council away from challenging inequality.

The rise and decline of local authority sport

The key provider of sport facilities and participation opportunities in the last 20 years have been local authorities. Could it be argued that the Government's and the Sports Council's shift towards the development of performance has been rendered academic by the contribution of local authorities to *Sport for All*?

Indeed, in an open letter to the Sports Council, the former Secretary of State for National Heritage, Peter Brooke, referred to the emergence of local authorities' sport provision to justify the Government's support for a shift away from the promotion of mass participation and *Sport for All*, explaining that there had been:

> ...many significant developments since the inception of the Sports Council in 1972, when it was the sole agency for the development of sport. For example, local authorities have taken up the lead in the intervening period in providing opportunities for sport and recreation for the general public as part of their wider leisure strategies. (Brooke, 1994: p. 2)

It is certainly true that during the period from 1971 to 1989 local authority sports facilities expanded. The number of sports halls mushroomed from 20 to 1,200, and the number of swimming pools increased from 500 to 1,200 (Audit Commission, 1989: p. 3). Although it would be erroneous to draw a causal link between availability of facilities and levels of participation (there are many other factors), there was a steady but significant increase in levels of participation during this period. In any case, the Sports Council (1988: p. 58) acknowledged that it was the local authorities who "made the most significant contribution to extending the 'sporting franchise'".

This was achieved under the umbrella of Sport *for All* through a complementary but piecemeal strategy of a) facility expansion and b) community outreach and animateur management strategies. It was out of these strategies that the sports development profession emerged to offer the 'sporting franchise' to those people resistant or unable to access the range of facilities available.

However, the 1990s have seen a progressive financial erosion of local authority sport and recreation services, which has undermined their ability to provide a comprehensive service. Research conducted by Taylor and Page (1994: p. 9) into 308 local authorities concludes that there is a crisis in local authority financing of sport and recreation; a clear majority of local authorities in the UK have suffered cuts of typically between 5% and 15%

in their recreation expenditure in the last two years Concretely, this has meant a virtual halt in those capital programmes which do not attract extraneous financial support -and worse, in some places the closure of facilities has occurred.

In terms of local authorities maintaining the mass participation goals of *Sport for All*, the situation is also deteriorating. The Sports Council own commissioned research (Macintosh and Charlton, 1985; Rigg, 1986) has demonstrated that the key to achieving genuine 'sport for all' lay in appropriately managed outreach strategies; that is community recreation sports development. Sports development was the means, and 'sport for all' the end. However, in a survey of 269 local authorities by Taylor and Page (1994: p. 3), over half reported threats of reduction or elimination of services in sports development and community recreation services.

However, at the same time, the emergence in the last decade of an estimated 2000 Sport Development Officers (Collins, 1995: p. 20) principally within local authorities, would suggest that the philosophy and objectives of *Sport for All* are in safe hands. But this is no paradox. First, the number of sport development officers (SDO) posts has undoubtedly reached a plateau, and within local authorities is probably now in decline. Secondly, the symbiotic relationship between sports development and *Sport for All* that developed in the 1980s, is increasingly the exception rather than the norm in the 1990s.

Therefore, the Government's claim that its sponsorship of *Sport for All* has been made obsolescent by the emergence within local authorities of a maturing sports development profession, is premised on a mistaken view of either the nature of *Sport for All*, or the nature of contemporary sports development, or both.

Sports development and *Sport for All*: from symbiosis to anti-thesis?

The general context then, is a Government shifting the terrain of sport policy away from any notion of improving the quality of life, to an obtuse instrument for creating discipline in schools (Hargreaves, 1995) and reasserting national pride and patriotism. The response of the Sports Council, which is funded by the Government, is to fall obsequiously in line behind their paymasters. Local authorities, faced with increasing financial and legislative constraints, have been forced to move towards contracting their services out to competitive tender, which in sport and recreation has diminished their power and influence to set and attain public policy objectives. In short, an environment exists which is at best indifferent to, but mostly hostile towards a *Sport for All* concept of sports development.

This hostile environment may begin to explain the claim, outlined in propositional form in the introduction, that the sports development profession is turning its back on the mass participation goals of *Sport for All*. It does not, however, give any clues as to how sports development can also be a fetter on increasing opportunities for participation, the second claim made at the outset of this paper. This requires a debunking of the notion that sports development and concepts like the sports development continuum, are technically neutral tools, in favour of a more sociological understanding of the emergence of the sports development profession and its conceptual apparatus.

Sports Development is not a static concept, it is constituted by, and constitutive of, the totality of historically specific social relations. Although as a concept, sports development had its roots in community development in the 1970s, it was originally given concrete form by the 15 Action Sport programmes in London and the West Midlands between, 1982 and 1985 (Eady, 1993; Lentell, 1993; Rigg, 1986) These were partly products of two social policy concerns in the late 1970s.

Firstly, the Sports Council recognised that despite the mushrooming of facility provision under the banner of *Sport for All* in the 1970s, overall rates of participation had increased, but specific groups, such as women, the elderly, ethnic minorities, the disabled, and the unemployed were still under-represented (McIntosh and Charlton, 1985). Traditional facility-based delivery methods tended to attract only a narrow proportion of the population — i.e., young white relatively affluent males. The response of the Sports Council was a policy of encouraging intervention and positive action in the community, through community recreation (Sports Council, 1982).

Secondly, Action Sport programmes were a direct political response to the Birmingham, Brixton and Toxteth riots of, 1981. Despite the long list of target groups it was clear that the Sports Council was directed by the Government to focus Action Sport predominantly on the perceived protagonists of social disorder; urban black youth and young working-class males. Sports Development, and therefore *Sport for All* were applied and justified primarily by an inner-city rationale of control and containment.

By the late, 1980s and early, 1990s however, political priorities changed. Inner-city rioting (but not deprivation) was sufficiently contained. Increasing financial and legislative restraints on local authorities, such as the introduction of compulsory competitive tendering (CCT) of sports and leisure management, forced a more commercial approach to the delivery of their leisure services. The net result is that as the Government has reduced its financial support for inner-city sport initiatives, the burden for funding community recreation projects has fallen on local authorities who, rather than taking on extra expenditure, sought to streamline their recreation services in order to stay within shrinking budgets.

Right on the heels of CCT came the publication of the Audit Commission's report Sport for Whom (1989). The report attacked most local authority leisure departments for prioritising social objectives over financial accountability. The need for cost-efficiency was stressed which meant curtailing 'profligate' social programmes.

For a nascent sports development profession to survive in the austere financial and free market ideological climate of the 1990s, a broader definition of sports development which went beyond community recreation was considered necessary. The lifeline was thrown by the Sports Council who had outlined a sports development continuum (SDC) during the 1980s. The aim of the SDC was to locate mass participation within a broad, strategic approach to sports development. It identified four relatively discrete but incremental building blocks which classified levels from 'lower' stages, *foundation* and *participation*, to 'higher' stages, *performance* and *excellence* (Eady, 1993: p. 11-15). Although the Sports Council originally conceived the SDC merely as an explanatory tool, it has undergone a process of reification to assume the status of the primary definer of 'proper' sports development. So, unless the activity is located within the SDC it can be deemed beyond the remit of 'proper' sports development, a classic case of the tail wagging the dog.

This reinterpretation of sports development based on the SDC has facilitated a conceptual slippage which is increasingly antithetical to *Sport for All*. Correspondingly, sports development practice has moved:

> ...away from community recreation, both towards a greater concern with the development of specific sports and sporting performance, and towards a greater dependence on market related factors. (Lentell, 1993: p. 44)

Even when community recreation does feature within the SDC, it is as an emasculated concept. SDC-based sports development, usually labels 'community recreation' as 'foundation' and 'participation' levels. However, these levels are almost always defined in terms of pathways for young people to access the competitive structures of specific sports. But this is far removed from the original concept of community recreation, which Haywood (1992: pp. 42-3) has characterised as exhibiting the following qualities:

> — a commitment to working collectively with the community in the process of identifying and meeting social needs;
>
> — placing a premium on 'community resources' in the development and operation of leisure and recreation services;
>
> — focus on disadvantaged and minority social groups as those least likely to benefit from market orientated and/or paternalistic provision.
>
> — understanding of the potential role that leisure and recreation participation may contribute to 'community' development.

The current ideological emphasis on developing performance means that the incongruity which exists between Haywood's characterisation of community recreation and SDC-based sports development, is resolved in favour of the SDC by redefining and narrowing the concept of community recreation.

The emasculation of community recreation is compounded in facility based sports development because of the technical requirements of compulsory competitive tendering. The Gradgrind demand in contract specifications for precise measurement of leisure services and quantifiable 'outputs', militates against services geared towards qualitative goals. When local authorities do stipulate that social objectives must be met through community initiatives, the response of contractors is often to organise periodic facility based 'community' recreational programmes that are devoid of any sense of real individual or community empowerment. This is called sports development (in the community) but it is not, in practice, *Sport for All.*

The Sports Council has been influential in orchestrating this shift in sports development. Apart from developing and promoting the SDC as the framework for sports development, it implicitly endorsed CCT with the publication of Developing Sport through CCT. (Sports Council, Scottish Sports Council, 1994) More recently at a conference for sports development officers, Rodney Walker (1995) called on delegates to support the Sports Council's work:

> In accordance with the new Government policy, the Sports Council and its successor bodies (the UK Sports Council and the English Sports Council) will be concentrating its resources in three areas ...young people in sport...the development of excellence...the use of national lottery funds.... Any current function of the Sports Council which does not directly contribute to these three key areas will have a question mark over their future. And we ask the ***whole*** *of the sports development network to join us in this endeavour.* [my emphasis] (Walker, 1995)

Given the traditional authority and influence of the Sports Council over the sports development profession, both Rodney Walker's speech and the publication of Developing Sport Through CCT, were blows against sport development officers striving to maintain the profile of community recreation. In the words of one community sports development officer in East London, Developing Sport Through CCT 'has done us no favours'.

It seems that in the political and economic climate of the mid-1990s, community sports and recreation development have an increasingly diminished place within the SDC and, by extension, in sports development.

It was community recreation that spawned the concept of sports development. Then, with the success of Action Sport, the number of sports development officers increased, particularly within local authorities. However, as we have seen, the concern to consolidate coupled with and related to an incipient professionalism, has resulted in the construction of the sports development continuum as the primary definer of sports development. The economic and ideological climate of the 1990s context has meant that only a narrow concept of sport could fit within the SDC superstructure. The rhetoric of 'community' has not totally disappeared, but where it persists, both the SDC and CCT tend to produce an emasculated version of community recreation.

This is the sporting equivalent of the survival instincts of *Theridion Impressum*, part of the Black Widow spider family, whose continued existence is ensured by the offspring devouring their parents. If *Sports for All* is the grandparent, then sports development is the parent to the sports development continuum. It has been argued above that the parent has now been swallowed up by the SDC. Antithesis, rather than symbiosis, therefore characterises the conceptual relationship between the mainstream work of the sports development profession and *Sport for All*. In short, sports development is becoming more of a fetter rather than a facilitator of *Sport for All*.

Municipal sports development in London

a) The research

Much of the theory and general analysis outlined above has been based on knowledge gained from field work on sports development undertaken during the summer months of, 1995 in all 32 of the London Boroughs (excluding Corporation of London). At the time of writing, there are only 3 boroughs (Barnet, Barking and Dagenham and Havering) that are not mentioned in this study due to a lack of information[2].

However with 29 boroughs included, a reasonably representative picture of the current state of play, and nature of local authority sports development in the capital is possible. Information on the respective boroughs was gathered from council reports and documentation, promotional literature, sport and recreation strategies, local newspapers, but most important of all, from interviewing key personnel. In all, of the 29 boroughs successfully approached, taped face to face interviews, most lasting between 75-90 minutes (none were less than 75, but some were longer than 90!) were conducted with 26 sports development managers/officers or their equivalent from 26 boroughs. In the remaining 3 boroughs, telephone interviews were carried out with senior sports development personnel.

The interviewees were selected because they have more strategic than direct day-to-day operational responsibility, and therefore have the knowledge and authority to release information relating to staffing numbers and responsibilities, work programmes, budgets, strategic issues, as well as an understanding and experience of a variety of political influences affecting their teams' operations. However, it was also recognised that their position as 'managers' might favourably colour their accounts of sports development in their respective boroughs, and so sensitivity to this possibility was required when interpreting the information received during the interviews.

(b) The Findings

The most striking characteristic that sums up the overall picture is fragmentation. This fragmentation highlights the fact that sports development in London cannot be understood simply by deduction from any meta-theory of contemporary sports development. As Marx once said, 'the truth is concrete'. But it is not satisfactory to ignore theory and say that there can only be borough specific approaches to understanding sports development. The inadequacies of theoretics does not legitimise rampant empiricism. However, the phenomenon of fragmentation does at least reflect one important influencing factor; the specifics of locality .

Fragmentation is partly a reflection of London's foible, that since the abolition of the GLC in 1986 it is the only British city without an elected statutory and strategic body. Instead it is split into 33 separate, elected municipal authorities, each possessing its own distinct characteristics of socio-economics and geography. This fact, coupled with the reduction in recent years of Sports Council funding of SDO posts, which has shorn sports development officers of a city-wide platform, has led to a parochialism in the outlook of many sports development teams. In the absence of a trans-borough voice, sports development agendas are set mainly by the exigencies and imperatives of borough councillors and officers.

Adopting the theoretical framework and analysis outlined in this paper it is possible to construct a typology of sports development approaches. Before doing so, two preliminary points can be made that are common to all boroughs amidst the general picture of fragmentation. First, the key shift that has occurred within the sports development profession in the last decade has been the move away from Action Sport type work and more generally from *Sport for All*. This shift is mirrored in London. Of the 25 boroughs that have sports development teams, it is clear that all have rejected any pretence of reaching the whole community, although none actively discriminate. However there are a minority of SDTs that maintain a focus on working within the community. But unlike Action Sport the manner in which these community oriented SDTs operate is less heavily reliant on the use of intervention and outreach techniques to establish face-to-face contact with people. This leads to the second general point.

The contemporary SDO is likely to be far more strategic in his or her mode of operation. Mirroring the changing rationale of local authority practice, SDOs are now busy 'enabling', 'facilitating', marketing and monitoring schemes from an office, usually in the civic centre rather than getting out and directly organising and delivering programmes. This 'managerial' method is common across all types of SDTs, and is widely recognised as a more systematic and effective approach to sustaining the development process. However, the real issue here is less to do with organisational 'forms', and more concerned with the social and political 'content' of their developmental processes.

For this study the first distinction drawn was between sports development teams (SDTs) with community based and non-community based philosophies. Then the non-community focus SDTs were sub-divided into three sub-groups; 'Income Generator', 'Sport Developer', and 'Niche Holder'. Table 1 shows that while 'Community Focus' SDTs are the largest single group, overall they are in a minority.

Table 1 A typology of sport development teams by London Borough

Community Focus		Kensington & Chelsea, Hounslow, Newham, Westminster, Southwark, Lewisham, Hammersmith & Fulham, Hackney.
Non-Community Focus		
(i)	Income Generators:	Merton, Waltham Forest(1), Enfield, Bromley, Ealing, Sutton, Camden.
(ii)	Sport Developers:	Greenwich, Wandsworth, Brent, Croydon, Redbridge, Richmond.
(iii)	Niche Holders:	Kingston, Tower Hamlets, Islington, Bexley,
(Harrow, Hillingdon, Lambeth and Haringey boroughs have no SDTs)		

Community Focus SDTs

Community Focus SDTs are closest in form and content to the philosophy of community recreation. These teams tend to operate outside the traditional facilities, relying more on parks, community halls, housing estates and open spaces. They also tend to interpret sport more widely than the other boroughs, as leisure, recreation or health, which is reflected in the sports development team titles of Hounslow (Community Recreation), Southwark (Leisure Development) and Hammersmith and Fulham (Community Learning and Leisure).

The most significant indicator of their community orientation was the negligible level of income generation. Only Newham and Westminster raised significant amounts (respectively just under £100,000 and approximately £350,000). This was because the Westminster team also have managerial control over a major sports and educational centre (Westminster Sports Unit, 1995), and Newham have a swimming development officer (Newham Borough, 1995). However, it was clear that for all the SDTs the role of sport was to improve the quality of life. Income generation targets were considered a fetter on this.

There are a number of important factors in these SDTs maintaining their community focus role. The political persuasions of the councils, perhaps unexpectedly, is not significant, as the Royal Borough of Kensington and Chelsea and the City of Westminster both have staunch Conservative councils and traditions. This points to the importance of agency as individual officers can develop policies which are, at least ostensibly, at odds with their employers. Two inter-related, though speculative reasons can be offered to explain the relevance of agency. First, a degree of autonomy is often possible because of the relative smallness of sports development within borough-wide structures and budgets. This can then dovetail with a level of complicity by the local authority in the 'subversion' of their political philosophies, probably because of the net-gain in kudos within their localities derived from the often high profile activities of sports development officers in perceived potential, and actual areas of high tensions.

In addition to personnel, tradition is also significant. Of the original 9 authorities involved in Action Sport, 5 (Hackney, Hammersmith, Lewisham, North Kensington and Southwark) are still community oriented, which identifies the final point, the importance of socio-economics. Action Sport was specifically designed to operate in disadvantaged inner-city areas. All of the 'Community Focus' SDTs are located in parts of London that have serious degrees of poverty and have disadvantaged communities. As one SDO said, 'Even if we wanted to raise income, we couldn't'. This may be an influencing factor behind the community focus, but therein also lies the threat to community recreation. Most of the SDTs are under pressure to save money, in particular Hackney, whose team are required to offer a cut every year, and Lewisham, where an imminent wholesale cost-cutting restructuring of the borough is perceived ominously by the local SDT.

As financial constraints increase, so will the vulnerability of sports development, especially as it is a loss-making non-statutory service. The existence of 'Community Focus' SDTs may demonstrate that alternative interpretations of sport development to the dominant discourse can exist; however, it is difficult to be optimistic about their long term existence in the absence of a significant challenge to this discourse.

Income Generator SDTs

Income Generator SDTs are characterised by the premium placed on revenue generating activities. This does not mean that these SDTs eschew loss-making activities in principle, but often these are compensated for by the use of cross-subsidies. Most activities that are offered are determined by those that pay their way, for example coaching courses, holiday sport camps and playschemes and the provision of sport-specific courses.

Attention to cost-efficiency leads to a tendency for activities to be course-based rather than session-based, and organised rather than casual.

These types of provision and activities tend to act as a disincentive to such people as those on low incomes, single parents, certain minority ethnic groups and the less active 14 -18 year olds'.

A striking feature of many of the 'Income Generator' SDTs is their managerial mode of operation. Bromley SDT, which is one of the largest in London, epitomises this approach. Its strategy document (Bromley Sports Development, 1994: p. 3) states that:

> Sports Development Officers' roles have become that of managers and/or enablers who are facilitating a development process.

The actual delivery of programmes are carried out by 'agency' or staff on a sessional basis, as and when required. This is clearly a more cost-effective use of SDO time if the aim is cost-efficient and commercially viable activities that generate income. Bromley, as the exemplar managerial 'Income Generator' SDT, even expresses its policy in terms of prudent financial management (Bromley Sports Development, 1994: p. 7):

> With the investment in a team of qualified coaching and sessional staff who are currently trained in service delivery, a wide portfolio of products encompassing a range from Active Lifestyles through to Sports and Events, can be delivered to a sustainable quality to target groups and within specified areas.

Working towards creating sporting opportunities for all, especially for low income and less active people is contingent on financial viability. Where this viability requires a fee or a cost-efficient programme structure, then social objectives become at best a secondary benefit. 'Income Generator' SDTs maybe on the entrepreneurial edge of the public sector and in the vanguard of managing the developmental process, but this has more to do with adapting to the changing culture of local authorities than responding to and serving any social objectives of *Sport for All*. Indeed it is possible to argue that the long term interests of these two constituencies are contradictory.

Sport Developer SDTs

By definition, the development of specific sports is the self-evident characteristic of Sport Developer SDTs. In respect of their mode of operation (enabling and facilitating rather than actually delivering), and the attention to cost-efficiency (though to a lesser extent), they bear similarities with the 'Income Generator' SDTs. However, the focus on the development of specific sports brings them into much closer relationship with sport governing bodies and more in line with the Sports Council's current policies than 'Income Generator' SDTs — for example, Greenwich runs the pilot scheme of TOP PLAY for 4-9 year olds which is part of the National Junior Sports Programme initiative.

Unsurprisingly, 'Sport Developer' SDTs are most reliant on the sports development continuum to provide the guiding principles and organisational framework for their work. Most of the officers are, as expected, characterised as sport specific, performance and target group SDOs (see Table 3 below).

As the aim of the 'Sport Developer' SDTs is to improve the opportunities for players to scale the ladder from participation to excellence, the main target group tends to be youth. Successful performances at the annual youth sports festival, the London Youth Games, is critical to boroughs like Brent and Wandsworth. Significantly, both are Conservative controlled councils, and as this event is taken as an indicator of progress or otherwise in raising standards of performance. Often the rhetoric surrounding sport, notably in the boroughs just mentioned, echoes that of the Government's. So the character-building virtues of competitive sport, its contribution to crime prevention, and the creation of civic pride are emphasised.

Brent have been the boldest in following this 'Sport Developer' route, aiming to become, "quite simply the best sporting Local Authority in the Country", where, "you can see the best, become the best, have the opportunity to do your best" (Brent Sports Development, 1995: p. 41).

Delivery of physical education as a part of the National Curriculum in schools is perhaps one of the biggest growth areas for 'Sport Developer' SDTs, which has been given added impetus by the *Sport: Raising the Game* document. Clearly there is a demand in schools for the kind of expertise offered by suitably qualified SDOs and coaches, and some SDTs, such as those in Brent, Croydon and Greenwich have already responded in depth to these demands. With youth as the main target group, and with the continuing amalgamation of leisure directorates with education, the prospect of school sport development officers increasing in number is probable. Haringey sport development team, which is not a local authority organisation, but an independent charitable trust funded from a combination of business sponsorship and council and charity grants, is effectively contracted to service the boroughs schools. It has a high level of penetration into Haringey schools, delivering holiday schemes, extra-curricular activities as well as the curriculum, but its budget is a fraction of the cost of most local authority SDTs.

The cost efficiency and effectiveness of Haringey sports development, raises the spectre of contracting. If the SDT has neither community recreation role, nor an income generation imperative, but exists primarily to develop performance and sport-specific opportunities, then the question of whether this is a legitimate area of public policy is raised. If the answer is in the negative then there is no intrinsic reason why it should be totally part of the local authority structure. Partnership (often a euphemism for local authorities to pass the responsibility for funding onto other agencies) is the organising principle of sports development in Croydon. Most of its funding comes from non local authority sources, most notably business sponsorship. Brent Sports Development also plans to detach itself from local authority political control, by becoming a charitable trust (Brent Sports Development, 1995: p. 38). Although the intention would be to continue to receive core funding from the local authority, it would 'liberate' sports development from any municipal responsibility that may detract from their quest to 'become the best'. The general issue at stake is the visibility of 'Sport Developer' SDTs within local authorities.

Niche holder SDTs

Niche Holder SDTs are a small but heterogeneous group. They are SDTs who are defined by specific orientations that fall outside the remit of the other categories. In Islington this means servicing the borough schools physical education requirements, and administering and monitoring the whole process of CCT. Organising inter and intra-borough events constitute the substance of work conducted by SDOs in Bexley and Tower Hamlets.

The fourfold typology of 'Community Focus', 'Income Generator, 'Sport Developer', and 'Niche Holder' summarises in broad terms the nature of sport development teams in London's boroughs. Of these four types, the 'Community Focus' SDTs have the most consistent orientation towards low income and disadvantaged social groupings, although this is still (in most cases) a far cry from the philosophy of community recreation. The majority of 'Community Focus' SDTs also face financial pressures which are pushing them yet further away from community recreation and towards one of the other three 'types' of SDT.

A closer analysis of the number and type of sports development officers in the team 'types', allows a more nuanced account of the fourfold typology. Table 2 confirms the predominance of SDOs operating within non-community focus teams with a breakdown of the number of full-time officers according to SDT type.

Table 2 Number of sports development officers (based on 25 boroughs)

Community Focus (8 boroughs)	49
Non Community Focus;	
(i) Income Generators (7 boroughs)	36
(ii) Sport Developers (6 boroughs)	28
(iii) Niche Holders (4 boroughs)	9
Total based on 25 boroughs	122

A more detailed breakdown of the individual sports development officer 'types' is outlined in table 3 below.

Table 3 Types or specialism of sports development officers (based on 25 boroughs)

SDT 'Type'	Community Focus (8)	Income Generators (7)	Sport Development Operators 6)	Niche Holders (4)	Total
Strategic/ Management	8	7	5	3	23
Generalist	8	12	1	0	21
Community	14	0	1	0	15
Sport Specific	4	5	8	0	17
Target Group	10	7	7	0	24
Performance	0	3	6	0	9
Other	5	2	0	6	13
Total	49	36	28	9	122

The definitions of sports development officer 'type' in this table can be defined in the following way (Eady, 1993: pp. 51-66):

Senior/Management SDOs are involved at policy-making level, and are therefore responsible for strategic planning, monitoring and evaluation.

Generalist SDOs (sometimes referred to in local authorities as generic officers) normally manage a multi-disciplinary programme incorporating a wide range of responsibilities.

Community SDOs tend to centre their work on participation, often delivering the programmes, using outreach techniques.

Sport Specific SDOs work to develop a particular sport, often with youth as a target group, based on the sports development continuum.

Target Group SDOs usually work with one of the traditional Sports Council priority groups; elderly people, people with disabilities, women, young people, and people from minority ethnic groups. The specific nature of this work will depend on the type of SDT this officer is located in. This is further explained and illustrated below.

Performance SDOs are often involved in coach education as part of their work of raising performance across a range of sports.

Other. Within this category are SDOs whose functions include organising events, marketing, or providing information.

The data in Table 3 indicate that are only 15 community SDOs. This understates the level of community recreation activity, because the nature of different 'types' of officer will be shaped by the 'type' of SDT that they are located in. For example, the 8 'Community Focus' strategic managers may have the same title as the 13 'Income Generator' and 'Sport Developer' strategic managers, but the nature of their work will relate to the 'type' of the SDT under their control.

Also the nature of the target group SDOs is very different between 'Community Focus' SDTs and 'Sport Developer' SDTs. For example, in relation to 'Community Focus' SDTs, there were specific target group officers in Hounslow and Newham. In both, ethnic minorities were the target group with the rationale based on health and participation. Contrast this with target group officers in two 'Sport Developer' SDTs, Croydon and Wandsworth where youth is targeted with a rationale based on creating pathways to enable young people to raise their standards of performance. Forty and Fifty plus are target groups that create revenue for officers in two 'Income Generator' SDTs, Ealing and Bromley respectively.

It is clear from the research that municipal sports development in London, while fragmented, displays certain patterns that both confirm and enrich the theoretical analysis outlined in this paper. There is little evidence of Sport *for All* as a living and relevant concept, although its legacy is found within the significant minority of 'Community Focus' SDTs. But for the majority of the borough SDTs ('Income Generator', 'Sport Developer' and 'Niche Holder'), extending the sports and recreational franchise to all sections of the community regardless of their age, cultural identity and socio-economic position on the basis of 'need', is not even on the agenda. Caught between the pincers of national sport policy and local authority imperatives the response of these SDTs is to emphasise either income generation or the development of focus sports. Correspondingly, the tendency is for sport to be interpreted in accordance with the rationale of the SDT. Therefore programmes are either beyond the fiscal means of lower socio-economic groups, especially in boroughs with 'Income Generator' SDTs, or they are culturally irrelevant and physically unappealing to many in the wider community in boroughs with 'Sport Developer' SDTs. However, the conclusion that these SDTs are therefore more of a fetter than a facilitator of increasing levels of participation should not be interpreted as a criticism of their practice because this is not their primary intended purpose. It is a criticism however of those national policy makers and commentators who deny that the mass participation goals of *Sport for All* are compromised by tightening local authority purse-strings and the ideological (ab) use of sport by the Government.

Concluding thoughts

There is an urgent need to debate the principles and politics of sports development, which would enhance the current preoccupation with practical issues. The early indications from the recently established Institute of Leisure and Amenity Management Sports Development Panel are that the wider conceptual and political issues fall outside their frame of reference. And yet the case for establishing clarity on the social principles underpinning sports development can be gauged from Eady's comments that:

> The development of the local authority role as enabler rather than direct provider of leisure facilities and opportunities will, both philosophically and practically, lead to sports development becoming the primary raison d'etre of local sport and recreation departments. (1993: p. 74)

If this is correct, then the call made here to challenge and debate the hidden or assumed principles and politics of municipal sports development becomes an academic question of significant practical and policy relevance. At stake is the sport and recreational disenfranchisment of countless individuals, especially from disadvantaged communities.

By theorising the relationship between different conceptions of sport, with sports policy and sports development, it has been argued that the sports development profession is not only moving way from *Sport for All*, but that its adherence to the present national sports policy agenda fetters rather than facilitates the opportunities for all sections of the population to participate.

However, this study of local authority sports development in London, demonstrates that the shift from 'community' towards sport-specific development and income generation is uneven, reflecting the importance of agents, local conditions and strategies articulating with and within the wider social sporting and political context. This means that in London at least, a community focus still prevails to a significant extent in many areas, but the prevailing ideological, political and financial environment places increasing limits on the autonomy of these sports development teams.

If those committed to the mass participation goals of *Sports for All* within the sports development community are to survive and exert influence, then understanding and discussing the nature of sports development as a political construct which embodies particular social values is a task of considerable importance[3].

Notes

1 The official designation for 'Minister of Sport' is 'Minister of State for Department of National Heritage'.

2 Waltham Forest has a system of devolved administration which is split between northern, central and southern areas. Only the northern area is included in this study.

3 The author is indebted to all of the following people; Byron Miller (Brent), Bernie Hammell (Bromley), John Mann (Camden), Mick Pittaway (Croydon), Sarah Wiseley (Ealing), Paula Hines (Enfield), Jeff Davies (Greenwich), Ann Holdway (Hackney), Terry See (Hammersmith & Fulham), Burk Gravis (Haringey), Phil Mead (Harrow), Gordon McLeod (Hillingdon), Pat Kirkwood (Hounslow), Tom Bogie (Islington), Mary Mackle (Kensington & Chelsea), Caroline Fraser (Kingston upon Thames), Bob Downham & Wendy Davies (Lambeth), Annette Stead (Lewisham), Sarah Teasdale (Merton), Leslie Jones (Newham), Anne Dolby (Redbridge), Angela Francombe (Richmond upon Thames), Rohney Malik (Southwark), Heather-Ann Worrell (Sutton), Madonis Darroux (Tower Hamlets), Mike Dulin (Waltham Forest), Lenny Kinnear (Wandsworth) and Carol Isherwood (Westminster), for giving up their time during a busy period in the sport development calendar to assist in this study. Thanks also to Jenny Hargreaves for correcting my mistakes and Claire Ozanne for finding out the name of the spider.

References

Allison, L. (1994) 'Sport for all or for the best', *The Guardian*, 25th September.

Audit Commission (1989) *Sport for whom? Clarifying the local authority role in sport and recreation*. London: HMSO.

Benington, J. and White. J (eds) (1991) *The future of leisure services*. London: ILAM/Longman.

Bramham, P. and Henry, I. (1985) 'Political ideology and leisure policy in the UK', *Leisure Studies* Vol. 4, No. 1: pp. 1-19.

Brent Sports Development (1995) *Sports quest 2000*. London Borough of Brent.

Brooke, P., MP (1994) *Review of the Sports Council*. Open Letter to Chairman of The Sports Council. Department of National Heritage. 8th July.

Bromley Sports Development (1991) *Working together.* London Borough of Bromley.

——— (1994) *Partnership in action.* London Borough of Bromley.

——— (1995) *Building partnerships through sport.* Bromley Leisure and Community Services.

Coalter, F., Duffield, B., and Long, J. (1988) *Recreational welfare: The rationale for public sector investment in leisure.* London: Avebury/ Gower.

Coghlan, J and Webb, I. (1990) *Sport and British politics since 1960.* London: Falmer Press.

Collins, M. (1995) *Sports development, locally and regionally.* Reading: ILAM/Sports Council.

Council of Europe (undated) *European Sports Charter.* London: The Sports Council.

Croydon Sports Partnership (1995) *Annual Report and Financial Statements for the Year ended 31st March, 1995.* Croydon.

Croydon Sports Partnership (1995) *Sports development plan.* Croydon Sports Partnership.

Department for Education (1995) *Physical education in the national curriculum.* London HMSO.

Department of Education and Science (1991) *Sport and active recreation.* London: DES.

Department of Environment (1989) *Sport and active recreation provision in the inner cities.* London: HMSO.

Department of National Heritage (1994) *Sport for the 21st century.* London: HMSO.

Department of National Heritage (1995) *Sport: Raising the game.* London: DNH.

Eady, J. (1993) *Practical sports development.* Essex, Longman Group.

Elvin, I. (1993) *Sport and recreation.* ILAM/Longman.

Enfield Leisure Services (1995) *Annual Report, 1993-94.* London Borough of Enfield.

Greenwich Leisure (not dated) *Sport and recreation strategy: A sporting chance.* Greenwich Leisure Services.

Hargreaves, J. A. (1994) *Sporting females: Critical issues in the history and sociology of women's sports.* London: Routledge.

Hargreaves, J. A. (1995) 'Gender, morality and the national physical education curriculum', in S. Parker, E. Murdoch and L. Lawrence (eds) *Professional and development issues in leisure, sport and education*, LSA Publication No. 56. Eastbourne: Leisure Studies Association, pp. 3-19.

Hargreaves, J. E. (1986) *Sport, power and culture.* Cambridge: Polity Press.

Haringey Sports Development (1995) *Schools sports development programme, 1995/96.* London: Haringey Sports Development.

Haywood, L. (1992) 'Community recreation and local government in the 1990s', in J. Sugden and C. Knox (eds) *Leisure in the 1990s: Rolling back the Welfare State* (LSA Publication No. 46). Eastbourne: Leisure Studies Association, pp. 41-44.

——— (1994) *Community leisure and recreation.* Oxford: Butterworth-Heinemann.

Henry, I. (1993) *The politics of leisure policy.* London: Macmillan

Houlihan, B. (1991) *The government and politics of sport.* London, Routledge.

Islington Sports Development (1993) *A sports development strategy for Islington.* London Borough of Islington.

Kingston Leisure (1994) *Sports and recreation strategy, 1994-99.* Royal Borough of Kingston upon Thames.

Lentell, B. (1993) 'Sports development: Goodbye to community recreation?', in Brackenridge, C. (ed) *Body matters: Leisure images and lifestyles* (LSA Publication No. 47). Eastbourne: Leisure Studies Association, pp. 141-149.

Lewisham Leisure (1993) *Lewisham sports development plan: 1993-96.* London Borough of Lewisham.

London Sport (1994) *The sporting capital: The regional recreation strategy for London, 1994.* London Council for Sport and Recreation.

——— (1994) *Young people and sport — a strategy.* London Council for Sport and Recreation.

McIntosh, P. and Charlton, V. (1985) *The impact of Sport for All policy, 1966-1984 and a way forward.* London: Sports Council

Newham Borough (1995) *Swimming development plan.* London Borough of Newham.

Newham Leisure Services (1994) *Sports Development Section: Work programmes/performance review and development plans.* London Borough of Newham.

Ravenscroft, N. (1992) 'The future role of the public sector in the provision of leisure facilities in Britain' in J. Sugden and C. Knox (eds) *Leisure in the 1990s: Rolling back the Welfare State* (LSA Publication No. 46). Eastbourne: Leisure Studies Association, pp. 21-32.

Rigg, M. (1986) *Action Sport — an evaluation*. London: Sports Council.

School Sports Forum (1988) *Sport and young people: Partnership and action*. London: Sports Council.

Southwark Leisure (1995) *Annual Report, 1993/94*. London Borough of Southwark.

Sports Council (1972) *Provision for sport*. London: HMSO.

——— (1983) *Sport in the community: The next ten years*. London: Sports Council.

——— (1988) *Sport in the community: Into the 90s*. London: Sports Council.

——— (1993) *Sport in the nineties: New horizons*. London: Sports Council.

——— (1994) *Developing sport through CCT*. Sports Council, Scottish Sports Council.

——— (London Region) (1995) *Sportsnews*. London: Sports Council (June).

Sproat, I. (1994) cited in *Daily Telegraph*, 28th February, p. 39.

Sugden, J. and Knox, C. (eds) (1992) *Leisure in the 1990s: Rolling back the Welfare State* (LSA Publication No. 46). Eastbourne: Leisure Studies Association.

Sutton Leisure Services (1995) *Sport and Recreation Strategy: 1995-97*. London Borough of Sutton.

Taylor, P. and Page, K. (1994) *The financing of local authority sport and recreation; A service under threat?*. Sheffield. ISRM.

Walker, R. (1995) Keynote speech to the 4th UK Sports Development Seminar, February 1st, Nottingham.

Walker, R. (1995) Keynote speech at the 4th UK Sports Development Seminar. Nottingham. 1st February.

Westminster Sports Unit (1995) *Business plan, 1995/6*. City of Westminster.

Whannel, G. (1983), *Blowing the whistle: The politics of sport*. London: Pluto Press.

——— (1993) 'Sport and popular culture: The temporary triumph of process over product', *Innovation*, Vol. 6, No. 3: pp. 341-349.

Wolfenden Committee on Sport(1960), *Sport and the community*. London: CCPR.

The German Government and the Politics of Sport and Leisure in the 1990s: An Interim Report

Udo Merkel

University of Brighton

Introduction

Several recurrent themes dominated the political discussion of sport and leisure in Germany in the 1990s. One of these — sport's contribution to the process of nation building — has been running through the history of German sport and has been revitalised due to the political collapse of the German Democratic Republic. A second is the integration of the East German 'sports miracle' into the organisational structures of West German sport; and a third is the noticeable and constantly increasing lack of involvement in, and commitment to the voluntary sector — one of the three pillars of German sport, caused by changing sporting priorities of many Germans. This paper is not intended to give a comprehensive and evenly balanced account of these three major and outstanding contemporary developments. Rather, it is intended to highlight a number of important aspects of these developments whilst placing them in their socio-historical context.

Germany is one of the twelve member states of the European Union, home of almost 88 million people. Of these, 17 million are so called "*Ossis*" (a fairly derogatory and patronising term for East-Germans used by West Germans) whilst the other 64 million are the so called "*Besser-Wessis*" (a term for 'know-it-all' West-Germans used by the East Germans). In addition, there are about 6.8 million foreigners living in Germany; 97% in the territory of what was the Federal Republic of Germany before 1990, whilst the remaining 3% live in the territory of the former German Democratic Republic. 1.92 million people of these foreigners (27.9%) are Turkish, the so called "*Gastarbeiter*" (guest workers).

By the end of 1995, Germany — or to be more precise, the latest version of the Federal Republic of Germany — will be about five and a half years old. Despite its youth, but due to its size and economic power, it is one of the most influential nation states in Europe. The ancestor of this Germany, the post World War II Federal Republic, was already a role model for many other European states, both admired and feared in equal measure. In sporting terms Germany, when divided or united, has done extremely well over the last five decades. Leisure — defined as free time — is equally important to the Germans. Thirty-five hour working weeks, an average of more than thirty days holidays per year, more than half a dozen bank-holidays, the option to take a year or even longer unpaid leave with a job guarantee — have all long since ceased to be exceptional working conditions in a society which abroad is still perceived as diligent, efficient and the last stronghold of the puritan work ethic (outside Germany). Although hedonistic tendencies do not fit into this picture, they feature prominently in modern German society.

Sport's contribution to nation building in Germany

This theme has been running through the history of sport in Germany since the foundation of the German nation state. More than ever before sport is perceived as and hoped to be, a major contributor to the national identity of a culturally, economically and socially divided nation which has gone through a varied history and many remarkable metamorphoses. The introduction of soccer as well as the staging of, and competing in the Olympic Games, reflect this instrumentalisation of sport very clearly and are briefly outlined in the two sub-sections that follow.

Soccer rules OK

The German Empire, the ancestor of the Federal Republic of Germany, was only founded in 1871, and since then has gone through a number of significant changes and developments affecting not only social and political structures but also sport and leisure. However, soccer has played, and continues to play a central role in the national culture of Germany, played by hundreds of thousands and watched by millions (cf. Merkel, 1994: pp. 93–119). The debates and arguments accompanying the initial introduction of soccer to German students in the last quarter of the 19th century clearly reflected the major concern and dilemma of the Germans — the question '***what is German?***' Soccer was mentioned for the first time in historical records in 1874, three years after the foundation of the German Empire. Hopf (1979: pp. 54–80) shows convincingly that the introduction of soccer instead of Rugby (the other well known game among sport enthusiasts in Germany) can be attributed to three causes, of which the third is particularly relevant for this theme. Of great political importance was the fact that soccer could be declared to be 'German football' while Rugby was considered to be 'English football'. Since the supporters of soccer were aware of the resentments that the introduction of an English game would provoke, they tried to provide evidence that soccer had a long tradition in

Continental Europe and that it had been played in 'Germany' in the Middle Ages.

In the last quarter of the nineteenth century and during the first decade of the twentieth century, soccer was primarily a middle class game. After the First World War it became the sport of the German industial working class:

> The key issue in an attempt to explain the enthusiasm for football clubs in working class areas and the degree of involvement going beyond the sporting activity is the potential to revive communal relationships in the increasingly differentiated society which Germany was about to become at the beginning of the 20th century. Looking at the history of the Ruhr area it becomes apparent that its inhabitants had to face two dilemmas, the rapidity of social change and the lack of a common cultural tradition. (Merkel, 1994: p. 97)

Equally remarkable is the success story of the West-German soccer team. Winning the World Cup in 1954, 1974 and 1990 is only part of this story. Particularly:

> Germany's first victory in the 1954 World Cup had an enormous social and national significance. After having been thrown out of FIFA in 1946 and being readmitted in 1950 the German success contributed significantly to the promotion of a national identity. (Merkel, 1994: p. 105)

Winning the 1974 World Cup in Germany, again, helped but equally significant and memorable was the 1-0 defeat of the West-German team by the East-German squad in the qualifying round, simply a political embarrassment of enormous magnitude.

The politicisation of the Olympic games

Although very often attributed to the Third Reich (1933–1945) it was during the Weimar Republic (1918–1933) that magnificent sport facilities were built in Germany (as part of the moral restoration after World War I), which the Nazis then took over. The Nazis were predominantly concerned with changing the organisational, administrative and legal structures of sport and with the staging of the 1936 Olympics in Berlin, which Hitler intended to use to express both internal unity as well as racial and national superiority. During this time fitness became an expression of patriotism. Vast sums of money and other resources were spent on *'Kraft durch Freude'* ('Strength through Joy') by the government of the Third Reich and Mussolini's *'Dopolavoro'* (cf. Holt, 1990: p. 344).

After World War II the defeated nations were excluded from the Olympic Games in London in 1948. However, sport was soon on the political agenda of the newly elected German government. Konrad Adenauer, the first head of German government (1948–1963), and his enthusiasm for sport made the 'Golden Plan' — to rebuild destroyed sport facilities, build new ones, and create parks and green areas for the public use of sportsmen and women — a successful project. He was also responsible for Germany joining the European Economic Community and NATO.

When Germany was readmitted to the Olympic community it competed as a united country from 1952 to 1964, representing both West and East Germany. But as Gratton relates:

> ...West Germany was far stronger in terms of both population and political importance and dominated the unified team, causing the East Germans to demand separate representation. (Gratton, 1990: p. 54)

For both, the Federal Republic of Germany (FRG) and the German Democratic Republic (GDR) sport played an extremely important role with respect to three major objectives:

- to demonstrate the superiority of their political system;
- to create a distinct national identity ; and
- to become internationally recognised and to establish a positive reputation.

In addition, it was extremely important for the GDR to overcome the worldwide political isolation imposed by the political and economic power and influence of the FRG, in particular the 'Hallstein Doctrine' — which meant that states acknowledging the political independence and sovereignty of East Germany would not be able to have diplomatic contacts with West Germany. The significane of sport in East-Germany can also be seen from the fact that one paragraph in the constitution was devoted exclusively to the meaning of sport in a socialist society.

Both states certainly achieved international recognition and established very distinctive reputations. It is difficult, though, to assess how much sporting success contributed to these achievements, in particular to the creation of two unique national identities, since as Houlihan describes:

> The political collapse of the GDR was so sudden and the willingness of the Germans to vote for the staunchly anti-communist Christian Democrat Party of Helmut Kohl so apparent that it must call into question the success of the GDR policy of using sport to contribute to the development of a new socialist national identity. (Houlihan, 1991: p. 48)

Yet, there is no doubt that the GDR did much better in Olympic Games than the FRG, particularly when international sporting success is related to the size of the population of 17 million people, the industrial output, or the Gross National Product. It was particularly the promotion of women in sport that both secured East-Germany a top position in the medal tables, and forced many Western societies to promote and support top-level accomplishments of women.

Hosting the Olympic Games in 1972 both supported and consolidated the process of nation building but the brutal killing of the Israeli athletes in Munich clearly undermined the positive effects.

The most recent political developments, in particular the end of the Cold War and eventually the merger of the two German states, had ambiguous consequences for the Germans and their identity. On one hand, they have had to come to grips with a very unexpected development: a new geographical shape and modified political and social structures. On the other hand, the merger of the two states has paradoxically caused an "us and them" feeling among the Germans. People in West-Germany have now started to insist that they are West-Germans, which before the wall came down was, according to the Conservative government, politically incorrect. In turn, the so called "poor brothers and sisters in the East" — for a long time the official jargon of the Conservative forces in the West — have also developed a kind of self-confidence and pride.

Gradually, many East Germans have started to acknowledge and to appreciate the many merits of their old Socialist system. Obviously, there is not only a touch of nostalgia involved when some now organise Trabant-meetings (the Trabant was one of the few available cars made in East-Germany), prefer to purchase products made in the East, visit museums and galleries displaying every-day objects of the Socialist era, and refuse to turn in their old GDR passports.

The Unification Treaty: license to dismantle the East German sports miracle

The most recent and — for more than half of the above mentioned 17 million East-Germans — regrettable moment in German history (cf. *Der Spiegel,*: 3 July, 1995, pp. 40–64) was the merger of the two German states, officially executed on 2 October 1990 at midnight, almost a year after a peaceful revolution subsequent to the mass exodus of East Germans via Hungary. Due to the large number of sportsmen and women among these refugees, a number of clubs ceased to exist and many scheduled competitions had to be cancelled due to the lack of competitors. Consequently, some sport organisations were among the first to call for 're-unification' in order to stop the mass emigration of top-level athletes.

Widely known and commonly used in both every-day and political discourse, this process is usually referred to as 'reunification'. However, the use of this term is politically incorrect as well as an ideological myth, simply because what happened in October 1990 was neither a political nor a geographical reunification but the take-over or integration [some even call it 'annexation'!] of the former German Democratic Republic. This process, obviously, has affected the sporting system in Germany, in particular top-level sport.

East Germany's pride, international reputation and recognition was based on sporting success. In its 45 years of existence, the German

Democratic Republic developed and applied a highly sophisticated system to produce top-level athletes and became renowned for its international sporting accomplishments.

Initial research undertaken by predominantly West-German sport scientists analysing the causes and structures of the 'sporting miracle' clearly identified the following as the four major ingredients for the recipe of success :

1. scientifically organised and rational selection of boys and girls in their early childhood
2. best possible facilities and an organised approach to coaching and training
3. extensive networks of support by highly qualified scientists from all relevant branches
4. efforts in a very restricted range of sports, particularly the Olympic sports, and those where there was some kind of evidence of a "German tradition".

However over the last three years the attention of the public and political discourse of the East German sport system has shifted and has been focusing upon other issues — for some, even more important than the organisational structuring of East German sport — such as the privileged status of top-level athletes, sportsmen and women serving as (informal) informers of the Ministry of Security [Staatssicherheitsdienst ('Stasi')] and the development of drugs and their use by top-level athletes.

When the Berlin Wall came down, what was a dream for some but a nightmare for others seemed to come true — the merger of two 'gold medal factories': the GDR's and the FRG's. However, this turned out to be a short-lived illusion. The image of the East German sport machine (for many a monstrous superpower) being taken over by the West-Germans worried West-German politicians so much that there was only one solution: to quietly dismantle and abolish it.

But it was not only concern about what the rest of the world would think of the West-Germans appropriating the advanced technology of the 'conveyor belt' production of Olympic champions. There was a sense that the destruction of the East-German sports miracle was also an act of revenge for all the humiliating defeats West German athletes (and with them politicians) had to suffer in the past, paired with the inability to appreciate the merits of the sporting system.

Although in the years immediately after the wall came down an average of about 40% of the sporting budget of the Home Office was designated to go into the New Five Regional States (the new name for the old GDR) (see Table 1), the sporting structures of the former GDR which made top-level sport so successful have ceased to exist. The Unification Treaty paved the way for this development since it clearly stated that the New Five Regional States had to adopt the political structures of the FRG in all areas of societal life, including sport and culture. Consequently:

- the *Deutscher Turn- und Sport-Bund* (the German Gymnastics and Sports Union), the administrative and organisational heart of the East German sport system, was dissolved and all its staff made redundant;
- most of the relevant research centres and sport institutes were either closed down or could only continue their work on a very reduced scale in terms of staffing and budget;
- more than 90% of the about 10,000 highly qualified coaches were made redundant;
- over 80% of the 12,000 support staff were made redundant within the first year after the Unification treaty came into force;
- top-level athletes were left on their own and did not receive any state support (which in the "good old times" of the German Democratic Republic included monthly grants, equipment, total access to sport facilities and support staff, travel expenses, etc.);
- the majority of sport boarding schools were privatised and almost all centres for excellence closed down.

In addition, the majority of the remaining administrative and management positions in East-German sport were taken over by Western staff, whilst athletes and remaining coaches were East-German, which created a great deal of tension.

Table 1 Financial support for sport in the new five regional states (in million Deutsch Mark)

	1991	1992	1993
Sport Budget of the Home Office of the Federal Republic of Germany	233.1	252.5	212.6
Amount alloted to financial support for the new states	87.3	100.5	88.4
(Percentage Proportion of Sport Budget)	(37.4%)	(39.8%)	(41.6%)

Source: Federal Office for Statistics (1994)

This dramatic transformation of the East-German sports miracle was caused by the reluctance of the Federal government to keep up payments for this complex system. To be more precise, the central government in Bonn did not refuse to support sport in the Five New Regional States but argued that sport — like all other cultural institutions — is under the administration of the regional states and, thus, the regional states should provide the necessary funds. [This is one of the many half-truths of the so-called reunification process since there is a clear division of labour and responsibilities in German sport: top-level sport in Germany is organised and looked after at the Federal level under the Home Office, whilst recreational sport and Sport for All are the responsibility of the regional states and their Ministers of Culture or Education.]

I would argue that this almost complete dismantling of the GDR sporting structures reflects and illuminates the arrogance and ignorance of the West-German Conservative government and its attitudes towards the achievements of the former East-Germany.

The former president of the FRG, Richard von Weizäcker, constantly urged his fellow party members of the Conservative Party to execute the unification process sensitively, smoothly and gently. Due to his firm belief in sports(wo)manship, the principles of fairness, and the integrative potential of sport, he suggested — soon after the wall came down — to use the merger of the two sporting systems as a role model for the unification process. As it turned out, this process was not a role model but a mirror image of the whole development.

However, other people find it "hardly surprising that the quasi-modern sports culture of the former GDR could not easily be transformed into the modern or even postmodern tendencies in the FRG" (Damklaer, 1994: p. 267). Although there is some evidence that physical culture and sport in West Germany can be characterised as modern or even postmodern it is, in my mind, problematic to generally categorise the sports culture in the former German Democratic Republic as "quasi-modern". Although 'Sport For All' was very much neglected and thus underdeveloped and top-level sport was certainly not as commercialised as it was at the same time in most of the modern Western societies, it was definitely as professionalised — but in a different way.

From Sport For All to sport for individuals: modern vs traditional values

'Sport For All' has never been a major issue on the political agenda of the East German government, since from the beginning of the 1960s onwards the emphasis was almost exclusively on the production of top-level athletes. At the same time it is obvious that the claims made in the past concerning high participation rates (for the general population) are inaccurate.

In two sub-sections that follow, I want to briefly highlight the quantitative development of recreational sport after World War II, before changing the perspective to focus on the current situation and the meanings attached to sporting activities and the reasons why and how people participate in sport nowadays.

The rising star of sport in German cultural life

Even a superficial glance at empirical data concerning sport in post-war Germany clearly shows that sport has developed from being one among many forms of leisure to an important part of social, cultural and economic life. This refers not only to active and passive participation in sport but also to the appropriation of sporting themes, vocabulary, norms and values in other areas of social life, as well as the use of sporting characteristics and props for individual presentation (cf. Rittner 1994).

Surveys have repeatedly shown that between 50% and 60% of the German population are regularly involved in active sport. (Or, to be more precise, about 50% to 60% *state* that they are). Nevertheless, the four biggest sporting associations total more than thirteen million people, i.e. both active and passive members. These are

- the German Football Association — with 5.2 million members
- The German Gymnastic Association — with 4.2 million members
- The German Tennis Federation — with 2.2 million members
- The German Marksmen [!] Association — with 1.4 million members

Currently, there are about 84,000 sport clubs in Germany operating at grass root level: these are usually considered to be one of the three pillars of German sport. In 1990, people over the age of 14 spent, on average, DM 540 on sport per year (old FRG: DM 590; old GDR: 347). But differences between East and West Germany are gradually diminishing. Sport contributed 1.4% of the GNP of Federal Republic of Germany, with its overall value of DM 30 billion; and about 600,000 people are employed in the sport sector (cf. Weber, 1994).

These figures are the preliminary climax of the post-war development which is characterised by steady rates of increase. In 1950, the Deutscher Sport Bund (DSB, the German Sports Federation) had three million members; in 1970 ten million; in 1980 more than sixteen million; and in 1990 about 21 million. Over the same period the number of sports clubs, the organisational core unit of the sporting community in Germany, grew from 20,000 to almost 84,000. In 1993, about one quarter (26%) of West Germans over 14 years old were members of sports clubs.

These figures refer to the old Federal Republic of Germany and ignore the situation in the new parts of Germany. However, since October 1990 about 15,000 clubs have been founded in East Germany, providing an organisational framework for about 3.4 million people's sporting activities. But these statistics neglect the process of increasing individualisation of sports participation, and in particular the unorganised forms of active sports involvement in recreational activities such as swimming, cycling, jogging, badminton, body-building.

However the highest rate of increase since the late 1980s has been in the Fitness Sector. About 3.5 million Germans regularly go to a gym. The 5,500 facilities have a turnover of about DM 3 billion per year (*Die Welt*, 5.4.1995: p. 13).

Freizeitsport, individualisation and de-sportification in the 'new Germany'

In a nutshell, the development of *Freizeitsport* (literally translated as *leisure sport* referring to all kinds of recreational sporting activities and Sport for All) in post war Germany is a success story. What are the reasons and causes for this success? Why is sport more successful than singing in a choir, collecting stamps, breeding racing pigeons or even tending one's allotment? Why are sports clubs — despite all the difficulties and problems they have been encountering for some time now and despite the competition from the private sector — more successful than other voluntary organisations? Obviously, there are no general, universal answers to these questions. The meanings attached to sport, both spectating and participating, as well as the subjective and objective experiences of individuals are the result of a number of factors, such as the *Zeitgeist* ('spirit of the time'), the socio-economic background and the political climate.

In the 1990s, for the Social Democratic Party in Germany, "sport is a significant part of culture contributing to both quality of life and individual happiness" (SPD, 1993: p. 4). For the Conservative government in Germany, "involvement in sport means to declare one's solidarity with and support for a free and human society, ... to feel a sense of belonging and to gain an identity" (*Presse und Informationsamt der Bundesregierung*, 1992: p. 3).

Despite a lack of qualitative investigations into the meanings individuals attach to and live through sport, Rittner (1994) argues that in order to understand the popularity of sport in Germany the following three sets of themes concerned with the aims and objectives of individual involvement, have to be addressed:

(i) Health and fitness as a precondition for individual happiness;

(ii) Fun, enjoyment and relaxation;

(iii) Aesthetic self-realization and the presentation of "subtle differences".

The motives 'health' and 'fitness' clearly demonstrate the radical denial and rejection of the norms of the classical (competitive) sport. In particular, these motives show that active participation in sport is geared towards functional and usable merits and effects for the individual. The emphasis on health is no longer linked with the very general idea of "*mens sana in corpore sano*". Fitness predominantly refers to the utilisation of physical efficiency (developed through sport and exercise) in non-sporting contexts.

This also explains how the commodification of recreational sport and its integration in the commercial service sector became possible with a redefinition of the term fitness and an extension of its meaning. Once a physiological concept, it became a social virtue, sought after by very different social groups. In other words, recreational sports — the traditional monopoly of voluntary organisations — became marketable when the traditional definition of 'fitness' (as a prerequisite for sporting success) was replaced by a very open interpretation. The preliminary climax of the semantic career of this term allows people nowadays to equate it with, and to use it as a synonym for individual happiness, health, youth, success, well being, sociability, attractiveness etc.

Two more general conclusions can be drawn from the analysis of this process:

1. Since fitness has become a general social virtue its meaning has lost its physiological exclusiveness. This indicates an undermining and weakening of the aesthetic norms and values of traditional sport.
2. This process also displays the rise of a sport and body orientated terminology and aesthetic in every day culture. Furthermore it indicates the appropriation of an additional set of props for one's self presentation.

The motives of 'fun' and 'enjoyment', too, stand in unbridgeable contrast to the traditional forms of affiliation and loyalty of athletes to the club representing communities organised along the themes of class and region. In addition, the use of sporting symbols in the world of marketing, public relations and advertising is significantly contributing to the creation of new realities replacing those features which helped to constitute modern sport in the first place, e.g. the tradition of voluntary work as expressed in honorary positions and the principle of amateurism.

However, these developments have not yet manifested themselves to the same extent in East-Germany. The EMNID Study (1991) of youth in East and West Germany analysing the subjective meanings of sport in comparative perspective clearly shows "that gratification and motives such as performance, effort, and competition find much more approval with the East German youth than with their peers in the West. On the other hand, West German youth put more emphasis on well-being, relaxing, and having fun" (Brettschneider, 1994: p. 256).

These contemporary developments, particularly the increasing dominance of non-sporting values contradicting and undermining a traditional understanding of sport, have caused some German sport sociologists (Cachay 1990, Heinemann 1989) to label the current phase 'the de-sportification of sport'. Whilst Rittner argues that these developments are caused by far reaching changes of the ideal perception of physicality and personality, Bette (1993) states that these changes have occurred due to the constantly increasing individualisation affecting the relationship between individual, body and sport. Drawing on Bourdieu (1979), Bette shows how the body has been captured by the general process of individualisation and is now used to demonstrate 'subtle differences', to present unique and distinctive features of a person and to manifest as well as to celebrate the individuality of human beings with the help of sporting metaphors and props. Those sports involving the extraordinary, the extreme, risks and adventures must therefore be understood as initiatives to escape from the ordinary, the trivial, the normal and the every-day world.

The search for unique and distinctive identities through sporting activities is certainly one factor explaining the steady growth of sport. This process of individualisation as reflected and pursued in sport and leisure is equally relevant to explain the major problem the voluntary sector is currently facing in Germany: the unwillingness of people to take on voluntary work and honorary positions. However, apart from the process of individualisation, there are other factors which have caused this problem.

Since this development could already be foreseen in the late 1980s, the first lively debates on the future of the voluntary sector had already taken place prior to the collapse of the German Democratic Republic. Currently a number of different policy initiatives to make the commitment to the voluntary sector more attractive are being discussed in Bonn. It has been suggested that changes should be made to:

- increase tax allowances and/or the pensions for people committed to the voluntary sector;
- provide these people with additional holidays per year;
- increase the public acknowledgement and recognition of voluntary work through the distribution of honorary titles and medals;
- provide free use of transport and reduced admission fees to public places, such as swimming pools, museums, adult education centres, galleries, etc.

However, since the decrease of interest in contributing to the voluntary sector is not only a problem of sport but of most other forms of leisure provision and social services it will be a major task for the future for the German government to provide the right circumstances and conditions as well as a positive climate for the voluntary sector to survive the increasing commercialisation of and individualisation in sport and leisure.

Conclusion

Sport in Germany in the 1990s has up to now been dominated by two major developments: the dismantling of the East-German 'sports miracle' which has transformed this part of the country into a sporting desert, and the emergence of a new type of sport consumer who increasingly rejects the responsibility of social duties and commitments within the voluntary sector and prefers to pay for certain services and to do sports on an individual basis outside the traditional organisational frameworks.

Obviously, the current developments in East-Germany can only be adequately understood against the background of the post-war rivalry between the two German states as part of the Cold War period. The dismantling of East-Germany's sporting system is still an ongoing process, yet over the last two years the focus of political debates has shifted. The emphasis is now on, firstly, the development and use of performance-enhancing drugs (providing an additional justification for the dismantling of the sporting structures) and, secondly, on the 'Golden Plan East' and 'Rebuild the East' — both concepts dealing with the future of sport in East-Germany, the necessary investments to upgrade old and build new facilities, and the promotion of the club as the core unit for community. The central government in Bonn is supporting these plans but has repeatedly stressed that it is not prepared to provide any additional finances. The governments of the regional states have, however, started to allocate funds to sport, but (due to other problems they have to tackle, e.g. the disproportionately high unemployment in the East) only in a very modest way. Consequently, due to the lack of sufficient and attractive facilities and the absence of successful athletes as role models — the majority have moved to the West to compete for the (financially) stronger clubs there — general levels of participation are at an all time low and will remain there if the Western propaganda machine continues to constantly associate the sporting success of the former German Democratic Republic with doping, exploitation of children, athletes serving as informers to the Ministry of Security, etc.

Whilst the central government of the new Federal Republic of Germany is, by and large, responsible for the destruction of the organisational structures of top-level sport in East-Germany, the Kohl government is very concerned about the declining role of the voluntary sector in sport, and in particular the reluctance of people to take on voluntary work and honorary positions. It does seem, though, to be prepared to tackle this issue which clearly shows that voluntarism still appeals to the Conservative government, particularly in times of economic and social problems which were caused, paradoxically, by the Kohl-government itself misjudging the challenge and burden facing the German economy, society and culture after "reunification".

References

Beck, U. (1986) *Risikogesellschaft — Auf dem Wege in eine andere Moderne.* Frankfurt: Suhrkamp.

Bette, K.-H. (1993) 'Sport and individualization', *Spectrum der Sportwissenschaften*, Jg. 5: pp. 34-55.

Bourdieu, P. (1979) *La Distinction.* Paris: Les editions de minuit.

Brettschneider, W. D. (1994) 'Unity of the nation — unity in sports?', in R. C. Wilcox (ed) *Sport in the global village.* Morgantown: Fitness Information Technology, pp. 251-259.

Cachay, K. (1990) 'Versportlichung der Gesellschaft und Entsportung des Sports — Systemtheoretische Anmerkungen zu einem gesellschaftlichen Phänomen', in H. Gabler and U. Göhner (eds) *Für einen besseren Sport — Themen, Entwicklungen und Perspektiven aus Sport und Sportwissenschaft.* Schorndorf: Hofmann, pp. 97-113.

Damklaer, S. (1994) 'The unification of German sports systems' in R. C. Wilcox (ed) *Sport in the global village*. Morgantown: Fitness Information Technology, pp. 261-268.

Gratton, P. (1990) 'The production of Olympic champions: International comparisons', in A. Tomlinson (ed) *Sport in society: Policy, politics and culture* (LSA Publication No. 43). Eastbourne: Leisure Studies Association, pp. 50-67.

Heinemann, K. (1989) 'Der "nicht-sportliche" Sport', in K. Dietrich and K. Heinemann (eds) *Der nicht-sportliche Sport. Beiträge zum Wandel im Sport*. Schorndorf: Hofmann, pp. 11-28.

Holt, R. (1990) *Sport and the British*. Oxford: Oxford University Press.

Hopf, W. (ed) (1979) *Fussball — Soziologie und Sozialgeschichte einer populären Sportart*. Bensheim: Päd-extra.

Houlihan, B. (1991) *The government and politics of sport*. London: RKP.

Merkel, U. (1994) 'Germany and the World Cup: Solid, reliable, often undramatic — but successful', in J. Sugden and A. Tomlinson (eds) *Hosts and champions*. Aldershot: Arena, pp. 93-118.

Presse und Informationsamt der Bundesregierung (1992) *Sportpolitik der Bundesregierung*. Bonn.

Rittner, V. (1994) 'Die "success-story" des modernen Sports und seine Metamorphosen', in Bundeszentrale für poltische Bildung (ed) *Aus Politik und Zeitgeschichte*. Bonn: Das Parlament, Vol. 24, pp. 23-30.

Schulze, G. (1993) *Die Erlebnisgesellschaft. Kultursoziologie der Gegenwart*. Frankfurt and New York: Campus.

Social Democratic Party (1993) *Das neue Sportprogramm der SPD: Lebensqualität und Lebensfreude*. Bonn.

Weber, W. (1994) *Die wirtschaftliche Bedeutung des Sports*. Paderborn.

Sports Policy in the People's Republic of China

Tan Ying and K. Roberts

University of Liverpool

The leap forward

World sport has been startled by the recent leap forward by Chinese athletes. Their pace of progress and levels of success across so many forms of competition are unprecedented. The achievements of Chinese runners in the 1992 Olympics was merely one of several peaks. The rapidity and scale of China's achievements have been sufficient to arouse suspicions that the means must have been unorthodox, and very likely illegitimate. Considering China's particular political status, now the world's most powerful sporting socialist nation, coupled with the country's large number of actual participants and the even larger number of potential players, there is understandable worldwide interest in the sport system and policy that has been responsible for the leap forward.

The following passages proceed by sketching the organisational framework within which China's sport has developed since the foundation of the People's Republic of China (PRC) in 1949. China's strategy towards sporting excellence during and since the 1980s is then discussed along with the current situation as regards mass sports participation. The concluding section outlines China's current reform plans and the changes that can be expected in the near future.

Administration of Chinese sport

Since the foundation of the PRC, sports adminstration has been thoroughly entwined with China's centralised political regime. The National Sport Federation, founded in 1949, was the first government sport body and was charged with national responsibility for sport affairs. At that time the government began to form its basic strategy in sport and to develop an organisational framework. It was emphasised that sport in the new China would be nationalised and scientific. A senior government leader, Zhu De, was appointed to be the chairman of the National Sport Federation, and his appointment signalled high-level official involvement in the organisation.

An important event during that period was the establishment of the National Sport Committee in November 1952, which superseded the Federation and became and remains a leading department under the State Council with responsibility for producing state strategies, directing, supervising and coordinating all national sport affairs. In 1952 the State Council appointed another senior government leader, He Long, to be the first Minister of the National Sport Committee. It was at this stage that the framework of China's sport administration system was created and this basic system has endured to the present day. Up to the 1990s there were no basic administrative changes. China's recent leap forward has been achieved by its established system of sports government; it is not a product of administrative reform.

A noteworthy feature of the administrative system is that it is highly centralised. Up to now it has been the central government in China that has made all major provisions for sport including financial investment, the organisation of national games, and the management of most national teams. Local authorities, mainly at provincial level, have some responsibilities for sport. A regional sport fund is raised mainly by the local authorities. A Provincial Sport Committee is charged with producing regional sport strategies under the direction of central government as well as administering local sports teams and organising provincial games. But it is obligatory for local sports organisations to supply their best athletes for selection by China's national teams, and it is at national level that decisions are made about which provinces' athletes qualify for international competition.

There are some minor sport organisations in separate government departments such as the Department of Education, Department of Health, Department of Civil Administration and Department of Culture which have interests and responsibility for sport within the departments concerned but they play no role in the organisation of national or international sport.

Until the 1980s the principal government organisations directly ran virtually all sport in China; there was no voluntary or commercial sector involvement. Even now, through all levels, the government, in another word, the National Sport Committee, is the dominant and by far the most influential body in sport affairs in China.

Sporting excellence in China

Excellence in sports development

China was a closed or a semi-closed country for a long time. Modern sport was introduced into China in the late nineteenth century, but it developed slowly and was unpopular at that time (Zhang Cai-zheng, 1985). Modern sports began to move forward only in the 1950s after the National Sport Committee was created. In addition to following the model of organisation in the Soviet Union at that time, China also adopted its theory and techniques in training and competition. Many foreign specialists in coaching from the Soviet Union, and also from Hungary, were invited to China to teach Chinese coaches and to train Chinese athletes. Simultaneously, some teams were sent abroad to participate in international competitions to gain experience, and, as a result, apart from the establishment of an organisational framework, as well as rules and regulations of competition, there was a significant improvement in performance in many modern sports compared with China's relatively poor standards in the past. Individual competitors achieved success in one or two sports including weightlifting, men's breaststroke and the high jump.

Throughout the 1960s and 1970s China's sport bodies were dedicated to hard work towards raising standards while evolving modern approaches to training in which both theory and practice embodied some Chinese characteristics. Through these new approaches remarkable progress was made in events such as table tennis, volleyball and gymnastics. Later China was to become a leading nation in these events. However, China's sporting progress inevitably suffered from the unstable political situation at the time of the Cultural Revolution. The National Sport Committee was placed under military control for five years, and many outstanding athletes were subjected to persecution and death. He Long, the former Vice Premier and Minister of the National Sport Committee, suffered this fate.

The period since the 1970s has been a dramatic phase in the history of China's sport. Some sports have blossomed. In many sports Chinese competitors have achieved outstanding international success. The Chinese female volleyball team has won the World Championship five times. The national table tennis team returned to China victorious after collecting gold medals in all sections of table tennis during the thirty-sixth International Table Tennis Championships thereby breaking all records in the 55 years' history of world table tennis. The Chinese men's gymnastics team became world champions and the women's gymnastics team won the silver medal. The high jump record has been broken three times by Chinese athletes. The men's and women's diving teams have been ranked among the top four in the world. Until the 1980s Japanese teams dominated swimming in Asia, but in recent years Chinese swimmers have made great strides. In 1982, 1986 and 1990 China achieved first place by taking the most gold medals in the Asian Games, thereby becoming the most powerful sporting country in Asia. China's performances in the 23rd, 24th and 25th Olympic Games have been even more startling, a reflection of the country's leap forward on the international athletics circuit. Within eight years of China's return to the International Olympic Committee in 1979, the country became one of the most powerful sporting nations in the world.

Olympic Strategy

There have been innovations in China's national sporting strategy, though not in the system of sports administration, since the political reforms in

1978. For many years after the foundation of PRC it was emphasised that the development of sport was a political task. So the government promoted sport, among other reasons, in order to improve the public's health and the country's social well-being. Especially during the Cultural Revolution it was proclaimed before all events that, 'The first thing is friendship, second is competition'.

The gulf that was then growing between China and the rest of the world in athletic levels was widened by the disruption of training and competition during the Cultural Revolution. At that time investment in sport per head of population was extremely low (see Table I). This reflected China's relatively undeveloped economic situation at that time and large population, and also the fact that sporting success was not a political priority. This changed during the implementation of reforms and the more open policy after 1978. This resulted in a switch in domestic priorities towards economic affairs. It was then decided at the Annual Sport Conference in 1979 to place particular emphasis on sporting excellence by creating nationwide sporting committees above the provincial level.

As can be seen in Table 1, since the late-1970s government spending on sport has risen steeply. Sport has become a means whereby China has sought to demonstrate her capabilities to the rest of the world. There was a historic breakthrough in China's international sporting status when the country was admitted to the International Olympic Committee in 1979 having withdrawn for 21 years. Since then China's sport has met the full force of international athletics competition with astonishing success.

After its successes in 23rd (1984) Olympic Games China defined its strategy towards sporting excellence as the 'Olympic Strategy' which set the highest possible targets and gave the country the task of becoming one of the most powerful sport nations in the world by the end of the century. A series of reforms were implemented during the 1980s including a reduction in the number of non-Olympic events in the National Games, making athletes' records in their events (not political criteria) the overriding consideration when selecting national teams, and increasing the number of events in Olympic sports such as swimming, and track and field. There was an adjustment in the ratio between Olympic and non-Olympic events in the National Games from 4:1 in 1986 to 9:1 in 1991, as well as related changes in training strategies centred on the Olympics (Zhang Cai-zheng, 1992).

As part of its Olympic Strategy the National Sport Committee listed China's major sports. These were track and field, swimming, diving, gymnastics, weight-lifting, fencing, judo, wrestling, shooting, archery, rowing, table tennis, badminton, basketball, volleyball and football. Like other communist countries that were seeking international sporting success at that time, China decided to concentrate upon a limited number of sports. The National Sport Committee decided to reduce its responsibility for, and loosen its control over, other sports while taking more responsibility for the administration of, and financial investment in, major (Olympic) events.

Table 1 Central Government Expenditure on Sport 1952-1991

Year	Total £ million	Pence per head	Percentage of budget
1952	3.0	0.5	0.17
1957	3.8	0.6	0.12
1962	5.4	0.8	0.18
1965	9.1	1.3	0.20
1970	3.7	0.5	0.06
1975	17.4	1.9	0.21
1978	25.4	2.7	0.23
1980	30.3	3.1	0.25
1981	34.4	3.5	0.31
1982	41.4	4.1	0.35
1983	45.5	4.5	0.41
1984	59.9	5.8	0.45
1985	75.3	7.3	0.58
1991	100.0	9.1	0.73

Source: National Census Yearbooks

Local sports organisations and some other government departments were charged with the responsibility for lesser events.

The Olympic Strategy is an important part of China's present-day sports policy. It has already made a great impact on China's sport development and has been responsible for the achievements listed in Tables 2 and 3 (overleaf). The post-1978 strategy has been responsible for 83 percent of all world records set by Chinese athletes since the foundation of PRC. More than 95 percent of China's all-time world champions have appeared since 1979. The peak of all these achievements was China gaining fourth place in the 25th (1992) Olympic Games by taking 54 medals including 16 gold (Xie Ya-Long and Wang Ru-Ying, 1992). This favourable situation, and encouragement from the successful organisation of 11th Asian games in 1990, gave China's government the confidence to bid to host the 27th Olympic Games in the year 2000, but this bid was frustrated partly for political rather than strictly sporting reasons.

Table 2 China's athletes breaking international records (1956-1992)

Year	No.
1956-1978	61
1979 *	13
1980	7
1981	8
1982	11
1983	13
1984	12
1985	5
1986	7
1987 **	22
1988	33
1989	36
1990	14
1991	31
1992	42
1993	57

1979 * The year of China became a member of IOC
1987 ** The year of announcement of the Olympic Strategy
Source: National Census Yearbooks

Table 3 China's athletes becoming world champions (1959-1993)

Year	No.
1959-1978	30
1979	12
1980	3
1981	25
1982	12
1983	37
1984	33
1985	42
1986	26
1987	64
1988	54
1989	80
1990	54
1991	88
1992	80
1993	103

Table 4 Number of international sporting contacts (1985-1992)

	Visiting China	China's delegations sent out
1985	466	476
1988	244	563
1989	211	597
1990	364	607
1991	518	876
1992	394	1006

Source: National census yearbooks

China is now a leading competitor in international events and can envisage a future as a powerful sporting country. The country has done extraordinarily well in sport compared with its backward status in some other areas. Its athletes' achievements have not only resulted in a higher status for China's sports in the international Olympic movement, but also a broader enhancement of the country's international reputation as can be seen from its widening international sporting contacts indicated in Table 4. Since the mid-1980s there has been a steady rise in the number of Chinese teams competing outside their own country.

iii. Features of China's superior sports

The sports in which China has already excelled, or clearly has the potential to do so, are table-tennis, badminton, women's volleyball, women's basketball, gymnastics, diving, weight-lifting, swimming, and track and field (Xie Ya-Long and Wang Ru-Ying, 1992). These events can be classified into three groups (see Figure 1).

Figure 1

1. Skill-based	a. Difficulty and beauty: gymnastics and diving
	b. Accuracy: shooting
2. Power-based	Judo, female
	Weight-lifting, light-weight
	Swimming, short distance men and female all distances
	Shot put, female
	Walking and middle-long distance races, female
3. Power and skill-based	Table tennis and badminton
	Female basketball, volleyball and football

Up to now, China's female athletes have made a greater contribution than males by taking more medals and breaking more international records, and the women's football, basketball and volleyball teams are now among the best in the world. Chinese athletes have made some strides in skill-based events, but even moreso, especially among the women, in events requiring moderate physical power.

Public sports participation

It is not surprising that the government's concern for public sports participation in China should be closely related to its concern for public health and fitness, particularly its interest in the healthy growth of children and young people, as well as the need to control non-work time. "The government should develop the sporting cause", and "educate and train the youth and children to grow healthily in morals, intelligence and physical constitution", are quotations from the Constitution of the PRC.

Alongside the emphasis on excellence, China's government has played a positive role in promoting the development of mass participation by steadily increasing capital investment in building programmes (see Tables 5 and 6).

Table 5 New-built sport facilities (1985-1992)

Year	Field	Gymnasia	Swimming Pools	Basketball Courts
1985	47	29	135	137
1988	77	86	366	220
1989	24	19	70	61
1990	27	34	105	60
1991	23	36	87	44
1992	54	45	128	94

Source: National census yearbooks

The number of sports facilities in the country is now more than 20 times the total before the foundation of the PRC. Excellence has been built upon a base of mass participation which, in the case of modern sports, has required the construction of new facilities. China now has an impressive number of modern facilities, enough to sustain a sufficiently broad base of participation to produce top-rank athletes, though provision remains modest relative to China's huge population.

Table 6 Capital budget of sport construction (1952-1985)

Year	Total (£ million)	Percentage of Budget
1952	0.1	0.02
1957	2.3	0.16
1962	2.0	0.03
1965	1.2	0.07
1975	5.1	0.12
1978	4.2	0.08
1980	7.8	0.14
1981	7.7	0.17
1982	10.0	0.18
1983	11.7	0.20
1984	19.0	0.26
1985	41.6	0.39

Source: National Census Yearbooks

Faced with great pressure on extremely limited financial resources, in recent years the government has adopted a realistic strategy. This encourages different social sectors, ranging from state organisations to the private sector, to sponsor and organise sports activities. These now include events based on the principle that the 'investor has a right to make a profit'. The National Sport Committee increasingly exercises its responsibility for public sports by trying to encourage and direct other organisations into a self-investing, self-consuming and self-entertaining trajectories. One of the most important programmes encouraging mass participation is 'The Criterion of National Exercises'.

The Criterion of National Exercises

This criterion is a set of performance targets, and is aimed at "encouraging and promoting the masses, especially the youth and children, to be active in sports and to build up their health, as well as enhancing competition levels to serve socialist construction and defence". This Criterion has been re-issued and adjusted many times since it came into being in the 1950s, and the most recent adjustment was in 1990.

The Criterion divides the population into children (9-12), juveniles A (13-15), juveniles B (16-18) and adults (over 18). Thus there are four age groups. The Criterion specifies performance standards for different events based on age and sex. Performances in all events are grouped into excellent, good or poor. Individuals are retested every year. All primary and secondary schools, as well as colleges and universities, are required to practise this Criterion. Students at primary school who fail the test are not allowed to graduate and are barred from entering secondary school. Up to 1994 the total number passing the test annually was over 500 million nationwide, mostly students.

Broadcast Exercises

Another important activity in schools and colleges is The Broadcast Exercises which began in the 1950s. All students are required to do these exercises during breaks, twice a day during terms.

The One Dragon System

After several decades of effort, China has formulated a training system which consists of elementary, middle and high levels in order to select and train excellent sporting competitors. Training schools are a fundamental part of the so-called 'One Dragon System'. By 1992 2,578 children's spare time sports schools, 94 middle sports and athletes schools, 13 sport colleges, and another 16,000 sports schools which laid emphasis on particular sports events, had attracted more than 5.5 million children and young people to participate in training since the foundation of the PRC. All China's gold medal winners in 24th and 25th Olympic Games had some training experience in the above schools.

The expansion of basic training has not only supplied competitors for higher levels, but has also given an impetus to younger participants, and has contributed to the improvements indicated in tests administered by the Departments of Education and Medicine. These have shown an average increase of 10 centimetres in height and one kilogram in weight every 10 years among 7-18 years olds. Successive cohorts have been healthier and stronger than their parents.

Mass sports participation

A survey of adult (16 and above) sports participation was conducted by The National Sport Committee in 1991 in two of China's major cities, Nanjing and Shengyang, where 22,000 residents completed a questionnaire, and the results of this survey provide recent evidence on sports participation in urban China (Liang zhen-shou and Yan shi-duo, 1992).

The findings show that 34.9 percent of all citizens were taking part in sports activities regularly (three times a week, thirty minutes each time). This suggests that for around one third of China's urban population sport has become an important part of their leisure. The 35 percent adult participation rate is impressive, but walking was the most common 'sport' in which people were participating three or more times per week, and this exercise probably owed more to the necessities of daily life than enthusiasm for sport or the pursuit of health and fitness.

Around 10 percent of citizens are aged people in China and in the above study they recorded high levels of sport activity. Their high participation rate, slightly higher than in all other age groups, was probably due to their steady pensions, more leisure time after release from looking after the younger generation, and concern for their health. A reason for the 'younger' adults' relative low participation was probably their lack of leisure time (see Table 7) under the pressures of paid work and housework.

Table 7 Daily leisure time in several countries

	Males (Hours)	Females (Hours)
China	2.5	1.7
Soviet Union	4.8	3.6
U.S.A.	4.5	4.1
France	4.1	3.1
West Germany	4.2	3.2

Source: China's Sports Daily, 8 May, 1988

Restricted by their relatively low incomes, poor transportation and limited access to sports facilities, most citizens were participating in simple, non-facility, low cost and family based sports activities such as are displayed in Table 8.

Table 8 The most popular sports in China

Sport	Percentage participating
Walking	28.58
Football, basketball, volleyball	15.26
Badminton and Table-tennis	12.39
Jogging and running	7.00
Qi-gong and Taijiquan	4.77
Swimming	2.20
Fishing and Dove-raising	0.82
Chess	2.24

Source: Liang zhen-shou and Yan shi-duo, 1992

In all the above sports, except that more females (33.2%) were taking part in walking than males (24.03%), there was always a tendency for there to be more male participants.

The two city study revealed several factors (see Table 9) which drive people in China to become involved in sports. Albeit to different degrees, all age groups are driven by a desire to improve their health and fitness. Aged people and intellectuals are especially likely to have this motivation. All participants tend to be driven by the pleasure and enjoyment that comes from strenuous exercise. 'Propaganda' is another important factor which increases participation, especially via television. The rapid spread of television in China during the 1980s made it an important part of most citizens' lifestyles. Statistics show that city residents in China now spend more than half of their leisure time watching TV including various sports programmes. The major televised sports in China are football, volleyball and basketball followed by track and field, swimming and martial arts. It seems that working class citizens and junior school students are particularly affected by this 'propaganda'. Intellectuals and others with high educational backgrounds are less likely to be influenced by this, maybe because they have less time to watch television, though their individualism could be another reason. Social networks including families and friends are further influences. It seems that friends are rather more influential than families; among regular participants (at least once a week), 7.5 percent claimed to have been initiated by friends compared with 4.5 percent by their families. Young people and students were especially likely to have been introduced to sport by friends.

Table 9 Factors promoting participation (in percentages)

		Fitness	'Propaganda'	Family	Friends
Gender	Male	34.86	17.62	2.16	4.82
	Female	37.03	15.89	3.83	4.51
Age	16-30	23.37	17.81	3.60	8.01
	31-35	30.35	16.81	3.29	3.53
	51-60	39.40	14.86	2.01	2.23
Occupation	Workers	31.24	20.45	3.11	5.44
	Intellectuals	44.77	12.00	3.43	4.03
	Students	25.63	12.27	3.39	8.30
Education	Primary	24.45	16.33	2.33	2.56
	Junior	25.22	21.64	3.14	4.37
	Senior	30.72	15.98	3.15	5.78
	University	45.50	9.92	2.95	4.90

Source: Liang zhen-shou and Yan shi-duo, 1992

The survey provided other evidence on the positive social functions of sports which include social relationship improvement among family members and neighbours, and making new friends.

Rural and ethnic minority sports

China has 56 national minorities and more than 80 percent of its people live in rural areas. Most of the territory is remote and undeveloped. China's rural population is generally poor and has no access to local, purpose-built sports centres. In order to promote sport development in rural areas, The National Sport Committee has adopted 'The Criterion of Advanced Sporting County' which lists detailed standards including facilities, financial investment and some other requirements for local authorities to meet. The National Sport Committee has the right to inspect, re-test and approve all local authorities every two years. The purpose of this is to sustain their efforts to maintain the title. Nearly 10 percent of China's 2000 or so counties nationwide have been titled 'Advanced Sporting County'. 'Peasants Games' have been held regularly every four years since 1988 to draw attention to sports in rural areas.

Another important sport event is the 'Ethnic Minority Traditional Games' which have been held every four years since 1982. These Games are geared to retaining and developing China's traditional events, and promoting unity between different minorities thereby helping to stabilise the political situation.

Economic change and lifestyles

Chinese lifestyles are currently in flux due to the country's rapid economic development. They are moving from ways of life geared to satisfying basic needs to being comparatively well-off. Private savings have now risen to 15 billion Chinese Yuan (£1.1 billion) according to the Department of Finance. Besides this, the capital-oriented present-day economy is producing a large number of *nouveau riche* who are able to afford expensive sport activities. Spending on sport has increased progressively during the last 10 years or so. Companies and enterprises, based in China and abroad, have fed some of their profits into sport. Income from lotteries run by central and local government has reached a considerable figure, some of which is channelled into sport. In addition to this, during 1994 all state owned organisations and enterprises reduced weekly work hours from 48 to 44, and all of this should give an added impetus to China's sport.

Non-government funds released into sport nationwide, around £100 million up to 1994, amount to only a tiny fraction of the government's annual sport budget. In the immediate future public investment is certain to continue to be the main source of sports funding in China. While most citizens' incomes have risen in recent years, the gap and between rural and urban areas has widened. According to a report from the state-run China Daily, the rural-urban wage gap is widening. In 1992 rural wages averaged only 44 percent of urban earnings. In 1993 there were 80 million residents in rural China whose living standards were below the official poverty line of 18.5 USA dollars per month. This was despite the government's efforts towards lifting up China's poor population. During the next six years these efforts will intensify according to the government 'Support for Poverty' programme which was announced at the 1994 People's Congress. Nevertheless, the rural-urban imbalance will persist for quite a long time if only because of the 130 million surplus workers in China's countryside, while four million were employed in loss-making enterprises in urban China in 1994.

Clearly it will be a long term task to improve public sports participation in China nationwide, especially in remote rural regions. The realistic way will be to provide the majority of citizens with low cost services and to increase publicity for sport facilities, to continue the capital building programmes of extending and upgrading facilities by obtaining funds from public authorities and the private sector, as well as introducing commercialisation into the administration of facilities in order to cover their costs, and providing luxurious modern sports accommodation and entertainment to attract the *nouveau riche*. In 1993 The National Sport Committee planned to establish a 'Whole Nation Healthy Plan' with the aim of further promoting public participation.

Reform programme

As already mentioned, in recent years there has been a nationwide trend to create a role for private enterprise in sport so as to raise performance levels and widen participation still further. This trend has been pronounced since the 1980s when China's 'opening' and reform began to promote the market economy. However, as much as anything else, the trend has been a response to the government's own financial problems. Despite the amazing leap forward in recent years, China's sports have been facing mounting financial pressure. After more than 10 years of consistently rising investment from the government, the central government's 1994 financial deficit, reported at around 20 billion Yuan, as well as the sharp decline in its budget as a proportion of national income from 37.2 percent in 1978 to 19.2 percent in 1988, meant that the release of yet more funds for sport from the government was unlikely (Wu Shao-zhu, 1993). Hence the trend towards sport committees at all levels seeking non-governmental sponsors. Having achieved international success, China has begun to change its system of sports administration. The government hopes that the new policies will give sport another boost, but radical changes will inevitably place China's achievements at some risk.

Devolution

A major reform programme comprising general principles and targets was issued at the 1993 Annual Sport Conference by the National Sport

Committee. It was announced that there would be a series of adjustments in the administrative system. The new system is to be controlled by the government but supported by the society, a combination of government and society, centralisation and de-centralisation. The most important step in the reforms will be making independent sport associations the key organisations which will co-ordinate training, competition and finance. It is intended that a half of the national associations of individual sports should complete this transformation by 1996 while the rest will be required to complete the change before the end of the century.

In line with the decentralised reform policy, the National Sport Committee is to transform the government's function in sport from direct administration to macroscopic control by handing over implementation to related institutions. In order to lay emphasis on investigation and policy planning, sports committees at all levels are to adjust their inner-structures based on the principles of streamlining, unification and efficiency. In order to promote cost effectiveness and encourage competition, there are to be changes in the organisation and selection of national teams. These changes will devolve responsibility for some national teams to local authorities and departments, and will thus break-up the existing highly centralised administrative system.

It is planned to introduce three kinds of administrative structures consisting of centralised, a combination of centralised and decentralised, and totally decentralised organisational patterns. The government will take responsibility for investment and administration in fewer Olympic events. These will be the events in which local authorities find it most difficult to fulfil the task due to their generally poor facilities, namely, diving, gymnastics, table-tennis and badminton. Most Olympic events will adopt the second pattern where national and local authorities share the duties. These events are track and field, swimming, weight-lifting, shooting, archery, fencing, judo, wrestling, boxing, cycling and some winter Olympic events. In team sports and other Olympic events such as football, basketball and volleyball, all local teams will entitled to contribute players to the national teams through fair selection following national competitions. All departments, enterprises and universities will be able to compete in the National Games in Olympic events. The administration of non-Olympic events will be totally decentralised. In other words, China's national government will relinquish all responsibility for these sports.

Marketing and commercialism

It is intended to introduce commercialism into low and middle level training by charging training fees so as to ease the financial pressures on China's sports. Another proposal is to introduce the professional club system into football, tennis and weights in order to reduce the government's contribution.

In line with the marketing policy announced by the central government in 1992, a plan of sport commercialisation is coming into force. This is designed to gradually develop a sport marketing structure which will consist of multi-systems of ownership. The main steps are to be as follows:

a. The government will take advantage of the booming market economy to encourage the operation of all kinds of sport clubs including entertainment installations imported from Western countries, and high-cost facilities to cater for the demands of the more affluent sections of the public.
b. The government expects to quicken commercialisation in the training system by an expansion of paid training and paid transfers of professional athletes between associations and regions.
c. It is intended to stimulate the production and marketing of sports goods, advertising, lotteries, tourism and fitness to promote swift sport development.
d. Another major plan is to establish China's Sport City which will include a high tech zone, an entertainment district, press and bookshops, commercial and trade facilities, and official buildings. This city will occupy 2.5 square kilometres in Beijing.

Convergence

China is beginning to benefit from its 'opening' and reform policies. The highly centralised system was capable of strengthening sports rapidly when fired by political will, and scored remarkable achievements in sporting excellence. The Olympic Strategy achieved great success in not only raising standards but also gaining international recognition, encouraging mass participation, and boosting Chinese confidence which has subsequently become a positive factor in the country's all-round development.

The government now hopes to sustain and build on this success by introducing marketing and commercialism into sport. In the future, in line with the economic markets policy, decentralised sport reform may eventually speed up sport development by attracting investment, introducing more competition and generating quality service. As yet, however, the reform process is unbalanced due to the different economic situations in different areas and the widening gap between east and west, coast and inner-land. Thus the new flexible policy may cause some turbulence. Athletes in poor regions may migrate to rich areas thereby further aggravating regional inequalities. Further imbalances will arise from the trend towards favouring a few high profile Olympic events. Personal reward may become the main impetus instead of national glory. Talented athletes will certainly become dollar millionaires. Commercialism may lead to more drug abuse and bribery.

Restricted by economic backwardness in many areas, lack of leisure time and limited sport facilities, as well as the huge poor population nationwide, the reform process will be a long term task especially as regards mass participation. The goal of increasing participation in rural areas will be difficult to achieve. Effective monitoring will be difficult since as yet there are no clear targets in many fields. Targets will have to be set according to the particular situations in different areas. Developing effective organisational structures and improving efficiency while relying more on markets and commercialism will depend on broader economic development, the depth of China's political reform, and the establishment of a social security system which will enable 'surplus' workers not only to survive but to pursue broader life goals. However, the main factor on which the success of the reforms will depend will probably be whether China can remain socially and politically stable. In the 1990s the security of the entire socio-political system has become less dependable than the performances of China's athletes at the next Olympics.

References

Liang zhen-shou and Yan shi-duo (1992), *Survey of Chinese Citizen's Sporting Activities*, Chinese People's Press, Beijing.

National Census Yearbooks, Beijing.

Wu Shao-zhu (1993), Minister of China's National Sport Committee's New Year Speech, *China's Sports Daily*, December 28.

Xie Ya-Long and Wang Ru-Ying (1992), *The Laws of Winning in China's Superior Sports*, Chinese Sports Press, Beijing.

Zhang Cai-zheng (1985), *History of Chinese Sports*, Chinese People's Press, Beijing.

Zhang Cai-zheng (1992), *On Olympic Strategy*, Chinese Sports Press, Beijing.

II

The Politics of Participation and Provision: Target Groups

Sport and Leisure and the Active Elderly: a Case Study of Hove

Peter Green

Chichester Institute of Higher Education

This study was prompted by a recognition of a number of trends indicating the growing needs of the older person in society, and the growing awareness of the physical, social and psychological benefits to be gained from an involvement in sport, exercise and leisure for this group. The elderly have been for some time identified by the Government and the Sports Council as an increasing proportion of our population with a range of needs in relation to health, exercise, sport and leisure.

Discussions with health professionals and sport and leisure providers locally supports the need to research this increasingly significant target group. National policies such as the Sports Council's *Sport in the 90s: New Horizons* (1992) and the Department of Health's *The Health of the Nation*"(1992) refer to the need to make provision for the elderly. At the local level the recently published *Leisure Life: a Local Authority code of practice for the effective provision of leisure to older people* (1992) provides a useful framework on which to build.

This study is a collaborative venture between Chichester Institute and Hove Borough Council Leisure Directorate which aims to:

- identify the active elderly of Hove and their sport and leisure needs;
- investigate the role and responses of planners, policy makers and providers in meeting the sport and leisure needs of the active elderly within the wider policy framework of general provision for the elderly in Hove Borough;
- evaluate the effectiveness of policies for sport, leisure and education aimed at older people in the Borough;
- examine the assumptions underlying policy formulation and suggest ways of improving their effectiveness.

In consultation with the Director of Leisure Services at Hove the following steps have been undertaken:

- Desk research into the demographic structure of Hove and current levels of provision of sport and leisure for the active elderly and the take up of those opportunities in the Borough;
- Interviews with the key policy makers, planners and providers for the elderly in the Borough;
- Interviews with the main agencies representing older people in Hove;
- A small number of interviews with older people actively involved in sport and leisure in the Borough.

At an empirical level there is a growing body of literature which has evaluated the benefits of sport and leisure policies for older people. This is particularly the case in relation to the value of sport and exercise in maintaining health and physical well-being. Norton (1993) cites medical evidence, and opinion supporting this at the ILAM Leisure for the Third Age seminar. There is also increasing evidence of the social and psychological benefits of sport and leisure, including education, for older people. Mobily and Bedford (1993) have identified the positive effects and social benefits of leisure consistent with other researchers.

A review of theory by Fennell, Phillipson and Evers (1988) refers to the Activity theory developed by Havighurst who claimed that:

> Research has established the fact that activity in a wide variety of social roles is positively related to happiness and good social adjustment in old age and also that a high degree of activity in a given social role is positively related to happiness and good social adjustment. (1954: p. 309)

An alternative view of old age put forward by role and disengagement theorists suggests that people withdraw from social and economic life as a result of retirement and ageing.

These theoretical perspectives can be paralleled by models of ageing developed by Wilson (1991) which she relates to assumptions made by policy makers and service providers. She identifies two contrasting models referred to as "downhill all the way" and "terminal drop". The former model she refers to as: "an inevitable and irreversible slide downwards into dependency" (1991: p. 43).

This correlates with the role/disengagement perspective. It also conforms with the notion of structured dependency developed by Townsend and Walker, cited in Fennell *et al.* (1988), whereby dependency is imposed on old people by society. Wilson claims that the result of the "downhill" approach is a need for increasing levels of care with age. This model encourages dependency and discourages independence and rehabilitation.
This "downhill all the way" model:

> ... assumes that most people have a large surplus over and above the necessary physical and mental capacities to maintain satisfactory independent living. Even though, as medical research and common observation shows, some physical and mental attributes may decline with age, dependency does not automatically set in. People continue in their ability to function in the community until there is a marked change in their health status and they die. (Wilson: 1991: p. 44)

This relates closely to the Activity perspective and suggests that dependency is not inevitable as a general rule and that the terminal drop model is the norm for the majority of older people. This view is consistent with the Government's care in the community approach following the NHS and Community Care Act 1990. The challenge to policy makers and service providers at the local level is to maintain active independence for the increasing elderly population living at home.

Older people in Hove and their sport and leisure needs

National demographic trends indicate a 40% increase in those of pensionable age over the next 40 years. Those aged 65 years and over represented 15.7% of the population in 1991. Within East and West Sussex the proportion of people of retirement age and over is 23.7%, accentuating the national trend considerably. The 1991 Population census recorded a population of over 85, 00 in Hove Borough of which 23,339 (just over one quarter) were 65 years or above. If this group is extended to those of 50+ then the proportion of the total population increases to around 40%. Over the total number of pensioners, 32% are male and 68% female. Again these proportions vary for different age groups. There is a higher proportion of males among younger pensioners. The 1991 census indicates that 99.4% of Hove's retired population are white, with the remainder being of mainly Indian or Asian descent. Eight thousand five hundred (8,500) pensioners live alone in the borough, representing 21.5% of all households. These households are concentrated in those wards covering the older parts of Hove south of the railway line.

Of those households having one or more pensioner, 60.6% do not have a car compared with 40.7% for the population as a whole. In terms of mobility this is clearly significant in relation to sport and leisure activity. In terms of social class (SC) of head of household there are proportionately fewer pensioners in the professional, managerial and technical categories (SC 1 and 2) and proportionately more in the semi-skilled and unskilled manual categories (SC 4 and 5). General Household Survey data on sport and leisure participation suggest higher levels of participation generally among those in SC 1 and 2 compared with those in SCs 4 and 5. (Central Statistical Office, 1995).

Table 1 shows that the '45 year to retirement' population, whilst declining in absolute terms over the last decade, is due to increase by over one fifth between 1991 and 2001. This is significant in recreation terms, as it is this group that is most likely to engage increasingly in active sport and leisure pursuits. In contrast, the marked decline in early retired age group identified in the eighties is set to continue at a greater pace in the nineties. The size of the 75-84 age group was relatively static in the eighties but is set to decline dramatically in the nineties. Conversely the large increase in the proportion of very elderly will stabilise up to 2001. Overall the retired population decreased by 10% in the eighties and will decrease by 27% from 1991-2001. This compares with the steady increase for the population as a whole over the two decades.

Table 1 Age Structure Change: 1981, 1991, 2001

Age	1981	1991	% change 1981-91	2001	% change 1991-2001
45-RA	15, 863	14, 603	-7. 9	17, 740	+21. 5
RA-74	15, 322	11, 861	-22. 6	7, 930	-33.0
75-84	8, 279	8, 321	+0. 5	6, 030	-27. 5
85+	2, 290	3, 157	+37. 9	3, 162	+0. 2
Total popn.	83, 418	85, 364	+2. 3	89, 546	+4. 9

Source: Hove Borough Council, Planning Department.

In a recent study of the main national data source for participation in sport in Britain, the General Household Survey, (Gratton and Tice, 1994) showed that age acted as a lower barrier to participation in 1987 than it did in 1977. Furthermore:

> ...the average age of participants increased across all activity groups; the percentage of participants that were retired increased dramatically across virtually all activity groups. (Gratton and Tice, 1994: p. 49)

They found that sports participants comprise more retired people than ever before and the rate of increase is faster than would be expected purely on the basis of the increase in the proportion of retired in the population.

Furthermore, argue Gratton and Tice, the study gives some support to Rodgers' (1977) theory concerning age and participation in sport. He suggests that the conventional view — that people drop out of active recreation when they get older — is wrong. He argues that many older people were never participants in their youth. Increasingly older people nowadays have been exposed and conditioned to exercise and active recreation from their youth — they are sports literate. If this is the case Gratton and Tice suggest that:

> ... between 1977 and 1986 as a more "sports literate" generation got older, they continued to be involved in sport, so that many more older people were regular sports participants in 1986 than ten years earlier. If this interpretation is correct the implication is that the average age of participants will continue to rise gradually over the foreseeable future. (1994: p. 60)

With regard to the second finding, the most rapid increases in the proportion of retired people have been in indoor sports, particularly swimming. However in absolute terms it is outdoor sports, particularly walking, which attracts the highest numbers of retired sports participants. The study also suggests that frequency of participation is also higher than average. An earlier paper by the same authors indicates that participants both subjectively perceive themselves as healthier, as well as appearing healthier based on a range of objective indicators. It was reported that older sports participants also have a much wider range of other non-sport leisure interests than non-participants.

Interviews with older participants in sport and leisure activities in Hove support the concept of sports literacy and the concepts of internal and external continuity developed by Atchley (1993) whereby:

> Applied to activities, continuity theory maintains that adults gradually develop stable patterns of activity and that, in adapting to aging, adults engage in thought and take action designed to preserve and maintain these patterns in their general form. (1993: p. 5)

A small sample of ten members of the Young at Heart club for the over 50s was interviewed in April 1995. The club is based in the King Alfred Leisure Centre and operates on Monday and Thursday mornings and provides opportunities for swimming, badminton and the use of exercise equipment. Some of the badminton players were interviewed on the following themes:

- why they attended the sessions and how frequently;
- their history of sport and exercise participation and the current activities they engage in;
- the perceived benefits of participation;
- their type of participation.

The people interviewed invariably played badminton for health and social reasons and usually attended sessions once or twice per week. The majority had been involved in sport since school, usually court and pitch sports and swimming. A minority had been introduced to sport via the Young at Heart Club. The majority also took part in other sport and leisure activities, especially swimming and walking, but also sailing, skiing, skating and golf.

The majority perceived the benefits of sport to be for health and fitness: some mentioned suppleness and exercise as preventive measures. Others mentioned the mental benefits as well. One individual said it gave him affirmation of his abilities. An important secondary benefit was the social/friendship dimension of physical activity and sheer enjoyment.

Virtually all the respondents were retired and almost all had worked in the professions. Former occupations included accountancy; engineering; planning consultancy; insurance; charity work.

Another perspective on the sport and leisure needs of older people in Hove was given by the Director of Age Concern, Hove and Portslade. She indicated that leisure activities run throughout the organisation's various clubs and programmes. these include day clubs, lunch clubs, social clubs, arts and craft clubs. An exercise class to music is the most active recreation activity on offer. She suggested however that, for many, voluntary work is their main and most fulfilling leisure pursuit. This provided a sense of worth and independence. Age Concern has over 250 volunteers of whom 95% are over 65 years old. It is a case, she said, of the mobile helping the less mobile. She identified a range of key issues affecting older people which have implications for sport and leisure:

- Isolation, depression and loneliness;
- Lack of mobility;
- Accessible venues which are safe to get to and cheap at suitable times of the day. There is a resistance to going out after dark;
- Coming to terms with bereavement, retirement.

An older person facing some of the issues above was interviewed at a relaxation class operating at the 52 Project in Portslade, a Health Promotion outreach scheme. This octogenarian had led a lonely and isolated life for some years following the death of her husband until she noticed an advertisement in a shop window for an adult education class in art at the Connaught Centre. By pure chance she met someone who was attending the class and offered to take her along. Since then she has developed a lively social life and has made a number of friends. This elderly woman contrasts vividly with the articulate and well-connected members of the Young at Heart Club and typifies the problems facing policy makers and providers in meeting the needs of outsiders who have little or no contact with the system.

The providers and the policies

The research identified a range of statutory and voluntary agencies providing services either directly or indirectly for older people in the Borough. The role of commercial organisations was very limited with regard to the elderly.

Statutory agencies

The main players in the statutory sector are: Health; Social Services; Leisure; and Adult Education.

1. The East Sussex Health Authority

The Authority has developed policy, planning and funding in relation to the health needs of older people via two strands:

East Sussex Community Care Plan 1995-1998;

Health of the Nation Group.

The key target of the Community Care Plan relevant to the role of sport and leisure is to promote preventive services for older people across Brighton, Hove and Lewes.

It is recognised that preventive services for older people can improve not only health but also quality of life. Services for older people concerned with the needs of the active elderly and health promotion should be encouraged and publicised. Each locality group will review the range of preventive services available and seek the support of statutory agencies, including leisure services to ensure a full range of services is available to older people within each locality (East Sussex, 1994: p. 42.)

In relation to Brighton and Hove specifically the 1995-1998 draft plan refers primarily to the major achievements and targets which relate to the overwhelming priorities of older people who are: frail and confused; have mental health problems; require residential care; endure poor housing; and who may themselves be carers. Achievements relate to provision for older people with mental health problems and the development of preventive health care services, in particular health screening for people over 75 years. Targets for the plan period include: respite care; support at home; day centre provision; crisis services for evening and weekends and specialist residential care.

The local East Sussex Health Authority planning team has a budget of £300,00-400,000 p.a. for pump priming (£160,000 for Hove). Inevitably with the priorities outlined above there is little money available for preventive health projects.

The Health of the Nation Group has a budget of £120,000 p.a. to allocate to projects which work towards Health of the Nation policies. However not much has been done for the elderly — dealing mainly those with mental health problems and children.

An exception has been the recent funding of a Hove Borough Council, Leisure Services Department application, "Hove Actively" for £5,000 to enable the Hangleton and Knoll project to encourage and facilitate people of pre-retirement and retirement age to participate in appropriate sport and exercise activities and to provide information and advice on the key risk factors associated with Coronary Heart Disease and strokes.

2. East Sussex Social Services Department

The Area Office in Hove attempts to provide and manage care services for the elderly identified by the Assessment Section. Of financial necessity there is heavy prioritising of cases and inevitably Social Services is more concerned with the frail elderly in the population. There is now hardly any emphasis on preventive measures with resources being channelled into remedial, crisis work. As such the Department has no resources for sport, leisure or education policies except for the community development work it undertakes in partnership with the voluntary sector. The main focus in Hove is a pilot project working with mentally ill elderly who do not or will not go to day centres. There is some work with carers providing a place to meet and engage in learning and leisure activities such as arts, drama and computing. The other relevant service is that of transport which is mainly tied to day-centre trips although there is some limited use at off-peak times.

3. Leisure Services Directorate

The Directorate provides both directly and indirectly for older people. Direct provision includes the Young at Heart Club at King Alfred's Leisure Centre where a GP Referral Scheme is operating. Other aspects of provision include golf, tennis and bowls. The Council funds upwards of 50 voluntary organisations. A number of these cater specifically for sport and leisure needs, and others work for the general benefit of older people. Through grant aid the Council is seeking to empower voluntary groups to make their own provision. For instance, Hangleton and Knoll Community association has adopted a community development approach to identify leisure needs of the elderly and provide opportunities for them to be met. Short mat bowls is an example of this.

The current policy statement is contained in the Borough's recently adopted Sport and Recreation Strategy (1994). This document realises the barriers and constraints which beset older people's leisure and goes on to state:

> Recognising the physical, social and psychological benefits of participation, sports development initiatives must seek to encourage and facilitate participation for the 90% of elderly people who do not participate and in particular recognise the potential of the community centres. (Hove Borough Council, 1994: p. 15)

The main policies/proposals of relevance to older people are as follows:

Policy:	Through a community development approach, address the barriers to participation for low participant groups. (p. 36)
Proposal:	To promote activities for elderly people which address issues of cost, transport, alienation and motivation. (p. 37)
Policy:	To extend the operation of a GP referral scheme in Hove. To provide an holistic approach to preventative healthcare. To facilitate adherence to regular exercise. (p. 45)
Policy:	To develop community networks which enable information exchange and co-ordination of service delivery.
Proposals:	Investigate establishment of Hove Sports Forum consisting of users and providers and opportunities. To develop a series of issue based forum groups which could be responsible for taking forward and monitoring proposals in this strategy. (p. 46)

4. Adult Education

The Connaught Adult Education Service in Hove offers a full programme of day, evening and Saturday courses. In 1994-95 the total enrolment for the Hove area was approximately 7,000-8,000 of which 2,500-3,000 were retired people, predominantly women. There are over 50 courses in health and physical education alone of which a number are targeted at the 50+ group. There are also many more classes ranging from cooking, crafts, arts languages, music, dance and drama.

Voluntary Organisations

Hove has a large and diverse voluntary sector, some of which cater specifically for sport and leisure needs; others which work for the general benefit of older people.

Below several organisations are examined in detail under four headings which identify their role in providing older people with opportunities for sport, leisure and education.

1. Umbrella organisations representing older people

Age Concern is unique in its umbrella role in Hove and Portslade. The Director suggested that the major pre-occupation of care services and agencies is one of meeting crisis situations and that involvement in the preventive role of sport and leisure as a means towards health and improving the quality of life is a luxury which time, money and personnel does not permit. She went on to suggest a number of proposals which would help to improve this situation:

- Agencies need to work closely with the Borough, which needs to be more proactive;

- Need for a lot of facilitation of elderly. It is hard to overcome resistance to change. There is a need for older people to be exposed to attractions and activities in a non-threatening way;
- Move away from top-down approach of provision to one of bottom-up.
- Need for consultation and involvement of older people in determining sport and leisure pursuits.

2. Organisations catering for the specific needs of older people as clients

Community Transport Ltd. The office manager estimates that 90% of the passengers catered for are elderly people. There are two sides to the operation: (a) contract work for East Sussex County Council and (b) minibus hire.

a. There are two main contracts in Hove: Dial a Ride and Shoppers' Special. The shopping contract provides a door-to-door service to local supermarkets in low step/lift-equipped vehicles for those who cannot use buses. Dial a ride offers trips to the centre of Brighton and Hove for hospital appointments and other high priority visits between 10am and 2pm. Leisure trips are a low priority for this service. Also the limited time availability renders its use for leisure purposes severely limited. Other contracts include those for children with special needs and adults with learning difficulties. The office manager also acts as a broker for the County Rider Brighton and Hove bus routes. For people living within one quarter mile of the bus route she can organise a doorstep pick-up service for individuals with limited mobility, which the bus service can accommodate. This offers additional opportunities to travel over a wider time period each day.

b. 200 groups are members of a minibus hire scheme which for £6 enables groups to hire 16 seater accessible buses. Services can include driver hire, driver training and assessment and retraining. The bus rates are 60 pence per mile (35 pence per mile over 50 miles). Hirings are often weekly, by lunch clubs and day centres for instance, and it is used by Age Concern, Clubs for stroke sufferers and the blind and partially sighted. Service is also used extensively for summer outings.

Overall the service is likely to provide 60,000 passenger journeys per annum of which approximately half are for shopping. Community Transport Ltd. is a charity which obtains a small amount of statutory funding but which obtains most of its income from contracts. Rates are set low to be competitive and to meet need. It is felt that there is considerable unmet demand which cannot be met by existing provision.

Cruse Bereavement Care Social Club. The primary aim of the organisation is to provide one-to-one voluntary counselling service for those who are bereaved. However it operates two social clubs; one in Brighton and the other in Hove, to provide social support for bereaved people and an opportunity to make new friendships. The leisure activities include monthly meetings with speakers, walks, lunches and dinners, picnics, outings and holidays. There is a problem of transport for the members many of whom are women, who lose their access to a car when their partner dies. Some individuals make use of leisure centres and the local dog track for other sport/leisure pursuits.

Hove Victors Gateway. Gateway is the leisure arm of Mencap (the national voluntary organisation for the mentally-handicapped) and a number of clubs operate around the country for those with learning difficulties. These clubs are generally geared more towards the needs of younger people and this is true of the Hove club which runs on a Monday evening at the Aldrington Day Hospital. However the S. E. area adviser is seeking joint funding for a development worker to work with older people based at a local Centre.

3. Sport and leisure organisations

Hangleton Community Centre: Short Mat Bowls club. This small club of 20 retired members, with approximately equal numbers of men and women, is affiliated to the Centre and plays short mat bowls two afternoons per week. The club is in receipt of a small Council grant for purchase of equipment. Many involved in the club also make use of other bowling provision at, for instance, the King Alfred's centre. The Hangleton centre also provides a range of social and leisure activities such as bingo and lunch club.

Association of Retired Persons and over 50s: Brighton and Hove Friendship Centre. This is a local branch of a 130,000-strong national organisation. The centre has approximately 232 members and provides a wide-ranging programme of activities including meals out, walks, bridge class and club, dance club, theatre, 10 pin bowling. There is a regular monthly meeting of membership often with a talk provided. A current project of the centre is to stage a meeting on the theme of "Health and the over 50s". It is hoped to invite guest speakers from the medical profession and to be sponsored by local commerce. The Chairman feels that the Centre provides for an unmet need in the area by providing a broad range of leisure activities for the more active elderly. He stresses the importance of keeping both the mind and body active in the older person. The Centre provides this as well as a focus for friendship and socialising among the membership.

British Legion: Sussex. The County Field Officer for Sussex is mainly concerned with co-ordinating welfare for ex-servicemen and their wives in the County. He referred to the 110 autonomous local branches in East and West Sussex, 26 of which are in Hove and Portslade. Many of the larger branches have clubs and entertainments officers. The main focus of activity for these clubs is to provide leisure and social activities and comradeship for the membership. With regard to sport and leisure activities, there is a very active county bowling association and a county golfing association. County sports competitions are also arranged for snooker, darts and billiards.

4. Education organisations

University of the Third Age* (U3A): *Brighton and Hove. The Brighton and Hove branch of U3A has 217 members and offers a programme of 20 subjects at the Connaught Adult Education Centre including languages, writing, yoga, music and art. The membership consists of two-thirds women and one-third men, most of whom attend at least two groups. In addition there are monthly talks, a Christmas party and a summer festival of work in June. Outings and social events are organised in the summer vacation. There are also events arranged with other U3A groups in East and West Sussex. In the Chairman's view U3A has made a great difference to the lives of many elderly lonely people.

Commercial organisations

In general the commercial sector provides nothing specific for older people in Hove. No doubt a large number of the spectators at Brighton and Hove Albion Football Club, Sussex County Cricket Ground and Coral greyhound stadium are older people, reflecting the Borough's age structure. An unsuccessful attempt was made to organise a football special for older people by Brighton and Hove Albion's Football in the Community Scheme and Age Concern.

Discussion

The ageing population of Britain and most western countries and the issues this poses for service providers and planners are illustrated clearly in this case study. The number of active elderly will increase in the next decade and the challenge will be to enable older people to follow active, independent and fulfilled lives. Evidence from the Hove study suggests that apart from the frail elderly there is a large number of *potential* clients of sport, leisure and education but a continuing small number of *actual* clients. Generally the latter are articulate with an ability to access opportunities and are leisure literate with probably a history of involvement in sport, education and leisure pursuits. The former group includes many lonely, depressed and isolated people who do not have the knowledge, social skills or networks to access the opportunities available. They are the classic 'outsiders' identified by Elias and Scotson (1994) and others in early community studies.

In common with much service provision the voluntary clubs and statutory agencies provide opportunities aimed at older people which is up to them to use. The Young at Heart Club is patronised by those who would have no trouble in using sport and leisure opportunities on offer and probably already lead full and active lives. Those in the greatest need are least likely to avail themselves of these opportunities. Paradoxically the establishment of 50+ initiatives and the like will in fact reinforce divisions in the elderly population. Instead of attracting low or non-participants with real needs for sport, leisure or education the policy makers are unwittingly excluding these groups. Similarly voluntary clubs whether they are aimed at specific clients such as the bereaved, or are simply social and leisure organisations will attract the "clubbable" and those who wish to belong.

Faced with this situation the statutory agencies, without exception, have to devote their limited financial resources to mainstream services or in supporting crisis situations. The market-driven structure of community care, health and leisure services means that increasingly priorities are determined on the basis of finance and needs are subordinated to income generation. There is very limited money for development work and that which is available is directed to voluntary organisations or community development and outreach schemes. Those working in the statutory sector unanimously support the value of preventive work through community development as a long-term aim, a means of averting crisis and remedial work in the future. This approach is beginning to take off in a big way with regard to physical health through the GP referral scheme. With a bit of imagination and not too much additional expenditure it should be possible to apply this referral model to older people in general, not just for exercise prescriptions but to link people seeking sport, leisure or education outlets with appropriate clubs and classes. A key to the success of such an initiative is good quality information on what is available to enable agencies in contact with some of the lonely and isolated elderly to refer them on to appropriate clubs and courses.

The voluntary sector identified the need for closer networking between all agencies. However this of itself is not enough. It was generally agreed that older people require considerable support and facilitation in taking up new activities and are generally highly resistant to change. The message of Atchley's work (1993) is clear: older people are most likely to become involved in activities which relate in some way to values, skills and backgrounds acquired earlier in life. At the referral stage some counselling about activities appropriate to their previous experience may ensure greater success in taking up those activities.

This points strongly to a need overlooked in the main by policy makers, which is the need for self-determination and empowerment among the elderly in choosing what they want to do and feel comfortable with. Research by Kurtz and Propst (1991) identifies the psychological benefits of being in control and independent when making leisure choices. Hove Leisure Services are seeking to establish forums to enable consultation and involvement by older people so that they can determine policy and provision with support from the "professionals". There is considerable scope for voluntary involvement by older people in making opportunities happen.

Age Concern noted that many older people are happy and fulfilled in the service of others and can use their talents and skills effectively to this end. Support for volunteers could be developed more fully through community development and outreach projects.

A consistent constraint identified through discussion with a number of voluntary and statutory agencies is the problem of personal transport and venues which are safe, cheap and easily accessible. A further constraint is a resistance to going out after dark. Opportunities for transport for leisure or education are severely limited and only 40% of Hove's retired population has access to a car. Women are often most disadvantaged, as their access to a car often ceases on the death of their partner. There is a challenge to pursue further voluntary transport schemes using private cars more effectively. Again the solution probably lies with older people themselves in determining their own leisure activities and their related transport needs.

The above reflections on the Hove study represent some thoughts on possibilities for developing policies and provision for older people. With some input or redirection of human and financial resources, the improvement of information networks and frameworks for consultation and self-determination it should be possible to make policies and provision more appropriate to the needs of older people. Inevitably as time goes on a greater proportion of the elderly population will be leisure literate and will actively seek involvement in sport, leisure and education. In the meantime there is still a need to unlock opportunities and empower individuals hitherto denied access to a fulfilled and active old age. If this is not done then the problems identified by Abrams will become more acute as time goes on:

> The lack of social interaction and the abundance of empty 'free' time experienced by many of the elderly, largely due to constraints discussed earlier, not only induce in many of them acute feelings of loneliness, but may also seriously affect their longevity. (Abrams, 1990, 1995: p. 86)

Note

1 Respite care provides a break for a carer, either on a regular basis or occasionally. May be just a few hours, or one or more weeks. May be provided in a person's own home or in a residential or nursing home or hospital (Meredith, 1993: p. 151).

References

Abrams, M. (1990) (1995) 'Leisure time use by the elderly and leisure provision for the elderly', in C. Critcher, P. Bramham, and A. Tomlinson (eds) *Sociology of leisure — a reader*. London: E and FN Spon, pp. 78-87.

Age Concern/Chief Leisure Officers Association/Help the Aged (1992) *Leisure Life*. Age Concern/Chief Leisure Officers Association/Help the Aged.

Atchley, R. C. (1993) 'Continuity theory and the evolution of activity in later adulthood', in J. R. Kelly (ed) *Activity and ageing: Staying involved in later life*. London: Sage, pp. 5-16.

Central Statistical Office (1995) *Social Trends* 25. London: HMSO.

Department of Health (1992) *The health of the nation: A strategy for health in England*. London: HMSO.

East Sussex Family Health Services Authority, East Sussex Area Health Authority, East Sussex Social Services (1994) *East Sussex Community Care Plan 1994-1997*. East Sussex County Council.

Elias, N. and Scotson, J. (1994) *The established and the outsiders: A sociological enquiry into community problems*. 2nd revised ed. London: Sage.

Fennell, G. Phillipson, C. and Evers, H. (1988) *The sociology of old age*. Milton Keynes: Open University Press.

Gratton, C. and Tice, A. (1994) 'Trends in sports participation in Britain: 1977-1987', *Leisure Studies*, Vol. 13, No. 1: pp. 49-66.

Havighurst, R. J. (1954) 'Flexibility and the social roles of the retired', *American Journal of Sociology*, No. 59: pp. 309-311, cited in G. Fennell, C. Phillipson and H. Evers (1988) *The sociology of old age*. Milton Keynes: Open University Press.

Hove Borough Council, Planning Department (undated) 1991 Census Ward Data for Hove. Hove Borough Council.

Hove Borough Council (1994) *Sport and recreation strategy: Consultation draft*. Hove Borough Council.

Kurtz, M. E. and Propst, D. B. (1991) 'Research note: Relationship between perceived control in leisure and life satisfaction: a study of non-institutionalized older persons', *Leisure Studies*, Vol. 10, No. 1: pp. 69-77.

Meredith, B. (1993) *The Community Care handbook: The new system explained*. London: Age Concern.

Mobily, K. and Bedford, R. (1993) 'Language, play and work among elderly persons', *Leisure Studies*, Vol. 12, No. 3: pp. 204-220.

Norton, D. (1993) 'Leisure and the Third Age', *Leisure Manager*, May: pp. 23-24.

Rodgers, B. (1977) *Rationalising sports policies: Sport in its social context*. Council of Europe: Strasbourg, cited in C. Gratton and A. Tice, 'Trends in sports participation in Britain: 1977-1987', *Leisure Studies*, Vol. 13, No. 1: pp. 49-66.

Sports Council (1992) *Sport in the 90s: New horizons*. London: Sports Council.

Wilson, G. (1991) 'Models of ageing and their relation to policy formation and service provision', *Policy and Politics*, Vol. 19, No. 1: pp. 37-47.

Empowering Disabled People Through Leisure: A Case Study

John Handley

Sheffield Hallam University

Introduction

In community health and development, 'empowerment' has been described as the individual's or community's ability to become actively involved or 'participate', which introduces the notion of ownership and enables people in non-power, non-policy making levels to feel that they have more influence in determining personal and community health (The United Kingdom Health For All Network, 1991). This process of involvement and building a sense of belonging and ownership has also been termed 'citizen involvement' and 'citizen participation' (Bracht and Kingsbury, 1990). Such principles were adopted by the Healthy Sheffield 2000 Project which emphasised the value of giving people "...more power over their lives..." so that they are able to "...control the factors which affect their well being" (Healthy Sheffield Support Team, 1993: p. 14).

In education, teachers have been encouraged to develop those processes which would 'empower' future adults, such as nurturing initiative, enquiry, decision making and co-operation through problem-solving activities. It has been postulated that the use of more democratic approaches to education, ultimately, would prepare children for life within a democracy and contribute to their development as autonomous agents (Beattie, 1984; National Curriculum Council, 1990; Bremberg, 1991; Tones, 1986). Leisure educators, also, have called on teachers to 'empower' children by exposing them to situations in which personal competencies are nurtured through participation (Raven, 1982; Mundy and Oldam, 1979; Hendry, 1985; Hemming, 1981; Plaskow, 1981; National Curriculum Council, 1990). Hemming (1981) described these competencies as "inner resources". He stressed that we need to develop our inner resources in relation to the use of leisure time because of the economic and employment changes in the future. Leisure competencies would help us to 'survive'.

So, within the context of taking control over everyday life, and more specifically, leisure, the notion of empowerment is well justified, but, seemingly, only applies to the majority. When the literature is concerned with the delivery of leisure for disabled people, perspectives and attitudes change.

The Council of Europe (1987) emphasised the importance of leisure in relation to quality of life and endorsed the right of disabled people to experience leisure opportunities which would afford them that quality of life. Current opinion, however, suggests that the way in which leisure provision for disabled people has been organised and delivered has actually inhibited progress towards this vision of owning, using and choosing leisure as freely as the majority. The principal justification for this situation is that leisure provision has been dominated by the biomedical model which has utilised leisure from a purely therapeutic perspective (Russell, 1995). This model perceives disability as some sort of 'personal tragedy' in which the victim strives to adapt to the environment with the assistance of medically trained professionals (Williams, 1994). The Minister of Sport's Review Group (1989) confirmed that one of the main barriers inhibiting the development of sport for the disabled was a misconception that sport was part of some medical programme, rather than an activity undertaken through choice. This therapeutic perspective has perpetuated the notion that disabled people are an homogeneous group and their sport and leisure programmes need to be organised and delivered within a framework of 'care' (Russell, 1995). According to Russell the antidote to this model is the implementation of person-centred approaches to leisure provision that are based on people's hopes and ambitions for their own lives.

In other words, leisure for disabled people should be organised and delivered in a way which embodies democratic principles. One such person-centred approach is through the facilitation of the development of self-advocacy skills, which is concerned with disabled people gaining greater autonomy, making decisions and choices in all aspects of life including leisure (Cooper and Hersov, 1986; Clare, 1990; Sutcliffe, 1991; Williams and Shoultz, 1982).

A small number of initiatives aimed at 'empowering' disabled people within the context of leisure have emerged in recent years (Russell, 1995; Federation For Disability Sports Organisations, 1994; Robertson, 1993). However, little or no research has been undertaken to determine the effectiveness of these initiatives. If disabled people are to achieve varying levels of empowerment through the medium of leisure, there is a need for researchers to examine the organisation and delivery of leisure programmes and identify the sorts of activities and practice that inhibit the development of personal competencies.

Objectives of the study

In 1993 four sport development charities serving the Yorkshire and Humberside region merged to form the Federation of Disability Sports Organisations. The first charity was DISPORT, formerly known as the Yorkshire and Humberside Sports Association for People with Mental Handicap. The other three charities were: British Sports Association for the Disabled; British Blind Sports and; British Deaf Sports Council. The aim of the Federation is to support and develop sport and recreation for and by disabled people.

During the first few months of 1993, under the patronage of the Federation, a sports and leisure club for disabled people called SEQUALS (an acronym for sports equals) was launched at the Ponds Forge International Sports Centre in Sheffield. SEQUALS was to provide sports and leisure activities for disabled people over the age of 15 years. The club takes place on one evening per week for two hours. Importantly though, one of its principal aims was to empower disabled members by offering them the necessary support and training that would enable them to become involved in the management and operations of their club.

The purpose of the study was threefold. The aim of the first part was to ascertain the Federation's views on the extent to which the empowerment of the disabled members of SEQUALS had been achieved and the degree to which empowerment had been influenced by the steering group and the volunteers. The aim of the second part was to determine the accuracy of their views. The aim of the third part was to ascertain the disabled members' attitudes towards and perceptions of empowerment and their role as members. It was important to find out whether the Federation's goal to empower was justified. Did disabled members actually want to take on new roles and vary their contribution to the club?

Methodology

In order to achieve the first aim, the two members of the Federation responsible for initiating SEQUALS were interviewed separately. The objectives were as follows:

1. To appreciate their vision of SEQUALS and the role of disabled members.
2. To ascertain their views on the extent to which the empowerment of disabled members had been influenced by the membership and functioning of the steering group when the club was being set up.
3. To ascertain their views on the extent to which the empowerment of disabled members had been influenced by the knowledge, attitudes and skills of the volunteers, since the club had been in operation.

In order to fulfil the second aim, it was necessary to acquire data from the members of the steering group and volunteers.

The steering group

Each of the nine members of the steering group was invited to respond to a questionnaire and two members of the steering group were interviewed separately. The first interviewee was a parent from a non-professional background. She has two disabled children who regularly attend SEQUALS. The second interviewee came from a professional background and has no disabled children. The two interviewees were selected because it was anticipated that as a consequence of their contrasting backgrounds and experience with disabled people they would appraise the membership and operation of the steering group from different perspectives. It was important to obtain a broad range of views. The objectives were as follows:

1. To ascertain the members' motives for joining the steering group.
2. To estimate the extent to which the membership and operation of the steering group affected the progress of issues relating to the empowerment of disabled club members.

In addition to the questionnaire and the interviews, the minutes of the steering group meetings recorded over a period of two years were scrutinised. The purpose was to monitor the progress of and importance attached to issues of empowerment and the role of disabled members.

The volunteers

Each of the 17 regular volunteers were invited to respond to a questionnaire. The objectives were as follows:

1. To ascertain their motives for becoming a volunteer.
2. To assess the extent to which their attitudes, knowledge and experience would influence the empowerment of disabled members.

To achieve the third and final part of the study, five club members were interviewed. The objectives were as follows.

1. To ascertain the disabled members' attitudes towards and perceptions of the role of a club member.
2. To ascertain the disabled members' attitudes to taking on new duties and varying their contribution to the club.
3. To ascertain the extent to which the aspirations of individual club members had been considered in relation to their role in and contribution to the club.

The five were selected because they possessed a broad range of disabilities. It was important to find out whether the type or severity of a disability influenced the member's position in the club.

Parts one and two of the study were completed by the Summer of 1995. The third part was scheduled for completion during the autumn of 1995.

Results and discussion (of completed phases/ parts)

The two members of the Federation asserted that empowering members within the context of the SEQUALS sport and social club was an extremely important objective. They wanted members to be able to "... make decisions and choices about leisure". SEQUALS would act as a centre for the co-ordination of the members' leisure activities.

It was intended that members would meet at the beginning of the evening and decide what they wanted to pursue. For example, they could visit the ski village or become involved with the Youth Service. Importantly though, in addition to disabled members making choices about leisure activities, the Federation wanted them to become empowered so that they could involve themselves in the running and management of their club. For example, some members would be making coffee whilst others might be involved with the steering committee. Levels of contribution and roles within the club would evolve given the appropriate support and training.

When asked if 'empowerment' was taking place, both members of the Federation gave a clear negative response:

> "Members are just turning up, participating and going home. Activities are decided by non-disabled people and run by non-disabled people."

Views as to why the vision of empowerment had not come to fruition can be considered from two perspectives, namely, the steering group and the volunteers.

The steering group — recruitment, training, and communication

Members of the steering group came from diverse backgrounds. The Federation considered this diversity to be problematic for two reasons. Firstly, not all members of the steering group would have understood the term 'empowerment' and even fewer would have been aware of the sorts of activity and practice which would facilitate empowerment. Secondly, achieving a consensus of views of the best way forward might have been difficult because of the different philosophies, personalities and levels of understanding.

Responses from the members of the steering group supported the views of the Federation in that the members did come from diverse backgrounds and had different motives for joining the steering group. For example, a lay Pastor joined the group because she was searching for a special social club for her learning disabled children. A Day Centre Officer joined the group in order to help create a resource for his day centre. A consultant surgeon joined the group because he had gained experience over many years working with disabled people in a professional capacity. The extent to which diversity of background related to knowledge of empowerment prior to the inaugural meeting and how this affected progress within meetings is unclear. However, doubt as to whether members of the steering group were aware of the sorts of activities and practice that facilitated empowerment was expressed by one of the interviewees from the steering group. The interviewee believed that the sorts of activities that facilitated social development and independence were not considered:

> "For example, how do you get 30 disabled people with 30 different personalities to mix and form friendships? All people [steering group members] said was 'Well we will all have a drink in the bar at the end of the evening'. This did not work because not all of the volunteers and not all of the disabled members could or wanted to stay. Playing badminton or table-tennis against people standing on the other side of the net is limited in its contribution to social interaction. Disabled members are not encouraged to do independent social things like making a cup of coffee because people buy their coffee at the coffee bar."

Sport was provided, but, according to the interviewee, not in a way that facilitated independent thinking and certainly not within a social context. So does this mean that members of the steering group were not the 'best' people to undertake the task of guiding the development of SEQUALS? In response to this question, both members of the Federation declared that in future they would be looking to put together a steering group that consisted of a higher proportion of disabled people. This would be achieved by targeting the right people and not by contacting non-disabled professionals and representatives of organisations. They want to recruit people "Who are clued into disability issues and not just sport" and who are "...involved in sport and disabled forums".

Three of the five members of the steering group also expressed doubt as to whether they were the best people to undertake the task of guiding the development of SEQUALS. Despite the fact that members of the steering group were aware of the aim to empower disabled members, one of the interviewees felt that the steering group members were:

> "...treating the club as a night out...to keep them [the disabled members] occupied in sport type activities and were not thinking of the wider social context such as making friends."

Unlike herself, the other members of the steering group did not have disabled children and consequently, "...did not understand the real issues". She felt that there was a need for more parents to be involved in decision-making. The second interviewee also expressed some reservation concerning the appropriateness of the membership of the steering group. He also felt that more parents needed to be involved.

The two interviewees from the Federation were of the opinion that certain members of the steering group were not adequately prepared for meetings. For some members of the steering group (in particular, the two learning-disabled members) the discussion progressed too quickly. There was a need to brief certain members as to the topics of discussion that were likely to arise. This would:

> "...allow them time to prepare their views and how they were going to put their views forward."

The two interviewees also had doubts about whether the members of the steering group were clear on what was expected of them. This view was supported by the members of the steering group because only half of them were clear on what was expected of them. Before the inaugural meeting the first interviewee recalled how she felt intimidated by the boardroom environment and the professional looking men in suits. Not only was she unclear on what was expected of her, she also felt "...insecure and out of place". The second interviewee also was unclear on his role. He felt that his experience and skills were not utilised and he should have been more centrally involved in the organisational process.

The results indicate that those members of the steering group who did not come from a professional background were disadvantaged in that they lacked confidence in the 'boardroom' atmosphere. The non-professionals had the relevant experience needed to promote the needs of disabled people, but not the confidence to assert themselves and articulate their views. Even though one of the interviewees felt that the professional people did not truly understand the wider issues of social empowerment, it was the professional members who directed the course of events. Discussion, therefore, was driven by 'professional expertise' and the desire to plan, provide and manage activities within the constraints of a sports facility. As a result, the needs and aspirations of disabled members and the wider issues of social empowerment were not adequately considered. The results also suggest that clearer lines of communication between the steering group and the Federation need to be established. Members of the steering group need to know why they have been recruited, and to be briefed upon their role and what is expected of them in terms of personal commitment. They also need to have clear terms of reference so that discussion is focused and progress can be more easily monitored.

Minutes of the steering group meetings

Tracing the development of SEQUALS through examination of the minutes of the steering group was a difficult task. The frequency of meetings was difficult to determine because not all of the minutes were dated, and the progress of many issues was difficult to follow because the minutes lacked substance. In addition, hand-written notes and other pieces of information without dates or adequate headings were, seemingly, inserted in an ad hoc manner into the steering group file.

Investigation revealed that, over a period of two years, on only three occasions did the minutes of the steering group meetings refer to disabled members taking on positions of responsibility. The first steering group meeting was held in January 1993, but it was not until August 1993 that the representative of the Federation of Disability Sports Organisation referred to disabled club members at SEQUALS taking on positions of responsibility. The minutes read as follows:

> "Information on SEQUALS to be distributed to all society/clubs. This to encourage the facilitation of activity sessions at SEQUALS by club members."

One month later in September 1993 in a "Draft Format of SEQUALS" the project co-ordinator stated that one of the principle aims of SEQUALS was:

> "To be self sufficient, being organised and co-ordinated by a committee made up of members."

Finally, in an undated "Project Update" held at the Ponds Forge International Sport Centre the project co-ordinator asserted that:

> "Every effort will be made to involve young people with disabilities in the staffing and management of the club."

Importantly, on each of these occasions when notions of empowerment were raised, no details were provided to clarify or add substance to these statements and it appears that over a twelve month period little or no progress was made on issues concerning the role of disabled members in the management of their club. This supports the view of the two members of the Federation that members of the steering group might have been aware of the importance attached to principles of empowerment but did not have the knowledge or experience to consider and implement the sorts of activities and practice that would enable disabled members to make choices and take on positions of responsibility.

The results point to a weak link between the Federation and the steering group. It appears that the Federation's project co-ordinator did not have the experience or knowledge to allow the concept of empowerment to evolve through productive discussion. If this deduction is accurate it would serve to confirm the views of the interviewees from the steering group that the needs of disabled members were not adequately discussed.

The volunteers — backgrounds, motives and perceptions of role

Both members of the Federation affirmed that volunteers were highly valued as they had a "...serious skilled role to play". They believed that volunteers, like members of the steering group, came from a range of backgrounds and had different motives for becoming volunteers. However, it was important that "...they did not just accept anybody...". There had to be an effective screening mechanism, where, for example, applications would be supported by references and applicants would be required to clarify their motives for wanting to become a volunteer.

Results of the questionnaire revealed that the volunteers did not come from a broad range of backgrounds. Most of them were either students or retired. Eight out of the 13 respondents became volunteers because they would personally benefit in some way. For example, "Filling in time in retirement", "Enjoyment", "Gaining knowledge". Of the 5 remaining responses, 4 volunteers merely wanted to "...assist...", or "...help...". Only one volunteer provided a response which focused on the needs of the disabled members. He declared that his motive was to help disabled members "...realise their potential".

The results tend to support the Federation's scepticism regarding the motives of some volunteers. Over half of the respondents disclosed that they volunteered in order to gain some personal benefit from what the club could do for them, rather than what they could do for the club. However, it would be reasonable to suggest that if the volunteers had undergone a programme of training, the responses would be different. In fact, the only volunteer who mentioned something about developing his own personal competencies was one of only two volunteers who had received some form of disability training[1].

So, what were the Federation's views on volunteer training? The responses were unequivocal. Training for volunteers was:

> "...too little too late. More time was needed for planning and thinking through the content of training regimes. Training has not been what it should be i.e. normally two days of disability issues including empowerment."

Responses from the volunteers demonstrated that the notion of volunteer training being "too little, too late" was a misperception, because only 2 of the 13 volunteers working at the club had received any form of disability training. This lack of training was illustrated by the results, as volunteers did not possess the sort of vision or attitudes that embodied democratic principles and would empower disabled members.

When asked to describe their role in the club, 12 out of the 13 volunteers described their role as something to do with helping or assisting. For example, "Helping swimmers", "Helping and providing activities", and "Volunteer in sports hall". No volunteer perceived her/his role as concerned with facilitating empowerment or enablement. Similarly, when asked to describe their most important duties, 12 out of the 13 volunteers referred directly or indirectly to helping or caring for members. For example, "Helping members to enjoy themselves"; "Checking members are safe"; "Helping with safety"; and "Dressing and undressing members".

Interestingly, the same volunteer who described his motive for becoming a volunteer as helping disabled members "...realise their potential" was the only volunteer who perceived his role as something to do with facilitating personal growth. He felt that his duty was "To enable members to achieve their potential".

Results established that all but one of the volunteers perceived their role as something to do with 'caring'. There was no vision in relation to individual needs, hopes and aspirations, potential, progression and development. Disabled members, therefore, were perceived as an homogeneous group. This supported the view of Russell (1995) who claimed that leisure provision for disabled people still focused on the provision of planned programmes within a framework of 'care'.

With regard to the benefits the club offers its disabled members, 11 out of the 13 volunteers believed that the club offered some social benefit. From those 11 respondents, 10 perceived these benefits as short term. For example, "A good night out", "A chance to get out", "A social outing", "Meeting others with disabilities", and "Meeting others with disabilities". One volunteer described the social benefits from a more long-term perspective, stressing the impoprtance of "Making friends with people with disabilities". Eight out of the 13 respondents also referred to the physical benefits to be gained from the club — for example, "Healthy activity", "Exercise", "An active environment", and "Sport participation".

The volunteers' descriptions of the benefits that disabled members would gain from the club smacked of physical and psychological therapy — members would be having a night out and participating in 'healthy' activity. These results support the postulation of Russell (1995), Williams (1994) and The Minister For Sport's Review Group (Department of the Environment, 1989) that sport and leisure for disabled people is perceived as some form of therapy. and is part of a wider medical programme.

When the volunteers were asked if they believed that the disabled members were involved in the running of the club, 9 out of the 13 respondents replied "Yes", 2 replied "No" and the remaining 2 were "Unsure". However, when the volunteers were asked to explain their response to this question it became clear that the volunteers did not have a common understanding of the term 'running the club'. Some volunteers believed that members were involved in running the club merely because they were allowed to choose the games they wanted to play. Other volunteers felt that because the volunteers did everything members were not involved in the running of their club.

When asked if disabled members had the ability to contribute to the running of their club, ten out of the 13 volunteers gave a positive response. However, from those 10 positive responses 6 volunteers believed that members were able to contribute to the running of their club, merely because they were able to choose the activities they wanted to play. The remaining 4 volunteers did not respond. Three volunteers believed that members were not able contribute to the running of their club because they were "Slow learners", or "Not capable.".

The volunteers, therefore, did not possess a common perception or understanding of the phrase "...members running the club". Half of the volunteers believed that merely being able to choose activities constituted a contribution to the running of the club. The other half believed that running the club meant more than just choosing activities, but they were unable to identify the sorts of activities and practice needed to achieve different levels of 'ownership', that is, levels which might range from coffee maker to representative on the steering group.

Conclusion and recommendations

This study found that the sorts of activities and practice taking place at the SEQUALS leisure club did not correspond with notions of empowerment, such as nurturing personal competencies in preparation for life in a democracy (Hemming, 1981 and Meakin, 1990) and developing a sense of ownership and belonging and gaining more power and control over their lives (Healthy Sheffield Support Team, 1993). Approaches to the delivery of activities for disabled members did not respond to the call for more person-centred paradigms (Russell, 1994) or conform to the Federation's vision of volunteers facilitating the empowerment of disabled members. Results highlighted three particular factors which, directly or indirectly, contributed to the development of this situation.

Firstly, the Project Co-ordinator was successful in taking the concept of SEQUALS from its inception through to a thriving leisure club. However, he was not successful in communicating, exploring and developing notions of empowerment at the steering group and volunteer level.

Secondly, steering group members came from diverse backgrounds, which created disharmony, in that members had different motives for joining the steering group and, consequently, different goals and needs. Members from non-professional backgrounds who had relevant life experience of disability issues were not adequately prepared or sufficiently confident to challenge the views of members from professional backgrounds. On the other hand, members from professional backgrounds with less life experience of disability tended to dominate discussions, but to follow agendas which did not take account of the sorts of activities and practice that would empower disabled club members.

Thirdly, volunteers were not equipped with the knowledge or skills that would enable them to facilitate the empowerment of disabled club members, even though were committed to the concept of providing a programme of enjoyable, active and interesting activities. Results show that this was probably due to a lack of appropriate training and support.

If one of the principal aims of a club such as SEQUALS is to empower disabled members so that they are able, in varying degrees, to gain 'ownership' of their club and choose and use activities as the majority do in other sports and leisure clubs, the following recommendations need to be taken into consideration:

- The Federation and the steering group need to clearly define who they want as volunteers and what they expect in terms of commitment. They also need to decide what they can reasonably expect, particularly if long term volunteers are in short supply.

- Adequate training for all those involved in planning and delivering leisure activities must be promoted, so that people in positions of power are aware of the sorts of activities and practice that lead to empowerment.
- There must be appropriate support and training to enable volunteers at all levels to contribute with confidence to discussion and debate.
- There must be clear lines of communication between the governing body and the different planning groups, so that progress can be monitored more effectively. Therefore, there needs to be appropriate support and training for those responsible for directing the affairs of planning groups.

Note

1 Disability training for volunteers usually involves activities which raise awareness of the positive and negative effects of different types of disability. Ways of overcoming stereotyping and of developing positive working practices are explored.

References

Beattie, A. (1984) 'Health Education and the science teacher: invitation to a debate', *Education and Health*, Vol. 10, No. 1: pp. 9-17.

Bracht, N. and Kinsbury, L. (1990) 'Community organisation principles in health promotion', in N. Bracht (ed) *Health promotion at the community level*. London, Sage Publications, pp. 66-75.

Bremberg, S. (1991) 'Does school health education affect the health of students? A literature review', in D. Nutbeam, B. Haglund, P. Farley and P. Tillgren (eds) *Youth health promotion: from theory to practice in school and community*. London: Forbes Publications, pp. 89-107.

Clare, M. (1990) *Developing self-advocacy skills with people with disabilities and learning difficulties*. Redhill: Further Education Unit.

Cooper, D. and Hersov, J. (1986) *We can change the future: self advocacy for people with learning difficulties*. London: National Bureau for Handicapped Students.

Council of Europe (1987) *The European charter on sport for all disabled persons*. Brussels: The Council of Europe.

Department of the Environment (1989) *Building on ability: Sport for people with disabilities*. London: HMSO. [Report of the Minister of Sport's Review Group]

Federation For Disability Sports Organisations. (1994) Work audit April 1993-May 1994. Presented as an Annual Report to the Annual General Meeting of the Federation For Disability Sports Organisations (Yorkshire and Humberside), Ossett, Yorkshire.

Healthy Sheffield Support Team (1993) *Combine development and health: the way forward in Sheffield*. Sheffield: Healthy Sheffield 2000 and Sheffield City Council.

Hemming, J. (1981) 'Education for self development', in W. Bacon (ed) *Leisure and learning in the 1980s* (LSA Publication No. 14). Eastbourne: Leisure Studies Association, pp. 21-29.

Hendry, L. (1985) 'Young people, school and leisure: developing meta-cognitive skills?', in L. Haywood and I. Henry (eds) *Leisure and youth* (LSA Publication No. 17). Eastbourne: Leisure Studies Association, pp. 1.2.1-1.3.1.

Meakin, D. (1990) 'How physical education can contribute to personal and social education', *Physical Education Review*, Vol. 13, No. 2: pp. 108-119.

Munday, J. and Oldam, L. (1979) *Leisure*. New York: Wiley.

National Curriculum Council (1990). *Curriculum guidance 8. Education for citizenship*. York: National Curriculum Council.

Plaskow, M. (1981) 'The pleasure principle: or why the curriculum doesn't work', in W. Bacon (ed) *Leisure and learning in the 1980s* (LSA Publication No. 14). Eastbourne: Leisure Studies Association, pp. 31-37.

Raven, J. (1982) 'Education and the competencies required in modern society', *Higher Education Review*, Vol. 15, No. 5: pp. 47-57.

Robertson, A. (1993) *Community sports initiatives for young disabled people*. London: United Kingdom Sports Association in conjunction with the Sports Council and the British Sports Association for the Disabled.

Russell, J. (1995) 'Leisure and recreation services', in N. Malin (ed) *Services for people with learning disabilities*. London: Routledge, pp. 155-169.

Sutcliffe, J. (1991) *Adults with learning difficulties. Education for choice and empowerment*. Leicester: The National Institute of Adult Continuing Education in association with the Open University Press.

Tones, K. (1986) 'Promoting the health of young people: the role of personal and social education', *Health Education Journal*, Vol. 45, No. 1: pp. 14-19.

United Kingdom Health For All Network. (1991) *Community participation for health for all.* Liverpool: United Kingdom Health For All Network, Healthy Cities Centre, Department of Public Health, University of Liverpool.

Williams, P. and Shoultz, B. (1982) *We can speak for ourselves. Self-advocacy by mentally handicapped people.* London: Souvenir Press.

Williams, T. (1994) 'Sociological perspectives on sport and disability: Structural functionalism', *Physical Education Review*, Vol. 17, No. 1: pp. 14-21.

Local Authority Leisure Policies for Black and Ethnic Minority Provision in Scotland

John Horne

Moray House Institute/Heriot-Watt University

> Black people can know facts of injustice for years but they are not real until white research validates them. (Kaliani Lyle, Church of Scotland Working Party Report, 1990, cited in M. Edward, 1993, p. 134)

Introduction

Mounting evidence in the 1980s and 1990s has demonstrated the existence of serious and widespread forms of prejudice, discrimination and oppression against black and Asian people "north of the border" (Armstrong, 1989; Bell, 1991; CRE, 1994)[1]. Yet the existence of racism in Scotland has often been denied, or at least played down. Subsequently, whilst non-white minority ethnic groups constitute a small, though significant, proportion of the Scottish population (OPCS, 1991) there has been no systematic research into their involvement in leisure and sport. This paper forms part of a series of investigations into ethnic minorities and their involvement in sport and leisure in Scotland (Horne, 1995). Research is at an early stage, and, although it is not my intention to confirm Kaliani Lyle's observation, my primary goal here is to contribute to the spread of greater awareness of the situation of ethnic minorities in Scotland.

Research into ethnic minority participation in sport in England has focused some attention on local authority responses to the needs of a multi-cultural society (Verma and Darby, 1994; Carroll, 1993). Carroll (1993: p. 107) stressed the importance of local authority provision of leisure and sport for all ethnic minority groups. In his research, local authority provision of facilities accounted for 50 per cent of usage by African, Caribbean, Indian, Bangladeshi, Chinese, Pakistani, East African and Asian minority ethnic groups. Clearly they relied upon local authority provision and programmes fairly heavily. Carroll's study focused upon the ten local authorities in the Greater Manchester area. Nine had formal Equal Opportunity (EO) policies and one had a policy in progress. Only 3 of the Leisure Service Departments had specific policies for ethnic minorities and leisure. These mainly related to employment and service delivery.

As we reach the end of one form of Local Government, with reorganisation scheduled to take place in Scotland in April 1996, it is timely to attempt to assess the equal opportunity policies adopted by Scottish local authorities. This paper considers the local authority response to the specific leisure needs of ethnic minorities and equal opportunities policies more generally in Scotland. It asks: to what extent have local authority leisure services in Scotland operated equal opportunity policies and specifically policies which recognise the diverse needs of their populations? To what extent have Scottish local authorities sought to discover and provide for the specific leisure needs of their non-white ethnic minority populations? To what extent might we hope for an improvement in provision after reorganisation?

All the 56 local authorities in Scotland responsible for leisure and recreation were contacted in May 1995. Initially a letter was sent to the Head of Recreation, or equivalent person, which asked for information about equal opportunities policies in general, racial equality policies and policies specifically designed with sport and leisure in mind. A request was also made for examples of codes of practice and illustrations of good practice in the particular authority. Comments were also invited on the likely impact of local government reorganisation — scheduled to take place on April Fools Day 1996 — on leisure provision. A follow-up letter in July 1995 and telephone calls in August and September 1995 secured a 100 per cent response rate. It is intended subsequently to focus on eight or nine of these as case studies, interview key personnel and gather more information about the genesis of the policies, the "key players" in their implementation, and examples of good practice.

This paper considers the results of the postal survey and makes some observations on the information collected. The next two sections provide some contextual information for those not aware of the situation with respect to local government and the ethnic minority population in Scotland. Next the findings of the survey are presented using illustrative extracts from policy documents and letters received from Leisure Service departments. A final section draws some tentative conclusions about the state of sport and leisure provision for ethnic minorities "north of the border".

Scottish Local Government and Leisure

Since 1975 local government in Scotland has consisted of 9 Regional Councils, 53 District Councils and 3 Island Councils. The division of responsibility has been that the regions have provided major strategic services — such as education, social work, roads, water and sewage, police and fire — like the County Councils in England. The District Councils (DCs) have been responsible for local services, such as cleaning, housing, environmental services, tourism, libraries and leisure and recreation. The DCs are currently grouped into nine Regional Councils: Borders Region (4 DCs); Central Region (3 DCs); Dumfries and Galloway Region (4 DCs); Fife Region (3 DCs); Grampian Region (5 DCs); Highland Region (8 DCs); Lothian Region (4 DCs); Strathclyde (19 DCs); and Tayside (3DCs). This will alter in April 1996 when 29 "unitary authorities" will replace the existing Regions and Districts. The three Island Authorities — Western Isles (Comhairle nan Eilean); Shetland Islands; and Orkney Islands — are already unitary authorities and will be largely unchanged by the clumsily titled Local Government Etc. (Scotland) Act 1994. Unlike the rest of Great Britain, where leisure is only a discretionary responsibility, the 53 District Councils and 3 Island Councils have had a statutory responsibility to provide sport and recreation opportunities since the *Local Government and Planning (Scotland) Act 1982*. Section 14 (1) of the Act states that district and island councils:

> ...shall ensure that there is adequate provision of facilities for the inhabitants of their area for recreational, sporting, cultural and social activities.

Despite the statutory responsibility, the vagueness of the 1982 Act, particularly the notion of "adequate provision", plus the variations in size of the DCs has always made provision highly variable (Byrne, 1994). Nonetheless local government in Scotland has been central to the provision of sport and recreation opportunities, as it has in England and Wales (Audit Commission, 1989; Association of Directors of Recreation, Leisure and Tourism, 1987, 1995)[2].

The black and ethnic minority population in Scotland

As a result of distinct patterns of immigration the composition of ethnic minority populations in England and Scotland differs considerably. Accurate data on population flows has been difficult to obtain until recently. The Scottish population has often been considered in terms of emigration rather than immigration yet along with England since 1945, and especially during the 1960s, the black and especially Asian population has been growing. Basic data on the ethnic minority communities in Scotland has only been systematically available since the 1991 Census as it was only in the last dicennial population census that a question on ethnic origin was included. Prior to this various estimates had been made (Smith, 1991).

Details of the ethnic minority population for the whole of Great Britain (see Table 1) showed that ethnic minority groups made up 5.5 per cent of the total G.B. population, 6.2 per cent of the population of England, but only 1.3 per cent of the Scottish population (CSO, 1994: 25).

Table 1 GB population: by ethnic group and region, 1991

	Black (000s)	Pakistani, Indian or Bangladeshi (000s)	Other ethnic minority (000s)	*Ethnic minority groups as % of total population*
Great Britain	891	1,480	645	*5.5*
England	875	1,431	605	*6.2*
Wales	9	16	16	*1.5*
Scotland	6	32	24	*1.3*

Source: adapted from Social Trends, 24, January 1994, Table 1.9, p. 25

In 1991 Scotland's non-white ethnic minority population totalled 62,634 out of the total population of just under 5 million. The largest non-white ethnic minority group in Scotland is Pakistanis (21,192 or 0.42% of the total Scottish population), about one fifth of ethnic minorities is Chinese and a small fraction is Afro-Caribbean (Bailey *et al.*, 1995). Almost two-thirds of the non-white population are concentrated in specific areas of the two largest cities, Glasgow and Edinburgh.

The black and ethnic minority population of Scotland is therefore mainly to be found in Strathclyde and Lothian regions, with smaller proportions in Grampian, Tayside and Central Region. The proportion ranges from 1.7 per cent in Lothian and 1.6 per cent in Strathclyde to 0.3 per cent in the Borders and the Orkney Isles. Table 2, adapted from the Commission for Racial Equality *1994 Annual Report* shows this very clearly.

Table 2 Scottish ethnic minority population by police force region

Police Force	Ethnic Minority Population
1. Strathclyde	35,121
2. Lothian & Borders	12291 (Borders only 300)
3. Grampian	4,458
4. Tayside	4,439
5. Fife	2,519
6. Central	1,947
7. Northern (including Highlands)	1,421
8. Dumfries & Galloway	528
Total	62,724

Source: Commission for Racial Equality, Annual Report, 1994

Equal Opportunities Policies in Scottish District Councils and Island Councils Survey Findings

As Carroll (1993: p. 107) notes, the development of Equal Opportunity policies in local authorities is fairly recent. No attempt has been made to identify the "age" of the policies as yet, although it is apparent that some have only recently been adopted by the Scottish authorities. Some authorities without policies actually stated that they were awaiting the reorganisation of local government before proceeding with adoption of an EO policy.

As mentioned earlier, all the Heads of Recreation, or equivalent persons, were sent a letter which asked for information about equal opportunities policies in general, racial equality policies and policies specifically designed with sport and leisure in mind. A request was also made for examples of codes of practice and illustrations of good practice in the particular authority. Comments were also invited on the likely impact of local government reorganisation on leisure provision. Responses to the last question have been variable in quality and hence are not discussed in detail here.

The responses to questions about EO policies have been placed into one of four categories: general equal opportunities policy only; racial equality policy; leisure /sport specific policy; or no equal opportunities policy. As Table 3 shows, from 56 responses 40 (71%) local authorities had a formal written equal opportunities policy, whilst 16 (29%) local authorities did not.

Table 3 Equal opportunities policies in Scottish District and Island Councils 1995

Region	General Equal Opp. (EO) Policy	Racial Equality Specific	Leisure or Sport Services Specific	No Formal Written EO Policy
Borders (4 DCs)	1			3
Central (3 DCs)	3		1	
Dumfries & Galloway (4 DCs)	3		1	1
Fife (3 DCs)	2		2	1
Grampian (5 DCs)	5			
Highland (8 DCs)	2			6
Lothian (4 DCs)	4	1	2	
Strathclyde (19 DCs)	16	3	4	3
Tayside (3 DCs)	2	1	1	1
Island Authorities (3)	2			1
Totals (56)	40	5	11	16

Of those 40 local authorities that had a formal equal opportunities policy 11 (28%) had a specific sport and leisure equity policy or strategy whilst only 5 (13%) authorities had a specific racial equality policy applying to sport and leisure.

By region the vast majority of authorities with formal equal opportunities policies are in Strathclyde (16 out of 19 DCs). With Lothian, Strathclyde comprises one half of the DCs with formal EO policies (20 out of 40). Adding the other two major population areas with minority ethnic communities of any size, Grampian and Tayside, 27 out of the 40 EO policies (68 per cent) come from the DCs covering these areas. Reflecting the urban location of minority ethnic group living, the five DCs with EO policies with specific reference to racial equality are all responsible for urban areas. With respect to equity policies in leisure and sport, or sports strategy documents, seven out of the eleven authorities with them were in Strathclyde, Lothian or Tayside. In contrast, over half those DCs without any formal EO policies (9 out of 16) were in rural areas — the Borders and Highlands regions. Only four out of the thirty-one DCs in the major population areas, Grampian, Lothian, Strathclyde and Tayside, had no formal EO policies.

Equal opportunity policy statements: proactive, reactive or merely gestural?

One means of distinguishing between the 40 Councils which had EO policies was to consider which policies applied solely to employment and which included service delivery as well. Sixteen of the 40 DCs with EO policies dealt with employment only (40 per cent), and hence might be described as having "gestural" EO policies; 13 of the 40 (33 per cent) could be described as "reactive" in the sphere of sport and leisure and 11 were "proactive" (28 per cent). These latter DCs had adopted action plans (Positive Action) and were involved in identifying target groups (Targetting) and assessing their performance through surveys and other means (Monitoring).

The eleven DCs identified as proactive had usually adopted a sport or leisure strategy, campaign or other form of action plan. This could include measures dealing with: training — to overcome the effects of discrimination; targetting — in both employment (by aiming for a specific proportion of staff from ethnic minorities or other disadvantaged groups) and service delivery (activities arranged for those with specific needs); and monitoring — the local demographic figures (for example the Small Area Census statistics), the number of job applicants and the number of those attending activities. Again the rural-urban division is apparent. Urban DCs were to the fore in Racial Equality-specific or Leisure and Sport-specific equity policies, whilst the more rural authorities tended to be either reactive or gestural. The following quotations from letters or policy statements illustrate the range of responses.

Gestural or no formal policy statements

Councils A, B and C all illustrate the thinking behind those Councils without EO policies: the Council is "fair", without the need for producing specific policies. Sometimes it is assumed that equal opportunity policies are only applicable to employment issues, rather than service delivery as well. Councils C and D exhibit the tendency to infer from my request for information that "positive discrimination" was legally possible. Of course, positive discrimination is illegal, unlike "positive action" as the extract from Council E's policy explains.

Council A — "is committed to being a fair employer with equal opportunities for all, but does not have any specific policies relating to equal opportunities in general or racial equality in particular. Needless to say, the Leisure and Recreation Department also has no such policies or, indeed, codes of practice ... It is possible that the situation may alter once the new Authority is in place next year ... ".

Council B — "took a decision some years ago advising that it was an equal opportunities employer as a statement of fact and has subsequently chosen not to expand upon those statements ... To date I am not aware that this has given rise to any difficulties either in respect of staff recruitment and relationships or use of premises or facilities by the community".

Council C — "This department and indeed authority embraces fully the provisions of laws on discrimination ... Equal opportunities in employment and in regard to access to Local Authority facilities for ethnic minorities have always been available without the need to produce specific policies. Ethnic minorities in this part of Scotland are indeed very much in the minority and accordingly it has also not been considered necessary to discriminate positively".

Council D — "does not have a policy of positive discrimination relating to any groups or individuals."

Reactive racial equality and general equity statements

These statements reflect a more generalised awareness of the need for some strategic action, an awareness of different needs and a responsiveness to them or a focus on other disadvantaged groups (e.g. Council G). Some of the replies are nonetheless illustrative of the "There's no problem here" viewpoint (e.g. Council I).

Council E — "I enclose the Council's Equal Opportunities Policy which includes the racial element ... I am afraid I have no further thoughts on the racial equality aspect as it is not perceived as a problem in the (region) as yet".

"(P)ositive action should not be confused with *positive discrimination/reverse discrimination* which is illegal. It is not legal to appoint a person solely because he/she belongs to a particular group. Selection must always be based on merit and related specifically to the genuine requirements of the job".

Council F — "The promotion of opportunities within (the District) is carried out on an equal basis without identifying groups which require positive discrimination with the exception of those considered disadvantaged" (unemployed 16-17 year olds, and 18 years and over in receipt of benefit, the long-term sick, physically or mentally disabled adults and children, single parents with children under 16 or still attending school, Family Credit — adults, and War pensioners and war widows).

Council G — The "policy on racial equality is contained within the Equal Opportunities Policy Statement ... this policy relates specifically to staff and not recipients of service delivery".

"A policy is contained within our department's Community Services Strategy and its aim is: To serve towards equality of opportunity for all members of the community to enable physical, cultural and personal development on a safe and secure environment".

"I am glad to reveal that an example of good practice ... has been implemented at (the district's) leisure centre and exists in the form of "women's only" swimming sessions. During these sessions all life guards and pool attendants are females and only females are allowed into the spectators area ... it was implemented in response to a request by Muslim women who would otherwise be unable to participate in swimming during normal swim sessions due to religious reasons".

Council H — "Our Department does not have a specifically stated policy relating to equal opportunities. However the department is required to apply the Council's race relations policy and equal opportunities policy ... The percentage of the population in (the district) from ethnic minorities is quite small and has therefore not been a major issue for the District Council. In saying this we try to assist local groups' requests to help themselves whatever part of society they represent".

Council I — "The only policies (the district) have with regard to equal opportunities and racial equality are those concerned with the recruitment of personnel. Racial discrimination is not an issue in this part of the country, simply because few people from ethnic minorities have chosen to live in the (region) of Scotland". "Nevertheless, I do not believe that anything we do will prevent people of ethnic minority from participating in sport: we certainly have not received any complaints relating to racial discrimination. However, we have no record of how many people of ethnic origin take part in sport in this area, so perhaps I am misreading the situation".

Council J — "The department does not have a particular policy regarding Racial Equality ... I can add however that we do make special arrangements at one of our swimming facilities for a group of Asian women who for religious and cultural reasons are only allowed to bathe within sight of females. We do therefore make specific arrangements for this particular group. I should add however in the past I have received complaints from individuals indicating that public facilities are programmed to meet specific groups of this nature and that the facilities should be used by everyone at all times".

Council K — "I enclose herewith, for your information, a copy of the District Council's Equal Opportunities Policy, but would have to say that this area does not have any problems with ethnic minorities".

Council L — "The Council has a general policy statement that it should strive towards ensuring equal access to opportunities for sport and leisure for all sections of the community. There is no specific statement on racial equality; indeed the major priority in this area is felt to be the needs of the low-waged and the needs of those people living in small communities remote from the specialist central facilities".

Proactive racial equality and leisure and sport specific equity statements

These statements reflect a more activist approach to racism, either as part of a sport and leisure strategy or with sport and leisure as the driving force in a campaign against racism. The most proactive council has appointed a Recreation Officer with specific responsibility for the needs of black and ethnic minorities and put in motion a series of initiatives to be accomplished over a period of three years.

Council M — "is committed to the provision of a comprehensive community orientated Leisure Service and will positively encourage participation from all irrespective of race, colour, religion or ethnic origin.

"The District Council through its Leisure Services Department will actively seek the support of local clubs, individuals and organisations in removing barriers to participation in sport and will identify measures to combat racism and sectarianism".

"The Scottish Professional Footballers Association (SPFA) officially launched its "Let's Kick Racism Out of Football" campaign in Scotland on 13th January 1994 ... The senior management within the Leisure Services Department believe this campaign should be supported, but widened to extend to all areas of sport and further, consider that local authorities, as the major providers of sports facilities in Scotland and throughout the U.K. have a principal role in ensuring that racist behaviour and activity is unacceptable within the facilities and services provided for local communities".

Council N — "will target lower participant groups in order that all groups can have an equal opportunity to take part in the sporting opportunities available. Its target groups will be women, unemployed, young people, middle aged and beyond, socially and economically disadvantaged, ethnic minorities and people with a disability."

"[The Council] recognises the ever changing nature of the demographic characteristics of the District and will ensure that such characteristics are continuously monitored to enable the appropriate groups to be targeted".

Council O — (Training Targets) "1. Ensure that all staff in Sport and Leisure and catering DSO and Leisure Management Unit receive training in: working with target groups. 2. Include in the Staff Development Scheme — contribution to equal opportunities policies. 3.Include in new Training Officers brief requirement to identify training needs to progress Equal Opportunities Action Plan".

Council P — "To lead the way in securing equal opportunities for all (the District's) citizens in terms of employment, access to services and participation in social activities"

"Equality of opportunity exists where the benefits of society are held in equitable proportion by the groups which make it up and when unfair treatment of particular groups has been eliminated."

"Target groups: this term is applied to women, black and ethnic minority people, people with disabilities, lesbians, gay men and people who have been unjustifiably discriminated against because of Trade Union activity, ethical or religious belief, long-term unemployment or because they have AIDS or are HIV positive"

Council Q — "Different sections of the ethnic community in (the District) have different needs and different ethnic groups may want different activities. It is essential that whatever the ethnic group or sub-group e.g. Asian women, the Council must be aware of and address their particular recreational and sporting aspirations and needs."

"In addressing this target group the Council will appoint an Ethnic Minority Sports Development Officer; increase training and education opportunities; ensure equal opportunities are carried out in service delivery; establish a programme of outreach work and target promotion/publicity of opportunities/activities in ethnic languages e.g. a "Women's Only" programme for Asian women."

"Major Objectives: 1. To heighten awareness amongst the ethnic minority community of the employment/career opportunities available within the Parks and Recreation Department. 2. To promote and monitor awareness of contractor and client responsibilities with regard to the Race Relations Act and combat racial discrimination. 3. To encourage greater participation in sport amongst ethnic minority groups".

Conclusions

Three questions were posed at the beginning of this paper: to what extent have local authority leisure services in Scotland operated equal opportunity policies and specifically policies which recognise the diverse needs of their populations? To what extent have Scottish local authorities sought to discover and provide for the specific leisure needs of their non-white ethnic minority populations? To what extent might we hope for an improvement in provision after reorganisation?

Over one-third of the DCs in Scotland had no formal EO policy. Most of these were in rural areas with low numbers of ethnic minorities. In the absence of EO policies and certain remarks in letters from these authorities there is evidence of some complacency about the existence of racial disadvantage and racism. The assumption that racism only occurs in towns and cities where numbers of black and Asian ethnic minority residents are large is not borne out by research conducted in England (Arnot, 1995; Myers, 1995). Surveys carried out on ethnic minorities in rural areas in England have found the lives of non-whites in small towns and villages marred by marginalisation, racial prejudice, abuse, attacks and lack of support networks. Commission for Racial Equality (CRE) researchers have compiled reports with titles such as "Keep them in Birmingham" and "Not in Norfolk" reflecting comments made to them by white people in rural areas. Yet in Scotland the debate about "rural racism" has hardly begun. Most of the DCs in rural areas appear to continue to see racial equality as a non-issue simply because they do not have large black and non-white ethnic minority communities in their areas.

Whilst over two-thirds of DCs have adopted formal EO policies their engagement with them and the implications for Leisure Services varies considerably. The DCs with EO and Racial Equality-specific policies are very much in the minority, but they have adopted some practices which could serve as a model for others. There has to be a greater sense of a proactive role for leisure services, requiring more effort to investigate and provide for the specific leisure needs of the non-white ethnic minority groups as well as for the white ethnic majority population.

Many of these extracts illustrate forms of denial of prejudice which have often underpinned the response of the white ethnic majority to ethnic minorities in Scotland. These have been identified by other writers as including: the argument over numbers; the notion of shared oppression; and the assumption that the "problem", if it exists at all, is confined to certain (urban) areas and is due to the presence of ethnic minorities (Armstrong, 1989; Cant and Kelly, 1995):

i). Numbers — "There is no problem here because there are so few black people" (p. 9)

ii). Shared oppression — "The Scottish people, belonging to an oppressed (stateless) nation, are not prejudiced against ethnic minorities" (pp. 11-12) iii). Confined problem — "If there is racism in Scotland it is confined to a few people and a few areas where the ethnic minorities live." (p. 19)

We would suggest that each of these assumptions is part of the logic of racism in contemporary Scotland.

Those departments responsible for leisure services in the new unitary authorities should look more closely in the future at the needs and interests of the so-called "New Scots" (Maan, 1992). According to research conducted for the Sports Council in England soccer is more popular amongst Asian youth than white youth — with 60% Bengali, 43% Pakistani, and 36% Indians playing regularly (Verma and Darby, 1994: 120ff). There are estimated to be 300 Asian soccer teams in Britain, many of them formed by temples and community centres when Asian youth have felt discriminated against elsewhere (Chaudhary, 1994). Further research will be needed to reveal the full extent to which these teams exist in Scotland and if Black and Asian players face the same forms of racist exclusion in soccer that research south of the border has uncovered (Highfield Rangers, 1993)[3]. In relation to other team games in England, historical and anecdotal evidence suggests that patterns of exclusion and inclusion similar to those in soccer have emerged (see for example, on cricket, Williams, 1994).

It is vitally important that the new authorities permit the articulation of black and Asian perspectives on these and related matters in sport and leisure. As Fleming (1994) argues, it is essential that anti-racist and racial equality policies avoid the problem of "false universalism" by acknowledging both black and Asian *hetereogeneity*. Here there is a need for increased collaboration and consultation with ethnic minority community groups — a practice evident in some of the more proactive authorities.

In this respect it is also vitally important to begin to investigate more thoroughly the position of both ethnic minority and ethnic majority *women* in leisure and sport in Scotland (Arshad and McCrum, 1989; Raval, 1989). A gender audit of Scottish society conducted by Engender (1994: p. 17) revealed that:

> ...ethnic minority women in Scotland compared to ethnic minority men, are less likely to be employed; less likely to speak English fluently; less likely to have educational qualifications; less likely to participate in activities, whether religious or community based, outside the home; more likely to have friends of the same ethnic group; and less likely to have white friends.

Their report acknowledges that there are significant differences between ethnic minority groups, yet compared with white women, ethnic minority women are:

> ...less likely to be employed; more likely to be at home looking after the family; likely to have more children; more likely to be married; and much less likely to be divorced, separated and single parents.

They note however that despite these differences in circumstance there has been "virtually no research focusing specifically on ethnic minority women" in Scotland (Engender, 1994: p. 17).

At the same time, the demographic structure of the non-white ethnic minorities is different from the white majority in Scotland. At either end of the life course specific issues may be arising for ethnic minorities which need to be addressed now: young Asians will soon be a large proportion of certain areas of the cities and towns where they live, and at the other end of the life course, older Asian people have specific needs that may remain underestimated by social and leisure services because of assumptions made about the role of the extended family in catering for them.

It is still too early to make any clear cut predictions about the impact of local government reorganisation on leisure provision, and EO policies specifically, in Scotland. Further research will yield more information here. The Association of Directors of Recreation, Leisure and Tourism (1995: 70) has recognised the need for awareness of racism:

> ...racism can imperil community relations in Scotland; many black and ethnic minorities remain disadvantaged in education and employment; and consequently "leisure equity" is not a reality for many black and ethnic minority people.

Yet at the same time it is recognised that leisure services are under threat in Scotland, as elsewhere, from Local Government Reorganisation. Reduced from 56 to a potential 29 departments, some Leisure Departments are already being subsumed under other headings, such as "Community Services" or "Education" in the reorganised local authority structures. Whether these will be able to develop what, for some, will be essentially new priorities remains to be seen.

The complexity of racism (in Scotland)

In Scotland racial and ethnic divisions are complex. Although nowhere near as significant as in Northern Ireland, institutional support for sectarianism remains in place in Scotland through separate schools, housing areas and the "auld firm" rivalry which helps sustain anti-Catholic/Irish sentiments (see Murray, 1984; Bruce, 1988; Moorhouse, 1993; and Finn, 1994, for contrasting views on Scotland, and Sugden and Bairner, 1993, on Northern Ireland)[4]. Compared to England the black and Asian population is small. Anti-racism campaigns or attempts to introduce EO policies based simply upon a "we-tooism" response (i.e., if England does it, "we-too" should) may not be adequately sensitive to the specific set of "racialised relations" in Scotland. Yet racism and other forms of discrimination exist in Scotland, even though it may sometimes take a different form from that in England.

Partly because of the small number of black and Asian people in Scotland, especially compared to the South East, Midlands and Northern regions of England, it has been possible for issues such as racism to be kept off the political agenda in Scotland. Yet it is a highly selective view of the past and the present that sustains the myth that racism does not exist in Scotland. (Armstrong, 1989; BBC, 1988).

The conclusion that there is no racist problem in Scotland, still voiced by some institutions of government in Scotland — most notably the Scottish Office and some local authorities — is ultimately mistaken because there always exists the potential for a process of "racialisation" to occur: racist attacks, racist abuse and racist chanting at soccer matches being examples of this. It was during the 1980s that anti-black racism entered the Scottish political agenda more explicitly than hitherto. Verbal abuse, physical assault, and other forms of racism have become a common experience for black people in Scotland (Armstrong, 1989; Bell, 1991; Scottish Eye, 1994). Since 1984 there has been an annual anti-racist march and rally in Glasgow. Between 1988 and 1990 racial incidents reported to the police increased by 100 per cent in the Lothian and Borders regions and in Strathclyde — which includes Glasgow — by 283 per cent (figures cited in Younge, 1993). The "black presence" in Scottish sport is undoubtedly much less evident than in England. Full-time professional football, for example, is essentially still a "white man's game" in Scotland compared with England — although this does not mean that racism is absent from the terraces or stands (Horne, 1995).

It is in this context that we can understand why there has been no research into the sport and leisure participation of ethnic minority groups in Scotland comparable with that carried out in England by Verma *et al.* or Fleming. Yet without more proactive monitoring and research — and despite the cynicism which this call sometimes attracts (such as that expressed by Lyle, cited in Edward, 1993: p. 134) — then the situation will not get any better.

Notes

1 "Black" and "Afro-Caribbean" are often used interchangeably within the research literature, and sometimes "Black" is also used inclusively to signal a politically forged identity between Afro-Caribbean and Asian people. Most "black" people in Scotland are Asian.

2 According to the Chartered Institute of Public Finance and Accountancy (CIPFA, 1989) spending on sport and recreation in England and Wales accounted for over 60 per cent of the total net expenditure on leisure and spending gradually rose in the 1980s to just below £400 million. In the report *Sport and the economy of Scotland*, research consultants Pieda (1991: p. 13 and p. 17) estimated that local government in Scotland spent £320 million on sport-related activities alone in 1990 and employed 11,000 people in sport-related jobs.

3 Tahir (1995) on the football team formed by the Scottish Asian Sports Association (SASA) in Glasgow. Another area where research could usefully replicate work already carried out in England concerns how far and in what forms racism permeates school sport in Scotland (on England see Fleming, 1991, 1993a, 1993b, 1994).

4 For a discussion of these complexities see Miles & Muirhead (1986); Dunlop (1993) and Horne (1995).

5 The extent to which the sectarian divide still has salience in contemporary Scotland is the subject of continuing debate, as recent events in Monklands District Council and in the response to footballer Paul Gascoigne (miming a flute player as in an Orange Order marching band after scoring for Rangers at Ibrox Lane) illustrated (Clouston, 1994; MacMahon *et al.*, 1995; Donegan, 1995).

6 Following Miles (1993: p. 41) it is our contention that to properly understand racism in Scotland we must dispense with the idea that the only or most important racism is that which has "black" people as its object. It is more helpful to consider racism in Scotland with the distinction proposed by Modood (1994) between "cultural" and "colour racism" in mind. Modood is critical of the emphasis upon "colour racism" since it excludes groups whose identity is felt most keenly through religion and culture, rather than colour. "Cultural racism" assumes that a group identified as culturally different is internally homogeneous and imposes 'stereotypic notions of "common cultural needs"' upon them (Brah, 1992: 129).

7 Carroll (1993) suggested the Sports Council should set a lead by encouraging good EO practice in those agencies with whom they work in partnership, or for whom they provide grants or advice. The Sports Council in Scotland, whilst developing initiatives such as the Sports Development Advisory Group (in conjunction with ILAM, Scotland), Team Sport Scotland, and explicitly targetting women, young people, the over 50s and the disabled, has not so far focused specific attention on the needs of minority ethnic groups (Scottish Sports Council, 1995, personal communication).

References

Armstrong, B. (ed) (1989) *A people without prejudice? The experience of racism in Scotland. London*: The Runnymede Trust.

Arnot, C. (1995) 'Race hate among the hedgerows', *The Observer*, 9th April.

Arshad, R. and M. McCrum (1989) 'Black women, white Scotland', in A. Brown and D. McCrone (eds) *The Scottish Government Yearbook 1989*. Edinburgh.

Audit Commission (1989) *Sport for whom? Clarifying the Local Authority role in sport and recreation.* London: HMSO.

Association of Directors of Recreation, Leisure and Tourism (ADRLT) (1987) *Leisure focus*, Association of Directors of Recreation, Leisure and Tourism.

——— (1995) *Leisure Matters: the role of leisure in Scotland's new local authorities.* Association of Directors of Recreation, Leisure and Tourism.

Bailey, N., A. Bowes and D. Sim (1995) 'Pakistanis in Scotland: Census data and research issues', in *The Scottish Geographical Magazine*, Vol. 111, No. 1: pp. 36-45.

Bell, A. (ed) (1991) *Aspects of racism in Scotland — information and sources.* Edinburgh: Moray House College.

Brah, A. (1992) 'Difference, diversity and differentiation', in J. Donald and A. Rattansi (eds) *Race, cultre and difference.* London: Sage.

BBC (British Broadcasting Corporation) Scotland (1988) *It doesn't happen here: Understanding racism in Scotland.* Glasgow: BBC Education.

——— (1994) *Kicking It*, BBC Multicultural Programmes Department, broadcast 28th September, BBC2, part of the All Black series.

Bruce. S. (1988) 'Sectarianism in Scotland: A contemporary assessment and explanation' in A. Brown and D. McCrone (eds)*The Scottish Government Yearbook 1988.* Edinburgh.

Byrne, T. (1994) Local Government in Britain. Harmondsworth: Penguin.

Cant, B. and E. Kelly (1995) 'Why is there a need for racial equality activity in Scotland?', in *Scottish Affairs*, No. 12, Summer, pp. 9-26.

Carroll, B. (1993) 'Sporting bodies, sporting opportunities', in C. Brackenridge (ed) *Body matters: Leisure images and lifestyles*, LSA Publication No. 47. Eastbourne: Leisure Studies Association, pp. 106-114.

Chaudhary, V. (1994) 'Asians can play soccer, too', *The Guardian*, 17th August.

CIPFA (Chartered Institute of Public Finance and Accountancy) (1989) *Leisure and recreation statistics — estimates.* London.

Clouston, E. (1994) 'Struggle for power reopens old wounds', *The Guardian*, 2nd July.

CRE (Commission for Racial Equality) (1994) *Annual report.*

CSO (Central Statistical Office) (1994) Social Trends: 24, HMSO, London.

Donald, J. and A. Ratansi (eds) (1992) *Race, culture and difference.* London: Sage.

Donegan, L. (1995) 'Gazza pipes up for King Billy', *The Guardian*, 31st July.

Dunlop, A. (1993) 'An united front? Anti-racist political mobilisation in Scotland', *Scottish Affairs*, No. 3, Spring: pp. 89-101.

Edward, M. (1993) *Who belongs to Glasgow?: 200 years of migration*. Glasgow City Libraries.

Engender (1994) *Gender audit*. University of Edinburgh.

Finn, G. (1994) 'Faith, hope and bigotry: Case studies of anti-Catholic prejudice in Scottish soccer and society', in G. Jarvie and G. Walker (eds) *Scottish sport in the making of the nation*. Leicester University Press.

Fleming, S. (1991) 'Sport, schooling and Asian male youth culture', in G. Jarvie (ed) *Sport, racism and ethnicity*. London: Falmer Press.

——— (1993a) 'Schooling, sport and ethnicity: A case study', *Sociology Review*, Vol. 3, No. 1: pp. 29-33, September.

——— (1993b) 'Ethnicity and the physical education curriculum: Towards an anti-racist approach', in G. McFee and A. Tomlinson (eds) *Education, sport and leisure: Connections and controversies*. Chelsea School Research Centre Topic Report 3. Eastbourne: University of Brighton, pp. 109-123.

——— (1994) 'Sport and South Asian youth: The perils of "false universalism" and stereotyping', *Leisure Studies*, Vol. 13, No. 33, July: pp. 159-177.

Highfield Rangers (1993) *Highfield Rangers: An oral history*. Leicester City Council.

Horne, J. (1995) 'Racism, sectarianism and football in Scotland', *Scottish Affairs*, No. 12, Summer: pp. 27-51.

Maan, B. (1992) *The New Scots: The story of Asians in Scotland*. Edinburgh: John Donald.

MacMahon, P., D. Scott and T. Crainey (1995) 'Monklands catalogue of abuse revealed', *The Scotsman*, 20th June.

McCrone, D. (1992) *Understanding Scotland*. London: Routledge.

Miles, R. (1993) *Racism after "Race Relations"*. London: Routledge.

Miles, R. and L. Muirhead (1986) 'Racism in Scotland: A matter for further investigation?', in D. McCrone (ed) *The Scottish Government Yearbook 1986* . Edinburgh.

Modood, T. (1994) 'Ethnic difference and racial equality: New challenges for the Left', in D. Miliband (ed) *Reinventing the Left*. London: Polity Press.

Moorhouse, B. (1993) 'Bigotry and sectarianism', *The Absolute Game*, No. 33, May/June: pp. 12-13.

Murray, B. (1984) *The Old Firm: Sectarianism, sport and society in Scotland.* Edinburgh: John Donald.

Myers, P. (1995) 'Country Mutters', *The Guardian*, 21st March.

OPCS (Office of Population Censuses and Surveys) (1991) *1991 Census Report for Scotland.* HMSO.

Pieda (1991) *Sport and the economy of Scotland.* Pieda/Scottish Sports Council.

Raval, S. (1989) 'Gender, leisure and sport: a case study of young people of South Asian descent — a response', in *Leisure Studies*, Vol. 8: No. 3: pp. 237-240.

Scottish Eye (1994) Scottish Television, broadcast on Racism in Scotland, May.

Smith, P. (1991) *Ethnic minorities in Scotland.* Central Research Unit Papers, Scottish Office.

Sugden, J. and A. Bairner (1993) *Sport, sectarianism and society in a divided Ireland.* Leicester: Leicester University Press.

Tahir, T. (1995) 'Racism drives Asians into a league of their own', *Scotland on Sunday*, 30th July.

Verma, G. K. and D.S. Darby (1994) *Winners and losers: Ethnic minorities in sport and recreation.* London: The Falmer Press.

Williams, J. (1994) 'South Asians and Cricket in Bolton', *The Sports Historian*, No. 14, May: pp 56-65.

Younge, G. (1993) 'Races apart on the Celtic fringe', *The Guardian*, 6th January.

Disabling Countryside: An Investigation of Wheelchair Users' Experiences of Informal Recreation

Melanie Limb and Hugh Matthews
Nene College, Northampton
Peter Vujakovic
Canterbury Christ Church College

Introduction

There is a growing interest in the ways in which people's leisure experiences are affected by socio-cultural dimensions such as ethnicity and gender (Fleming, 1994; Deem, 1986; Wimbush and Talbot, 1988). For geographers interested in the ways in which people interact with their environment these socio-cultural perspectives have been developed in the context of a new cultural geography. The call from Mowl and Towner (1995) for geographers researching leisure to embrace humanistic approaches to the interrelationships between people's leisure experience and place is grounded in their conviction that "the subjective world of the individual is a legitimate and fruitful area of leisure research" (p. 103). Central to the new cultural geography is the idea that different people have different 'ways of seeing' the world (Berger, 1972) and that, although our individual subjectivities and personal geographies differ from one another, we share "many visions and actions with the people who occupy our cultural world" (Anderson and Gale, 1992: p. 2). There are in society 'textual communities' (Stock, 1983) holding similar visions of the world. Furthermore, certain groups within society have a greater influence on the design and management of landscapes than others. Mowl and Towner (1995) outline research on gendered townscapes and their importance in constraining women's leisure experiences. Anderson and Gale (1992) argue that dominant groups have the power to 'make over' the world in the image of certain interests, so much so that the dominant cultural view becomes accepted as 'natural' and taken for granted. Environments become documents of power, 'written' expressions of values which are dominant in society. For 'textual communities' who do not share the same view these landscapes can be constraining, even alienating. This is of great significance in the context of leisure as "the feelings that places engender determine whether what we experience is experienced as leisure or as something completely different" (Mowl and Towner, 1995: p. 104).

One group of people whose environmental perspective has only recently been studied by geographers is the disabled (Matthews and Vujakovic, 1995). The disabled are not an insubstantial group within society. The proportion of Western industrialised societies which may be classed as disabled is estimated to be 12 percent (O'Brien and McFetridge, 1992). In Europe this represents around 50 million people (Davenport, 1991), whilst in 1988 the disabled population in the UK was estimated at 6.2 million, 4.3 million of whom were affected by locomotor problems (Office of Population Censuses and Surveys, 1988). Disability takes a variety of forms and not all disabled people are in wheelchairs. In this paper our interest is in the perspective of the wheelchair user. In 1988 the estimated number of wheelchair users in the UK was 60 people per thousand of the population.

As the proportion of elderly people increases so will the proportion of disabled. In the UK the elderly account for three-quarters of the disabled population. While the population in general is predicted to grow at 4 per cent between 1990 and 2006, the number of people older than 65 is expected to increase by 8 per cent. The proportion of the population reaching an age greater than 85 will rise by 74 per cent. The number of wheelchair users therefore is also likely to increase.

Early studies of disability concentrated on physical impairment and the ways in which people adapted to their condition (Blaxter, 1990). More recently there has been a recognition that while physical impairment may be the result of a variety of factors, for example, disease or accident, many aspects of disability are created, or at least exacerbated, through the planning and management of the built environment. There have been a number of studies which have drawn attention to how wheelchair users experience place in urban contexts (Matthews and Vujakovic, 1995; Butler and Patterson, 1994). O'Brien and McFetridge (1991) suggest that while integration is identified as a goal, disabled people suffer from a 'benign neglect' as a result of inadequate consultation.

In the context of leisure activity there has been some research on the ways in which disability constrains an individual's leisure experiences (Henderson *et al.* 1995). Research into the leisure experience of tourists, for example, indicates that barriers to their enjoyment undermine their sense of freedom and control and that some of these barriers are the result of externally imposed restrictions rather than their own personal limitations (Smith, 1987). The need to involve the disabled community more fully in leisure activities is acknowledged, and steps are being taken to encourage their wider participation in sport (Atha, 1991). At a recent conference on tourism the tourist industry acknowledged the need to make better provision for disabled tourists and their families, not least because in the U.K. the estimated market value of such custom is £25 million pounds (Davenport, 1991). Even the very specific needs of the wheelchair user can be met if leisure environments are designed with the wheelchair user in mind. Eurodisney for example boasts wheelchair access to all of the site and wheelchairs can be hired (*ibid.*)

There has been less research aimed at how wheelchair users experience the countryside. Studies have been undertaken to investigate problems of physical accessibility of the countryside for wheelchair users (for example, Gant, 1994) but there has been little attempt to see how wheelchair users perceive, value and use the countryside especially for informal recreation. There is some indication that countryside recreation is important to disabled people. Evidence given to the Snowdon Working Party includes comments such as "a lot of money is spent on disabled sports but not on woodland or riverside walks which some of us would like best" (McConkey and McCormack, 1983: p. 27). A similar view was expressed by a participant in workshops for the Irish Committees for the International Year of the Disabled, "I'd go for a long walk if I was let ... but there is so much traffic on the roads ... I'd prefer out in the country" (*ibid.*: p. 30) The Countryside Commission argues that "the freedom and refreshment of being out in the country is just as necessary and enjoyable to the minority of people who are permanently disabled as it is to able-bodied people-perhaps more so" yet goes on to acknowledge that "all too often the countryside experienced by disabled people is marred, not by their disabilities or mobility aids, but by an environment which has been modified by the able-bodied for able-bodied people" (Countryside Commission, 1981: p. 1). This acknowledgement is unhelpful in the absence of research which investigates disabled people's "ways of seeing" the countryside. The need for such consultation is all the more urgent at a time when restrictive practices abound. In the context of the countryside, strategic planning has emphasised restrictive recreational policies because of assumptions which have been made about growing recreational demand and possible damage (Curry and Pack, 1993). Access restrictions for bicycles and motor vehicles can have implications for the wheelchair user. If the views of wheelchair users are not taken into account during this debate, the access restrictions will still further reduce wheelchair users' opportunities to enjoy the countryside.

This paper is based on in-depth discussion groups with wheelchair users in Northampton. The methodology was chosen to investigate wheelchair users' recreational priorities in the countryside. Small group analysis of this kind has been used elsewhere to investigate the environmental values of able-bodied people (Burgess, 1986; Burgess et *al.* 1988). The small group setting was particularly suited for wheelchair users. Past research suggests that such groups allow the expression of important feelings and values for the countryside by people who might "otherwise never have a public voice" (Harrison *et al.* 1986: p. 20). In our groups, wheelchair users were able to share experiences and values with one another; expressing, confirming and sometimes challenging each other's views. In the process, the influence of the able-bodied researcher was diluted. The research method proved flexible enough to respond to perspectives we did not envisage when we began the research, and sensitive enough to reflect the, at times, highly emotional content of the discussions. We believe that the insight we have gained through this in-depth and intensive approach fundamentally challenges "able-bodied" perspectives on countryside recreation, and we are pleased that our participants so enthusiastically grasped the opportunity to be heard. In this study, in-depth discussion groups were combined with participant observation in outings to the countryside.

Two groups of wheelchair users were recruited with the help of the Northamptonshire Council for the Disabled. One group consisted of five wheelchair users, the other, of four wheelchair users and two spouses. Table 1 summarises the characteristics of the wheelchair users.

Table 1 Characteristics of group participants

Sex		
	Male	5
	Female	4
Age		
	35 or less	2
	36-50	3
	51 or more	4
Family circumstances		
	Living with parent	1
	Married, no children	2
	Married, dependent children	2
	Married, children left home	4
Length of time in wheelchair		
	From birth	1
	10 or more years	4
	Less than 10 years, more than 1	2
	1 year or less	2
Living location		
	Village	3
	Town	6

The small group size was determined by our desire to take the groups out on visits. Each group spent half a day in a local Country Park, and went on a day trip to the Peak District. The combination of in-depth discussion (four sessions of one and a half hour's duration) and outings was chosen to provide an intensive interpretation of their values and the difficulties they faced participating in countryside recreation. The volume of data (some 50,000 words) generated by such in-depth methods takes a great deal of time to interpret rigorously. To have added more groups would have made such a detailed interpretation more difficult. We see this study as a starting point for further research. Nevertheless, while we would make no claim that our group members are representative of the whole wheelchair-using community, we have no reason to expect that they are unusual in the problems they face.

Each of the groups met for two discussion sessions before the outings and two sessions afterwards. The general topics for discussion included places in the countryside they enjoyed (session 1), places they did not like and problems experienced (session 2), the outings (session 3) and suggestions for improving access for wheelchair users (session 4). As in previous studies of this kind the conduct of the group was carefully managed to encourage participation by all the group members while avoiding the exposure of vulnerable individuals. Tape-recordings of the sessions were transcribed in full. Methods of interpreting this kind of transcript data are discussed in Burgess *et al.* (1988).

Positive experiences and values

Wheelchair users' experience of and values for the countryside were the major themes of the first meeting of the group. Our intention was to concentrate on the benefits of visiting the countryside in the first meeting and then talk about participants' less favourable experiences and fears in the second discussion session. This division was based on previous experience of discussions with able-bodied people where some familiarity and security needed to be built within the group before negative experiences could be freely aired.

However, it was clear early in the first session that this separation was very difficult for wheelchair users. While there was evidence of pleasurable experiences and positive values held towards countryside, the negative experiences and feelings, either in the form of a sense of loss of "able-bodied" visits to the countryside or in terms of unwelcome restrictions and barriers inevitably surfaced in the discussion. We therefore allowed the participants to discuss the places they had visited in their own way and concluded from this that when it comes to countryside, pleasure and frustration are inextricably linked for wheelchair users. We had learned our first important lesson about their perspective.

In spite of this early discovery it is important to emphasise the positive aspects of visits identified by wheelchair users. The group participants valued the landscapes of the countryside and identified many of the pleasures recognised in studies of the able-bodied summarised elsewhere (Harrison *et al.* 1986). For example, the importance of sensory pleasures — sights, smells and sounds, contact with nature through both plant and animal life, a sense of escape, of peace and quiet and solitude and the importance of vistas were all reflected in the conversations.

Some aspects of countryside experience were qualified by confinement in a wheelchair. For those members of the group who rely totally on others to push them wherever they go, the attainment of solitude was very rare:

> *Dorothy:* It's not as easy because you've got to take someone to cope with every eventuality. I mean, I very seldom get time on my own. Time on my own is a very very unique experience. *(A1.624-6)*[1]

For others, aided by an electric wheelchair or an able upper body, some solitude was possible and greatly treasured.

Wildlife and plant life featured highly. The importance of connecting with nature: through the sounds of bird noise, the colour of autumn leaves, the flowers and trees, ducks, lapwings, deer and even domesticated animals such as horses and sheep was significant.

In particular there was an immense desire for the "difference" which the countryside provides, of an escape from the home and urban environment and an opportunity to exist in "another world" albeit for a very short time. Don and Graham describe this feeling during one of the outings:

> *Don:* ... it was being able to get out there and dropping into a valley wasn't it, basically, and you'd lost all sounds of traffic and the rest of the world if you like. That had gone because you were sort of in your own world. You hadn't got the sounds of the traffic and things like that which was beautiful.
>
> *Graham:* It was like being in a different place wasn't it? *(B3.81-87)*

That sense of escape was only possible for those participants with some degree of independence. For others such opportunities were rare and only possible as a result of negotiation with others.

The desire for a "view" has been explained by Appleton in terms of prospect- refuge theory (Appleton, 1975). He identifies the need for vistas as very basic and rooted in our human history. The importance of vistas is supported by studies of able-bodied groups in which views play an important role in countryside enjoyment. For wheelchair users the achievement of such a vista is far more difficult because, in many cases, it means negotiating a steep hill. The pleasure derived from views is no less significant, although sometimes these pleasures must be snatched during a car journey because achieving them in a wheelchair is such hard work.

In spite of the close entanglement of pleasure and frustration in the context of the countryside experience, there is no doubt that visits to the countryside were treasured by wheelchair users. This is illustrated during a discussion about the extent to which seeing the countryside on television can act as a substitute for visiting it in person.

Don: I don't think you can beat on hands, you know, to go and touch and feel. It's like being blind or something like that. A blind person likes to go and touch and feel.

Mary: And smell it.

Don: And smell it. It's much the same as a person who is not able to walk, or is limited in his ability to walk. It's nice to get out there and feel it, you know. I can watch it on the telly. It's nice, but it makes you want to say 'well, I'd like to go there'. *(B3.981-9)*

As Dorothy concludes, the countryside "is important because a lot of people find a great sense of peace in the countryside and great enjoyment in going out and about" *(A1.234-5)*.

In some ways the group members' appreciation of the countryside seems idealised and romantic, perhaps a product of their infrequent visits and the immense value they placed on the rare countryside experiences they had.

Lost countryside

Environmental loss

For eight out of our nine wheelchair users, disability occurred in adult life. Interweaving their discussions of current experiences were references to the countryside they had lost. The loss of walking as a pleasurable activity in its own right was very important and perhaps symbolised most poignantly by the fact that two participants still kept their walking boots. Even the everyday walking which is a possibility in the lives of the able-bodied, such as walking to a neighbouring village to the pub or walking the children to school, was missed by the group.

In the context of the countryside, the opportunity to walk into the countryside rather than sitting in a wheelchair at the edge was a loss acutely felt. The process by which this loss occurs is illustrated by the experiences of Ann who was in a transition between walking and wheelchair use. At the beginning of the project she was able still to walk with crutches for short distances and she described a visit to a landscape which she realised she was on the verge of losing as her walking difficulties increased:

Ann: we went to Bodmin Moor ... and it was wonderful. I loved it, and I'd got my crutches then, and it was a long walk and I was having trouble picking my feet up, which

I thought, well you've got to carry on because there's no way I'm going to be able to use the wheelchair there. I mean that definitely wouldn't have been wheelchair friendly at all. It wasn't foot friendly really-sort of falling about on boulders all over the place. But I loved it. ... it was so quiet and that's what I loved about it more than anything-the peace and quiet. It was fabulous. And the views! *(A1.85-92)*

The contraction of her "accessible countryside" was accelerating as she became more and more dependent on a wheelchair and indeed, due to deterioration in her Multiple Sclerosis during the project, even short distances required a wheelchair. Her sense of loss and bewilderment at the prospect of having to review the environments available to her, especially in the countryside, was palpable. She described an occasion on a recent family holiday where she managed to struggle on crutches down into a valley to enjoy the trees in autumn colours:

Ann: ... especially over the last week or two I've resigned myself-tried to resign myself to the fact that I'm not going to be doing that again, so I'm going to have to look into finding places that are wheelchair friendly, and I think, how do I find out? *(A3.186-90)*

In addition to the loss of walking, there was a loss expressed of particularly valued landscapes. For Sheila, these losses included Beachy Head and the uplands of the Lake District where she had hiked in the past. Unable to explore new wildscapes in her present condition, Sheila uses her imagination to recapture the landscapes visited by a friend on hiking holidays by looking at the photographs together on her friend's return. This vicarious enjoyment of countryside is something she now cherishes.

The countryside of childhood memory is often remembered with great affection and fondness, and 'rose-tinted' with nostalgia. For those in wheelchairs the importance of such memories is all the greater because they do not always have the ability to revisit the places concerned. The following comments from Don and Mary sum up their sense of loss:

Don: There's lots of beauty spots in it we'd all dearly love to go and look at. All over the country. I originate from Herefordshire and there's some beautiful country down there but I can't get to it, you know, except if I've got a motor car I can get there. But when I see my boys get out the car and sort of like go and run along a path or the hillsides or whatever being a Mary Poppins. Why can't I? (B2.579-84)

Mary: I feel as if I had quite a cherished childhood. I had the woods and the bluebells and the cowslips and the birds.

> Oxford was in the valley surrounded by woods and hills. Then there's the river Thames with the ducks, the coots, the moorhens, all different types of fish and the water meadows and the cattle and the plants ... .Now since I've come to Northamptonshire as a disabled person, apart from ploughing through Brigstock Country Park my experience of the countryside (apart from Rockingham Castle which is limited — that's nice there) is virtually nil. *(B1.553-61)*

Visiting villages were seen by some able-bodied visitors to the countryside as an important link in their values to a different (and older) way of life (Harrison *et al.* 1986). For wheelchair users negotiating village environments is very difficult. When asked if visiting villages was still a possibility in a wheelchair Mary responds:

> *Mary:* That's all in the past — gone. That's just memories because when you go to villages, like I live in a village, you get a real steep stone step, the doorways are old.
>
> *Graham:* And small, usually small, aren't they?
>
> *Don:* Usually catch your hands when you go through 'em. *(B3.456-60)*

For Don, the closest he can get is sitting outside a country pub or tea shop, but Graham points out how dependent that is on the weather conditions.

The loss of environmental experience extends to the mundane as well as the special visit. Even local countryside sites are restricted for the wheelchair user on summer evenings. Many Country Parks in Northamptonshire close the gates to the car park at 6pm and allow access only by kissing gate. While this prevents motorcyclists from tearing up the parks in the absence of the rangers, it also prevents wheelchair users from gaining access to the site. Mary summarises the frustration:

> *Mary*: If I go to my local Country Park, I'm able to sit there in the car. But in the winter and the summer the gates shut at six, so if it's a nice warm sunny summer's evening I can't go there. If I had use of my legs I could go there but because I drive the car and the ranger's gone, I can't go there. *(B3.1023-8)*

One suggestion made by the participants was that such gates should have a lock fitted which would allow access by a special key. This system is used to enable access to toilets and could be extended to gates.

The responsiveness of able-bodied countryside visitors to good weather conditions illustrates the extent to which able-bodied visitors can spontaneously visit the countryside on a sunny day as the opportunity arises.

Our own experiences of arranging the group visits to the Peak District and even the local Country Parks gave us an insight into the considerable amount of planning which is involved in such trips. Admittedly taking five wheelchair users at a time to the countryside is a more complex operation than one wheelchair user going on their own or with friends. Nevertheless the fact remains that spontaneous visits are more difficult for some participants. Dorothy was especially affected by this as she explains:

> *Dorothy:* You have to think logically about the things and whether it's possible and if you've got somebody to go with you ... everything I do has got to be done with somebody else. I can't just say 'I'm going to do that tomorrow' and hopefully I'm going to do it. It all has to be planned, therefore I can't suddenly say in the morning-get up and say 'I'm going in the countryside today'. *(A1.166-74)*

The seasons in the countryside are an important aspect of enjoyment. Here again people in wheelchairs are disadvantaged. The choice of path surfaces by many countryside site managers makes passage by wheelchair impossible at worst, and often restricted to the summer at best. This means that they lose out on the pleasures of early Spring because paths remain waterlogged, and find the colours of Autumn difficult to enjoy because soggy leaves combine with mud to make visits treacherous.

Social loss

An important aspect of countryside visits for some people is the opportunity for social activities. The family outing, the trip out with friends are highly valued by able-bodied people (Harrison, *et al.*, 1986). For the wheelchair user in a countryside environment designed for the able-bodied the social aspects of visits create feelings of conflict. They perceive themselves as a burden to their families, often requiring immense effort to push them along, and restricted in their ability to participate. On the one hand they enjoy the feeling of being in the country with others, yet they are frustrated by the barriers they encounter not only for their own sake, but on behalf of the others they accompany. Don describes a visit to a wooded area near the East coast:

> *Don:* ... it was beautiful to start off with because for about a quarter of a mile to half a mile it was downhill on a very slow gradient and it was quite wide and it was tar–macadam, it was. And I thought this is brilliant, this is. I've got all the woods. Wonderful! We've got the birds singing and the wood pigeons cooing and what have you and it was a nice place to be. And then we got to its bottom and there were a few seats there to sit on and it was beautiful. And then we started coming up hill. Dear, oh dear! And it went from tarmacadam to gravel to mud and then it went up hill like this and it was tree roots

> then ... it wasn't particularly far. It was probably 150-200 yards but my hands were dropping off by the time I got to the end and my wife had just about had it ... *(B2.685-97)*

Another exchange illustrates the conflicts wheelchair users feel.

> *Mary:* You've got to be a very selfish person to say to your partner 'take me to Irchester' or 'take me to Brigstock' or 'take me to somewhere else. I want to go'. Because ... they're going to have a hard job getting down round there.
>
> *Don:* You've met my wife haven't you, Melanie? Size of her, she'd have no chance of pushing me would she? Not round Irchester.
>
> *Mary:* There's another thing. When you get back, your wheelchair's dirty. The car boot's dirty. They're not going to want to take you. Yes, I know we can't expect town centre standard but I do honestly believe they can make a bit more effort. *(B3.377-89)*

In many instances wheelchair users take the decision not to burden their spouses or children in this way. In Harry's words, "there are limits that I apply upon myself on her behalf" *(B1.217)*.

On several occasions the participants describe situations in which they traverse a path and then can go no further. Don tells of one such experience where a motorised vehicle and track were provided for the disabled. Unfortunately the track was unfinished and stopped abruptly:

> *Don:* By squinting I got a view down one valley out to the sea and that was about it. And of course my wife carried on and she'd got far better views than I ever got. *(B1.202-4)*

In such situations wheelchair users experience immense frustration and their companions are faced with the unenviable choice of turning round and going back or leaving the wheelchair user while they continue. The sight of able-bodied spouse or children disappearing out of sight compounds their sense of isolation in an able-bodied world. Whilst such an experience cannot be prevented in all situations, some improvements are possible.

Phantom accessibility

One of the most disappointing aspects of our findings was the extent to which areas advertised as accessible to the disabled are not. Derek described a visit to Boddington reservoir, near Daventy in Northamptonshire, where there was a signpost welcoming disabled visitors, shortly followed by a gate which prevented wheelchairs from passing. On the day outing to the Peak District one group visited Tideswell Dale which was deemed wheelchair accessible by the Peak Park Planning Board and promised more than a mile and a half's access before a barrier would be encountered. In the event, we managed to traverse the path for only half a mile before it became impassable. Over that short distance the nettles and the poor surface made the experience unpleasant for some of our participants. The trip back up the hill to the car park was very hard work indeed, even for our pushers who were fit and healthy students. To attempt such a path with a spouse who is also supposed to be enjoying the day out is difficult to imagine. The following comments provide some insight into the difficulties of that day:

> *Don:* It probably is perfectly all right if you're on two feet and walking well, but when you're on four wheels in a wheelchair it's no joke. I felt sorry for the lads who were pushing me 'cause-it was probably easier going downhill ... but it was still difficult, and coming back, well, God bless your souls! When you're pushing sixteen and a half stone, it's no joke is it? I tell you what. My wheelchair's never been right since. It's always creaked.
>
> *Graham:* I had my wheels changed *(B3.57-66).*

And later:

> *Harry:* ... had I been able-bodied I'd have thoroughly enjoyed both walks, but I usually judge a walk by the state of my tail when I get back, you see, and by the time I got back, my tail was on fire! ... Also I have to judge it by whether my wife could take me. My wife couldn't have taken me. *(B3.200-7)*

The other group visited Dovedale which was certainly an easier path to follow and much less work for the pushers. But here also access is restricted to half a mile, before the route requires the negotiation of stepping stones. There is no further provision for the wheelchair user. The disappointment expressed by those on the trips represents the frustration other wheelchair users must feel. To make a long trip to the countryside is difficult enough when you are in a wheelchair, and perhaps uncomfortable. As Mary explains "what was available to us wasn't worth the trip" (B3.150). Most of the wheelchair accessible routes suggested by the Peak Park Authority's leaflets were little more than half a mile long. Tideswell Dale was one of the longer ones in theory but not in practice.

In the case of Dovedale other aspects of the facilities were problematic. It is advertised as wheelchair accessible and there is a disabled toilet but if you follow the signs from the car park you have to negotiate a difficult ramp with an uneven surface. There is a much easier way to gain access to the disabled toilet but no one has thought to change the sign to direct people to the easier pathway. Furthermore, there are no designated disabled parking bays. Dovedale is a well known beauty spot and on warm bank holidays becomes so busy that an adjacent field is used as a car park. Even on a sunny weekday in mid September the car park was half full. With no priority for wheelchair users they have little chance of getting parked in a place with easy access to the toilet and pathway. Many countryside sites do not have designated parking bays and for those that do there are no ways to enforce their proper use. Indeed it was not clear to the participants whether they had any legal rights whatsoever to these bays.

One might expect Country Parks to be more accessible than the open countryside. Certainly the group participants seemed to use the local countryside more frequently than wildscapes such as the Peak District. Even in Country Parks however, the issue of phantom accessibility was evident. The following exchange about Brigstock Country Park illustrates the problem.

Mary went with the ranger to evaluate the park from a wheelchair users' standpoint:

> *Mary:* The park ranger took me round there when he was doing his report, you know, for the Parks Committee and he pushed me about, and afterwards — and he was a strong athletic lad — and he was worn out and shattered you know half way through ... .Although prior to that he said 'I've pushed people about the park' ... and I worked it out afterwards. He'd pushed a 12 year old child around the park. *(B1.142-8)*

She continues in a later session:

> *Mary:* He (the ranger) thought they (the paths) were very good and I come back and my skirt, my coat, my, you know, shawl — everything was plastered in mud. *(B4.294-6)*

One of our half day outings was to Irchester Country Park where there is a circular route round the park. Again this is negotiable by wheelchair but only with considerable effort. One section of the path, not long after leaving the car park, was steep with an uneven surface. One of our pushers required two attempts to get one of the participants up the hill. Many a spouse or child of a wheelchair user may have been discouraged at that point fearing that the remainder of the path would be the same. Inthis case, some attention to that section would have made a difference. Alternatively the suggestion might have been made on the notice board at the ranger's station to traverse the path the other way round. This would mean going uphill on the tarmac road-not nearly so unpleasant.

The strength of feeling which is generated by phantom accessibility is summarised in the following conversation:

> *Don:* ... at the moment most of these Country Parks are a

feeling exercise aren't they? You've got to go there and test it to see if it's accessible for you. Em, if it's not-are you going to go again?

Mary: No because it's-it hurts me mentally when I read of the thing 'wheelchair accessible'.

Graham: Absolutely, absolutely.

Mary: ...and you go there and see what they think is wheelchair accessible ... They're trying to tell me I am insignificant. I'm not worth a second thought. I always take it personally. *(B4.727-39)*

As the examples illustrate, it is not enough to create a path wide enough for a wheelchair. The quality of the surface is critical in determining the extent to which an area is accessible. More important, in the context of outings which are supposed to be enjoyable, the path needs to allow both the wheelchair user and their pusher (if they require one) to enjoy the experience of going out. Otherwise the tendency is for people in wheelchairs to conclude that they are not welcome in the countryside. The fact that the leaflets advertising Country Parks imply access for the disabled by highlighting disabled toilets or car parks, comforts only the able-bodied. Perhaps the most disappointing outcome is that non-use by wheelchair users is likely to be explained as lack of interest on their part when it is actually the product of able-bodied managers creating disabling landscapes.

Vulnerability

The issue of vulnerability is evident among able-bodied groups visiting the countryside. The desire for escape and isolation is tempered by the fear of getting lost, hurt, or a car breaking down. For wheelchair users that vulnerability is multiplied. The fear of breaking down in a car while driving through the countryside is certainly evident.

For Jane, Graham's able-bodied spouse, this was a concern when they went on honeymoon:

Jane: When we went on honeymoon I had to drive from Northampton to Devon in a little mini metro ... it took us all day and I was worried in case we broke down. I mean I would have to walk somewhere to get a phone. *(B2.895-9)*

For wheelchair users themselves a breakdown would have even more serious consequences if they were alone. While some group participants such as Don and Derek were capable of getting their wheelchairs out of the boot and wheeling for help, for others this was not practical. As Mary put it, "When the car stops, I stop, because I can't push myself about" *(B1.168-9)*.

In addition there are genuine fears of falling out of the wheelchair and debate as to the usefulness of wheelchair seat belts. There is anxiety about getting stuck or venturing too far and then not being able to return to the car park. There are feelings of uncertainty about placing too much of an imposition on their helpers. Finally, there are the fears of embarrassment, of being stuck without appropriate toilet facilities or having to be lifted over a stile or a fence. While the general public are commended for their helpfulness at times, there are still those who abuse wheelchair users and belittle them.

In this context Country Parks were seen as providing some additional security because of the high profile of ranger stations in some parks:

Graham: ... the difference between Derbyshire and Irchester is, if you have any problems at all, you'd have had to do about fifty yards up the road to find what's it, you know, the warden. But in Derbyshire you wouldn't know where to go would you. *(B3.310-3)*

Unfortunately, in some cases to cut costs, staffing levels are being reduced. In these circumstances the wheelchair user's vulnerability is likely to increase.

Exclusion

A comment from one of our participants summarises very well the sense of exclusion from the countryside which participants felt:

Derek: I don't know any places that are easy in the countryside for a wheelchair.

Brian: Not in depth, when you really want to go in. You can look, on the outside looking in, which is enjoyable to a certain extent, but actually wanting to get in there, into the vales and what not. It's not on. *(A2.697-702)*

The need to belong to the wider community is a fundamental one for the group members. In the context of the countryside the desire to belong to groups interested in countryside is very strong. Sheila and Dorothy would like to be included in some of the outings organised by the Ramblers Association. In Sheila's words "it would be an idea if the rambling club could bear us in mind" (A1.822-3). Don mentions this too. Most especially, the wheelchair users long to share the pleasures of the countryside which able-bodied people take for granted. Part of this is a desire to cease being seen as separate and different. Don explains:

Don: I don't want people to feel sorry for me because I am in a wheelchair. I still want to get out and do. I still want to be able to drive my car. I still want to be able to go out and do the things that an able bodied person would go and do. Whether he wants to sail his boat or whether he wants to go down the Broads or whether he wants to go fishing. *(B4.779-85)*

For Graham and Jane, such integration is a forlorn hope. They are so frustrated by their experiences of disabling countryside that they are discouraged from going again. Jane explains:

Jane: To be honest with you, the places that we've been to — it's such hard work with little old me, 13 stone you and it's — the paths are uneven and you're going all over the place. I mean I don't have much pleasure at all, going to country parks or anywhere because of the hard work. *(B2.216-9)*

Derek explains their contradictory feelings as they struggle with the desire to improve access on the one hand yet not be seen to make a fuss on the other:

Derek: We've learned to put up with it and we laugh at it. If we didn't we'd never go out. So, perhaps we shouldn't ...

Sheila: You find ways round.

Derek: We can't stand there shouting and screaming can we? So we find ways round it on our own or we don't go to that place again. I tend to go to the same few places right or wrongly ... we don't like to be seen to be playing up do we? We like to disappear into the trees. *(A1.433-9)*

For the able-bodied, it is easy to conclude that it is the physical condition of people which make them unable to be part of the wider community who enjoy the countryside. They are outsiders because of the illness from which they suffer. This position can no more be sustained than the position held 70 years ago that their condition required an institutionalised existence. The extent to which they are outsiders is socially determined as the result of political decisions and priorities. The participants themselves were aware of this, quoting examples from other countries where the environment-even in the countryside-was more sympathetically managed.

Conclusion

Under the circumstances it would be understandable if the members of our groups gave up any attempt to visit the countryside. It is an indication of their strength of feeling about the importance of countryside to them that some still persist in their visits. They are well aware however that it is an uphill struggle which not all wheelchair users are willing or able to make. Furthermore, they fear that they will lose what access they have because of countryside managers' responses to recreational pressure on the countryside and financial restrictions. Moves to limit access (particularly for cars), the increases in car park charges and the growing tendency to site car parks some distance from villages or beauty spots; the use of gravels for path surfacing because of their low cost and the fact that they blend in with the "natural" environment; the reduction in park staffing levels; the introduction of stiles and gates designed to prevent cyclists and motorcyclists from gaining access to pathways — all these have implications for the group members and are likely to affect other wheelchair users.

At some countryside sites the changes required to encourage wheelchair access are immense. In others however, there are minor barriers which prevent wheelchair access and a small amount of money and thought would go a long way to solving the problems. The highest priorities must go to those sites which claim to be wheelchair accessible but are not. These require a rethinking by managers and planners to see the countryside from a wheelchair user's perspective. The group discussed ways in which this might be achieved:

Graham: Why on earth don't these rangers or whatever they are in these gardens — why don't they go round even themself in a wheelchair ... that would be an education for them.

Mary: But they're all fit, slim, healthy young men. If they pushed themselves around they wouldn't find it difficult to. They would say we're a load of moaners ...

Harry: And of course it's not the same as having an able-bodied person in a wheelchair because about two years before I had my head trouble, I had a small operation on my foot and I borrowed a wheelchair and I thought it was super fun. I could go everywhere-up and down the steps and everything in the damn thing because I was so strong. But of course as soon as I actually go into this situation, if I wasn't careful I fell out of it ... and when I fell out of it, it was a five man job to get me back in again. *(B2.708-724)*

If getting in a wheelchair provides only a partial understanding of the wheelchair user's "way of seeing" then how can managers of the countryside appreciate such a different perspective? It is clear from the group discussions that wheelchair users desire to be consulted and are capable of explaining the complexity of the difficulties they face.

Dorothy sums up her hope:

> *Dorothy:* What it boils down to is not a few of us knowing what the problems are, but lots of us. So the more things like this happen, the easier it will be to get around the countryside. *(A1.132-3)*

To be fair to the Peak Park Authority, it claims in its leaflets to have consulted disabled rights groups. In view of this the inappropriate provision seems all the more surprising and the consultative process perhaps needs to be re-examined. As Lifchez and Winslow (1979) suggest:

> ... the environmental needs of physically disabled people are complex and not readily understood by able-bodied people who do not have direct interaction with them. (p.129)

A genuine effort to consult wheelchair users requires managers of countryside sites to acknowledge that one important and often forgotten group of experts on wheelchair accessibility is the wheelchair users themselves. If consultation is to be effective it must involve interaction with the wheelchair user and be followed by action which results in more than piecemeal or token provision. Perhaps, most especially, there is a need for the symbol for wheelchair access to become more than a salve for the conscience of the able-bodied community.

Note

1 Bracketed notations following interview quotations identify group, session and line in transcript. For example:
A1.624-6 = Group A, Session 1, transcript lines 624 through 626.

References

Anderson, K. and Gale, F. (1992) *Inventing places. Studies in cultural georaphy*. Australia: Longman Cheshire.

Appleton, J. (1975) *The experience of landscape*. Chichester, Sussex, John Wiley.

Atha, B. (1991) 'Is sport for all?', *Sport and Leisure*, Vol. 32, No. 2: pp. 11-28.

Berger, J. (1972) *Ways of seeing*. Harmondsworth: Penguin.

Blaxter, M. (1990) *The meaning of disability. Sociology of social and medical care series*. London: Heinemann Educational Books Ltd.

Burgess, J. (1986) 'Crossing boundaries: a group analytic perspective in geographical research', *Group Analysis*, Vol. 19: pp. 235-44.

Burgess, J., Limb, M. and Harrison, C. M. (1988) 'Exploring environmental values through the medium of small groups. Part one: theory and practice', *Environment and Planning A*, Vol. 20: pp. 309-26.

Butler, C. H. and Patterson, A. (1994) 'The disabling environment: constraints on the mobility of the physically impaired in the urban high street', *West London Papers in Environmental Studies No. 2*: pp. 35-46.

Countryside Commission (1981) *Informal countryside recreation for disabled people*. Advisory series No. 15, Cheltenham: Countryside Commission.

Curry, N. and Pack, C. (1993) 'Planning on presumption: strategic planning for countryside recreation in England and Wales', *Land Use Policy*, Vol. 10, No. 2: pp. 140-150.

Davenport, K. (1991) 'Wheel in change', *Leisure Management*, Vol. 11, No. 5: pp. 36-40.

Deem, R. (1986) *All work and no play? The sociology of women and leisure*. Milton Keynes: Open University Press.

Fleming, S. (1994) 'Sport and South Asian youth: The perils of false universalism and stereotyping', *Leisure Studies*, Vol. 13, No. 3: pp. 159-178.

Gant, R. (1994) 'Disability matters: A Cotswold perspective', *Scottish Association of Geography Teachers Journal*. School of Geography: Kingston Polytechnic.

Harrison, C. M., Limb, M. and Burgess, J. (1986) 'Recreation 2000: views of the country from the city', *Landscape Research*, Vol. 11: pp. 19-24.

Henderson, K., Bedini, L., Hecht, L. and Schuler, R. (1995) 'Women with physical disabilities and the negotiation of leisure constraints', *Leisure Studies*, Vol. 14, No. 1: pp. 17-31.

Lifchez, R. and Winslow, B. (1979) *Design for living: The environment and physically disabled people*. London: Architectural Press.

Matthews, H. and Vujakovic, P. (1995) 'Private worlds and public places: mapping the environmental values of wheelchair users', *Environment and Planning A*, 27: pp. 1069-1083.

McConkey, R. and McCormack, B. (1983) *Breaking barriers: Educating people about disability*. London, Souvenir Press (Educational and Academic) Ltd.

Mowl, G. and Towner, J. (1995) 'Women, gender, leisure and place: towards a more "humanistic" geography of women's leisure', *Leisure Studies*, Vol. 14: pp. 102-116.

O'Brien, L.G. and McFetridge, M. (1992) 'Mapping geographical space for the disabled', in K. Rybaczuk and M. Blakemore (eds) *Mapping the nations*. London: International Cartographic Association: pp.157-163.

Office of Population Censuses and Surveys (1988) *The prevalence of disability, Reports 1-4*. OPCS, London: Her Majesty's Stationery Office.

Smith, R.W. (1987) 'Leisure of disabled tourists: barriers to participation', *Annals of Tourism Research*, Vol. 14, No. 3: pp. 376-389.

Stock, B. (1983) *The implications of literacy*. Princeton, New Jersey: Princeton University Press.

Wimbush, E. and Talbot, M. (eds) (1988) *Relative freedoms*. Milton Keynes: Open University Press.

Problems of Public Perception of Sport and Physical Recreation in the Prevention of Reoffending and the Rehabilitation of Juvenile Offenders

Fiona McCormack

Buckinghamshire College

During the 1990s the problem of juvenile delinquency has continued to be one of public concern. While media articles have suggested a need for recreational opportunity as a diversion from youth crime, the use of youth recreation activities (particularly adventure-based activities) in the rehabilitation process has led to strong media criticism. The problem appears to be that such projects are perceived to reward juvenile offenders. This paper will consider this problem of negative perceptions which threaten to reduce support for sport and recreation at post-offending (tertiary level) intervention. Negative public perception has already led to cuts in government funding, with a move away from support for the use of mainly adventure-based projects. The problem facing providers was summarised by King, describing the less exotic outdoor activities provided at tertiary level by Glenthorne:

> ... the outlook for this rock climbing is not sunny. The clouds, literal and metaphorical, are closing in. (*The Guardian*, 11 Sept., 1994)

Providers of all recreation projects aimed at juvenile crime prevention need to consider how best to justify their approach in the face of increasing public attention.

I will briefly explore some of the key issues. To begin I will consider the theoretical benefits of sport and recreation as they relate to preventing the expression of juvenile delinquency. Having established the theoretical base, I will consider how these ideas can be compatible with current philosophies regarding tertiary intervention. If sport and recreation is compatible with tertiary objectives, then why have these schemes been subject to criticism? Finally, I will consider whether criticism is justified.

What is the theoretical basis for the use of sport and physical recreation in juvenile crime prevention?

It is essential to consider the benefits of sport and recreation projects as related to juvenile crime prevention since, in the past, research into schemes has revealed little connection between the theory and practice. Robins (1990) concluded after a study of selected projects that:

> ... a gap exists between straightforward assertions about the capacities of sports and outdoor adventure programmes to ameliorate social problems such as juvenile delinquency, and the scale, scope and variability of what happens on the ground. (Robins, 1990: p. 88)

What are these 'straightforward assertions'? Since there is a variety of activities which are encompassed under the broad field of sport and recreation, and different activities have their own rationale and uses in reducing juvenile delinquency, it is important to consider them individually. In this analysis I have chosen to consider adventure, sport and constructive leisure projects. If recreation is to be shown as a legitimate factor in reducing juvenile delinquency it will firstly be important to recognise the causes of juvenile crime in contemporary Britain. Research by Cooper (1989) and Webb and Laycock (1992) provides evidence which supports the motivation theories of a search for fun and entertainment, of boredom and frustration, of status-seeking behaviour, and of peer pressure and poor parenting. Schemes which are based on participation in sport and recreation will need to demonstrate an ability to counteract these causes of delinquency.

Firstly I will consider outdoor activities and adventure. The basis for the use of outdoor activities and adventure in the personal development of young people can be found in the theories developed by Kurt Hahn, founder in 1934 of Gordonstoun School. The school was based on the philosophy of education to:

> ... develop the righteous and the active citizen, with a strong emphasis on leadership and service. (Hopkins and Putnam, 1993: p. 24)

These objectives were to be achieved through the use of expeditions into the hills and on small boats, as well as through physical training and community service. A second major influence in the development of outdoor recreation for young people was Baden Powell, with his emphasis on outdoor activities for character building within the Scouting and Guiding movement.

The impact of adventure on individuals was summarised by Everard (1987) as the development of self-concept. The positive development of self-concept is central in evaluating Outward Bound projects. Unfortunately, self-concept is difficult to define and to measure, particularly in the long term. The outcomes of improved self-concept are often seen as self esteem, reduced anxiety and improved self-confidence. Many attempts have been made to offer empirical evidence in support of these claims. Roberts (1974) concluded in a study of the " character training industry" that:

> Following their training most young people feel "different", more mature, self confident, and better capable of handling relationships. (Roberts, 1974)

The use of adventure as a therapeutic tool for social work and counselling has been predominantly developed in America. In "Adventure Therapy" (1993) Gass explains the rationale for the use of adventure in the 1990s from a sociological perspective. Taking the basic idea from Kurt Hahn that young people who feel unneeded will behave in a variety of inappropriate ways, Gass considers the role of adolescents in western culture. He suggests that they require certain life skills such as self-confidence, self discipline, judgement and responsibility. However, the social structure of the 1990s no longer offers the same opportunity as in previous decades for these skills to develop naturally. In analysing this problem he concludes that:

> Outward bound and its derivative, wilderness therapy, can be seen as educational processes where adolescents are initiated into prosocial values that form the basis of western culture. (Gass, 1993: p. 19)

Therefore adventure and outdoor pursuits were developed to encourage personal development and are now applied not only to adolescents but also in several business management applications. In more recent years adventure experiences have been used more controversially as a forum for therapy, such as the work of Bryn Melyn.

Sport has a strong historical background in personal development. In Britain the value of sport in terms of socialising young people was identified by the headmaster of Rugby School, Thomas Arnold, in the nineteenth century. A concept of 'Muscular Christianity' was evolved as an attempt to quash or divert attention away from immoral activities through introducing a vigorous programme of athletics and team sports. The rationale to support this idea is found in the definition of sport as physical recreation which involves developing physical or psycho-motor skills and which takes place within a competitive but rule-bound structure. From this, participation can be seen to require acceptance of rules and authority as necessary. This acceptance by young people, it is suggested, will lead to a general acceptance of the need for rules within society. This has been expanded by Snyder and Spreitzer (1978):

> Sport is a social institution which has its primary functions in disseminating and reinforcing the values regulating behaviour and goal attainment, solutions to problems in the secular sphere of life.. This channelling affects not only perspectives on sport, but, it is commonly assumed, affects and aids in regulating perceptions of life in general. (Snyder and Spreitzer, 1978)

This more recent assessment can be linked to the early theories of Muscular Christianity with a strong emphasis on its power to develop a moral code. An acceptance of fair play in sport will, in theory, lead to a general acceptance of society's moral code. The role which sport can play in the socialisation process comprises the transmission of social values, mastery of skill and good character, moral definition of behavioural problems thus facilitating social order.

The value of traditional sports was not solely exploited for the expected moral results of Muscular Christianity, and adherence to a moral code, but also the importance in constructive opportunity to use up surplus energy. The Surplus Energy Theory, developed by Herbert Spencer (1855), stressed the need to burn excess energy not used at work. Sport would offer a satisfactory medium for this release and without a suitable outlet such as sport, the energy would be released in pursuit of, as Robins summarises this perspective, "... dysfunctionality in the form of delinquent behaviour...." (Robins, 1990: p. 12). Sport and physical recreation projects have been used to encourage personal development, but their main rationale has more often been to assist in the socialisation process.

Finally, more recent projects have sought to encourage positive use of leisure time. Constructive leisure activity has developed from Rational Recreation which was an early attempt to control the activities of the working class, through their leisure time being guided towards self-improvement. Almost a century later, contemporary applications advocate the power of constructive leisure activities as a tool for teaching social skills to young people at risk of offending. This relies on the concept that recreation is an effective tool with which to instil the values and behaviour accepted by society in general, and which helps young people to develop self-respect and a sense of physical well being. Examples such as the Scouting movement are used to support this idea. Constructive leisure behaviour can therefore be defined in terms of activities which offer positive outcomes to the individual and to society. Examples can be either participating or creative. Non-constructive use of leisure time includes activities which harm society or the individual, such as vandalism and drug abuse. Constructive leisure behaviour continues to be encouraged through public sector subsidised provision.

Generally, politicians and government policy in recent years have embraced this idea. The Scarman Report (1982) suggests that the Brixton riots were closely linked to a lack of constructive leisure opportunities for young people. In the 1990s this argument can be supported by the high levels of youth unemployment in Britain, which leaves thousands of young people with no direction, little money and plenty of free time.

Constructive leisure participation offers benefits in terms of interest, opportunity for self-expression, and social interaction. Unlike sport and physical recreation, constructive leisure need not test physical ability, nor offer an enforced sense of competition. The common link between all of these types of activity is that they seek to divert the young offender from delinquency by offering challenge, excitement and a release from boredom.

Are the benefits of participation in sport and recreation compatible with tertiary intervention philosophies?

The discussion of theoretical benefits of participation in adventure, sport or constructive leisure demonstrated that such participation has been seen as a means of countering the causes of delinquency. In order to achieve these proposed benefits, sport and recreation projects have been used at various stages in the intervention process. Much of the criticism of schemes has been directed at the tertiary level of intervention with known offenders. In order to understand why, it may be helpful to briefly review the philosophy of intervention.

The roots of intervention are commonly considered in terms of primary, secondary and tertiary interventions (Brantingham and Faust, 1976). For the individual, crime prevention can be focused at pre-offending and existing offending groups, through secondary and tertiary prevention. Primary prevention, on the other hand, is not directed at individuals, but at the environment and social structure which may encourage crime and delinquency. At the secondary level, crime prevention is based on theories of preventive intervention before offending occurs, for example, directed at socialisation (affecting positive attitude development), diversion and deterrence. At tertiary, or post offending phase, the intervention theories are based most commonly on deterrence, punishment, rehabilitation, education and diversion. If we are to understand and respond effectively to criticism of tertiary level schemes, then it is important to look at intervention philosophies for this area more closely. This can be achieved by considering rehabilitation and punishment.

Rehabilitation to alter attitudes and behaviour

The philosophy of rehabilitation is centred around efforts to address the causes of delinquency in young people, and to help them to change their behaviour and attitudes. Within the rehabilitation process adventure, sport and constructive leisure activity have been applied. The use of outdoor activities and adventure has been developed over several decades by the British probation service. Pointing (1986), reporting on the account by

Maitland of Inner London Probation Service's use of these experiences, explained its rationale for addressing deficiencies in the offender's lives which were:

> ... often lacking legitimate outlets for energy and excitement. The use of client's leisure was often described as being over-reliant on money-consuming, mechanical sources of entertainment, which were without challenge and unable to provide a lasting source of satisfaction. (Pointing, 1986: p. 147)

The courses were used as a way of working with clients as therapy:

> ... such activities would appear to be a useful way to facilitate the client/officer relationship. (Pointing, 1986: p. 160)

They were also used as a measure of diversion from delinquent activities through widening their horizons. Maitland concluded that, as part of a rehabilitation programme, adventure activities can offer positive outcomes to a wide range of clients. These include one-off experiences to improve client/officer relationships and longer-term participation to develop social skills, which may contribute to overcoming a history of lack of self-confidence or a propensity to commit acts of violence. At a tertiary level, in a rehabilitation process, adventure activities provide evidence to support their use as both diversion and as a forum for individual and group therapy.

However, in efforts to rehabilitate offenders, the use of traditional team sport faces problems of acceptability. The role of sport in developing acceptance of rules and moral codes may be proven for long-term preventative approach throughout childhood. Group or individual treatment may be successful in using sport to instil socially acceptable behaviour patterns, if the young people targeted are not already in or on the edges of delinquent sub-cultures. This is because the values of sportsmen and women, which stress perseverance, success through competition and rewards for hard work, fair play and loyalty, may put off potential delinquents as they would resist activities which conform to the wider conventions of society. Sport with it's hierarchy, rules and authority can in one formal manifestation represent a microcosm of everything which the young delinquent resents in society. Therefore, sports projects as diversion may also be unsuccessful. However, sport does offer opportunities for excitement, release from boredom, potential status and a feeling of belonging. If resistance, on the basis just identified, can be overcome then sport projects may be successful. This could be demonstrated by evidence of continued participation over several years.

Constructive leisure projects have become increasingly important in probation service provision for juveniles. The use of these programmes seeks to introduce young offenders to alternative interests to occupy spare time and to improve their job prospects. The most thoroughly evaluated tertiary scheme is the Solent Sports Counselling project. The results are probably the most important British evidence to date of medium-term benefits. Its monitoring process considered reports from probation officers and sports leaders. The probation reports can offer insights for the longer term, such as:

> ... the scheme has given K(19) a considerable boost in confidence and self esteem and the change has been noticeable to see. I am sure it helped her gain employment and has given her a more positive view of life.... (Extract from probation officer's reports on completion of the scheme) (Hampshire Probation Service, 1993: appendix 2)

Punishment for offending against society

Society is conditioned to expect punishment for wrong doing. Retribution will deter further offences and other potential delinquents, while the public can feel satisfied that the offender has paid his price to society. Both adventure and sport have to some extent been used within a punitive regime.

Although modern practitioners shy away from terms such as 'character-building', the adventure experience in certain physically severe conditions can meet one requirement of advocates of a punitive regime. Where adventure experiences stress physical endurance, challenge and lack of home comforts their use has been established within the punitive regimes of character building. An early experiment by the Rainer Foundation in 1960 and 1961, can offer evidence to support this role. Day (1967) reported that adventure activities can help to reinforce an acceptance of the need for discipline, since the circumstances are created by natural dangers not arbitrarily imposed from without. The experience was restricted to boys between 14- 18 years who were physically fit and not severely disturbed. His research concluded that:

> ... a period of outdoor activity away from the normal school setting could be a beneficial part of reformative training. (Day, 1967: p. 188)

Post-offending interventions with juvenile delinquents have used sports-based projects as part of punitive regimes and rehabilitation. In terms of punishment, hard physical exercise and its inherent discipline has been frequently used in custodial sentences. In recent years this has been demonstrated in the USA and in two trials in Britain of the 'boot camp' concept; however, evaluation of the American schemes shows little evidence of a reduction in reoffending. Constructive leisure activity provision has little place in the punitive aspects of tertiary prevention.

From this analysis it is possible to identify the rationale for sports and recreation intervention at tertiary level in juvenile delinquency. The main relationships which link the benefits of various recreational programmes to both the causes of delinquency and the objectives of various forms and stages of intervention are:

1. As diversion from delinquent activity at both secondary and tertiary stages, through offering legitimate opportunities for challenge, excitement and status; thus providing relief from boredom.
2. As a form of informal education and treatment at both secondary and tertiary stages of intervention to counteract poor socialisation, lack of parent support and peer group pressure; through improved self esteem and therefore perceived status and worth.
3. As a form of punishment to instil discipline and physical fitness.

The main link between the benefits and the objectives is found at both secondary and tertiary levels in the form of diversion. However certain characteristics of each type of activity make it compatible with other objectives such as atonement and education or treatment. The weakest connection is with the objective of retribution at a tertiary level and it is for this reason that such schemes have been subjected to media criticism recently.

Why are tertiary schemes criticised and are these criticisms justified?

There are several basic lines along which tertiary recreation schemes have received particularly strong media criticism. Reports use individual cases to highlight: cost, management, lack of results and activities chosen. However there appears to be one central problem facing such schemes, that society expects punishment for delinquency and views leisure as a reward. This has led to a mistrust of many adventure and sports based projects for young offenders. *The Guardian*, reporting on Portillo's Fife speech, quotes:

> ... the quiet majority dismayed by yobbos sent on sailing cruises.
> (*The Guardian*, 23 April, 1994)

At the preventive levels, primary and secondary, the dilemma is one of achieving a balance between intervening to improve the situation, and intervening as a form of social control. For tertiary intervention there is a dilemma, to punish or to rehabilitate. The question remains whether these two philosophies are mutually exclusive, or whether some satisfactory compromise can be achieved. Both have merits and some supporting evidence. In a society conditioned to expect punishment for wrong doing, the policy of radical non-intervention or reparation is frequently seen as unjust. Media headlines exposing young delinquents " rewarded" with adventure holidays to exotic places increase public concern to see some punishment for wrong doing. Nonetheless, evidence also shows that the punitive regime of custodial sentences often acts as a school for delinquents, releasing hardened criminals into society. What is more interesting for recreation and leisure, is that both the punitive and atonement regimes utilise sport and recreation during the process.

In order to assess the areas of criticism I will refer to two recent surveys of the work of the probation service and the Prince's Trust Report (Coopers and Lybrand, 1994).The Home Office (1994) has produced a report — *Demanding Activities For Offenders In The Community* — which presents the results of Probation Circular no.72/1994, a survey into the use of sport and recreation. The second survey was conducted as part of my research. In March 1994 a self-completion questionnaire was distributed by post to all of the head offices of the English Probation Services as listed in the 1994 NAPO Probation Directory. Of the forty seven services contacted there were 32 returns, giving a response rate of 68%. Of the returns, half of the services were using recreation, and the remainder either gave incomplete information, or were not using recreation.

Activities used — demanding physical recreation, community based constructive activity or luxury holiday?

A central issue for media attention has been the type of activity selected. These are frequently described as 'holidays'. *The Guardian* (13 August, 1994) reported on the use of Centre Parcs as a venue for a 14 year old offender, questioning the rationale in sending him to a luxury holiday site. Overseas trips, as used by Bryn Melyn, have focused attention further on the rationale for offering holiday style treats to young offenders. *The Times* (1994) comments that the young offender "never understood what his trip to East Africa and Egypt, which included climbing the Pyramids and cruising the Nile, was supposed to do for him". Although a clear rationale for such activities has been developed through the concept of adventure therapy, providing a conducive atmosphere for personal change, to the general public such trips will undoubtedly be perceived as rewards for offending. This concept now colours public perception of sport and recreation at tertiary level and according to practicians has already restricted the use of such schemes. My research has however shown that these luxury activities are the exception, and that the general picture of provision is one of traditional sports and outdoor activities within a fairly local area. Indeed responses showed that most of the probation services used a wide range of activities with no single respondent using only one type of intervention. Sail Training was the least popular possibly due to the more costly nature of the activity, lack of awareness of opportunities and the fact that activities may reflect the interests of the staff and volunteers. Other activities mentioned include work with disabled groups, use of all community resources, Community Sports Leaders Award and the Duke of Edinburgh Award. My findings are supported by the results of the research presented in Probation Circular no.72/1994 which showed that of 54 areas:

> ... Many of the activities seemed to be run for offenders in probation hostels and probation day centres. It appears that much of the activity which is taking place is generated by local staff initiative... (Home Office, 1994: p. 66)

Indeed 64% of the probation services were including physical activity in their 3 year operational plans. Therefore, perceived holiday style activities represent a very small percentage of recreation at tertiary level, with the main emphasis being on local activity and the constructive use of free time.

A criticism of many residential recreation interventions is that substantive changes in client attitudes and behaviour can only be achieved in the long term project. Pressure has therefore been placed on such projects to offer longer contact and follow up. For probation services shorter projects may be used as part of the counselling process with an officer. My survey showed great variety in the duration of recreational intervention. The majority of respondents (32%) indicated that courses were of variable duration to suit client needs. For fixed duration courses the length varied between one week residential to 8 months non residential. The trend in terms of provision seemed to be for continuous programmes, which avoids delay in introducing new clients to the schemes.

Further criticism has been directed at tertiary intervention for using organisations to provide the activities which lack training and experience in this field. Research reported in the Probation Circular 72 showed that a number of partnerships in the field of provision existed, mainly through Fairbridge, Duke of Edinburgh Award Schemes and leisure centres. The research also showed that 38% of providers were voluntary sector. This may present more cost-effective provision but may also require funds to be made available to develop specific training initiatives to ensure professional standards are communicated effectively.

Costs — expensive treats provided by the tax payer?

Since media reports usually highlight overseas or residential courses such as Centre Parcs, a familiar theme for criticism is the cost of such activities to the public. My research showed that although cost per client was relatively low, no service was able to give a breakdown as requested in the questionnaire for staff and other costs. However one did indicate a 3:1 client: staff ratio. Three respondents indicated that a total budget was allocated and the details given were £200 per month for 30 clients which is £6.60 per client per month. Another indicated an annual budget of £1,000. Yet another gave the cost of a residential course as £750, while a non-residential week was £70. One respondent suggested that since activities were directed to encourage constructive use of leisure, all activities were low cost and could be continued after the projects.

These figures are significantly lower than those cited in articles such as *The Independent* (18 October, 1993), which reported on the work of a residential school, Winestead, which stresses the use of outdoor activities, sports and leisure activities in the rehabilitation of young offenders. Their fees were quoted as £44,000 per year. *The Times* (1994) suggests that the £1,600 per week cost for Bryn Melyn was described by one young offender as "a waste of money". In some cases longer-term residential care is required to satisfy sentencing requirements. In these cases the adventure course costs are often significantly less than custodial care. This concept was highlighted by Gloucestershire social services when explaining the choice of Bryn Melyn. It was stated that this option, rather than costing more than custody, actually saved the public £700 per week.

The Prince's Trust Report (Coopers and Lybrand, 1994) was centred on a cost and benefit analysis of sport and recreation projects with youth work. Their case study results would support the findings regarding probation service expenditure on schemes. In their study the cost per client per annum for non-residential community based initiatives was between £165 and £440. Their findings regarding the cost effectiveness of schemes will be considered in the next section.

It is important for the future of recreational projects at tertiary level to communicate the fact that the majority of activities are low cost and community based as part of non custodial sentencing. If the public continues to perceive recreation intervention as costly treats for offenders then government policy may make funding for all projects more difficult in future.

Ineffective schemes which cannot demonstrate success?

Examples of young people returning swiftly to crime after or even during a recreational project have been used to question the effectiveness of schemes. Therefore it is important to consider the task presented to schemes working with recreation by considering their client base. The proportion of offenders who were juveniles was 46% in 1990. It has been established that frequently a single young offender can be responsible for a large proportion of the reported crime. Therefore, when considering juveniles involved in tertiary provision, it is essential to realise that to reduce the proportion of total crime, a small group of persistent offenders needs to be targeted for detection, indictment and treatment. Since crime statistics show that most first-time juveniles never reoffend, the process of cautioning has been sufficient deterrence. Juvenile justice and probation will be more likely to contact regular or serious offenders. The type of offender/ young person targeted for recreation projects according to my research showed that most schemes are for persistent and serious offenders. Recreation intervention will therefore face the challenge of breaking an offending cycle and replacing the influence of a delinquent subculture. Therefore, expectations for success must be considerably lower than at primary and secondary stages of intervention. When setting targets for these schemes this problem should be considered and realistic goals set.

There are many different measures of effectiveness for tertiary intervention. Government policy and public interest in tertiary projects has up until now been restricted to the measures of recidivism after one and two years. Recreation intervention is required to demonstrate lower rates of reoffending among juveniles as compared to other interventions. Some projects have successfully demonstrated this performance; however, my research showed that despite operating under fixed budgets and increasing pressure for acceptability, little evaluation of the projects was identified. Of the 15 using recreation, only 3 had carried out a formal evaluation and one had just started the evaluation process. This is a serious problem as probation services are faced with increasing pressure to produce evidence on the effectiveness of these programmes.

The Prince's Trust Report (Coopers and Lybrand, 1994) has important implications linked to the cost benefit analysis of investment in sport and recreational projects. Their study highlighted the problems of any analysis of this type; reducing crime can have benefits in terms of community and personal well being, as well as reducing the financial cost of juvenile crime to society. However, one of their case study projects, the Pyramid Project, aimed at tertiary intervention was evaluated in terms of financial costs. Their results show:

> The Pyramid Project is cost effective if 13 of the 96 participants (approximately 1 in 7) are diverted from committing one average youth crime in the course of a 12 month involvement in the project.... (Coopers and Lybrand, 1994: p. 22)

This demonstrates not only that projects can be financially cost-effective even with low levels of success in reducing offending. However their research did not actually collate figures for recidivism and therefore this is still only a framework. If tertiary projects are mainly concerned with persistent offenders, recidivism (no offences) may not give a true financial reflection of the benefits. Schemes should consider their success not only in preventing further offences but also in their success at reducing the number or seriousness of offences for any individual client.

Conclusion

Since the benefits of recreational interventions are not simply aimed at recidivism but also the rehabilitation of young offenders and helping them to develop a more positive role within their communities, schemes must consider more seriously the need to provide evaluation and evidence. The scope for evaluation should however not be restricted to reoffending, but depending on the activities used and the philosophy of intervention, other measures could be considered. Most commonly improved self-esteem is cited as a reason for using both sport and recreation as intervention, and this could be assessed. However, tertiary schemes should carefully consider their objectives and may find that continued constructive use of leisure time, improved employment prospects and changes in attitude to their environment may all be relevant measures of success.

If schemes directed at tertiary level are to flourish and offer benefits as described in this paper in the rehabilitation of young offenders, it is essential that they examine their rationale carefully. In doing this, and by setting measures of success, providers may be more able to communicate a positive image of recreation in tertiary intervention with young offenders. Having clarified the rationale for the use of these activities in tertiary intervention I have explored the validity of the negative perception of these schemes. Research such as Coopers and Lybrand (1994) and Probation Circular 72/1994 (Home Office, 1994) shows that it should be possible to alter many of the negative perceptions but that currently schemes are not providing evidence to support claims to effectiveness. This leaves isolated examples to reinforce the publics view that these schemes are ineffective, costly treats. If this is to change, the most difficult task will be to overcome society's long established attitude that leisure and recreation are rewards. To communicate to society that there is a need to educate young people, particularly those at risk of offending, in the positive use of free time and providing well researched evidence of effectiveness will be fundamental in gaining better acceptance of these projects.

References

Brantingham, P. and Faust, F. (1976) 'A conceptual model of crime prevention', *Crime and Delinquency* , Vol. 22: No. 3: pp. 284-296.

Cooper, B (1989) *The management and prevention of juvenile crime problems*. London: Home Office.

Coopers and Lybrand (1994) *Preventative strategy for young people in trouble*. London: Prince's Trust.

Day, M. J. (1967) 'An adventure experiment with boys on probation ', in A. Mays (ed) *The social treatment of young offenders* . London: Longman.

Everard, K. (1987) Development training — progress and prospects. (private publication).

Gass, A.(1993) *Adventure therapy*. Iowa: Kendall/Hunt.

Hampshire Probation Service (1993) *Annual Report 1992 -1993.*

Home Office (1994) *Demanding activities for offenders in the community* (Conference Report). London.

Hopkins, D. and Putnam, R. (1993) *Personal growth through adventure*. London: David Fulton Press.

Pointing, J. (1986) '"Oh God, It's going to be awful": Clients and officer's perceptions of adventure activities', in P. Maitland (ed) *Alternatives to custody* (Ch. 9). Oxford: Blackwell.

Roberts, K. (1974) *The character training industry*. London: David and Charles.

Robins, D. (1990) *Sport as prevention.* Centre for Criminological Research, Oxford: University of Oxford.

Lord Scarman (1982) *The Scarman Report.* London: Penguin.

Snyder, E. and Spreitzer, E. (1978) *Social aspects of sport.* New Jersey: Prentice Hall.

Webb, B. and Laycock, G. (1992) *Tackling car crime: The nature and extent of the problem.* London: Home Office.

Newspaper articles:

The Guardian (1994) 'Quiet majority dismayed by yobbos sent on sailing cruises' (edited extract of Mr Portillo's Fife speech), 23 April: p. 5.

——— (1994) S. Boseley, 'Holiday crime 'knee-jerk' condemned', 13 August: p. 8.

——— (1994) T. King, 'Guide to social climbing', 9 November: p. 9.

The Times (1994) M. Hook, 'Youth taken to Africa says trip was a waste', 23 September: p. 6.

The Independent (1993) C. Arnot, 'Winestead', 18 October: p. 18.

The Impact of West Yorkshire Sports Counselling on Probation Service Clients

Geoff Nichols

Sheffield University

Introduction

The West Yorkshire Sports Counselling (WYSC) Project has been working with probationers since March 1993 with the aim of reducing 'offending' behaviour. It was developed from a model provided by the Solent Sports Counselling Project (SSCP) which has been in operation since 1985 and the West Yorkshire Sports Counselling Association (WYSCA), which is an independent trust. Initially WYSCA was funded directly by the Home Office but now it is funded by West Yorkshire Probation Service. It operates in all five districts of this probation service, with four sports leaders employed on a part-time basis by the project, and based in the sports development sections of four local authority recreation departments in West Yorkshire. This close link to sports development sections has had considerable advantages in linking the sports leaders to a network of locally available sporting opportunities.

Sports Counselling offers a 12 week programme of sports opportunities to probation service clients. Probationers are told about the project by their probation officers. Participation in the programme is voluntary and not a condition of their probation order. Thus, if a probationer did not attend the programme it would not constitute a breach of their order. This voluntary participation is important because it allows the probationer to have a different quality of relationship with the sports leader compared to that with their probation officer. It also allows for a real sense of achievement on completion of the programme, as completion is a measure of the participant's own commitment. A distinctive feature of sports counselling is the one to one contact between the individual sports leaders and the participants. When a participant starts on the project the sports leader will discuss the range of sports available and a programme is devised to match each individual's needs. In deciding this programme the sports leaders consider the present and past interests of the participant as well as the practicality of continued participation after the twelve week period. Ideally the programme will lead to an 'exit route' that involves each participant continuing to take part in sport independently. There are also some common elements of the programme for each participant, and these include an introduction to local sports facilities, obtaining a concession card for local facility use, and an outdoor pursuits session.

After the twelve week programme there is a possibility of some further contact between the sports leader and the participant. In some areas a weekly group session is organised, which may be attended by probationers waiting to take part in the programme; and which is a way of maintaining both their interest during this period, and also that of past participants. Sports leaders will also act as 'brokers' of opportunities by informing selected participants of opportunities to take part in training schemes or help as volunteers. For example, on completion of a 12-week programme, some participants have attended Football Association leaders awards or have assisted with sessions run by the sports development sections. This continued involvement after the twelve weeks is dependent on the levels of motivation and commitment of the individual participant.

The project is being evaluated by the Leisure Management Unit at Sheffield University. The first report was primarily concerned with the working relationships between WYSC, the local authorities and the probation service (Nichols and Taylor, 1994), and employed a variety of methodological tools: interviews with participants, sports leaders and probation officers; a questionnaire survey of participants (administered at the start of their involvement in the project, the end of the twelve week period of counselling and twelve weeks after this period), and a comparative reconviction rate study. The final evaluation report will focus on the impact of the project on participants, and this paper presents and discusses initial findings related to this. In particular, it argues that a combination of factors in the process of sports counselling can lead to a change in an individual's behaviour through a redefinition of their self-identity.

Methodological and conceptual problems

Previous evaluations of projects that aim to use sport and leisure activities to divert participants from offending behaviour have encountered several inter-related methodological and conceptual problems. Evaluations have been criticised for a lack of methodological rigour in defining what exactly they were measuring (see, for example, Coalter, 1990). The first reason for this was that the concept to be measured had not been defined clearly enough. For example, projects have attempted to reduce delinquency without defining exactly what delinquent behaviour is, and even when this has been done, definitions have not been consistent across projects, making comparison of findings from evaluations difficult. The second reason is that even when the measurement of reconviction rates would seem to be an obvious way of evaluating a project, there are several difficulties in doing this. A rigorous reconviction rate study would match project participants to a control group over a period of at least two years. Clearly, though, this would require sufficiently large samples in each group to produce statistically significant results. The selection of a valid and reliable control group is difficult because those who have volunteered to take part in the project may be less likely to commit crime than those who have not. Thus, differences in reconviction rates between the two groups might reflect differences in the propensity of group members to volunteer to take part in the project, rather than the impact of participation itself. Ideally a control group would be selected from people who have volunteered to attend the project but have not been able to. Even if a control group was successfully set up, results would be limited by the degree to which reconvictions measured offending behaviour because only 3 per cent of offences result in a conviction (Wilkinson, 1994). A reconviction rate study needs to be conducted with the full co-operation of the probation service.

These difficulties in using reconviction rates as the basis of project evaluation have led to research that has addressed other impacts of projects that may contribute to a reduction in offending behaviour. However, if research does not have a clear understanding of how the experiences of the participant on the project might lead to a reduction in offending behaviour (i.e., a rationale for how the project works), it is not able to justify its selection of what to measure. For example, if it was clear that a project reduced the propensity to offend by introducing the participant to a new peer group, then it would be reasonable to measure a change in the participant's peer group before and after participation in the project. However, as this relationship between a changed peer group and a reduction in offending behaviour has not been proven, and in general the understanding of why a project might work is limited, the choice of effects to measure has not been clear either. Programmes themselves frequently lack a clear rationale. In a recent review of 11 programmes, Robins (1990) found that the programme providers had assumed sports participation would reduce crime without analysing why it might do so.

One methodological route out of this dilemma is to combine qualitative and quantitative research to build up a progression of understanding of how a project works. Coalter's (1990) criticism of methodological imprecision was directed towards studies that had used a positivistic approach, using quantitative methods to measure the effects of programmes. Qualitative research, through interviews with participants, sports leaders and probation officers, as well as a review of previous research, can inform the selection and definition of variables to measure. The measurement of these can contribute to an evaluation of the project's effectiveness, but also to a refining of the understanding of how it works. Reconviction rate studies have their place in project evaluations, as a measure of a project's impact on offending, but their inherent limitations require them to be complemented with other research methods, especially when research aims to understand why a project has a particular effect as well as measuring that effect.

Reviews of previous project evaluations have been critical of the lack of reference to previous work. Understandings of how projects might affect offending behaviour have not always built on previous research. It has been difficult to do this because the existing research has covered a wide range of academic disciplines; criminology, sociology, education and the study of adolescence, and either the research has not been widely reported, or it has not been methodologically sound. Importantly, too, there have been few critical syntheses of existing work upon which the researcher could draw (Coalter, 1989; Ewart, 1983; Purdy and Richards, 1983).

As Roberts (1992: p. 11) illustrated, recognition of the value of qualitative research allows for the incorporation of 'common sense' understandings. The gist of Robert's understanding was that, for example, taking part in chases with the police in stolen cars is very exciting, but average citizens might not do this because they have too much societal status to lose. People who *do* have no status to lose.

However, a difficulty with incorporating qualitative understandings is that they reflect value judgements. The use of sport itself as a medium to divert offending behaviour has been justified by value judgements that emerged from the rational recreation movement of the last century and which still inform public policy. At a conference in April 1995 David Maclean MP, Minister of State at the Home Office illustrated this by his reference to, "discredited safari holidays". These sorts of activities were too easily understood by the public as a pleasurable reward for offending behaviour, and the Minister also referred to the need for projects with offenders to involve demanding physical activities, for projects to emphasise the need for offenders to take responsibility for their own actions, and for projects to increase participants' self-confidence. The Minister's comments reflected values judgements rather than research findings, and led to a condemnation of one approach and an advocacy of another. There is a well-reasoned rationale underpinning the 'safari holiday' approach (McNutt, 1994), but prevailing value judgements limit its rational consideration. The difficulties of conducting evaluative research, as outlined above, in a way that will be regarded as methodologically rigorous by both the sceptic and supporter of such projects, means that interpretation of evaluative research is itself more dependant on the value judgements of the interpreter. In this research, qualitative interviews with participants on the project, probation officers and sports leaders, have been very valuable in contributing to an understanding of how participation might reduce offending behaviour.

The development of the research methodology — building on past understandings

The starting point for this research was the rationale provided by WYSC itself and the results of the earlier Sports Council study of the Solent Sports Counselling Project (Sports Council Research Unit, North West.

1990). The rationale for WYSC stated that:

> ... the approach accepts that an individual can develop confidence, self esteem and social skills from the sports experience.... the attraction of such work for those working with offenders is the clear emphasis on constructive use of leisure time, which together with an element of positive involvement in the community may lead to a move away from offending behaviour. Less easy to measure, but of added value, is the potential impact of positive participation and achievement by the individual. (WYSC, 1993)

The main focus of the Sports Council study of the Solent Project had been the impact of the project on sports participation but the study also concluded that major benefits for participants were increased self-confidence and the relationship with the sports leaders. Participants perceived sports leaders as figures in a position of authority, but also as friends from whom they could seek support, in whom they could confide, and from whom they could freely seek advice. This relationship often contrasted with their relationship with probation officers and previous experience of other authority figures. The implications of this are that the sports leaders could provide an alternative role model.

Thus the questionnaire survey of participants aimed to discover changes in sports participation, changes to the context of sport participation, the importance of relationships with the sports leader, involvement in coaching or training sessions, and changes in self-esteem. Self-esteem was measured by a test instrument devised by Warr (Warr and Jackson, 1983) and administered at the start of sports counselling, at the end of the twelve week period and at a follow up meeting twelve weeks later (questionnaires one, two and three). Thus responses could be compared between these periods. Semi-structured interviews with probation officers and sports leaders were also used to explore the impact of the project, and interviewing with a small number of participants was also undertaken. These participants were selected because the sports leaders thought they had benefited significantly from involvement in the project, so they were not necessarily typical. These interviews were very open, allowing interviewees to identify the important benefits they had derived from participating in the project.

Results and discussion

The results reported in this paper are interim. Further interviews and questionnaires will be completed, as well as a comparative reconviction rate study, before the final report on the research is produced in March 1996. The discussion of the results draws on the data collected so far, as well as relating these to results of previous studies and other theoretical contributions. The effects of participation in the project are inter-related but together can contribute to a participant's reappraisal of their self-identity, which may lead to a change in behaviour.

The relationship with the sports leaders

As in the Sports Solent project probation officers felt that the relationship between the sports leaders and the participants on the project was extremely important. As one officer put it, the sports leader is unlike the people probationers would normally encounter in probation work, which confuses probationers at first, but is a good education, challenging the probation officer stereotype. This impression was supported by the participants who were interviewed. One described how she disliked her probation officer and would only turn up for meetings to avoid breaching her probation order, but on the other hand, she had confided a range of personal problems to her sports leader and had sought his assistance on several occasions. This participant's relationship with her probation officer might not be typical, but the relationship with the sports leader was. The contrast between the two relationships was in accord with findings from research into the Sports Solent project. The questionnaire survey also examined this relationship by asking on both the questionnaire completed at the start of sports counselling, and the one completed at the end, 'If you had a difficult problem to sort out and wanted to talk to someone about it, who would you talk to?'. In comparing responses to questionnaires one and two, ten percent (n=9) of respondents who had stated "the sports leader" in the second questionnaire, had not done so in the first.

Thus the sports leaders may be significant role models for the participants. A set of theories attempting to understand the relationship between sports participation and juvenile delinquency have stressed the importance of role models (for example, Purdy and Richards, 1983), though this has usually been in the context of sports coaches and fellow participants. Many of the participants can be considered to be coping with the key task of adolescence, identified by Hendry (1993) as establishing their own sense of self-identity, and in this, role models provided by 'significant others' will be important.

New peers

Alternative role models may also be provided by other sports participants. The sports leaders felt this was important for participants. While recognising that 'you can't get a person to drop all their old friends' there were examples of participants who had become involved in sports teams or clubs. Ten percent of participants played sport in a club at the end of the period of counselling, and had not done so at the start. A good example of this was a participant who now attended a private fitness gym once a week. He was an ex-professional boxer, with a strong personal commitment to personal fitness before he had become involved in drug related crime. At the gym he was able to make friends with other participants similarly committed to fitness training. This participant reported that a benefit of the fitness training was that it kept him away from his old friends who had influenced his drug taking. In some areas it had been possible to run weekly sports sessions for participants who had finished their twelve week period of counselling, and these sessions were also attended by participants on the programme at the moment and those that were waiting to take part. These sessions also provided a new group of peers.

Increased self-esteem

The measures of self-esteem on the questionnaires showed that between the completion of questionnaire 1 and questionnaire 2 there was a mean increase in the self-esteem score of 3.4, out of a possible maximum score of 40. Between the completion of questionnaire 2 and questionnaire 3 there was a slight drop in mean score of 0.7. Thus self-esteem had increased during the period of counselling and then dropped down slightly twelve weeks later on, but still remained above its original level. The relatively small number of participants completing questionnaires 2 and 3 limits this analysis; but the general picture of increased self esteem is supported by the sports leaders and probation officers. However, even if self-esteem is increased a link has to be made between this and a change away from offending behaviour. This may be through giving the individual greater confidence to experiment with alternative self-identities. This was the case for one participant who after being involved in crime since the age of 14 had now developed the confidence to take initial qualifications in youth work. This confidence had been nurtured by the sports leader and the youth worker in charge of the club where this participant was presently working voluntarily. Following the period of counselling the sports leader had invited this participant to attend further training courses in football leadership, first aid and nutrition, but had also attended himself. Without this support the participant would not have attended the courses but now the participant's confidence was sufficient to enable him to take on the course in youthwork himself. This illustrates the need to support participants through a progressively more challenging set of experiences.

It has not always been possible to provide this degree of support to participants after the twelve week counselling period. Another participant had been introduced to aerobics sessions while on the project, which she enjoyed and these had motivated her to get out of the house. Ideally the sports leader would have linked her to a voluntary support worker who would have continued to attend aerobics sessions with her until she felt confident enough to go on her own. This was not possible and lack of confidence, compounded with the difficulties of childcare, cost and travel, prevented her attending again.

Participants gained self-esteem from their completion of the programme, at which they are awarded a certificate. This certificate is very important for some participants — it can be the only such achievement they have had and represents the personal commitment required to complete the programme. Self-esteem may also be derived from sporting achievement itself. Many previous studies have reported the positive impact of programmes on self-esteem. For example, in an extensive review of research into the impact of Outward Bound courses in America, Ewart

(1983) reported a general finding that self-esteem was improved.

However, increased self-esteem might not necessarily lead to a change in an individual's behaviour. To help understand how this might occur self-esteem could be linked to the concept of locus of control. This concept describes the extent to which an individual feels able to control the outcome of their experiences and the extent to which they feel powerless in the face of external circumstances. It is measured on an internal-external scale. For example, an individual might feel that they would like to train to get a job and they have the confidence to embark on the training, but the prospect of getting a job is so remote that it is not worth doing it. In this instance the individual's locus of control would be low. The concept has been refined to differentiate between three 'spheres of influence' (Paulhus, 1983). These are: personal efficacy — which refers to control over the non-social environment (for example, personal sporting achievement); interpersonal control — which refers to control over personal relationships; and socio-political control — which refers to control over social and political events and institutions. This differentiation between 'spheres of influence' explains why an individual may feel that they have a considerable influence in one sphere of influence, for example, personal achievement in sport, but little influence over another, such as obtaining a job or government policy. A significant positive relationship exists between sporting achievement and high 'internal' locus of control (Paulhus, 1983). Some studies of the impact of Outward Bound courses have also reported an increase in locus of control (Ewart 1983). The relationship between self-esteem and locus of control may be important for understanding why increased self-esteem might lead to a reduction in crime. If an individual achieved a more realistic view of their locus of control, this might help them to recognise where apparent past failures were not a true reflection of their own capabilities, and therefore were less threatening to their self-esteem. For example, failure to obtain employment or educational qualifications might not have such a detrimental effect on an individual's self-esteem if the individual realised that they were significantly disadvantaged in the job or education markets. Without this recognition of disadvantage an individual who had experienced educational or social failure may have tried to protect their self-esteem by attributing their 'failure' to a system over which they had little control. In this instance they might subsequently underestimate their locus of control. A more realistic view of locus of control might help an individual to re-appraise their self-identity and allow them to be more selectively pro-active where they felt that they would gain the rewards of their own efforts. Thus participants need to be helped towards a more realistic perception of locus of control if they are to be able to take full advantage of increased self-esteem, and a change in locus of control may itself increase self-esteem.

Increased internal locus of control can be related to one of the sets of theories identified by Purdy and Richard (1983), explaining a link between sports participation and juvenile delinquency. These theories linked non-delinquent behaviour to a belief that the social system would deliver just rewards. Conversely, delinquency has been related to a belief in the injustice of the system. This is similar to Roberts' (1992) understanding of juvenile crime as promoted by a feeling of injustice in society. Therefore if increased internal locus of control reduced a belief that the system was unjust, it would also reduce offending behaviour. This research did not apply tests to measure changes in locus of control as they were considered too complex to administer. The relationship between locus of control and self-esteem could be explored in future research.

Increased self-esteem, and locus of control at the interpersonal level, could also lead to increased competence in managing interpersonal relations. Research by Ross and Fabiano (1985) in America and Canada has claimed to understand a large proportion of criminal activity as the consequence of 'cognitive deficiencies'. By this they meant; an inability to solve interpersonal problems and deal with social relationships; a lack of self control; a lack of the ability to reason abstractly; low locus of control; and an inability to feel empathy with other people. Ross and Fabiano reviewed 50 programmes designed to reduce offending behaviour which had been rigorously evaluated. They concluded that 21 of the 25 programmes that had been successful in reducing reconviction rates had attempted to develop participants' cognitive skills. From this Ross and Fabiano developed an understanding of criminal behaviour as being predisposed by a set of cognitive deficiencies. The research on WYSC did not attempt to measure explicitly changes in the cognitive skills identified by Ross and Fabiano, but the discussion above of the inter-relation of increased self-esteem and a more realistic locus of control suggests ways in which these effects could lead to a development of such skills.

Increased fitness

The questionnaires asked participants to rate their fitness on a 5-point scale. Over the twelve week period of participation in the project this had risen an average of one point. In a study of 10,000 young people in Scotland, Hendry et al. (1993: p. 72) found a significant relationship between participation in sport and perceived physical and mental health, for males. This was an especially strong relationship for males involved in team sports although the relationship was not significant amongst females. Improved mental health and fitness had helped one participant on the project to cope better with problems, and this had contributed to her stopping using heroin, which she had previously used as an escape when she could not cope. For another participant the commitment to personal fitness had become such an important part of his life that it was incompatible with drug use and it had provided an alternative central life interest.

Other impacts of participation in the project

Eighty seven percent of the participants were unemployed when they started sports counselling. The project gave them something to do and a significant boost to their general motivation. Just filling time with an activity can reduce the propensity to take part in offending and can give structure and purpose to peoples' lives. These findings are similar to those from studies of sports schemes targeted at the unemployed (Glyptis, 1989). Similar to participants on these sports schemes, sport may offer an additional dimension to someone's life without becoming a central life interest or a substitute for paid work. These effects are illustrated by a participant who was a single parent with two young children. She had moved to a new area to get away from her husband and knew nobody where she now lived. It was difficult for her to meet people. For this client the project had given her "something to do in the day, to get out of the house".

Conclusions on the overall impact of the project

The discussion above has indicated several effects of the project on participants and has considered how they might contribute to a reduction in offending behaviour. This is illustrated in Figure 1.

Effects will be of different relative importance for different participants but in any one case they may interact to contribute to a redefinition of the participant's self concept which may lead to a reduction in offending behaviour. The sports leader provides a role model of a person who has a stake in society and a degree of authority, but to whom the participant can relate and form a strong personal relationship. New peers, met in the context of sports participation or other exit routes after the twelve week

Figure 1 Contributions to a new self-identity

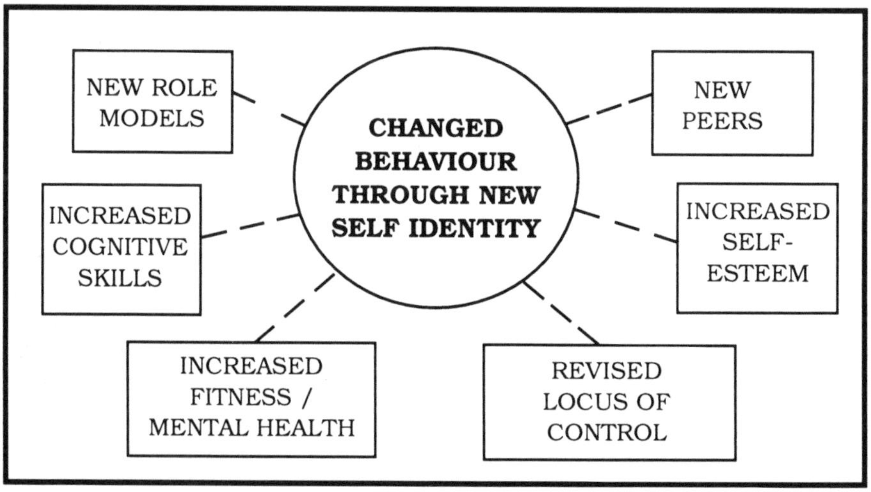

programme, can provide other alternative role models. Self-esteem may be enhanced through participation and, crucially, this will enable participants to take personal risks in trying out new self-identities. The exit routes themselves provide the opportunity for participants to adopt new roles. For example, one participant has taken a football leadership award and has now been invited to coach a woman's team. Another has started working as a voluntary youth leader and a third has become recommitted to a role that involves serious fitness training. The new roles have taken the participants away from former peers who are involved in criminal and drug cultures. Participants need to be nurtured through this increase in self-confidence to a stage where they can take charge of their own further development. A change in perceived locus of control could lead to a more positive outlook on opportunities and an increased willingness to move away from criminal behaviour. Increased fitness can lead to an increase in mental health, which could be related to increased self-confidence and an increased locus of control.

Much of this understanding of how the project might reduce offending behaviour is summed up in the observations of one of the participants. To paraphrase his observations:

> "The major effect of WYSC has to been to motivate me to do things, 'to get off my arse'. Crime is addictive. To get out of it you have to first get away from friends who are committing crimes and then move to a new area. When you have little money it is very tempting to commit crime when you see friends walking down the road with new clothes and things they have got as a result of crime the previous night. Once you have got into crime you realise how easy it is. So it is hard to break out of it."

The central concept in the understanding of the impact of the project offered by this paper has been the way in which a participant can be helped to change their behaviour through adopting a revised self-identity. This approach draws on sociological theory that stresses the ability of the individual to freely develop their own self-identity through social interaction, especially in leisure contexts (Kelly, 1983). However, the structural constraints remain considerable, especially for these participants. The circumstances of poverty and peers that predisposed them to criminal behaviour are still present. This was illustrated by a participant who stated on his questionnaire at completion of the programme that the project was "the best thing I've ever done". His sports leader regarded him as one of the project's best clients and his probation officer felt that sports counselling had helped him apply for a training course and successfully complete the interview. A couple of weeks later the participant was charged with a previous offence, went back their old peers in a different part of the country and died from causes related to drug use.

Conclusions on the methodology

The methodology employed in this study attempted to overcome, as far as was practical, the deficiencies of previous studies. The selection of effects of participation in the project to measure quantitatively was based on the findings of previous research. These measurements were complemented by qualitative interviews and case studies. The results of these two approaches have been interpreted with reference to other previous research and theoretical contributions from a broad range of work in criminology, sociology, psychology and the study of adolescence. This broad range of theoretical contributions has led to an understanding of the impact of participation in the project in terms of a participant's change in self-identity. This provides the starting point for future research, which could choose to measure quantitatively such changes.

References

Coalter, F. (1989) *Sport and anti-social behaviour, a literature review*. Edinburgh: Scottish Sports Council.

Coalter, F. (1990) 'Sport and anti-social behaviour: hits and myths', in J. Long, (ed) *Leisure, health and well-being*. LSA Publication No. 44. Eastbourne: Leisure Studies Association, pp. 145-154.

Ewart. A. (1983) *Outdoor adventure and self-concept: a research analysis*. University of Oregon: Centre of Leisure Studies.

Glyptis, S. (1989) *Leisure and unemployment*. Milton Keynes: Open University Press.

Hendry, L. B., Shucksmith, J., Love, J. G. and Glendinning, A. (1993) *Young people's leisure and lifestyles*. London: Routledge.

Kelly, J. R. (1983) *Leisure identities and interactions*. London: George Allen and Unwin.

McNutt, B. (1994) 'Adventure as therapy: using adventure as part of therapeutic programmes with young people in trouble and at risk', in J. Barrett (ed) *Adventure-Based interventions with young people in trouble and at risk*. Dumfries: Basecamp, Marthrown of Mabie, Mabie Forest.

Nichols, G. and Taylor, P. (1994) *West Yorkshire Sports Counselling Project, evaluation — first report*. Castleford: West Yorkshire Sports Counselling Association.

Paulhus, D. (1983) 'Sphere-specific measures of perceived control', *Journal of Personality and Social Psychology*, Vol. 44, No. 6: pp. 1253-1265.

Purdy, D. A. and Richard, S. F. (1983) Sport and juvenile delinquency: an examination and assessment of four major theories, *Journal of Sport Behaviour*, Vol. 6, No. 4.

Roberts, K. (1992) 'Leisure responses to urban ills in Great Britain and Northern Ireland', in J. Sugden and C. Knox (eds) *Leisure in the 1990s: Rolling back the Welfare State*. LSA Publication No. 46. Eastbourne: Leisure Studies Association.

Robins, D. (1990) *Sport as prevention: The role of sport in crime prevention programmes aimed at young people. Occasional Paper No. 12.* University of Oxford: Centre for Criminological Research.

Ross, R. and Fabiano, E. (1985) *Time to think: A cognitive model of delinquency prevention and offender rehabilitation.* Ottawa: T3 Associates.

Sports Council Research Unit, North West (1990) *Solent Sports Counselling Project final evaluation report.* London: Sports Council.

Warr, P. and Jackson, P. (1983) 'Self-esteem and unemployment among young workers', *Le Travail Human*, Vol. 46. No. 2: pp. 355-364.

Wilkinson, J. (1994) 'Using a reconviction predictor to make sense of reconviction rates in the probation service', *British Journal of Social Work*, Vol. 24. No. 4: pp. 461-475.

WYSC (1993) West Yorkshire Sports Counselling Project: Information Pack, available from West Yorkshire Sports Counselling, Five Towns Resource and Technology Centre, Welbeck St, Castleford, WF10 1DR.

The Role of Sport and Leisure in the Rehabilitation of Offenders

Alex Twitchen

Chichester Institute of Higher Education

In addressing public school headteachers at their conference in September 1994, Sir Roger Bannister spoke of the value that participation in sport may have on the education of young people. In his opinion, regular involvement in sport helps the young avoid developing into "immoral, uncouth, contentedly unfit and flabby adults" (*Daily Mail*, 23rd September 1994). The benefits he spoke of centred on notions of character building, improved health and the promotion of sporting excellence. These benefits are those in which the Minister for Sport, Iain Sproat, shares belief and has championed during a well publicised campaign to promote the place and status of sport, particularly team sports, in schools during both curriculum and extra-curricular time.

These sentiments reflect a deeply ingrained view of sport as a valuable tool, capable, amongst other attributes, of educating people towards sound moral citizenship. It has also been the keystone of the Government's recent policy document, "Raising the Game" in which the Prime Minister writes:

> It (sport) is one of the best means of learning how to live alongside others and make a contribution as part of a team. It improves health and it opens the door to new friendships. (Department of National Heritage, 1995: p. 2)

Similarly this perception of what sport is, and can do, has been used as a guiding principle for projects and schemes that seek to prevent delinquent behaviour and help avoid recidivism by those who have already offended. However, in the view of Coalter, "...much of this is based on a varying mixture of belief, conviction, intuition and ad hominem arguments, with little reference to systematic research findings", (1988: p. 1). This paper examines the role of sport and leisure in the rehabilitation of offenders. It will summarise the recommendations from past research and critically explore the effects of sports and leisure based schemes by drawing on the work of Michel Foucault (1977, 1980).

In assessing the value of sport as a means of preventing delinquent behaviour, Segrave and Hastad (1984a) illustrate the complexities of seeking causal relationships between athletic participation and delinquency. They are of the opinion that "the efficacy of sport...as an antidote to delinquency is by no means settled" (1984b: p. 37). This opinion is shared by Coalter (1988) in a review of the literature on sport and anti-social behaviour. Robins (1990) also concedes that there is a lack of substantive evidence, but suggests that from the schemes examined, which dealt specifically with young people:

> there is no evidence at all that participation...makes things worse. On the contrary, there is plenty of impressionistic and anecdotal evidence available that they do individual youngsters a great deal of good. (Robins, 1990: p. 94)

Coalter and Robins examined a variety of schemes and projects which aimed to prevent initial and further delinquency. The differing contexts within which the schemes were located, variations in concepts of what constituted "success" and different definitions of "sport" and "delinquency" made it difficult to draw out specific conclusions. However a number of general observations were made. Those which are most relevant to preventing recidivism may be summarised as:

1) **Appropriateness of activities used**: Some activities reflect competitive, formal and institutional aspects of a society in which offenders have little experience of success or fulfilment. As such these activities may not be the most effective to use. Non-competitive, individual, activities may be more appropriate. In light of this observation it is pertinent to consider concepts of sport in a "loose" and less specific manner than simply those of organised, competitive activities.

2) **Pursuing a client centred approach**: If the effectiveness of a physical recreation programme is to be maximised, individuals need to determine and be empowered to decide on their level of commitment and the type of activities in which they participate. This is the basis of the "sports therapy" approach which is employed at the Solent Sports Counselling Project (Coalter, 1988).

3) **Commitment to the programme**: Any form of formal or informal physical activity will not be effective in achieving its desired goal if the individuals concerned do not feel attached or committed to the programme. This reinforces the need to create programmes that empower the individual.

4) **Sphere of influence**: An offender's exposure to sports and physical activities represents just one source of values in a field of experience. As such, any positive benefits of participation may be outweighed by negative experiences elsewhere.

The key lessons to be learnt from previous experience would appear to be that: the type of activity needs to be carefully applied; each individual needs to be able to feel empowered and able to determine his/her choice of activities; and that formal sports are just one set of a much wider range of physical recreational and leisure activities that may be encompassed within any scheme or project. Perhaps most importantly the research points towards individual counselling and specifically dealing with each individual and matching any expressed interests to appropriate activities. This has been undertaken in West Sussex where the probation service has entered into a partnership arrangement with Youth Clubs Sussex to help clients participate in a range of activities that are already present in the community (Correspondence with West Sussesx Probation Service).

Clients are referred by their probation officer to the Leisure and Education Officer who then discusses what type of activities the client might wish to pursue. Any interest is then met by matching the client to a suitable person drawn from a pool of accredited volunteers. These volunteers receive training that deals with issues of confidentiality and health and safety. The ethos of the volunteer scheme is very similar to that of the "sports therapy" approach in that each individual is counselled and directed towards activities in which they have expressed an interest and would appear suitably motivated towards. The volunteer then accompanies the client to the sessions for the duration of the probation period. From anecdotal evidence and reports going back to probation officers this scheme appears to have been relatively successful in making an important contribution to clients self-esteem and confidence.

The use of volunteers and partnership arrangements has been one means of circumventing the financial constraints that the probation service currently experiences, a reflection of the hardships faced by all public services. It is also a means of accommodating the growing number of clients for whom the service is responsible. This has arisen partly as a result of the 1991 Criminal Justice Act which directed magistrates and judges towards using a greater number of community sentence orders (as opposed to custodial sentences) particularly with young offenders (Bretherton, 1991: Ian Nesbitt, 1993: Worthington, 1993). However research does suggest that in some cases supervision by volunteers may in any case be more effective than that conducted by probation officers. Andrews and Keissling (cited in McIvor, 1992) observed that for those who were assessed as having a high risk of re-offending, supervision by volunteers was more effective than supervision by probation officers. Hollin (1992: p. 134) cites the research of Fo and O'Donnell who devised a "buddy" programme where young offenders were paired with adult volunteers. A two-year follow-up study showed improvements in the offending rates of serious offenders but an increased arrest rate amongst those who had committed minor offences.

The pursuance of a client-centred approach (by the West Sussex Probation Service) using volunteers where appropriate, is identical to

the ethos of the "sports therapy" approach used by the Solent Sports Counselling Scheme. These share a common approach in that the individual body is the site and focus of the rehabilitation process.
Michel Foucault (1977) writes:

> ... we can surely accept the general proposition that, in our societies, the systems of punishment are to be situated in a certain political economy of the body:...it is always the body that is at issue — the body and its forces, their utility and their docility, their distribution and their submission. (Foucault: 1977: p. 25)

For Foucault the body becomes the site upon which power is invested and discipline instilled. This stems from the necessity of a specific set of historical conditions through which modern societies organise individuals into a productive and efficient economic system (Harvey and Sparks, 1991). In undertaking an analysis of this process, Foucault develops a series of conceptual tools for understanding the relationship between power, knowledge, discourse, and the body. Power is understood within a framework whereby it does not belong to a specific group or stem from economic and political foundations, but is omnipresent, agent-less and evident within all social relations. It is "fundamentally relational, which is to say that power is expressed in the multiplicity of day-to-day relations of people with social institutions, discourse and other people" (Harvey and Sparks, 1991: p. 166). Power, according to Foucault, is the term given to a strategy that is utilised to invest the body with the properties that make it pliable and receptive to technologies of control and normalisation. It permeates bodily gestures, what we say and the way we learn to work and live together (Foucault, 1980). In this respect power is approached from a micro level and its effects examined in relation to the specific contexts and locations that it is operating, but which at the same time form the links which uncover the broader macro effects of power. Foucault is also of the opinion that power is not inherently repressive, negative or alienating, rather it can be positive and productive. As he maintains, "We must cease once and for all to describe the effects of power in negative terms ... In fact, power produces; it produces reality" (Foucault, 1977: p. 194).

An analysis of discourse also plays a fundamental role in this concept of power. Foucault views discourse as being the socially defined modes of symbols, language and knowledge of everyday relations which are permeated with the effects of power. Furthermore discourse "produces" the body and has in the transition from pre-modern to modern societies changed so that its focus is not so much with the biological body but with the mind of the body. In his analysis of sexuality, Foucault explores how in the middle ages sex was primarily as act of the "fleshy body", but through the Reformation and Counter Reformation the church began to inquire into in the intentions of people as well as their actions and subsequently the focus of sexual discourse shifted from the physical body to the mind of the body (Shilling, 1993: p. 76).

Sport itself is imbued with discourse, not just generally but also specifically. All sports have their own language, gestures, knowledge and customs which become ingrained into the practices of individual participants. For example long distance runners will often become obsessive about the number of miles covered in weekly training, the type of "sessions" completed, the times for each "session", and the food consumed. The power of this discourse and its requirements shapes behaviour often resulting in very disciplined lives. Much of this discourse is consumed through a burgeoning array of images and signs that modern consumer culture communicates through the mass media. Whilst much of this focuses on the "fleshy" body, the discourse stimulates intention, to get fit, be active, achieve these goals, run this time, take this to help, eat this, drink this. The discourse focuses on the mind of the individual first and foremost, the biological aspect of the body being influenced by the intent of the mindful body.

Foucault (1977) also explores the transformation of punishment as a means of demonstrating the shifting focus of discursive practice from the biological body to the mindful body. In pre-modern societies punishment was often considered to be, necessarily, physically painful. Criminals would be executed in a public spectacle where the body was a highly visible object of repression. This is superseded by placing criminals in jails where their minds become the subject of discursive practices through which they become more self-restrained in their behaviour. Foucault takes the example of Bentham's Panopticon, a circular prison built so that prisoners can be observed by the guards without the guards being seen, as a means of illustrating the process by which discipline becomes instilled and self-regulating. In the Panopticon, the prisoners can always see the central watchtower but remain uncertain as to whether they are actually being watched. As a result of this uncertainty the prisoners are encouraged towards the voluntary exertion of greater self-control over behaviour. As well as prisons, institutions such as schools, hospitals, and factories act as forums whereby surveillance is undertaken and individuals become docile, disciplined bodies. Equally the discourse of non-institutionalised disciplinary technologies, such as the knowledge accumulated with respect to the health of human bodies, act as complementary structures of knowledge which contribute to the ethos of discipline (Andrews, 1993). The outcome of this process is the primacy of self-restraint and self-discipline over external regulation, where discipline provides the means by which appropriate and normal behaviour is learnt rather than imposed (Rojek, 1995).

The intensity, means and sophistication of surveillance has been a continually developing process which has promoted an increasingly disciplinary society. Contemporary means of surveillance involve ever more complex technical solutions which enable more individuals to be scrutinised without the knowledge (or at least uncertainty) as to whether their actions and behaviour are being observed. An example of this process is the casings in which speed cameras are fitted. These have proliferated on road sides but drivers cannot be certain whether the cameras are in fact fitted inside. However, the effect of spotting a camera casing is that drivers are encouraged to curb excess speed *in case* the camera is fitted. This reflects the permanence of the surveillance effect, even though it may be discontinuous in its action; and also that the perfection of power should be to render its actual use unnecessary (Foucault, 1977: p. 201) since, in this example, drivers exercise self-restraint in adhering to the speed limit.

Likewise, growth in knowledge has heightened individual awareness and disposition towards exerting self-discipline over many bodily actions. Smoking is now known to cause cancer, regular exercise is important to maintain a healthy body, diets containing foodstuffs with too much saturated fat can increase the likelihood of coronary heart disease. The accumulation and dissemination of this knowledge stimulates increased individual awareness about our bodies and the regimes required to keep the body fit and healthy. This is reinforced through the discourse of modern capitalist societies which promote a normal type of body shape that is intrinsically related to regular exercise and the consumption of a balanced diet. This requires varying degrees of disciplinary behaviour in aspiring to meet and fulfil the notion of what society defines as being a normal body shape. In modern consumer cultures anything that deviates from being an athletic, slim and fit body may be viewed as being deviant and in need of corrective treatment, unless it is the body shape required for a specific context.

In Foucault's opinion then, society is comprised of a series of inter-related disciplining technologies which make judgements about, exert power, and permeate everyday relations. This promotes normative behaviour through disciplined self-regulation of individual actions. Foucault suggests that we are situated within:

> ... the society of the teacher-judge, the doctor-judge, the educator-judge, the social worker-judge; it is on them that the universal reign of the normative is based; and each individual, wherever he may find himself, subjects to it his body, his gestures, in its compact or disseminated forms, with its systems of insertion, distribution, surveillance, observation, has been the greatest support, in modern society, of the normalising power. (Foucault, 1977: p. 304)

With these observations in mind the application of Foucault's work within the sociology of sport has focused on situating the human body at the centre of critical analysis whilst exploring the nature of disciplining mechanisms within sport. Hargreaves (1986) draws on the work of Foucault to develop a critical understanding of physical education which identifies how it operates to develop individual adherence to dominant conceptions of normative behaviour. Hargreaves details the ritual nature of physical education, the environment of control and discipline in which the subject is conducted, and the opportunities for surveillance that it affords. Heikkala (1993) interprets the discipline attached to competitive participation in sport through examining the specific means by which discipline is instilled into the bodies of athletes and through which athletes acquire the self-discipline necessary to complement external techniques of discipline and produce competitive performances. Examples include the production of training schedules, training diaries, conforming to set goals and targets, testing and the monitoring of performance and the conformity to the institutional customs and rules of sport. In the opinion of Heikkala (1993: p. 398), sport "is a prime example of the production of disciplined bodies". Foucault has also inspired a number of post-structuralist feminist writers to explore the means through which modern patriarchal power is exercised. This analysis involves mapping out the range of disciplinary practices that produce a recognisably female body and consequently maintain and reproduce patriarchal relationships (Theberge, 1991). In general, Foucault's ideas may be valuable wherever the disciplining, normalising mechanisms of sport are the central focus of examination (Maguire, 1993).

Interpreting empirical evidence within a Foucauldian framework would appear to offer a favourable avenue through which to explore and examine the efficacy of using sport and leisure amongst offenders. The probation service is an organisation that undertakes the surveillance of offenders and initiates programmes that may lead to a prevention of re-offending. It can be thought of as a type of "auxiliary institution" (Foucault, 1977: p. 270) facilitating the rehabilitation of the criminal. In this case the means by which recidivism is potentially averted becomes a critical issue in the work of the service. Furthermore, the effectiveness of the probation services' work is dependent upon the degree to which clients begin to assimilate a greater degree of self-regulation and self-restraint in avoiding patterns of behaviour that may have previously led to offences being committed. According to the West Sussex Probation Service Annual Review (1995: p. 1) "...probation officers' work is targeted at individual and group work programmes which tackle offending and motivate offenders to take more control over their lives." The probation service consequently plays an active role in facilitating the investment of disciplining discourses into individuals. The manner in which this is achieved and the techniques used will be dependent upon a number of factors, but the essence is to achieve the same outcome, that of disciplined and normalised bodies who no longer transgress societal notions of delinquency.

The extent to which a framework drawing on the thoughts of Foucault can be used to understand this process may be limiting in at least one central concern. Foucault's ideas proudly rejected any notion of grand or meta-narratives. For Foucault such grand theories try to piece together an understanding of human action, society and social change which is built on the premise of collective and universal principles that organise and are at the centre of modern societies. In Foucault's opinion there are no orienting principles that govern lived experiences, reality is a relativist construction in which principles that organise society are not in any sense real but produced themselves through discursive formations. This approach has led a number of commentators to interpret Foucault's work as a decentring of traditional sociological understandings of society and towards a relativism that precludes any sense of emancipatory change. Wapner (1989) states:

> ... decentring provides no countervision from which to criticise the status quo and towards which to orientate social change. It provides no notion of freedom or truth or the good life and hence offers no purchase point from which to criticise, or blueprint to consult for social reconstruction. Indeed, it is premised on the view that nothing can possibly play these roles. (Wapner, 1989: p. 106)

In this interpretation of Foucault's work there is, arguably, little value in trying to rehabilitate offenders. There is no sense of a real, better lifestyle that can be aspired to through the help of the probation service. All lifestyles, in this regard, are relative and any notions of freedom, choice, personal fulfilment, legitimate and non-legitimate leisure activities are the redundant baggage of humanism and the modernity theorists narrative of enlightenment.

By contrast, Michele Barrett (1991) argues that a more appropriate task is to review the "old conception of relativism" (p. 162) that relationships between discourse and the real world are cast in a different manner when viewed with ideas drawn from Foucault. Barrett reaches this conclusion through examining Foucault's theorising as primarily an attempt to counter the entrenched notions of ideology that derive from Marx and those who have developed ideas based on his writings and the spirit in which they were written. I feel that Barrett, in highlighting this context, steers a direction towards enabling an appropriation of Foucault's ideas for deriving a framework of analysis that can begin to understand how the use of sports and leisure activities can be of value to the probation service; and in particular, the ideological basis on which sports and leisure activities are deemed legitimate and purposeful means of rehabilitating offenders. I concur with Barrett's view that it is "better, perhaps, that we oblige ourselves to think with new and more precise concepts, rather than mobilising the dubious resonance's of the old" (Barret, 1991: p. 168).

What is initially apparent is that the probation service such as that in West Sussex has developed a range of techniques that operate to supervise its clients and that these can be carefully tailored to suit the needs of each individual. This somewhat follows from the development of a more disciplinary society in which the technologies of surveillance are sophisticated and highly developed. It is the body which is the site of this process and the subject of control and normalisation, and in particular it is the mind which is primarily the focus of attention as opposed to the biological body.

Foucault's ideas are also helpful in directing research to uncovering and examining the localised narrative in which probation service clients are located and dealing with the specifics of the context in which each individual engages in sport and leisure activities.

In dealing with sport and leisure specifically, I wish to investigate through further empirical work, the mechanisms by which the discourse associated with the undertaken activities may help offenders make positive changes to behaviour. Robins cites the comment of a sixteen year old member of the Walsall Wood Police Amateur Boxing Club, which was established to try and prevent crime, as a reflection of the effect participation in sport may have. It was the view of the member that:

> Before I took up boxing I always used to get into fights and everything. If anyone used to say anything bad to me I used to turn round and smack 'em one. But over the last few years I know that boxing has taught me to control myself because of the self-discipline. (Robins, 1990: p. 54)

This comment highlights the potential sport and leisure activities have for preventing recidivism. It also reveals the disciplinary and observational technology associated with the discourse of sport, and in this particular case boxing. However in my opinion the relationship between rehabilitation and participation is by no means as simple and straightforward as the assumptions some would have, which, ultimately, are based on the contingent notions of public school athleticism. In particular no one activity or group of activities are better than others, no one type of offender is more susceptible to changing their behaviour as a result of participation than another, no type of supervision is more effective than another. In my view there is a complex relationship between discourse, power and discipline, the tenets of Foucault's theory, with participation in sport and leisure. What I want to explore are the local narratives on which participation in sport and leisure activities are grounded — teasing out specifically, not generally, the effects of power and then mapping these formations into a more systematic picture — whilst, perhaps unlike post-modernity theorists, maintaining a commitment to a concept of emancipation. I would argue that social life goes beyond the mere relativist interaction of discursive formations, that it is organised around a moral framework, arguably what Foucault may have described as the extradiscursive, which is more fundamental and secure than layers of discourse that interlink and overlap.

Sport and leisure can play a role in the process of rehabilitation but how and why does involvement translate into exercising the effects of power, through discourse, into more disciplined and normalised individuals? How can the variety of opportunities be matched to individuals, soc genuinely empowering and enabling changes in behaviour which offer liberation from the oppressive effects of power?

References

Andrews, D. (1993) 'Desperately seeking Michel: Foucault's genealogy, the body, and critical sport sociology', *Sociology of Sport Journal*, Vol. 10, No. 2: pp. 148-167.

Barrett, M. (1991) *The politics of truth: From Marx to Foucault.* Cambridge: Polity Press

Bretherton, H. (1991) 'Partnerships in practice', *Probation Journal*, Vol. 38, No. 3: pp. 132-135.

Coalter, F. (1988) *Sport and anti-social behaviour: A literature review.* Edinburgh: Scottish Sports Council.

Daily Mail (1994) 'A sporting life curbs yobs, says Bannister', 23 September: p. 33.

Department of National Heritage (1995) *Raising the game.* London.

Foucault, M. (1977) *Discipline and punish: The birth of the prison.* London: Allen Lane.

——— (1980) 'Two lectures', in C. Gordon (ed) *Michel Foucault: Power/ knowledge.* Brighton: Harvester Press.

Hargreaves, J. (1986) *Sport, power and culture.* Cambridge: Polity Press.

Harvey, J. and Sparks, R. (1991) 'The politics of the body in the context of modernity', *Quest*, Vol. 43, No. 2: pp. 164- 189.

Heikkala, J. (1993) 'Discipline and excel: Techniques of the self and body and the logic of competing', *Sociology of Sport Journal*, Vol. 10, No. 4: pp. 397-412.

Hollin, C. (1992) *Criminal behaviour: A psychological approach to explanation and prevention.* London: Falmer Press.

McIvor, G. (1992) 'Intensive probation supervision: Does more mean better?', *Probation Journal*, Vol. 39, No. 1: pp. 2-6.

Maguire, J. (1993) 'Bodies, sportscultures and societies: A critical review of some theories in the sociology of the body', *International Review for the Sociology of Sport*, Vol. 28, No. 1: pp. 33-50.

Nesbitt, I. (1993) 'The Criminal Justice Act. 1991: Implications for young offenders', *Youth and Policy*, No. 41: pp. 44-46.

Rail, G. and Harvey, J. (1995) 'Body at work: Michel Foucault and the sociology of sport', *Sociology of Sport Journal*, Vol. 12, No. 2: pp. 164-179.

Robins, D. (1990) *Sport as prevention: The role of sport in crime prevention programmes aimed at young people.* Oxford: Centre for Criminological Research.

Rojek, C. (1995) *Decentring leisure.* London: Sage.

Segrave, J. and Hastad, D. (1984a) 'Interscholastic athletic participation and delinquent behaviour: An empirical assessment of relevant variables', *Sociology of Sport Journal,* Vol. 1, No. 2: pp. 117-137.

——— (1984b) 'Future directions in sport and juvenile delinquency research', *Quest,* Vol. 36, No. 1: pp. 37-47.

Shilling, C (1993) *The body and social theory.* London: Sage.

Theberge, N. (1991) 'Reflections on the body in the sociology of sport', *Quest,* Vol. 43, No. 2: pp. 123-134.

Wapner, P (1989) 'What's left: Marx, Foucault and contemporary problems of social change', *Praxis International,* Vol. 9, pp. 89-111

West Sussex Probation Service (1995) *Annual Review,* Chichester.

Worthington, M. (1993) 'The Criminal Justice Act 1991: New ways of dealing with adolescent offenders in England and Wales', *Youth and Policy,* No. 41: pp. 38-42.

III

Policy Challenges: Sport Spaces and Sites of Consumption

Responsible Tourism: A Model for the Greening of Alpine Ski Resorts

Simon Hudson

University of Brighton

Introduction

As the tourist industry moves into the next century it will face the increasing problem of achieving not growth but a quality of tourist experience that is consistent with sustaining both physical and social environments (Ryan, 1991). With an increasing number of conferences and publications dedicated to 'responsible' or 'alternative' tourism it appears that academics at least are addressing the key environmental issues arising from the impacts of modern tourism. The mountains are among Europe's most threatened wilderness, with the rapid growth of skiing central to the crisis. Skiing, in both practice and infrastructure, is causing numerous environmental problems which consequently give rise to serious challenges for the winter sports industry.

Impact of skiing on the environment

The Alps account for one quarter of the world's total tourism revenue. An estimated 100 million people visit the Alps each year and with them have come the problems of pollution and erosion. Despite its apparent strength, the Alpine environment supports a very fragile ecosystem. Any human impact is felt twice as strongly there than lower down in the valleys. Destruction has been caused by deforestation and altering the use of traditional Alpine land for construction of dams, skiing facilities and hotels and by the dumping of waste which has polluted nearby lakes. Though tourism has saved whole facets of Alpine culture and economy since the last century, death by tourism and over-development is one of the major threats hanging over the Alps.

The continual use of the same location and of the same runs, together with the pressure to expand the skiing areas, has brought skiers and conservationists into conflict. Unfortunately there is no way of compensating for the damage done on the ski slopes and it is often permanent rather than temporary. In the long term, the face of the landscape changes and the whole ecosystem is altered. It is not just a matter of physical destruction such as erosion, deforestation and the disappearance of rare habitats. There are also the problems created by building ski lifts and cable cars, new roads to allow coaches up the mountains, avalanche fences, car pollution and litter.

In March 1981, close to the purpose-built resort of Les Arcs, heavy rain and warm weather caused a small stream to turn into a torrent, destroying roads and bridges. Resulting landslides were responsible for 60 deaths. Repairs ran into several million pounds. The blame was put on tree-felling and the bulldozing of mountains to make pistes. There was much publicity about the heavy long-term ecological price paid for all the development undertaken in the French Alps for the 1992 Winter Olympics (Keating, 1991). The natural environment may never recover from the frantic construction and massive injection of funds the games brought about. The men's downhill piste in Val d'Isere and the women's downhill in Meribel will leave scars on the landscape which will take hundreds of years to heal. The bobsleigh run at La Plagne was plagued by controversy, having been built on unstable, marshy land. To make it usable, it was frozen with 40 tonnes of ammonia, a substance normally banned by French law for use in public places. Local residents were issued with gas masks to protect themselves against poisonous fumes.

There are also environmental problems caused by artificial snow. The Alpine lakes source four major European rivers and their enormous hydroelectric potential is already widely exploited by ski resorts. Over 5,000 snow cannons consume vast quantities of water using 2.8 million litres of water for each kilometre of piste (Grabowski, 1992). This artificial snow melts slowly and reduces the already short recuperation period of Alpine grasses and flowers during the summer months. Also, reduced river currents restrict upstream movements of trout, and there is a greater exposure of fish eggs to freezing.

There is a growing view that the landscapes of the western Alps in France, Switzerland and Austria are under serious threat from tourism, especially the development of higher resorts. The growing tendency for the Alpine pastures, and the pistes with them, to deteriorate could be attributed to the loss of peasant farming which traditionally has maintained the ecological balance and conservation of the natural beauty of the Alps. The very important mutual links between land use, forestry, landscapes and tourism can only be maintained if the people who manage the landscape, the peasant farmers, are encouraged to remain in the mountains (May, 1995).

Statistics documenting the tide of vacationers flooding into the Alps mask significant regional variations in the structure of the tourism industry and variations in economic importance. The statistics also obscure differences in cultural values and political organisations that determine the actions of governments and host populations (Barker, 1994). In the French Alps, over the last 30 years, the regional economic development policy of the central government has resulted in the construction of urban-style ski stations with high bed capacities. The Tarentaise for example has a quarter of a million beds and the most dense concentration of ski lifts in the world. Such stations are physically, economically and culturally divorced from the farming communities in the valleys. Inevitably there is a price to pay. The skiing facilities with hotels, lifts, car parks and roads leave a network of impermeable water surfaces where water will collect instead of gradually draining away.

In Switzerland and Austria, on the other hand, mountain agriculture and tourism have coexisted in a symbiotic relationship which has been strengthened by federal subsidies fostering local participation and control. But the issue of responsibility towards the environment is one which skiing authorities sometimes seem reluctant to accept. Some are even unwilling to admit the fact that skiing can damage the environment. Economic motives prevail, and the fear of losing business prevents them from making changes that could alter the whole nature of the sport. Unfortunately, too often, bottom line considerations have ruled over aesthetic ones.

Barker has highlighted four key issues in growth management in the Alps, suggesting that growth management and consolidation strategies tend to evolve through four phases along a learning curve:

1. An initial focus on quantitative growth witnessed in the 1960s and 1970s.
2. A shift in emphasis towards qualitative growth in response to market competition, sectoral problems, and emerging social and environmental impacts.
3. A recognition of the need for change once congestion, for instance, becomes unacceptable to hosts and guests.
4. A fundamental reorientation in an effort to break out of the uncontrolled growth spiral. Integrated regional management strategies focusing on sustainable development concepts and defining limits aimed at ensuring socially and environmentally compatible tourism.

In her article, Barker gives three examples from the Austrian and German Alps to illustrate a range of strategies being used to contain tourism's growth. She believes that over the past two decades there has been a major shift from local piecemeal solutions towards comprehensive regional management frameworks. However, mechanisms still must be developed to deal with transboundary problems such as transit traffic and acid rain, which affect the existence and quality of Alpine tourism.

Reaction to these impacts

A 1994 Roper survey on environmental attitudes in the United States found that public concern for the environment is very high (NSAA, 1995). Media attention given to the greenhouse effect, acid rain, oil spills, ocean pollution, tropical deforestation and other topics has raised public awareness about environmental issues. The survey discovered that skiers, especially, are worried about the environmental results of development and growth. Universal concerns regarding growth and development such as traffic, adequacy of utility infrastructure and effects on air and water quality are now beginning to focus on ski areas and their impact on surrounding communities.

In North America several dynamics have combined to create these environmental attitudes. Children are now educated on conservation and preservation subjects and are taught to respect the environment. Younger people are moving into positions of authority, with agendas to protect resources and to enforce environmental regulations. Also, corporate America has jumped on the environmental sensitivity band-wagon and companies have become 'green marketers' of their environmental commitment.

A model for the greening of ski resorts

If skiers are genuinely worried about the environmental impacts of development in the Alps, and resorts accept that sustainability is the only way to survive into the next century, then the 'greening' of resorts must be the goal. There are several variables that contribute towards effective greening of a destination, and these can be represented in a model (see Figure 1). The model shows the relationships between these variables. The strength of these relationships will differ from resort to resort, and the power of each group will vary depending upon the region and the country in which the resort resides.

Whilst each of the variables in the model will affect the greening of ski destinations in varying degrees (single-headed arrows), they will also influence each other (double-headed arrows). The relationships can be summarised as follows:

Responsible tourist — Responsible operators. The responsible tourist will demand a greener product and will look for the operator that can provide such a package. The responsible operator in turn can persuade skiers to travel with them for environmental reasons.

Responsible operators — Responsible marketing. The operator can use sustainability as a marketing tool and will seek to cooperate with resort marketers in order to communicate the right message to the consumer or media.

Responsible marketers — Responsible development and management. Marketers will be expected to keep management informed as regards

Figure 1 A model for the greening of ski resorts

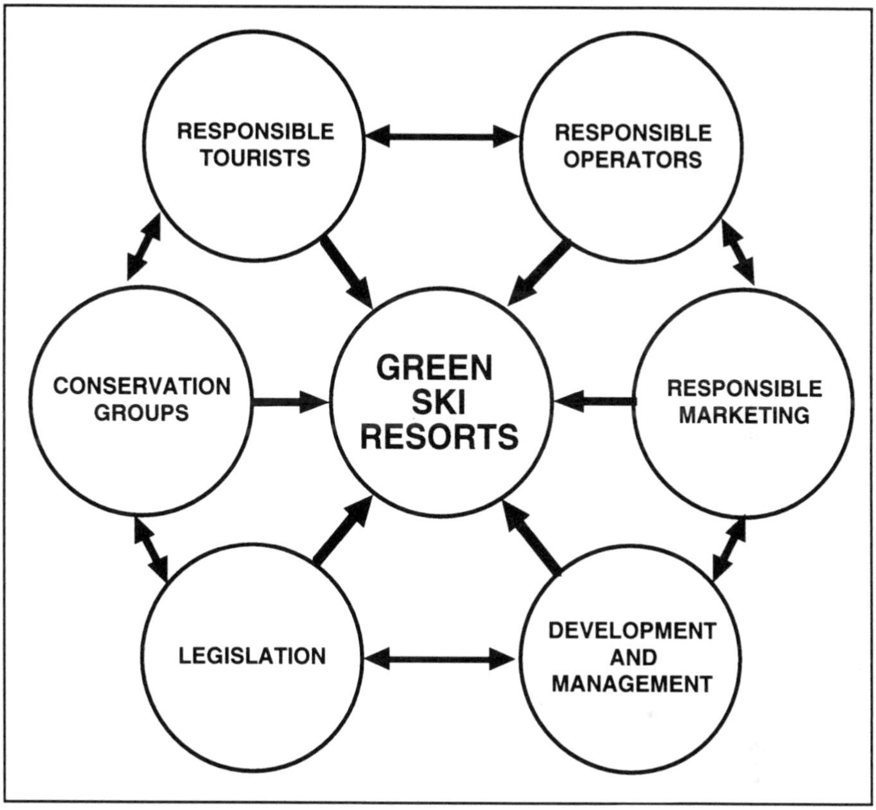

to consumer tastes, attitudes, desires and related matters. Management and developers will look to the marketers to inform the public of environmental efforts and use sustainability as a marketing tool.

Responsible development — Legislation. Management and developers must comply with any local, national or EC laws and in turn may lobby for rights to conduct their business in a responsible manner.

Legislation — Conservation groups. Conservation groups will use the existence of legislation as ammunition when exerting pressure on resorts. They will also lobby for new environmental legislation to curb irresponsible development.

Conservation groups — Responsible tourists. Conservation groups will influence tourists through the media and the tourists in turn may join, and even form such pressure groups.

The influence of each variable is discussed below.

Legislation

Although the Alpine ski industry is generally acknowledged to be mature, there are increasing concerns about its sustainability. In 1991 the European Union established an Alpine Convention which aims 'to safeguard and protect the Alpine region and its ecological balance, threatened by growing human intervention'. In the document, signed in Salzburg, the Alpine States and the EEC agreed on a framework convention for the protection of the Alps. By signing this document Austria, France, Germany, Italy, Liechtenstein and Switzerland committed themselves to cooperating on a strategy for development based on environmental goals. The Union now requires that before major developments take place there should be an assessment of the potential impact upon the environment, and the Alpine Convention stresses the need for signatory nations to put measures in place which will protect the environmental resources of the Alps.

Legislation will also affect ski operators, and organisations in the future may find that greening is no longer an optional activity, chosen with a view to improving one's competitive position. If the industry as a whole does not act decisively soon, it may find that greening is imposed through government and supra-governmental regulation. The EC Package Travel Directive may well be an indication of legislation to come that will address green issues in tourism (Swarbrooke, 1994).

Conservation groups

Membership of environmental organisations is growing. In Britain, there are 2.2 million members in the National Trust and 250,000 in Friends of the Earth. Surveys show that 60% of the public is sympathetic to environmental initiatives, whilst only 4% actually opposes them. The media is largely pro-green and tourism has been getting increasingly critical coverage.

In North America a variety of interest groups — ecologists and conservationists, farmers and ranchers, small retailers and fishermen, senior citizens and historic preservationists — are finding common cause in their fight to preserve their community's 'quality of life' (Beaudry, 1991). More than often that common cause is opposing more resort development in their backyard. From New Hampshire's Loon Mountain expansion to Colorado's proposed Mt. Catamount, shocked developers everywhere are finding their way barred by newly discovered environmental red tape.

As ideas filter over from North America, similar concerns are also being voiced in Europe. In 1995, Green Flag International, a Cambridge-based environmental group set up in 1990 with support from tour operators, is seeking £25,000 in sponsorship for a year-long study on the environmental impact of the tourism industry in the Alps.

Haid (1989) talks of community 'Alpine emancipation groups' who use voting rights to oppose local political leaders still committed to tourism expansion. For example, Lausanne in 1988 was the first town to have a referendum on whether to make a bid for the Olympic games. They rejected the event on environmental grounds. This was an acute embarrassment for the International Olympic Committee whose headquarters happen to be in the same town. More recently, both Davos and St. Moritz voted overwhelmingly against submitting a bid for the 1996 Winter Olympics. At the moment, many groups in Switzerland are not happy with plans to bring the 2002 Olympics to the Sion Valley, despite the organiser's promises to have a 'balanced' games, reconciling the games and the environment.

Mountain Wilderness, an organisation established in 1987 and known as the 'Greenpeace of the Alps', has dedicated itself to raising awareness of environmental problems and the prevention of further damage. It has succeeded in preventing the building of constructions such as the ski-circuit of Mount Pelmo, ski-lifts on the Chaviere glacier in the Vanoise and a ski resort at Saleve.

Community action is not limited to defensive stands, especially when outside assistance is available. In the Bavarian Alps for example, one commune of 5000 inhabitants has gone into partnership with Alp Action — a Geneva based conservation charity chaired by Prince Sadruddin Aga Khan — to provide synergy between Alpine tourism and agriculture. The Prince writes of this and other initiatives in a recent book on Ecotourism edited by Cater and Lowman (1994). In this particular area, the 'Hinderlang Nature and Culture Land', the entire community, along with Alp Action, has created a fund to help the farmers manage the environment. The farmers in return have signed an agreement whereby they will abide by a set of strict rules drawn up by environmental specialists and approved by the community.

Elsewhere, Alp Action has planted hundreds of thousands of trees in six Alpine countries with the support of Jacobs Suchard International. It is to encourage and perpetuate traditional mountain crafts by restoring some of the oldest Alpine chalets. And it has encouraged Clarins, a multinational cosmetics firm, to purchase land on behalf of the Swiss league for the Protection of Nature, to create Alpine butterfly sanctuaries. In fact since its launch in 1990, Alp Action has contributed to the implementation of many environmental projects with the support of its 25 corporate partners in conservation.

Responsible development and management

In addition to the higher incidence of citizen interest and participation in the planning process of ski resorts, more specialised jurisdictions and agencies are becoming involved in the approval of ski area development (Beeler and Wood, 1990). Local sewer and water authorities; state agencies with responsibility for ecology, wildlife and cultural resources; and federal authorities governing wetlands and threatened and endangered plant and animal species, all may have a role in the approval of ski area development.

The Aga Khan has campaigned for closer consultation and cooperation between the mountain communities, state tourism, transport and industry authorities, and competent environmental experts. When planning ski resort development, destinations should work with all interested parties in a team effort to find mutually satisfying approaches to development. Much can be gained through open discussion with the interested parties, particularly those who are ski resort critics or development opponents. If issues of concern identified by local communities, environmental advocates or other recreationists are brought out into the open, this information can be used to develop a stronger and more unified plan, rather than serve as a stumbling block during the approval process (Beeler and Wood, 1990).

It was mentioned earlier that more economic, social and environmental concerns should be addressed in the approval of ski area development projects. But these issues are increasing in their complexity. Rather than planning on a piecemeal project-by-project basis, ski areas need to consolidate their planning efforts in order to reduce the amount of negotiating required to gain approvals. Approval of a long-range master plan for development insures that step-by-step implementation of individual projects will go smoothly.

Responsible marketing

In the past ten years, ecotourism and sustainability have become buzz words used to sell a variety of tourism products, just like the tendency of manufacturers to label numerous products as 'green' or 'ecologically friendly'. The problem has been that the consumer did not know what they were getting, nor its impact on the environment and did not know how the product differed from others.

Wight (1994) identifies the need for a balance between commitment to environmentally responsible action and commitment to environmental marketing. A destination can be sold as green, but false claims should not be made. The destination should be developed sensitively with regard to the long-term future, and consumers must be made aware of the genuine concern for the resources concerned. This position should involve more than the idea of balance, which implies compromise and trade-offs. It should involve the complementary integration of economic goals and environmentally responsible or conservation goals. Conservationists should consider the implications of not developing further. Land already under pressure will suffer more severely as greater numbers of skiers compete for limited slopes, and habitats that have survived so far are likely to be irrevocably damaged.

At the Winter Olympics in 1994, set in Lillehammer, Norway, the organisers set out to market the first 'green' games. Acknowledging the negative impacts major sporting events can have, the organisers used sport, culture and the environment as the three pillars that formed the foundation philosophy of the Lillehammer Winter Olympics. They appointed executives responsible for environmental issues and invested extra time and money in an attempt to make the games the first in which the environmental challenge became an equal partner to the high profiles of sport and culture. As many people as possible were brought into the environmental programme, from schoolchildren to industrialists who could translate work done for the Games into marketable environmental products or services.

Responsible tour operators

According to Wood (1992), a large responsibility lies with tour operators and the skiing industry itself, which should be seeking alternative places to send their clients, and also be limiting the numbers present in any one season. She suggests that clients ask operators whether any type of monitoring is carried out; whether the company takes any active role in researching environmental damage caused by skiing; and, generally, what solution the company might offer by way of improving the situation.

Unfortunately, UK ski operators show little concern for the impacts of skiing on the environment. Very few have a financial investment in the host destination which means that their vested interest in the long-term sustainability of the destination product is low (Ryan, 1991). Alp Action surveyed ski operators who were members of the Association of Independent Tour Operators (AITO), a group which has always stressed its green credentials. Out of 29 companies, only one had an environmental policy and none had heard of Alp Action and its conservation projects to improve the mountain environment. At a Tourism Society/Tourism Concern conference in London on sustainable tourism (April, 1995), delegates agreed that the industry could not be trusted to regulate itself, and they called for government intervention to protect host destinations from 'use up and move on' type operators.

However, for many operators, sustainability could be a useful marketing tool. It will cost a little more, but will help maintain, or even increase market share in the long term. Ski companies could follow the example of UK operator Eurocamp, a mass market operator carrying over 40,000 families from the UK each year. Its main brochure carries a full page on environmental issues and describes the company's response to those issues. Before departure, clients receive detailed briefing packs outlining simple steps they can take to reduce their impact on the ecosystems of their destinations. On arrival, information is provided on locally made products, fauna and flora, environmental and community issues, and excursions on foot and by public transport.

Unfortunately in the skiing industry, many companies do not — and cannot afford — to think of the long term, and do not even consider environmental issues. However, there may come a time when they cannot afford to ignore them.

Responsible tourists

Can consumers be expected to put pressure on the operators to provide a greener product? A US Travel Data Centre survey (1992) has found that travellers, on average, would spend 8.5 per cent more for travel services and products provided by environmentally responsible suppliers. Kiernan (1992) says that reliable statistics about the environmental consciousness of UK tourists are hard to come by. In Canada it is estimated that 40 per cent of consumers consider the environmental track record of both holiday company and destination when booking a holiday. Kiernan believes this figure to be about 10 per cent in the UK but growing rapidly. Other figures from the European Tourism Institute claim that more than half of all travellers are willing to pay up to 20 per cent more for a holiday in a natural preserved environment.

Certainly in the States, the growth in special interest nature-orientated travel reflects the increasing concern for the environment. Data on the US ecotourism market substantiates this growth (Hawkins, 1994). US tour operators report that between 4 and 6 million Americans travel overseas for nature-related travel each year. These operators say that 63 per cent of the travellers would pay $50 and 27 per cent would pay $200 towards conservation of the area visited (Ecotourism Society, 1992).

Wood suggests that skiers are starting to ask more questions about the environmental policies of companies they travel with, and they believe that it wouldn't take too many people refusing to book with irresponsible companies before changes would have to be implemented.

The model in action: Verbier, Switzerland

Two hours drive from Geneva, close to the Italian border, lies the popular Swiss ski resort of Verbier. From a small farming community in the 1930s, Verbier has developed into a thriving tourist destination, with over a million overnight stays each year. Made-up of Chalet style buildings, giving it the atmosphere of a large village, Verbier has 25,000 beds divided between hotels, chalets and apartments. The resort is in the heart of one of the world's largest skiing areas, the "4 Valleys", boasting more than 400 km. of ski runs and 100 installations.

From the first festival of Alpine herdsman, organised in 1805 near Interlaken, tourism in the Swiss Alps has always been a part of an existing settlement scheme or land use system (Messerli, 1987). However, during the sixties and seventies the exponential growth of tourism in the mountain regions resulted in a physical and economic predominance of tourism in many places, including Verbier. The important investments were mainly oriented to the winter season, in order to increase the rate of return. During this period tourism became the leading industry for mountain areas and many now have a total economic dependence on tourism.

The Swiss Man and Biosphere programme (1978-85) points out that this unbalanced growth has not only increased the risk of economic failure but also biased the danger of disintegration of the local socioeconomic-ecological system.

Agriculture was identified as the most important linkage element in this system. As the basis for cultural identity, it also reproduces the traditional landscape, which was found to be a formula for ecological stability, biotic diversity and recreational qualities. Messerli therefore believes that sustainable development of Swiss mountain tourism requires the integration of mountain agriculture in the socioeconomic development. He suggests that sustainable development in a changing socio-economic and natural environment should be based on three principles; prevention (environmental policy), flexibility (supply structure) and quality (personal services).

Messerli highlights two significant events from the 80s that affected Swiss mountain areas. First, the stagnation of tourist demand indicating a saturation of the market in winter sports; second, some dramatic changes in the natural environment (floods, forests dying and a lack of snow). He believes that these two challenges call for immediate change of the old quantitative strategies toward a more qualitative and innovative orientation of further development. This not only implies structural adaption in many resorts but also a better regional coordination of further investments. Being an old and established resort, Verbier for one, is a ski resort that must face up to these challenges. Is 'greening' the answer? By applying the model, one may be able to draw some conclusions.

Legislation

The Swiss government was one of the first to adopt a policy of qualitative growth, the second of Barker's four growth phases discussed earlier in this paper. The Swiss Tourism Concept introduced in 1979 was aimed at restructuring and slowing down the rate of tourism growth and established an administratively binding framework for cantonal planning. But the policy and its implementation have been sharply criticised for the widening gap between stated objectives and reality. Jost Krippendorf (Krippendorf, 1986; Krippendorf *et al.*, 1988) in particular, attacked the policies of many resorts, including Verbier, and suggested that the only solution is 'Alpine recycling' or the active reduction of over capacity and assisted liquidation, instead of continued subsidisation of marginal operations. He believes that resorts sell their soil and their labour too easily, economic motives always being the strongest.

The Aga Khan (Prince Sadruddin Aga Khan, 1994) is in agreement with Krippendorf, and believes that competition must be frozen in the field of regional tourism. He says that in the Swiss plains, only 3.5 per cent of the land surface is uncultivated, and the shrinking of natural biotypes threatens half the indigenous species of flora and fauna. Some areas have been protected through the creation of reserves and natural parks. But between sanctuaries and concrete jungle, he believes there are alternative ways to reconcile economic and environmental interests which favour quality over quantity.

The Sion Valais in Switzerland is currently bidding for the 2002 Olympic Games. The organisers have the firm desire to reconcile the games and the environment. No major constructions are planned for short-term use within the sensitive Alpine environment, and priority has been given to using existing facilities.

Conservation groups

Conservation groups are a particularly pro-active force throughout Switzerland. For example, in Verbier, providing new lift facilities for the increasingly more discerning consumer is not easy. In France queuing problems are solved as soon as they emerge by developing new lift systems. If Televerbier (Verbier's powerful lift company), and its director Louis Moix, decide to invest in a new lift, plans must first of all be accepted by the environmental departments within the commune. When an announcement is made to the public about such plans, there are two powerful organisations that can block development. The first is the League Valaisan pour la Protection de Nature (LVPN), and the second is the World Wildlife Fund (WWF). Both Moix and Tourist Office Director Patrick Messeiller disapprove of the latter group's actions if not its motives — Moix because the WWF will not sit down at a negotiating table, Messeiller because if the WWF objects to Verbier's plans the onus is on the resort to conduct and pay for impact studies that the Fund can then use against the development. Messeiller believes that in coming years it will become almost impossible to get approval for new lifts unless it is proved to be absolutely necessary. It will be interesting to see whether plans to replace the old Chassoure lift, the major cause of Verbier's reputation for bad queues, ever get approved.

Responsible development and management

In Verbier, environmental issues are starting to play an important part in development plans. Francois Perraudin, local journalist and President of the Commission de la Zone Protegee — the protected zone of the commune — talks about 'developpement durable' (sustainable development) and the need to find a balance between the needs of the local economy and the needs of the environment. He believes that communities cannot ignore the economic benefits that lift operators bring to a resort such as Verbier, but the agriculture and natural resources must be given serious consideration in any impact analysis. He suggests that for all big projects, lift companies employ specialists or consultants, knowledgeable in countryside ecology. He, and Patrick Messeiller, believe that because half of their 300 square kilometre commune (the largest in Switzerland) is protected, Verbier can claim to be part of an environmentally friendly area.

Since the arrival of Louis Moix, (arguably Verbier's most powerful decision maker), there has been evidence of the lift company making changes to protect the environment. For example, under the main Medran lift, slopes have been fenced off to protect delicate shrubs and trees. However, because there is no communication with the public, no messages informing skiers of the reason for the fences, the skiers just duck under the barriers. Even in Meribel, a resort in the French Tarentaise where conservation is less overt, there are signposts indicating nature parks, and notices asking skiers to respect the environment when skiing off piste.

If Verbier is to make a commitment to reducing air and eye pollution, then long term plans must be set in place to bring about a reduction in resort traffic. Visitors should be encouraged to use public transport which means Verbier should make a move towards being a car-less resort. Eight Swiss mountain communities, including Zermatt and Wengen, have implemented a total ban on vehicular traffic. Of course, the decision is not always spurred by environmental concerns (such as confined physical settings), and a resort like Verbier has the infrastructure in place to accommodate thousands of cars whose owners may chose to drive elsewhere if they cannot bring their vehicles. For this reason alone, Tourist Office Director, Patrick Messeiller believes a move to ban cars would come up against strong opposition. This is a typical example of commercial and environmental interests in conflict.

Responsible marketing

If it decides to 'green' operations, Verbier will need to market its environmental programmes just as it marketed its new high speed Funispace lift that cost 27 million francs (this involved a large promotional campaign at home and overseas). It needs to create environmental education programmes as an added attraction or recreational opportunity at the ski area. Most importantly it must find ways to communicate environmental commitment to visitors and should publish environmental practices and results in all languages (the pamphlet produced recently by the Swiss transport companies on skiing and nature was published in French and German only).

Despite growing environmental awareness, both ski resorts and the skiing public have a long way to go before they really understand the benefits and necessity of sustainable development. Until this education is complete it will be difficult for a destination to gain competitive advantage by marketing itself as 'green'. It makes sense to use the fact that 'green sells' for marketing purposes, but only when the product-labelling conforms with both consumer expectations and industry standards. In North America, according to the National Ski Areas Association (NSAA, 1995), ski resorts that have laudable environmental programmes often fail to communicate their success to employees, skiers, the general public and especially the media.

Responsible tour operators

Switzerland is still suffering from the perception that it is an expensive destination, which is tending to limit volume growth at the moment, and the number of British skiers coming to Verbier has fallen by 50% over the last six years. However, despite a strong currency, and few economies to offer the skier, Switzerland will continue to sell on quality to a certain section of the market, especially advanced skiers who are looking for snow quality and variety. If Verbier can improve its quality, which includes adopting the principles of sustainable tourism, then committed skiers will continue to frequent the resort.

As yet, there is no evidence to suggest that any of the dozen or so UK operators in Verbier see a niche marketing opportunity in adopting the principles of responsible tourism. But without their cooperation, the green ski resort will be that much harder to achieve.

Responsible tourists

For most experienced British skiers, Verbier would be in the top five in Europe for the skiing 'experience', and certainly in the top five for expense. It could be argued that because Verbier attracts a more up-market, discerning and educated visitor, such clients will be aware of environmental issues, and will be prepared to pay more for a greener product. However, there is little evidence in Europe to suggest that skiers, especially those in the UK, will pay a higher price for a more environmentally friendly skiing holiday. In the early days of the environmental and ethical 'revolution' astute observers recognised that one of the greatest mistakes any marketer could make is to confuse what consumers say they will pay for with what they will actually pay for. Clearly, this is an area that requires further indepth research. However, Verbier should keep skiers informed about any efforts made to improve their environment, and tourists should be encouraged to play their part. This may involve requesting that guests keep their cars in the valley, educating skiers as to the problems caused by skiing off-piste, and pointing out the environmental and economic costs of dropping litter on the slopes.

The benefits and constraints for Verbier

There is a wide range of potential benefits which greening might bring for a destination such as Verbier (Swarbrooke, 1994). These include:

1. Reductions in the cost base of the destination, through savings from energy conservation measures for example;
2. Improving the public reputation of the resort and helping it project a quality image;

3. Allowing the destination to appeal to the more affluent customers, who tend to be the sector of the society more interested in green issues;
4. Enhancing the reputation of the resort with government regulators and peer groups;
5. Giving present and potential investors the impression that the management of the resort is sensitive to changes in consumer behaviour;
6. Making resort staff feel more positive about what they do for a living.

However, Verbier will face both constraints and dangers in greening the resort. Based on Swarbrooke's 'constraints on greening' (1994) barriers include:

1. The existing customer base may currently have little understanding or even interest in green issues and there is the danger that radical greening may alienate such customers;
2. The willingness to pay of customers who may need to be asked to pay a higher price for a greener product;
3. The initial capital costs of greening;
4. The resort's past behaviour and current reputation may make it difficult for it to establish a credible reputation as a green destination;
5. The culture of the destination and the attitudes of workers may not be sympathetic towards the idea of greening.

From the evidence provided in the first half of this paper, it is clear that the 'greening' of ski resorts is a necessity for sustainable tourism in the mountains.

Taking the definitions of sustainable tourism into account, a sustainable ski resort community will be committed to developing in only such ways as will protect and sustain the resort's natural assets for future generations. By staying true to this vision the pioneers of the first 'green ski resort' will become model examples on how to marry economics, recreation and the environment. By developing and applying a model for the greening of ski resorts to the Swiss destination of Verbier, the author has shown that this particular resort has a long way to go before it can claim to be green.

References

Barker, M. L. (1994) 'Strategic tourism planning and limits to growth in the Alps', *Tourism Recreation Research*, Vol. 19, No. 2: pp. 43-49.

Beeler, T. and Wood, J. (1990) 'Overcoming environmental obstacles', *Ski Area Management*, March: pp. 74-87.

Beaudry, M. (1991) 'The limits to mountain resort growth', *Ski Area Management*, July: pp. 39-63.

Cater, E. and Lowman, G. (eds) (1994) *Ecotourism: A sustainable option?*. New York: John Wiley and Sons.

Ecotourism Society (1992) *Definition and Ecotourism statistical fact sheet*. Alexandria, VA: Ecotourism Society.

Grabowski, P. (1992) 'White gold', *Focus*, Vol. 5: pp. 8-9.

Haid, H. (1989) *Vom neuen leben. Alternative wirtschaftsund lebensformen in den Alpen*. Innsbruck: Hayman.

Hawkins, D. E. (1994) 'Ecotourism: Opportunities for developing countries', in W. Theobald (ed) *Global tourism*. Oxford: Butterworth Heinemann.

Keating, M. (1991) 'Bad Sports', *Geographical*, Vol. 63: pp. 26-29.

Krippendorf, J. (1986) *Alpsegen — Alptraum. Fuer eine tourismusentwicklung im eeinklang mit mensch und natur*. Bern, Switzerland: Kuemmerly and Frey,

Kiernan, P. (1992) 'Earth-bound', *Marketing Week* August 21: pp. 26-30.

Krippendorf, J., Zommer, P., and Glauber, H. (eds) (1988) *Von der diskrepanz zwischen zielan und wirklinchkeit. In Fuer eeinen andern tourismus*. Frankfurt: Fischer Verlang.

Lane, B. (1992) 'Marketing green tourism', *Leisure Opportunities*, January: pp. 34-35.

May, V. (1995) 'Environmental implications of the 1992 Winter Olympic Games', *Tourism Management*, Vol. 16, No. 4: pp. 269-275.

Messerli, P. (1987) 'The development of tourism in the Swiss Alps: Economic, social, and environmental effects. Experiences and recommendations from the Swiss MAB Programme', *Mountain Research and Development*, Vol. 7: pp. 13-24.

NSAA (National Ski Areas Association) (1995) 'Enhance ski areas' environmental image', *Ski Area Management*, January: p. 73.

Prince Sadruddin Aga Khan (1994) 'Tourism and a European strategy for the Alpine environment', in E. Cater and G. Lowman (eds) *Ecotourism: A sustainable option*. New York: John Wiley and Sons, pp. 103-110.

Romeril, M. (1984) 'Tourism and the environment — towards a symbiotic relationship', *International Journal of Environmental Studies*, Vol. 25: pp. 215-218.

Ryan, C. (1991) 'Tourism and marketing — a symbiotic relationship?', *Tourism Management*, Vol. 12: pp. 101-111.

Swarbrooke, J. (1994) 'Greening and competitive advantage', *Insights*, May: pp. D43-D50.

Wight, P. (1994) 'Environmentally responsible marketing of tourism', in E. Cater and G. Lowman (eds) *Ecotourism: A sustainable option.* New York: John Wiley and Sons, pp. 39-55.

Wood, K. (1992) *The good tourist. A worldwide guide for the green traveller.* London: Mandarin.

Youth and Collegiate Soccer Participation in America — A Foundation For Major League Success?

David Hudson
De Montfort University

Robert J. Boewadt
Georgia College (USA)

Introduction

Soccer is a major league spectator sport in almost every country except one, the United States of America. Part of the deal which brought the 1994 World Cup to the United States was the commitment to Major League Soccer (MLS) in April 1996. The objective of MLS is to become the fifth major team sport in the United States.

Soccer exists in America as a participatory and relatively gender-neutral activity. Figures from the Soccer Federation suggest that youth soccer participation has grown considerably over the last ten years with soccer at collegiate level becoming the fastest growing sport in the National Collegiate Athletic Association (NCAA). The conundrum of soccer in the USA is that it is a popular participation sport yet appears to have limited spectator appeal.

For Major League Soccer to succeed in the USA it is important that the League management is aware of the factors that have prevented soccer from becoming a popular spectator sport. This paper firstly discusses US soccer's situation at both the youth/collegiate and professional level. It then proceeds to look at the influencing factors that are likely to determine the success of MLS and highlights the subsequent management and marketing implications for US Soccer.

Youth/collegiate soccer participation

There is ample evidence that soccer has increased as a participatory amateur sport since the demise of the North American Soccer League in 1985. A survey by the Soccer Industry Council of America (SICA) suggests that 16.4 million play soccer of whom over one third are female. 12 million are under 18, which is up 77% on the last decade (USSF, 1995). However it is highly questionable whether anyone who plays soccer only once in a year can be counted as being involved in the sport. Indeed less than a fifth of the 16.4 million players are frequent participants (52+ days).

Soccer is America's fourth most popular sport for youngsters under 18, behind basketball, volleyball and softball and ahead of baseball, football and ice hockey. For youngsters under 12 it is second only in popularity to basketball. According to the USSF more than 2.2 million young players are currently registered participants in organized soccer leagues (USSF, 1995).

The popularity of soccer in American colleges and universities has been growing tremendously during the past 15 years and has now become the quickest growing sport in the NCAA (Milk, 1993). The number of NCAA colleges playing men's competitive soccer in the 1993-94 academic year compares favourably with other major sports; 642 colleges play soccer, 582 play football, 793 baseball and 907 basketball. 529 colleges have women's teams (USSF, 1995).

Since 1972 the sport has had a national ratings system and a Senior Bowl game and scholarships have become increasingly available, which has further encouraged growth in the game at high school level. According to the National Federation of State High School Association, in 1988 more than 35% of American high schools featured soccer as a interscholastic sport compared to 2% in 1962 (Sugden, 1994). In 1994-1995 high school soccer participation increased by 14% compared with a 4% increase for high school basketball and football (USSF, 1995).

There have been several particular reasons for this growth in youth and college participation. Large numbers of parents have become increasingly unhappy with the expense, risk, specialist physical demands and violence associated with American Football. Soccer is an equal opportunity sport where everyone can be involved all the time. It is recognised as an ideal sport for the average-sized athlete as well as being a cheap and easy team sport to organise.

Converting youthful enthusiasm into paying and TV spectators has been a continual problem for the sport. It is often suggested that this continued growth in soccer participation will fuel soccer as a spectator sport and hence augment the chances of MLS success. Industry executives surveyed by Sporting Goods Business in January 1994 felt that the opportunity for success was much greater than during the era of the now defunct North American Soccer League (Pesky, 1994).

Professional Soccer in the USA

Interest in soccer in the United States as a spectator sport is noticeably small compared with other countries in the world. This relative indifference is reflected in the fact that what the rest of the world, virtually without exception, calls 'football', Americans know only as 'soccer' (Markovits, 1990).

Underlining soccer's status as a participatory rather than a spectator sport is the fact that, since 1960, six professional soccer leagues have come and gone in the USA (Grover, 1993). In 1995 there are currently two semi-professional leagues operating in the United States although neither can consider themselves to be of major league status. The American Professional Soccer League (APSL) which includes Canadian franchises has suffered from disappointing attendance totals and several barely viable clubs (Cohen, 1994). The current National Professional Soccer League (NPSL) (an indoor soccer league) comprises 13 teams who drew an average attendance of just 5,213 in the 1992/93 season (Lovejoy, 1993).

The last attempt to make soccer an integral part of the major American professional sports market came in the late 1970s and early 1980s in the shape of the North American Soccer League (NASL).

The NASL experience

In the late 1970s, in just two years, the NASL was transformed from being a minor league into one of the world's most exciting soccer leagues (Markovits, 1990). Initially it was a marketing success. Pele and a number of other great (if ageing) international players were brought in and the events and the rules were changed to make it more exciting (wrongly in some cases, but the precept was right). Events were made family affairs and were hyped up as though it was something special. Attendances doubled in just two years as a result, with New York Cosmos regularly attracting crowds of 70,000 people (Economist, 1986).

In 1978 the league decided to expand from 17 to 24 teams. Unfortunately the spiralling costs began to take their toll. Although New York Cosmos almost always attracted crowds in excess of 30,000-40,000 to their home games, average attendances for the league were between 10,000 and 14,000 and were not enough to sustain the wages being paid (Whitney, 1994). In 1981 the NASL began to collapse and lost 17 of its franchises in just four years. The league was eventually closed down in March 1985.

There has been a number of reasons put forward to explain why the NASL failed to impose the game on the country, some of these internal to the league, some external. Internal reasons range from poor financial and league management and over expansion to an over reliance on foreign players. Externally, a lack of playing base, public ignorance, competition from other sports and problems with Television are often cited.

The proposed Major Soccer League

In December 1993 Alan Rothenberg, president of the United States Soccer Federation announced its proposals for the new Major Soccer League. Rothenberg says that structuring will be towards the big bang theory. Ten franchise slots are proposed with eight sites already in place. MLS will have a Spring and Summer Schedule of at least 16 home league games, plus playoffs. The league will play from April to early October to avoid competing with the grid-iron season. The business plan is predicated on drawing modest average crowds of 12,00-13,000 (Saporito, 1994).

The proposed structural plan is to have five franchises run by operators-investors and five run by MLS under the single entity ownership plan. There will be a $1. 3 million salary cap per team. The league will allow a maximum of four to five foreign players for the first year or two then reducing to 3 per team. It is hoped that the semi-single entity structure will help avoid disparity in the financial stability of the clubs and allow the league to maintain strict financial control and gain economies of scale in purchasing power.

Hank Steinbrecher, Assistant President of US Soccer and former marketing executive for Quaker Oats' Gatorade sports beverage brand, intends to apply the marketing principles learned there to making soccer mainstream. He says "we have a sports entertainment product to sell, and the dynamic is no different from Gatorade going up against Coke or Pepsi" (Saporito, 1994).

Major League Soccer success — key influencing factors

If MLS is to emulate the success of Gatorade the league management will need to be aware of the factors that have so far prevented soccer from becoming a popular spectator sport.

A number of authors have considered the origins and manifestations of America's soccer exceptionalism (Waldstein and Wagg, 1995; Gardner, 1994; Murray, 1994; Sugden, 1994; Markovits, 1990). Whitsitt (1994) suggests that the question of why soccer has failed to achieve any significant success in America has not yet received a satisfactory answer. The following influencing factors may provide some possible explanations for America's reluctance to embrace the world's most popular spectator sport.

Competing sports/cultural influences

It could be argued that perhaps the biggest barrier to MLS success is the competing sports in the United States. Soccer has never posed any serious challenge to America's own 'big three' sports: baseball, basketball and football. These sports with their burgeoning and overlapping schedules keep the Americans more than busy (Thomas, 1994). Few, if any, countries have, like the United States, succeeded in developing three major team sports, all of which have attained national significance in their professional version (Markovits, 1990).

A number of authors (Gardner, 1994; Sugden, 1994; Markovits, 1990) argue that the particular nature of America's development as 'the first new nation' contributed considerably to the crowding out of soccer as one of the country's major spectator sports. At the turn of the century America was anxious to develop its own distinctive national identity and demonstrate that it was not a country built on other people's traditions. Soccer therefore became a victim of what Gardner (1994) terms 'The Americanisation process'.

The game of soccer is seen by many Americans as unpatriotic, a sport for foreigners, snobs or sissies. A USA Today journalist said that "hating soccer is more American than mom's apple pie, driving a pick up or spending Saturday afternoon channel-surfing with the remote control" (Barnes, 1994a). Whitsitt (1994) suggests that to be American and to play soccer are two mutually exclusive things. American sports draw upon certain traits which are fundamental to the culture that engendered it. The games embody many of the basic codes which determine how Americans understand themselves and their culture and are the product of the attitudes and beliefs of a White Anglo-Saxon Protestant (WASP) culture.

One of the problems for soccer is trying to convince Americans that the world's most popular sport is one that is played without using the hands. In American sports the emphasis is on the use of the upper body as opposed to the lower body. Whitsitt (1994) suggests that America will not play soccer as long as the WASP idea of the whole body, soaring upward, represented only by the upper half, continues to dominate America's cultural codes. What soccer proposes he argues "is simply un-American". He suggests that those who play soccer in America have to some slight but decisive degree slipped beyond America's dominant cultural codes. The difficulty of dislodging established sports codes makes Murray (1994) confident that, regardless of the 1994 World Cup success in the USA, the game will not succeed in establishing itself as a serious rival to American football, basketball or baseball.

Despite the growth of youth soccer participation in the USA its popularity is still regional and in a geographical sense still remains a minority sport. It is particularly popular in the west coast states and along the eastern seaboard but remains under-developed within the southern states and in the cowboy states of the plains and the mountain west (Sugden, 1994). It is questionable whether there are enough big soccer markets in North America to ignore Canadian participation from Toronto, Montreal, Vancouver and Edmonton (Deacon, 1994). So far, demand for professional soccer has not been overwhelming. In July 1994 seven cities had gathered pledges for 5,000 season tickets, less than the 10,000 league organizers initially requested but enough to win initial franchises (Grover, 1994).

At present American soccer is an overwhelmingly suburban middle-class, white sport. The kids actively involved in the sport and their families are more wealthy and more suburban than most collections of sports types (Saporito, 1994). There is minimal black involvement in USA soccer and there has been no great effort on the part of the USSF and other soccer bodies to recruit blacks (Gardner, 1994). Mason (1995) suggests that with so small a number of Afro-Americans either playing or interested in soccer a successful professional league is a long way off.

Although soccer has been popular in some USA suburbs for decades, it has failed to make any serious impact in the inner cities. Soccer's long term prospects may therefore depend, in part, on its ability to penetrate the inner cities. Programs such as the Chicago 'Soccer in the Streets' initiative have attempted to draw upon the rich vein of athletic ability in the inner cities where basketball is king (Deacon, 1994).

Nature of the soccer product

There is a number of problems inherent to the game that make it hard to sell in the USA. It has been suggested that the "reason why soccer has never been a big spectator sport in America is simple — it's boring to watch on TV, the field is too big, the games are too slow and the goals are too few" (Forbes, 1994). On the day of the 1994 US World Cup Final an ABC News poll found that only 22% of Americans found football exciting (Mason, 1995). This was after, what was by common consent, one of the most entertaining World Cups in recent history.

Home grown sports are uniquely tailored to American sensibilities and the needs of television and advertising. American spectators are used to sporting action coming in repeated explosions of drama with high scoring and regular halts for commercials. Soccer is a fluent, almost continuous sport demanding fairly prolonged concentration as the game ebbs and flows. America by contrast expects team sports to offer short, repeated bursts of action. Basketball, with its staccato bursts of excitement, regular halts for commercials and avalanches of scoring, effectively demonstrates the gulf in appetites and attitudes separating American sports fans from the majority elsewhere (Mcllvanney, 1993).

Entertainment

Soccer is considered to be overly geared to defense and in need of rule changes to favour offence (Forbes, 1994). Americans love high scoring games (hockey being the exception) and soccer is historically a low scoring game. One Wall Street Journalist suggested that when a goal does actually come it only seems so magnificent because the rest of the game is so terrible.

In America 'offense' sells tickets and makes people watch sports. It is no coincidence that some of the most popular sports figures in America today are stars like Ken Griffey Jr, Steve Young, Jerry Rice, Michael Jordan and Barry Bonds all known for their offensive prowess. One recalls the famous remark of the New York Cosmos (NASL) executive about Franz Beckenbauer:

> Tell the Kraut to get his ass up front. We don't pay a million for a guy to hang around in dee-fense. (Barnes, 1994b)

FIFA, the world governing body for soccer, has been notoriously slow in implementing rule changes to increase the entertainment level of the game. USA major league sports by comparison are never static. Rule changes have been gradually introduced to improve the entertainment and excitement level of the games. When pitchers became too dominant in the 1960s, baseball made it harder for them by lowering the height of the mound. American football is forever tinkering with its rules to make life safer for the quarterback and easier for the wider receiver and basketball has recently introduced the three-point shot and the time clock to encourage more attacking play.

There does seem however to be a world-wide demand for better, more exciting soccer (Gardner, 1994). It is widely held that the rule changes in the 1994 World Cup had a positive effect on the tournament in terms of excitement and goals. It is likely therefore that FIFA will be warmly receptive to further changes. The APSL and the NPSL are currently being used as a trial centre for a series of FIFA-backed experiments — for example, bigger goals, withdrawal of players after five fouls, and clock stop. MLS will look to be the world's 'proving' ground for affecting rule changes limiting overly defensive play, and promoting attacking, entertaining soccer (MLS, 1994).

Markovits (1990) points out that a lack of understanding and appreciation for any sport easily renders it 'boring' in the eyes of the uninitiated spectator. This suggests that apart from rule changes one of MLS's major tasks will be to educate the American public.

Statistics

Soccer does not lend itself easily to statistics so beloved by American commentators and fans in their insatiable desire to manufacture rankings and records.

Americans like sports in which people accomplish things, runs, touchdowns, birdies, baskets, therefore lending themselves to statistical analysis. They like high scores and are consumed by the statistics that lie behind the final score. Soccer can only provide a fraction of this numerical diet. Percentage possession is fairly meaningless in a game where most goals are scored from attacks that last less than 5 seconds (Edwards, 1994). Soccer fans are often unable to evaluate with numbers and rely on adjectives.

For all these reasons, American fans have greeted soccer with the same enthusiasm as the American public welcomed the metric system.

Quality of players/coaching

The quality of the players can obviously affect the attractiveness of a sporting contest. Successful players can galvanize interest in a sport. Michael Jordan in American basketball is a perfect example of this. A spectator sport in the USA cannot exist if it has no stars (Fynn and Guest, 1994). Americans associate sports with the personality of its players. Since Brazilian superstar Pele retired 16 years ago from the NASL there have been few big names for young players to emulate. The problem for American professionals is that, since the demise of the NASL, the best players have had to go to Europe to find work.

The quality of the American player has increased over the last ten years. John Polis, a former executive of both the NASL and the US Soccer Federation suggests that the quality of the American player is far superior to what was available during the days of the NASL (Pesky, 1994). Without a professional league the United States has been pursuing the policy of building the game through its national team which resulted in a creditable performance in the 1994 World Cup. However the team contains a number of foreign-born or bred players and as a result remains vulnerable to the same problems that helped cause the downfall of the NASL (Waldstein and Wagg, 1995).

The lack of a big-time college feeder system is one of the reasons why soccer has not progressed from a popular youth participation sport to a serious adult sport and a viable spectator sport (Grover, 1993). College sports, in particular basketball and American football, play a significant role in the development of recruits for professional sport in America. One of the reasons for the NASL's failure was its failure to bring on young Americans. Because the league did not initially limit the number of non-USA players there was no opportunity and motivation for young soccer players. This low American representation was compounded by the fact that colleges were increasingly recruiting overseas students on scholarships which meant that many of the better players being recruited by the NASL from the draft system were foreigners (Murray, 1994).

A professional league in the USA can only be based on high-quality soccer. It does seem however that, at youth level, there has been a lack of attention to the quality, as opposed to the quantity of soccer in the USA (Gardner 1994). The chances of colleges providing home-grown players of a professional standard are hindered by the relatively poor standard of coaching and the changes that have been made to the rules of the game. European style dominates at the expense of the Latin with an emphasis on physical power, size and strength. The colleges and high schools are only associate members of the USSF and have always published their own version of the rules.

One of the major variations in the rules is the use of substitutions with free substitution allowed at youth and high school level and up to 18 players in college soccer. This has resulted in a lot of soccer at youth league and high school and collegiate level places being played on the basis of an American Football mentality, with too much emphasis on physical strength (Gardner, 1994). Free substitution allows this physical emphasis to flourish as players can take multiple breaks. It also enhances the importance of the coach during the game which some will argue can lead to less creative play.

Gardner (1994) concludes that "a European style domination, plus the American football mentality, has saddled American soccer with an unsophisticated, coach dominated, hard-running athletic game that has a long track record of failure when offered to the American sports fan as a spectator attraction".

Media support

The media plays an important role in the sports industry both as a revenue provider and as a promoter of the sport. Markovits (1990) suggests that soccer's marginal existence as a major spectator sport in contemporary America probably has more to do with its inability to land a long-term television contract with one of the major networks than with it being crowded out by baseball and football. Sugden (1994) suggests a 'conspiracy theory' where the established major sports and the USA media have worked together to ensure that soccer continues to be marginalised as a professional sport.

One of the main goals of TV sports presentations undoubtedly lies in the entertainment factor (Lobmeyer and Weidinger, 1992). However it is because of the product features of soccer, outlined earlier, that many people believe that it does not sit easily as a TV spectator sport. Most Americans regard the game as recreational rather than a spectator activity, comparable with fishing. A poll carried out in 1993 to discover what sports Americans like to watch found that soccer was ranked 95th, below log rolling (Edwards, 1994).

Prolonged exposure in the USA World Cup led some media commentators to conclude that soccer does not televise well. Soccer is not easy for Americans to follow because the players are spread out for television compared to other sports (Triplett, 1994). There are no predictable wake-up-call lead-ins to scores such as the rallies in baseball or drives in football, and soccer's uninterrupted 45-minute halves overburdened many Americans television viewers' attention spans (Klein, 1994).

Over the years as the influence of the media in America has increased the major sports have tailored their games and schedules to suit the requirements of television and sponsors (Sugden, 1994). American football has become so accommodating to television that 60 minutes of playing time stretch, with interruptions, to over three hours. With soccer, play is continuous and there are no commercial time-outs, no injury time outs and no 20 second time outs. This does not give television many opportunities for action replays or advertising.

Playing facilities

The size and nature of the stadium is important to the sports-watching experience (Cohen, 1994). A core problem for professional soccer in the United States is the lack of suitable stadiums specifically designed for soccer. Alan Rothenberg considers the stadium situation to be the single biggest impediment to success (Gardner, 1994).

A suitable venue should have a capacity of around 20,000 to 30,000. Currently stadiums of this size, with the natural turf needed in soccer, are in short supply. Pending construction of new stadiums games will have to be played in facilities that are otherwise larger than currently needed (National Football League [NFL] and major college facilities, for instance). There will be attempts to 'downsize' the stadiums by draping off seating areas with flags and banners and tarpaulins (MLS, 1994). However the American football stadiums tend to be so large that even after 'downsizing' a modest crowd of 10,000-15,000 will be lost.

The size of the stadiums was considered by some to be a major factor in the demise of the NASL. The NASL had to make do with a combination of adapted football and baseball facilities and teams were attracting crowds of only 15,000-20,000 in stadiums with a capacity of 70,000 or over.

The World Cup factor

The 1994 World Cup was the biggest single-sport event the United States has staged and was a huge commercial and footballing success. The estimated economic impact of the tournament on the USA was $4 billion, with a direct profit of over $20 million to the US organizers (Fynn, 1994). The American team won their first World Cup match for 44 years and qualified for the quarter finals providing an upset by beating Columbia along the way.

The World Cup provided a terrific sampling opportunity among American viewers (event and television). Games were played in Los Angeles (Pasadena), San Francisco, Detroit, Chicago, Boston, Dallas, New Jersey, Orlando and Washington DC. The games drew an average gate of nearly 68,000. Up to America dropping out of the competition ABC viewing figures showed over 10 million households were tuning in. After America's exit 3. 5 million homes continued to watch regularly although the spectators were mainly American immigrants (Wilson, 1994). The World Cup Final was seen on television in ten million North American households, a bigger audience than for the first six games of the National Basketball Association (NBA) final (Mason, 1995).

The question for MLS is whether the World Cup has created an atmosphere in which a professional league can flourish or whether it has just been a transient success? (Gardner, 1994). It is hoped by the MSL that the strong showing by the American team has helped promote interest in the sport.

There is a concern, however, that America was less interested in the game than the event itself. It is probably significant that Alexi Lalas one of America's key players in the World Cup is not optimistic about the impact of the World Cup on the future of the game in America. "The circus comes to town", he says, "and then the circus leaves again" (Vulliamy, 1994). The Wall Street *Journal* perhaps summed it all up when they said, "It was great fun: was it just one of those things?" (Heylar and Harris, 1994).

Strategic management and marketing implications For MLS

MLS's management and marketing strategy should designed to avoid the mistakes made by the NASL. It can also learn from the marketing of America's other major league sports as well as the recent successful introduction of professional soccer in Japan. Sound management and marketing strategies combined with the game's growing popularity could very well make the MSL a success.

League Structure and Organisation

Introductory marketing budgets for Major League Soccer have been set at $50 million and another $50 million has been allocated for modification of existing stadiums. The budget figure is conservative in the opinion of many sports industry executives.

It is important that the league structure is designed to put all teams on equal financial footing to avoid the disparities between large and small markets that plagued the NASL and resulted in its collapse in 1984 amid disputes and money shortages (Reeves, 1993). MLS management must be able to make decisions that are in the best interests of the league rather than just one or a few teams. It is important that the new league is seen to be bigger than any one club and that financial parity, competitiveness and hence uncertainty of outcome is maintained.

MLS will need to impose external constraints similar to those introduced in other American major sports to prevent sport being entirely market-led. American football and basketball have a draft system, with the club that did worst in the previous season picking first in the draft. There are also other financial rules that try to retain league parity including total team salary caps and income sharing arrangements (sponsorship, merchandise and television).

Product modifications

Rule changes

It is important that MLS authorities are constantly looking to maintain the attractiveness of the spectacle without detracting from the traditions of the game. Some of the possible rule changes that MLS is considering to increase the entertainment levels are; making the goals larger, moving the offside boundary to the 35 yard line, changes in the point awarding system to encourage goal scoring and reduce the incentive to tie games. They are also discussing various sudden-death overtime schemes (Cohen, 1994).

Changing the laws is not a thing to be undertaken lightly, conservatism is deeply enough ingrained within any one football nation without trying to get a majority of them (and FIFA) to agree to any fundamental change (Murray, 1994). It has even been suggested by some American commentators that it is time to eliminate the goalkeeper position to induce more goals (Ostler, 1994)!.

Twenty years ago the NASL also adopted the 35 yard offside line in addition to a shootout for settling ties in the place of traditional penalty kicks. Although this brought more creativity to the game it also brought hard-to-define costs, as former Public Relations director for NASL's California Surf pointed out " Soccer is a global game and when you start changing the rules here, and the rules aren't changed somewhere else, then you lose a lot of the fabric of the game" (Cohen, 1994).

Player quality

It is important that enough money is made available to attract the top American players back from Europe as well as attracting some of the top foreign players. A handful of foreign players in each team will not only raise the quality of the product but also galvanise interest in the ethnic population.

An average of only $500,000 per player (£330,000) has been set aside for the transfer fees for foreign players and the proposed average wage will be a modest $70,000 a year (Lovejoy, 1994). It is unlikely that this sort of wage is likely to attract American players back for Europe or attract foreign players to America.

Gardner (1994) believes that any professional league in the USA must be largely populated by American players and it is the qualities of these players that will determine its success. The foreign player quota[2] is important as the American fan will be able to relate much better to the players, and the US soccer youth will be much more motivated to strive for professionalism (Pesky, 1994).

The one component that the USA must address is the situation at the college level. MLS needs to work closely with the NCAA on the issues of rule changes, coaching and a possible draft system. MLS should use the NCAA, as does the NBA, NFL and MLB. The colleges can not only provide players but also help in generating interest for the game. The NBA did not start to become popular until the NCAA Final Four became a major event in the 1980s.

In terms of coaching, a shift of emphasis is needed in training to skill rather than strength, to self-learning rather than coach-imposed drills and tactics (Gardner, 1994) This change in emphasis should result in a more skilful, attractive and exciting game, essential qualities for American Soccer if there is to be a successful professional league. MLS should follow the lead of the Japanese league which has a fair sprinkling of Latin American coaches and players.

Stadiums/event management

MLS should look to gain private and public financial support to build middle-sized, custom built soccer stadiums. Interestingly the average Japanese League stadiums can only hold 11,000 fans (Friedland, 1993) and this might have been a key factor in the successful launch by adding to the event atmosphere. The J. League is now looking to enlarge or build new stadiums.

The idea should be to stick to American sport's big selling advantage, namely its attraction as family entertainment, including pregame and postgame events.

International events

Though MLS projections involve audiences of 10,000-15,000 with a view to gradual expansion in the long term, in the short term, a more pragmatic view is that the new level of soccer consciousness can be kept high by hosting more prestige events and mini-tournaments. The football element of the 1996 Olympics in Atlanta is already being keenly anticipated. Fynn (1994) suggests that while a league grows organically FIFA should plan to hold big-event soccer tournaments and games in the USA on a regular basis to keep interest going — such as an annual world club tournament played over two weeks.

MLS can build on the success of the 1994 World Cup and further promote the sport and educate the population via the 1996 Atlanta Olympics. MLS can use the 1996 Olympics to promote the game. At the 1984 Los Angeles Olympics more people went to watch soccer than any other sport, more than 1.4 million tickets were sold for the soccer games, mostly to Americans (many Hispanic Californians, filling some 95% of seating capacity (Saporito, 1994). It is hoped by the MSL that a strong showing by the American Olympic team in 1996 could galvanize the country, much as the US hockey team did in the 1980 winter Olympics, and provide professional soccer with the springboard it needs.

Promotion of player and game image

Much of the marketing activity that will be necessary to win over the American sports fans to professional soccer will be educational in nature. It is important that efforts are made to change the way the game is perceived. To win interest, soccer must overcome action-loving America's innate aversion to a low-scoring, deliberately paced sport (Deacon, 1994).

In addition to the public education mission role of soccer advertising, a substantial amount of promotion must be directed to stimulate public enthusiasm in the game itself and its players.

It is important that soccer is branded as basketball and football and baseball are branded. The sport of soccer should learn from the lessons of the other professional leagues in the USA in terms of building personalities and interest for the sport. In other major league sports in America players are seen as entertainers and performers rather than just athletes. In both basketball and football TV networks have focused on players rather than the games themselves. When the Fox Network recently completed the NFC football deal it hired an advertising agency to create a star building promotional campaign. (Jenson, 1994).

Unless it can make inroads into the inner cities and the Afro-American community soccer is likely to continue to play a marginal role as an adult participation and spectator sport in the USA. It is important that there are successful black players who can serve as role models for up and coming generations of minority, inner-city youngsters. MSL should sponsor clinics around the country in the schools, colleges, inner cities and the community at large to help establish a general knowledge of the game as well as create excitement in the youth of America. These clinics will not only help promote good relations with the communities and the franchises but will also help in developing a spectator and playing base for the league.

Partnership marketing activities

If professional soccer is to firmly establish itself in America, there will be marketing activities necessary that will transcend mere media promotion. They will involve forming partnerships with various societal constituencies. The forming of such private-public alliances is generally credited as a major factor in the recent successful introduction of the sport to Japan (Leadbeater, 1993). The Japanese J-League forged long term partnerships with national and local sponsors as well as local government authorities. The J-Leagues's corporate backing means it will probably avoid the fate of the NASL.

For MLS soccer to succeed in the USA it is important that soccer's splinter organizations and their constituents are brought together by the US Soccer Federation. Several years of infighting over directions that soccer should be taking in the USA ended in 1990 with the election of attorney Alan Rothenberg as Chief Executive Officer of the United States Soccer Federation (Gardner, 1994). US Soccer Partners, set up as the marketing arm of US Soccer, will need to galvanize not only the corporations, but the splinter organizations in soccer around the country.

Media considerations

In order to hold any hope of commercial success, professional soccer in the United States must work in concert with the television industry in such a way that the game's format complements, rather than impedes, the delivery of commercial messages by potential sponsors. TV revenues must be the life blood of any fledgling professional sport.

Additionally, the sport will benefit from widespread media publicity and it is, therefore, beneficial for it to have good relations with the media. A television contract therefore is paramount to the success of the new league and MLS will need to sell itself to the major networks in order to succeed.

MLS will need to consider game changes that would allow better commercialization for sponsors and more entertainment for fans. Wraparound screen commercials are one way round the TV time-out problem for a game with virtually no breaks. Another alternative would be to take breaks when there are injuries — this could be done with the aid of a two way communication with the referee as is done in American football. FIFA-approved basketball style time-outs may soon be a reality. They were tried out at the 1995 Women's World Cup in Sweden, where team coaches were able to call two-minute time outs in both halves of a match in order to give their players tactical instructions and advice. These time-out tests have already being going on in regional leagues in Brazil (European, 1995).

There will be a need for more comprehensive statistical data so that spectators can follow their teams and favourite players in the sports pages. MLS will do well to learn from the mistakes of the American Professional Soccer League where the fans, the media and even the league have had problems with the points system. In short, the systems have been extremely complicated and confusing for fans, the media, teams and coaches and the leagues themselves (Allen, 1995).

Conclusions

Converting youthful enthusiasm into paying and TV spectators has been a continual problem for the sport, and acceptance of professional soccer as a major USA spectator sport will not be easily won. Cultural, competitive and promotional barriers must be overcome if the game, on the professional level, is to be embraced by American sports fans and media sponsors.

It is important that MLS is well financed and has significant corporate and media support from its inception. Organizational and structural issues will need to be considered as will the development of an effective marketing strategy. It will perhaps require modification of the game's current format but, to a greater extent, it will require a basic attitudinal change on the part of American sports fans and this may prove to be a formidable marketing challenge. Never the less these strategies, combined with the publicity for soccer generated by the 1994 World Cup and the 1996 Olympics, could provide an opportunity for a successful launch.

Notes

1 In the draft system, teams recruit players from the colleges before the start of each season.

2 The "foreign player quota" is set by the league, limiting the number of foreign players on any one team.

References

Allen, C. (1995) 'For a sensible American pro soccer scoring system': *Internet.* csallen@uga.cc.uga.edu

Barnes, S. (1994a) 'Episode of the Simpsons overshadows football's main event', *The Times* 17th June: pp. 45.

——— (1994b) 'World Cup's appeal invites a host of prejudice', *The Times.* 15th June: pp. 46.

Cohen, A. (1994) 'Elusive Goals', *Athletic Business*, May, Vol. 18, No. 5: pp. 22-28.

Deacon, J. (1994) 'Soccer comes to America', *Macleans*, 20th June: pp. 40-42.

Economist (1986) 'Association Football: A battered sport and a troubled business', *Economist.* 31st May: pp. 49-72.

Edwards, M. (1994) 'Dead on its feet; Football', *Sunday Times.* 19th June: pp. 10.

European (1995) 'Now women test time outs', *European*, 14th-20th April: pp. 14.

Forbes (1994) 'How to build on world cup euphoria', *Forbes*, 1st August: pp. 22.

Friedland, J. (1993) 'Japan shoots for goal', *Far Eastern Economic Review*, 17th June: pp. 48-50.

Fynn, A and Guest, L. (1994) *Out of time: Why Football isn't working.* New York: Simon and Schuster.

Gardner, P. (1994) *The simplest game.* New York: Macmillan.

Grover, R. (1993) 'The selling of the World Cup', *Business Week*, 30th August: pp. 80.

——— (1994) 'The World Cup is not running over', *Business Week*, 4th July: pp. 60-61.

Heylar, J. and Harris Jr, R. J. (1994) 'US refrain: It was great fun; Was it just one of those things?', *Wall Street Journal*, 15th July: pp. A6.

Jenson, J. (1994) 'All the sports world's a stage', *Advertising Age*, 24th October: pp. 1-5.

Klein, F. (1994) 'Among The Heathens, a Cup of Good Cheer', *Wall Street Journal*, 15th July: pp. A8.

Leadbeater, C. (1993) 'Japan adapts its winning strategy to soccer', *Financial Times*, 9th October: pp: W X-X1.

Lobmeyer, H and Weidinger, L. (1992) 'Commercialism as a dominant factor in the American Sports Scene', *International Review for the Sociology of Sport*, Vol. 27, No. 4: pp. 309-327.

Lovejoy, J. (1993) 'Football: The beautiful game's pleasant dawn in the USA', *Independent*, 19 June: pp. 52.

——— (1994) 'Why a better game is on the cards', *Sunday Times*, 24th July: pp. 2/5.

Mcllvanney, H. (1993) 'Football feels the heat in the US melting pot', *Sunday Times*. 19th December: pp 2/1.

Markovits, A. S. (1990) 'The other "American Exceptionalism": Why is there no soccer in the United States?', *The International Journal of the History of Sport*, Vol. 7 (September): pp. 230-264.

Mason, T. (1995) *Passion of the people?*. London: Verso.

Milk, J. (1993) 'Women's Soccer on a roll', *The Chronicle of Higher Education*, 3rd November: pp. 39.

MLS (1994) Major League Soccer Factsheet.

Murray, B. (1994) *Football: A history of the World Game*. Scolar Press.

Ostler, S (1994) 'Just too many saves: So lets get rid of the goal tender', *Sport*, April: pp. 10.

Pesky, G. (1994) 'League of its own', *Sporting Goods Business*, January, Vol. 27, No. 1: pp. 78.

Reeves, P. (1993) 'US launch $100m league', *Sunday Independent*, 19th Dec: pp. 18.

Saporito, B. (1994) How' US Soccer hopes to score', *Fortune*, 27th June: pp. 126-128.

Sugden, J. (1994) 'USA and the World Cup: American nativism and the rejection of the people's game', in J. Sugden and A. Tomlinson (eds) *Hosts and champions — soccer cultures, national identities and the USA World Cup*. Aldershot: Ashgate/Arena, pp. 219-252.

Thomas, D. (1994) 'The Americans took a working class winter sport and turned it into a middle-class, summer entertainment', *Daily Telegraph*, 10th March: pp. 10.

Triplett, T. (1994) 'Soccer league hopes to build on World Cup Marketing Success', *Marketing News*, 29th August: pp. 2.

USSF (1995) *Soccer 1995 Media Guide*. US Soccer Communications Department.

Waldstein, D. and Wagg, S. (1995) 'Unamerican Activity? Football in US and Canadian Society', in S. Wagg (ed) *Giving the game away*. Leicester: Leicester University Press, pp. 72-87.

Whitney, D. (1994) 'North American Soccer League 1967-1984: A statistical history of the NASL', *Internet*. Whitney@ames. arc. nasa. gov.

Whitsitt, S. (1994) 'Soccer: The game America refuses to play', *Raritan*, Summer, Vol. 14, No. 1: pp. 58-69.

Wilson, P. (1994) 'Jury is still out on American Soccer', *The Times*, 24th July: pp. 9.

Vulliamy, E. (1994) 'Masters of revel prove it's a mad, mad world', *The Observer*, 17th July: pp. 18.

The Football Stadium as Contested Terrain

Alastair Loadman

King Alfred's College, Winchester

Introduction

My initial interest in this subject stemmed from living in an area where an extensive new sports and leisure complex had been planned. It was obvious from the amount of local press coverage, and the strength of feeling clearly evident, that this was a far more important issue than just a decision to be made about where the local football team should or ought to play. Plans had been tabled by Southampton Football Club to build a new "Community Stadium" at Stoneham, an area of green fields surrounded by arterial trunk roads, motorway, factories and privately owned housing. If the complex was going to be built, provision would be made for such activities as tennis, athletics, and bowls as well as Premiership football. A cinema screen and a concert hall have also been mooted. Therefore, it is claimed, the proposed development would fulfil the role of a multi purpose community stadium.

These proposals caused much anguish and anxiety amongst some local residents, some of whom have been mobilised to respond with sustained and conservative resistance. Prominent in this respect have been The Stoneham Association and the Swaythling Residents' Association. At a public meeting held on 7 September 1995, both groups presented thoroughly prepared and clearly articulated objections to what they argue would be a noxious facility (cf. Bale, 1993). It is precisely this kind of struggle and conflict over land use which is the focus of this paper, with the main aim being to explore what the planned new stadium would mean to individuals in the local community, and to unravel some of the micro-political processes which are at work.

This task also relates directly to my own biography as a player of dubious quality and as a lifelong aficionado of football. It is not stretching a point to say that as an adolescent growing up in Liverpool, three o'clock on a Saturday afternoon became the defining moment of the week. These details are significant because, as Hammersley and Atkinson (1983) argue, biographical dimensions are key to the complex and interrelated processes of research design and data collection. They are also crucial to the interpretation of material and to the subsequent textualization of those interpretations. Far from being a neutral or value free activity, it is suggested that research is laden with personal, political and ideological imperatives (Sparkes, 1992: p. 42). Further aspects of research methods will be addressed later in this paper.

Sport as a cultural practice

The claim that sport is an important cultural activity has been made so frequently as to become something of a truism. The fact that sport occupies the attentions, and perhaps the consciousness of large numbers of people; and that media coverage of sport, already immense, continues to grow, is usually cited as sufficient evidence to support this proposition (Whannell, 1992). There is in Britain a specialist Radio Station (BBC Radio 5) given over exclusively to news and sport, a specialist channel on Sky television (Sky Sports) and enormous amounts of time are given to sport on terrestrial television. There are very few other areas of human activity which receive such attention. In the summer of 1995, for example, it was reported on the front page of *The Times* that an estimated 10 million people watched England play New Zealand at Rugby Union and, after the match, that jubilant 'Kiwis' performed the *Haka* 'war dance' on the streets of London (Gorman and Jenkins, 1995).

Few writers would now dispute the statement that sport and politics are inseparable. The fact that John Major, despite being elected as Prime Minister of Britain, speaks wistfully of his vision of England as land of warm beer and long shadows across the county grounds, shows that cricket not only embodies Major's conception of a certain kind of Englishness, but also that sports discourse is rooted deeply in the political psyche. Complaints about "moving the goalposts", pleas for "a level playing field" and admonitions about ministerial "own goals" can be heard with alarming regularity. The long-awaited document from Downing Street: *Sport: Raising the Game* (1995: p. 2) makes it clear that "sport is a central part of Britain's National Heritage". The fact that Nelson Mandela opened the 1995 Rugby World Cup in South Africa shows how sport has a fundamental role to play in the making of a nation and the forging of a new national identity. Sport and politics are closely enmeshed.

Yet sport is also experienced in different ways and at different levels, and the meanings and experiences which people gain from and bring to sport do not always coincide. Indeed, as soon as it is acknowledged that a diversity of meanings exist then the contested nature of sport becomes apparent. For example, on a recent cricket tour of Australia, one section of

English fans began to support their team in a much more voluble and demonstrable way. There was banter with outfielders positioned near the boundary, there was chanting, singing and "Mexican Waving" — in short, a carnivalesque atmosphere. The English cricket establishment was not impressed. Former Test player Trevor Bailey was one individual heard to bemoan this perceived decline in standards of behaviour. Further research is necessary to explore the dynamics of this contestation over the ways in which cricket is popularly watched and appreciated; and, given the volumes which have been written about football spectating and hooliganism, there is a comparative dearth of work which considers the behaviour of cricket followers.

It is necessary to establish the all-pervasive influence of sport in order to develop the view put forward by Stephen Jones (1989) that any attempt to make sense of or understand sport is properly done within the overall framework of work, politics and community. In this paper, the word politics will be used to refer not only political parties, State legislation and the activities of central government but also to the processes of decision making at a grass roots level. In this sense, politics would include, for example, the direct and indirect actions of individuals or groups who seek to bring about or resist change.

The word 'community' also requires further elaboration. Used in the sense in which I think Jones (1989) intended it, this word can be interpreted as referring to a specific section of society in which members share a certain commonality, set of beliefs, interests, skills or geographical location. It makes sense to speak in this way about an African Caribbean community, a local artists' community or a working class community. In this paper, the word community will be taken to mean a shared sense of place or belonging. It became clear from an analysis of the interview transcripts that one of the main objections to the Stadium 2000 complex is the fear that it would close the "strategic gap" which exists between Eastleigh and Southampton, and would destroy the sense of distinctiveness which some, perhaps older, residents find desirable.

Other writers have questioned the existence of the concept of community. For example, Benedict Anderson (1983) argues that this is a mythical notion dreamed up by the powerful business elite. For Anderson, the idea of community is not just about the physical and cultural characteristics of bodies in certain spaces, but is rather about the construction of the community at an ideological level in order to generate a sense of wellbeing and catharsis. Thus, although Chairmen of successful football clubs, such as Sir John Hall at Newcastle United, may speak of the "whole town buzzing", and make great claims on behalf of football, the extent to which this reflects social reality would be questioned by scholars such as Anderson. Nevertheless, primary evidence suggests that this is a live and important theme which has a real impact on the way in which people interpret their surroundings and construct their own identities.

Changing experiences of football spectating

Watching football has, arguably, become an increasingly cosmetic and passive activity. Concerns for safety and the legal requirements to provide all seater stadia have meant that spectators are often severely limited in their freedom of movement once in their seats. Glass screens separate those watching from the air conditioned executive boxes from the atmosphere which is unique to every stadium. Although much publicity is given to the new generation of "super stadia" (at Old Trafford, Newcastle and Liverpool for example), this is not a new phenomenon.

The perceived need for ground improvements was in fact already gaining momentum in the 1980s with the rapid increase in mass consumption of leisure products and an aggressive right wing ideology which emphasised materialism and the values of the free market. The language of business came to permeate many areas of life with sport and leisure being one such area. Football clubs found it necessary to ensure that the customer was comfortably accommodated and catered for. A seemingly irreversible trend was established away from cheaper terrace accommodation towards more expensive executive suites and antiseptic hospitality boxes.

In the case of Southampton, the current ground capacity of 15, 000 ensures it remains one of the smallest grounds in the Premiership. There has been compliance with the all-seater requirement, but very little scope exists for further development or refinement because of the densely populated residential streets on all sides. The current trend is to relocate stadia away from all residential areas, which Bale (1994) has described as the 'rationalization of sport space'; though in this particular instance that solution has not been possible.

For Bale (1994), the dual concerns of modern clubs are corporate profit and crowd control. In his book Landscapes of Modern Sport he draws on insights from Foucault (1970) and applies the concept of panopticism to explain this controlling strategy. According to Foucault, one particularly powerful technique of crowd control was to place prisoners in a central courtyard from which they could be surveyed on many sides. This experience of being surveyed, whether actual or perceived, was thought sufficient to intimidate and constrain prisoners. As Bale (1994) points out, the parallels with crowd control techniques in sports stadia are quite marked.

The forms that this new generation of stadia adapt are of interest to diverse groups, including sport sociologists, social geographers of the humanist tradition, environmentalists, land managers and politicians (Bale 1993). This is largely because debate and controversy over stadia redevelopment can be perceived as ideological struggles over public space and public values; and our commercial and leisure practices. The importance of such struggles should not be underestimated, especially if one accepts Nagbol's (1994) suggestion that the final product can be interpreted as a collective symbol of people's relationships with each other — a form of cultural staging.

On one level, decisions made about where football teams should or ought to play merely represent the culmination of a democratic process concerning the allocation of scarce resources. On quite another level, they might be said to represent the ability of powerful individuals or groups to influence hegemonically the ways in which public spaces are regulated and controlled. The decisions surrounding the proposed community stadium should be seen in this context.

However, merely gaining access to a setting does not guarantee access to the dynamics of the decision making process, as crucial interactions and encounters remain obscured from the public view. For whilst it may be possible to be in attendance at Council meetings by being situated in the public gallery, the lobbying, wrangling and political manoeuvring which may have preceded the council vote was obfuscated from all but the privileged few.

A number of key questions therefore persist: who would provide the funding for Stadium 2000? Would the community genuinely benefit or would the complex simply provide an arena for elite level performers and performances both in sport and the arts? Whose interests would really be served by the venture? These are important but as yet unresolved issues which will be discussed in the concluding section.

Research methods

As stated earlier in this paper, the intention was to explore the meanings and importance which were attached to the Stadium 2000 project by people living in the community. As this is a sensitive and emotive issue, it was felt that the local press would provide a fruitful source of information. The back copies of the local paper, The *Evening Echo* were analyzed for the month of November 1994, and any contributions relating to the proposals were noted. This time period and date were chosen since this was the month in which the Stadium 2000 proposals were particularly newsworthy items and therefore likely to be high in the public consciousness. A total of 17 contributions were noted, ranging from a terse letter written by "Impatient of Fareham" to more substantial editorial pieces. The *Echo* was selected because it had given much greater prominence to the story than the weekly Hampshire Chronicle, and because it had sought actively to contribute to the debate through the editorial and features columns.

The *Evening Echo* was also used as a means of "advertising" for interviewees willing to talk about their views on the proposed sports complex. A press release which was sent to the paper generated a rather disappointing total of four responses. This led to two interviews at the homes of local residents, one of whom was overtly "for", and the other who was clearly "against" the proposals. The interviews were tape recorded and lasted for 40 minutes and 30 minutes respectively. There was no formal structuring to the conversations, but the themes of biography, community and sport experiences in a broad sense were central to the discussions. Given more time, an interview schedule would have been posted in advance to the interviewees.

Both interviewees were retired and were able to make adjustments to their daily routines in order to fit the appointments in. This would have been much more difficult, if not impossible, for a single parent to have done. The second interview was in fact delayed considerably by the over running of a Council Meeting which the researcher was attending. Further interviews would clearly be necessary to represent the views of all ages and groups in the community. It was also unfortunate that no interviews were conducted with members of Southampton Football Supporters Association or contributors to Saints' Fanzine. This would have enabled a more rounded picture to have been developed including the views of the most committed fans. Further work will be necessary to explore the possibility that fans would experience a sense of loss brought about by the demolition of the old stadium or of alienation from any new development (Bale 1994).

A third source of data was derived from attending a public meeting of the County Council in Winchester on Thursday 7 September 1995. Observational notes were taken from the public gallery throughout the morning when a number of deputations were being heard, and also in the afternoon when a vote was taken to see whether land should be released by Hampshire County Council to enable developments to go ahead. It was noted that the first public speaker was one of those interviewed the previous day in response to a message being left at College. It was considered that qualitative details observed, and comments made by viewers in the gallery, would provide a rich seam of data which statistical methods would not perhaps reveal. Once again it is worth repeating that the aim was not to attempt to obtain simple "for" or "against" responses — although obviously these would come to light — but rather to try and explore the meanings which lay behind people's fears and aspirations for stadium development.

Discussion and conclusion

Sporting facilities in the area are reasonable, with a number of school/ community clubs providing opportunities for the general public (road running, aerobics, netball and junior football) and a newly opened Tennis and Health club offering scope those able to afford the membership fee. However, anecdotal evidence from several visits to the local Sports Centre suggests increasing demand for facilities, with usage being extremely heavy in the evenings during the week.

Given these sorts of pressures, and the fact that the current football stadium is far too small, the case for a new community stadium appears to be a strong one. As Sleap and Walker (1992) argue:

> Community sports centres offer a flexible and comprehensive range of sporting possibilities. (p. 66)

However, the community itself must welcome and feel comfortable with the development if it is to be a successful long term venture. As one interviewee put it: "the stadium would have to be open for three hundred and sixty five days of the year in order to pay for itself; otherwise it would just become a white elephant ... and I just think you have to say when enough is enough". The interviewee went on to speak about the quality of life being affected detrimentally by the developments around the town of Eastleigh, and that in her view the associated disadvantages, in terms of traffic noise, pollution and congestion now outweighed the benefits. She was also acutely aware of the close connection between sport and business, stating that: "sport is now right in the marketplace".

In many ways this neatly summarizes the dilemma. Stadium 2000 cannot realistically be expected to be all things to all people. It cannot, on the one hand offer opportunities for elite level sport and at the same time purport to offer local people the chance to make decisions about their own sport and leisure practices. The defining features of *community* activities are that they spring from, and actively engage, people within that community, and this entails empowering local people to make decisions about what forms of sport will take place and how those activities will be administered. There is a danger that Stadium 2000 will produce a top-down, hierarchical model of sport and leisure because it will be driven by the dynamics of the market place rather than local needs and concerns.

Perhaps it is true that a successful football team would bring kudos to the area. The Southampton supporter to whom I spoke claimed that people in Quebec had asked him about the player with a French-sounding name (Le Tissier). But this interviewee went on to offer an essentially functionalist perspective, in which certain forms of sport (in this case, football) were given precedence over competing ones. It may be appropriate to recall Bruce Kidd's (1990: p. 32) description of the Toronto Skydome as "The Men's Cultural Centre". Kidd went further, arguing that this physical structure symbolized wider patterns of subordination/domination in a patriarchal society. No women's voices could be heard at County Hall in support of the community complex, yet the County Council agreed to release the land for the development of a community Stadium. No women supporters were obvious in the public gallery when the debate was being heard. This silence and absence might be interpreted as evidence of the gendered nature of struggles over recreational land use.

The theme of male dominance in sport decision making has recently been reported by Duncan (1995) in an article concerning the bidding process for the new national stadium. Duncan observes that the steering group currently charged with allocating National Lottery money includes only one female member. Furthermore, it is stated that "seven of the ten committee members are football men and they recognise that football supporters do not want a stadium with a permanent athletics track". Thus it would appear that in the most significant example of sport stadia development, women are at the margins of the decision-making process, and that some sport forms take precedence over others.

Fundamentally all these struggles are about the use of power. In the case of Stoneham, further research is clearly necessary to explore the meanings which the sports complex holds for different groups and individuals, and to question the taken- for-granted assumption that all the community will automatically benefit from such a development.

Acknowledgement

I am grateful to Gill Clarke for her comments on an earlier draft of this paper.

References

Anderson, B. (1983) *Imagined communities*. London: Verso.

Bale, J. (1993) *Sport, space and the city*. London: Routledge.

Bale, J. (1994) *Landscapes of modern sport*. Leicester: Leicester University Press.

Department of National Heritage (1995) *Sport: Raising the game*. London: HMSO.

Duncan, J. (1995) '"No support" for national stadium bids', *The Guardian*, 16 September 1995: p. 22.

Gorman, E. & Jenkins, L. (1995) 'England's World Cup bid eclipsed by a superstar', *The Times*, 19 June 1995: p. 1.

Jones, S. G. (1989) *Sport, politics and the working class*. Manchester, Manchester University Press.

Kidd, B. (1990) 'The men's cultural centre: Sports and the dynamic of women's oppression/men's repression', in M. Messner and D. Sabo, (eds) *Sport, men and the gender order*. Champaign: Human Kinetics.

Nagbol, S. (1994) 'Helgoland on Aamer: An attempt to achieve a scenic understanding of a sports environment', *International Review for the Sociology of Sport*, Vol. 29, No. 1: pp. 85-96.

Short, J. R. (1991) *Imagined country*. London: Routledge.

Sleap, M. & Walker, (1992) 'Usage of community sports centres by adolescents: A case study of a secondary school', *Physical Education Review*, Vol. 15, No. 1: pp. 61-71.

Sparkes, A. C. (1992) 'Validity and the Research Process: An Exploration of Meanings', *Physical Education Review*, Vol. 15, No. 1: pp. 29-45.

Whannel, G. (1992) *Fields in vision*. London: Routledge.

IV

The Politics of Professionalism: Courses and Careers

An Investigation into Employment Levels within the Leisure Industry

Mike Lowe

Bolton Business School

Introduction

The principal purpose of this paper is to provide a comprehensive review of the current state of employment within the leisure industry. To this end the analysis and evaluation of numerous secondary sources of statistical information is made, with the primary acting as a backdrop for an up to date analysis of current employment trends within the leisure industry (Morgan, 1995). The results of this research, will be of particular interest to Careers Offices, education providers, and students, who seek to identify employment opportunities within the leisure industry.

The nebulous nature of leisure requires a cautious approach in attempting definitions of a leisure industry. Therefore the initial focus of the paper is to provide a template for the classification of a variety of activities, which may constitute employment within a leisure industry. Only when this has been achieved can there be a detailed picture of the distribution of employment. Inevitably, this process exposes the difficulties encountered in carrying out such research, as well as emphasising the importance of this type of research in the current climate of accountability.

A leisure template ?

Researching employment statistics for the leisure industry, is as difficult as, and clearly connected to, attempts to define what exactly is meant by leisure, and what constitutes a leisure industry. A plethora of authors, Torkildsen, Coalter, Henry, etc., have commented upon the problems in defining leisure and consequent attempts in identifying a leisure industry. In a similar vein, sources of statistical information, predominantly from various government departments, differ considerably in their methods of research, interpretation and presentation of data, thus compounding problems associated with any investigation.

Preliminary background research uncovered a mass of statistical information regarding specific areas of employment, e.g. hotel, tourism etc. A major obstacle is that these specific areas of employment which maybe construed as leisure disciplines, are not contained within a separate leisure classification. Leisure as an industry is not recognised in government statistical sources, and the specific areas of employment highlighted above, appear under a variety of industrial classifications. This creates problems in defining a leisure industry and subsequently attempts to extrapolate the relevant statistical information. In an attempt to define or rationalise what constitutes a leisure industry, the broad definition of leisure used by ILAM is helpful:

> In ILAM ... we are interested in leisure and recreation in the broadest sense, so we have the lead body for sport and recreation, for amenity horticulture, for the environment and conservation, for the arts and entertainment, for museums and you could include hotel and catering, travel, transport and so on. (Fleming 1991)

Hence the research reported in this paper encapsulates the above disciplines commonly associated with the leisure industry and redefines these disciplines through use of the following template: Cultural Recreation; Sport and Physical Recreation; Tourism, Hotel and Catering; Countryside and Amenity; and Horticulture.

Whilst not exhaustive, this template provides a basis for classifying specific areas of employment. It is recognised that certain employment opportunities may fall between two or more specified areas presenting difficulties in classification, but this does not impinge upon, or adversely affect, the overall trends identified on the discussion that follows. Similarly employment within these specified areas relates to the industry in terms of direct provision and excludes associated industries, or industries where employment attributable to leisure is impossible to distinguish, e.g. manufacture of books, clothing or food production. These points and other issues associated with the analysis of employment statistics are investigated further.

Methodology

An initial analysis of published data has revealed a hierarchical structure of available statistical information:

1. **Government statistics** — The main sources of up to date employment statistics, which in many cases are the key statistics utilised by a variety of leisure organisations.
2. **Professional research organisations (general)** — Organisations

whose primary function is to provide a variety of general statistical information for other organisations.

3. **Professional research organisations (leisure specific)** — Organisations whose primary function is to provide leisure specific statistical information.
4. **Leading leisure organisations** — Organisations which represent a particular discipline(s), and may be seen as a leading body.

Whilst this classification is artificial, it has been constructed as a means of highlighting the hierarchical structure. Professional research organisations (general and leisure specific) utilise government statistics as part of their research. Leading leisure organisations utilise professional research organisations statistics as part of their research. Whilst government statistics provide the major source of statistical information, the information gained from other sources sought to reinforce or provide further details on levels of employment, (a record of organisations contacted appears in appendix 2)

Due to the volume of data, the rationale for this research, and the methodology a number of problems were encountered. These problems are associated with attempting to rationalise the leisure industry, and are discussed in the section following under the headings: (1) Leisure as an industry; and (2) A review of published data.

Problems associated with developing a leisure template

Leisure as an industry

The difficulties encountered in attempting to rationalise leisure as an industry for can be summarised as:

i. The classification of leisure disciplines within a template whilst assisting in rationalising the industry also creates anomalies e.g. why include Tourism with Hotel and Catering? Or should recreation in the countryside appear under Sport and Physical Recreation or Countryside? The classifications are attributable in part to the source of statistical information — e.g. Employment Department, Industrial Lead Body, and a "best line of fit" using ILAM's definition.
ii. Problems in obtaining statistics for specific leisure disciplines presented problems in providing accurate employment figures.
iii. The government employment research apparatus fails to recognise leisure as an industry. Neither the Employment Department's statistical information nor the SOC (Standard Occupational Classification) or SIC (Standard Industrial Classification) refer to leisure as an industry. Leisure employment statistics have been ascertained by

extrapolating this information from a range of SOCs/SICs. [Note: new Standard Industrial Classifications 1992, are at present being applied to the Employment Department statistics. Not yet published in September 1995, it is not yet clear if they will identify leisure separately.]

iv. Employment in the manufacture, wholesale and distribution of leisure goods may be seen as part and parcel of employment in the leisure industry. These, however, have been excluded for three reasons::
   - Difficulty/impossibility of distinguishing/extrapolating these statistics for the leisure industry from all other industries
   - Lack of statistical information regarding manufacture, wholesale, or distribution of leisure.
   - Lack of direct relevance to this discussion, especially in view of the focus and definition of leisure employed here.

v. Whilst certain statistical sources distinguished between full and part time employment, very few sources distinguished between temporary, short term, seasonal employment, etc.

vi. In a similar vein, voluntary employment, whilst a major contributor to a number of leisure disciplines have been omitted. Only paid employment has been included.

In light of the above factors, employment statistics incorporated for this paper refer to those people who are employed within "direct provision" of leisure.

A review of published data

As highlighted earlier, the methods of collection, collation, interpretation and presentation vary amongst the different research organisations, which in turn presents problems of the analysis of such information.

Major Sources of Data — Governmental

After initial consultation with the Department of National Heritage (DNH), it was evident that there was a lack of statistical information which referred to leisure as an industry. Subsequently the DNH relied on extrapolating specific information from general industrial statistics, from a variety of sources (usually other government departments).

The two most prominent sources utilised for this paper, regarding employment statistics are based upon either the General Household Survey (GHS), or the Census of Employment.

i. The GHS incorporates SOCs which provide details on the status of occupation — for example: Professional, Skilled Manual. The Census of Employment however incorporates SICs which provide details on the nature of the occupation e.g. Hotels and Catering.

ii. Likewise the Geographical area covered by each survey also differs: GHS represents UK and GB, Census of Employment represents GB, thereby providing differences in numerical figures, as population statistics for these areas vary.

iii. Certain publications referring to the same survey reflect discrepancies in statistical information, e.g. two governmental publications referring to employment figures:

    Employment Gazette [Rest., Cafes, Snack Bars] 296,500 (1993)
    CSO Annual Abstract [Rest., Cafes, Snack Bars] 298,000 (1993)

iv. The Census of Employment (*Employment Gazette*) reflects employees' PAYE returns and in certain cases omits the self-employed, which according to the BTA accounts for a considerable amount of employment especially with respect to Farm tourism. Whilst this may present problems, self-employed figures have been extrapolated from other sources for certain disciplines — especially for Tourism, Hotel and Catering statistics.

v. Other statistical information from various government departments revealed a lack of leisure employment statistics, differing industry classifications, including varying dates of collection and publication of data.

In the light of these difficulties, more valid and reliable data can be obtained from statistics contained within the Census of Employment (*Employment Gazette*). Hence this survey formed the basis of employment statistics, for though the Census of Employment is undertaken triennially, the actual statistics are regularly updated on a quarterly basis by carrying out sample surveys on 30,000 organisations.

Other sources of data — non-Governmental

i. Professional Research Organisations rely mainly on an extrapolation of government statistics (e.g. BTA, ETB, KEYNOTE) and utilise the statistics from the Employment Department as the basis of their statistical publications.

ii. Similarly, the majority of leading leisure organisations are unaware of employment statistics for their own discipline. Some failed to see the relevance of such statistics to their own organisations; in addition, a small number of organisations (for one reason or another) would not divulge any statistical information. Certain leisure organisations are in the process of undertaking a detailed analysis of employment within their particular discipline, e.g. SPRITO, The Arts Council.

iii. An 'overlapping' of statistical information from different sources caused repetition in statistical presentation, for example:
    - *Employment Gazette*, 1995 — Hotel Trade (including campsites, holiday camps, and short stay tourist accommodation) = 301,700
    - ATB-Land Base, 1995 — Rural Tourism (including campsites,

holiday camps, and short stay tourist accommodation) = 400,000 (unsubstantiated)

In this instance, although one source lacked substantiation, the fact remains that there is an overlap in statistics. Rural Tourism, according to some definitions, includes all aspects of tourist activity within the countryside (West Country Tourist Board, 1995), which will also overlap with Countryside statistics. In cases such as these, in the analysis that follows the overlap is acknowledged, but is not extrapolated further.Whilst these statistics may overlap, in part they also include other employment activities which do not overlap, and so both the substantiated and unsubstantiated data are presented.

iv. Statistical information differed dependant upon the source referred to. For example, Forestry:

Forestry Commission (1995) unsubstantiated = 4,000
ATB — Landbase (1995) unsubstantiated = 42,000
Employment Gazette (1995) = 7,700

In these instances, where there is no overlap of statistical information — e.g. employment attributable solely to forestry activities — only the substantiated data are presented.

After analysing and evaluating the secondary sources of statistical information it is evident that:

1. Leisure as an industry fails to be recognised by government, and there is conflicting statistical information.
2. There is an overall lack of information regarding employment within the industry as a whole.
3. There is a lack of information regarding employment within particular leisure disciplines.
4. It would appear that a detailed analysis of employment levels within the industry has never been undertaken.

A sector analysis of employment

Given the difficulties presented in defining leisure, rationalising the leisure industry and accepting the fragmented nature of statistical information regarding employment within the leisure industry, any attempt to give a detailed analysis is fraught with difficulty. However an attempt has been made to register the employment distribution within separate segments in the leisure industry.

1. SPORTS RELATED EMPLOYMENT IN THE U.K.

(Sources include: Employment Department, ISRM, CCPR, Sports Council, ILAM, SPRITO, FIA, DNH, NCF, TLC.)

Sports Council, Henley Centre (1990)	*467,218*
Employment Gazette March (1995)	342,600
Total Employment within Sport and Physical Recreation	342,600

The difference in figures is attributable to the difference in definition of sport and recreational employment. The Henley Centre's figure includes Voluntary sector employment, Police, and Central/Local Government transport. The Employment Department's figure includes sections 9791-SIC 1980. Due to this fact, the Employment Department's figure for employment within Sport and Physical Recreation has been used.

2. TOURISM, HOTEL AND CATERING

(Sources include: Employment Department, HCIMA, ETB, BTA, ILAM, Hotel and Catering Training Company, Keynote Publications, DNH.)

Hotels and Catering Restaurants, Snack Bars, Cafes and Other Eating places (Eating places = supplying food for consumption on the premises) (SIC 1980, 6611,6612)		304,200
Public Houses and Bars SIC 1980, 662)		335,900
Night Clubs and Licensed Clubs (SIC 1980, 663)		135,800
Canteens and Messes (SIC 1980, 664)		117,900
Hotel Trade (SIC 1980, 665,667)		301,700
Self Employed (SIC 661, to 667) (Employment Gazette 1991)		168,300
Visitor Attractions		
Gardens	3,800	
Wildlife	6,000	
Historic properties	20,400	
Other (Leisure/Theme Parks, etc.)	40,600	
Total =		70,800
Total employment within Tourism, Hotel and Catering		1,434,600

3. CULTURAL RECREATION

(Sources include: Employment Department, Museum and Galleries Commission, Arts Council, PSI-Cultural Trends, DNH, ILAM.)

Film Production, Distribution and Exhibition (SIC 1980, 9711) (1991)	*23,900*
Radio and TV Services, Theatres, etc. (SIC 1980, 9741) (1991)	*74,500*
Authors, Music Composers, and Other Own Account Artists (SIC 1980, 9760) (1991)	*10,900*
Libraries, Museums, Art Galleries etc. (SIC 1980, 9770) (Employment Gazette March 1995)	*68,100*
Arts Council (including cultural occupations, and art industries, and also including the self-employed) (Arts Council 1995)	650,000
Museums and Galleries Staff (including 1,875.5 temporary staff) (Museums and Galleries Commission 1995)	12,080
Total Employment within Cultural Recreation	662,080

(The Art Council's figure is seen as a more accurate figure as it represents a more detailed analysis cross referencing SIC's and SOC's and including self-employed, which since 1990/1991, has seen an increase of 135%.)

4. COUNTRYSIDE

(Sources include: Employment Department, CC, CMA, ILB-COSQUEC, DNH, FASTCO.)

Forestry (SIC 1980, 020-0200) (Employment Gazette March 1995)	7,700
English Heritage (English Heritage 1995)	1,568
Countryside Employment (including countryside management, National Trust employees and 3,000 Archaeologists) (Ecotec Consultancy 1989/90)	15,000
Total Employment within the Countryside	24,268

5. AMENITY AND HORTICULTURE

(Sources include: Employment Department, ILB-Agricultural and Commercial Horticulture, ILB-Amenity and Horticulture, Institute of Groundsmanship.)

Garden Centres	20,000 **
Horse Industry (riding, stabling, racing)	35,000 **
Fishing Husbandry	5,000 *
Countryside sports (angling, shooting, etc.)	20,000 *
Environmental and Conservation	114,000 **
Rural Tourism (farm based tourism etc.)	400,000 **
Parks (Private, Public, sports pitches) (Institute of Groundsmanship 1995)	85,000
Horticulture (ILB Amenity and Horticulture 1995)	106,000 **
Total Employment for Amenity and Horticulture	= 785,000
(* Cobham Resource Consultants as featured in ATB-Land Base briefing paper 1995)	
(**ATB-Land Base 1995 based on a variety of sources but considered unsubstantial)	

6. Summary of employment within the leisure industry

Sport and Physical Recreation	342,600	
Tourism Hotel and Catering	1,434,600	
Cultural Recreation	652,080	**662,080**
Countryside	24,268	
Amenity and Horticulture	785,000	
Total Employment	3,238,548	**3,248,548**

(This figure is greater than Fleming's (1991) which may be attributable to an overlapping of certain leisure disciplines; or it could be a reflection of a more accurate analysis of the industry; or the overall employment picture in the leisure industry may have changed; or any combination of these factors.)

Conclusion

An analysis of employment levels within the leisure industry is fraught with difficulties which can in part be attributed to the nebulous nature of leisure. Given the complexity in defining a leisure industry a totally accurate picture of employment is highly improbable. Statistical sources are many and varied and they contributes to the complexities associated with measuring levels of employment. The difficulties are summarised below :

- Lack of agreement as to what constitutes a leisure industry;
- Failure to recognise leisure as an industry;
- Confusing classifications of employment;
- Lack of statistical information;
- Overlapping/repetition of statistical information;
- Conflicting statistical information.

Despite these difficulties, a comprehensive picture of employment within the leisure industry has been attempted.

It could be argued that the above difficulties are symptomatic of a relatively new/immature industry, and that as the industry matures these problems will dissipate. However what is alarming is the fact that a number of leisure organisations fail to recognise the importance of employment statistics within the industry or within their specific discipline. An illustration of this is provided by the current situation where the move towards market led principles by the public sector requires them to be more accountable to be competitive for funding.

Bidding for funds usually incorporates an economic analysis, employment statistics are an integral part of this analysis .

Certain organisations such as The Arts Council and SPRITO are in the process of mapping out employment for their particular discipline. Others have yet to realise the importance of employment statistics. Clearly the difficulties in extrapolating statistical information and rationalising leisure as an industry may present problems for leisure organisations in their attempts to carry out an analysis for their particular discipline.

As long as successive governments continue to fail to recognise leisure as an industry, a significant contributor to employment 3,248,548 (approximately 20% of employment within the service sector — 15,429,300 Employment Gazette, 1995); and whilst certain organisations within the industry fail to recognise the importance of such statistics, these problems will be magnified.

With respect to the Department of National Heritage, it is recognised that there are difficulties in researching employment statistics, and that an analysis of the industry has not yet been undertaken. Indeed, they incorporate the same sources of information that have been utilised in this paper. In the light of this information, it is suggested that the DNH, in its role as co-ordinator of the industry, should —

- provide a comprehensive definition as to what constitutes a leisure industry;
- carry out a detailed analysis of the industry;

— which will alleviate the problems highlighted throughout this paper.

References

Audit Commission (1994) *Leisure services, parks and open spaces: The quality exchange.* London: Audit Commission.

——— (1994) *Museum Service,* section 11, detailed findings of the survey. London: Audit Commission.

British Security Industry Association (1994) *Guidelines for the surveying, planning and operation of stewarding services in stadia and sporting venues.* 24pp. Worcester: British Security Industry Association.

British Tourist Authority (1994) *Tourism Intelligence Quarterly,* Vol. 15, No. 4, 74pp. London: BTA.

Bromley, P. (1990) *Countryside management.* London: E. and F.N. Spon.

Central Statistical Office (1992) *Annual abstract of statistics,* No. 128. London: HMSO .

——— (1991)/92 *Key Data.* London: HMSO.

——— (1991) *Regional Trends 26.* London: HMSO.

——— (1993) *Regional Trends 28.* London: HMSO.

——— (1994) *Social Trends 24.* London: HMSO.

Cheers, A. and Sampson, A. (1991) *The Leisure Environment.* London: Macmillan.

Coalter, F. Celts (1990) *Recreation Management Training Needs — Summary Report.* London: Sports Council.

Eckstein, J. (1993) *Cultural Trends, 20, employment in the cultural sector, books, libraries and reading.* London: Policy Studies Institute.

Employment Department (1991) *Employment Gazette.* London: Government Statistical Service.

Employment Department (1994) *Employment Gazette,* London: Government Statistical Service.

English Tourist Board (1994) *Getting it right: a guide to visitor management in historic towns.* London: ETB.

——— (1993) *Sightseeing in the UK 1992*: a survey of the usage and capacity of the United Kingdom's attractions for visitors.

Feist, A. and O'Brien J. (1995) *Employment in arts and cultural industries.* London: Arts Council of England.

Feist, A. and Hutchison, R. (1989) *Cultural Trends* (1). London: Policy Studies Institute.

Fleming, I. (1991) in *Employment and training opportunities.* Careers in Sport and Recreation Seminar. Birmingham: Sport and Recreation Information Group (SPRIG).

Henley Centre for Forecasting (1991) *Leisure futures.* London: Henley Centre.

Keynote (1992) *Market review, industry trends and forecasts*: UK tourism and travel. London: Keynote.

——— (1992) *Tourist attractions*: Keynote report, a market sector overview. London: Keynote.

——— (1993) *Key note market review, industry trends and forecasts*: UK sports market.London: Keynote.

Morgan, D. (1995) 'An investigation into employment trends in the leisure industry', in this volume.

Office of Population and Censuses Surveys (1991) *General Household Survey 1991:* an inter-departmental survey carried out by OPCS. London: HMSO.

——— (1994) *General Household Survey 1992*: GHS, No. 23. London: HMSO.

Sports Council (1992) *Sport in the nineties, new horizons:* a draft for consultation. London: the Sports Council.

Tourism Research and Marketing (1994) *Theme parks: UK and international markets.* London: Tourism Research and Marketing.

1 GOVERNMENT STATISTICS	2 PROFESSIONAL RESEARCH ORGANISATIONS (GENERAL)	3 PROFESSIONAL RESEARCH ORGANISATIONS (LEISURE SPECIFIC)	4 LEADING LEISURE ORGANISATIONS
EMPLOYMENT DEPARTMENT EMPLOYMENT GAZETTE 1994/5 CENSUS OF EMPLOYMENT 1991 LABOUR FORCE SURVEY 1995 NEW EARNINGS SURVEY 1994 CENTRAL STATISTICS OFFICE ANNUAL ABSTRACTS 1991-95 SOCIAL TRENDS 1994-1995 REGIONAL TRENDS OFFICE OF POPULATION AND CENSUS SURVEYS — VARIOUS PUBLICATIONS GHS. 1991-93	MINTEL — GENERAL MARKETING STATISTICS LEISURE MARKETING STATISTICS KEYNOTE PUBLICATIONS - VARIOUS PUBLICATIONS 1992-93 OECD — QUARTERLY LABOUR FORCE STATISTICS 1995 CIPFA — CHARTERED INSTITUTE OF PUBLIC FINANCE AND ACCOUNTANCY -VARIOUS PUBLICATIONS AUDIT COMMISSION -VARIOUS PUBLICATIONS	POLICY STUDIES INSTITUTE — VARIOUS CULTURAL TREND PUBLICATIONS 1989-1993 LEISURE CONSULTANTS -LEISURE FORECASTS ENGLISH TOURIST BOARD — SIGHT SEEING IN THE UK 1993 TOURISM RESEARCH AND MARKETING -THEME PARKS, UK AND INTERNATIONAL MARKETS 1992-94 HENLEY CENTRE FOR FORECASTING -LEISURE FUTURES 1991	ILB (INDUSTRIAL LEAD BODY) -AMENITY AND HORTICULTURE — IMPLEMENTATIO N PLAN 1994-97 ENGLISH HERITAGE — ANNUAL REPORT AND ACCOUNTS 1993-94 ILAM — VARIOUS PUBLICATIONS 1990-95 ARTS COUNCIL — FACT SHEET ILB — ATB LANDBASE — AGRICULTURE & COMMERCIAL HORTICULTURE FUTURE TRAINING NEEDS — A BRIEFING PAPER 1995 ILB — HOTEL AND CATERING TRADING COMPANY — FACT SHEET MUSEUM AND GALLERIES COMMISSION — FACT SHEET SPORTS COUNCIL — VARIOUS PUBLICATIONS INCLUDING — SPORT IN THE 90s — 1992

Appendix 1 Organisations providing secondary sources of information

* SOURCES ARE LISTED IN HIERARCHICAL ORDER

1 — KEY SOURCE, 4 — SUPPORTIVE SOURCE

ORGANISATION	CONTACT & Nº
ABTA	0171 637 2444
ARTS COUNCIL	0171 3330100 0171 973 6463
ATB LANDBASE — ILB AGRICULTURE & COMMERCIAL HORTICULTURE	01203 696996
CAREERS & OCCUPATIONAL INFORMATION CENTRE	0114 259 4563
CCPR	0171 828 3163
COSQUEL ILB	01452 840825
COUNTRYSIDE COMMISSION	01242 521381
COUNTRYSIDE MANAGEMENT ASSOCIATION	01565 633603
DNH	0171 211 2110
EMPLOYMENT DEPARTMENT	01928 715151 ext 2563 Census Division 01928 792690
ENGLISH HERITAGE	0171 973 3000
ENGLISH TOURIST BOARD	0181 846 9000
FASTCO (ILB)	0131 334 0303
FIA	01276 676275
HCIMA	0181 672 4251
HENLEY CENTRE FOR FORECASTING	0171 353 9961
HOTEL AND CATERING TRAINING COMPANY ILB	0181 579 2400
ILAM	01491 874222
ILB AMENITY & HORTICULTURE	01225 852518
INSTITUTE OF GROUNDSMANSHIP	01908 312511
ISRM	01664 65531
LOCAL GOVERNMENT TRAINING BOARD	01582 451166
MINISTRY OF AGRICULTURE, FISHERIES AND FOOD	01645 335577
MUSEUM AND GALLERIES COMMISSION	0171 233 4200
NATIONAL COACHING FOUNDATION	0113 274 4802
NATIONAL OUTDOOR EVENTS ASSOCIATION	0181 669 8121
NATIONAL PLAY INFORMATION CENTRE	0171 383 5455
SPORTS COUNCIL	0171 388 1277
SPRITO	0171 388 3111
TICK (FORMERLY TRAVEL SERVICES LEAD BODY)	01483 740854
TLC	0171 233 6868

An Investigation into Employment Trends in the Leisure Industry

Dan Morgan

Bolton Business School

Introduction

The purpose of this paper is to analyse recent employment trends in the leisure industry by researching one source of information, the weekly job advertisements service ("Appointments") supplied by the Institute of Leisure and Amenity Management (ILAM). The information generated will form a more concrete picture of the recent employment trends within the leisure industry and identify various characteristics of the job market.

At the outset it must be emphasised that the empirical data are derived from a single source, and one that is patently restricted in its coverage. The source has a built in bias which must be taken into account when making any observations. This feature of the research and others are discussed in the research methodology. Consequently, it is clearly not prudent to make bold assertions about employment trends throughout the leisure industry. However this does not detract from the efficacy of this information in providing one barometer of employment trends within the industry and in providing substantive information on job characteristics.

A guiding objective steering this research is to recognise ways in which it may contribute to the Higher Education (HE) experience of students wishing to pursue a career in the leisure industry. To this end a number of lines of enquiry have sought to identify whether the jobs advertised require 'graduate' competencies and also to determine whether there are specific skills, knowledge or qualifications being sought. These questions are appropriate when recognising the seemingly tenuous links between industry and education at this level, particularly when compared to more conventional professional groups e.g. medicine, law, finance etc... The reasons behind this 'weakness' appear to revolve around three key features, the relative immaturity of the industry, the historical background to much HE provision in this area, and a consequent lack of awareness between industrialists and education.

Added to this lack of liaison is the possible disparity between the needs of the industry and the demands of HE in terms of employee/ student numbers. It is clear that HE establishments have regarded Leisure Studies/Management courses as a lucrative area for the expansion of student numbers. A movement which has its roots in much of the residual hyperbole resulting from unsubstantiated claims from leisure forecasters in the last decade (Jenkins and Sherman, 1980). But perhaps also in the more pragmatic 'bums on seats' approach which has developed as a result of recent government directives.

This research is intended to contribute to the body of knowledge that informs the debate about appropriateness of HE provision, and to eliminate some of the confusion and myths surrounding employment trends within the industry. It seeks to add to the information required by HE course managers when developing courses, and to enhance the quantity and quality of the information they can pass on to their students in terms of career prospects. The results of the paper may be used by students and careers officers in determining characteristics of employment at a particular moment in the industry.

The amount of literature immediately relevant to this study is minimal and the emphasis is laid upon the research data generated. The results of the research are then displayed and briefly described. This is then followed by a fuller discussion which centres upon two main objectives: firstly, to provide an overall picture of employment trends and the characteristics of the job market; and, secondly, to relate this information to graduate prospects.

The conclusion emphasises the caution that must be applied when using these data whilst at the same time recognising their usefulness. There are clear indicators relevant to job prospects for graduates and these are discussed in the broader picture of employment trends within the industry. Pointers are also given as to how this research should be advanced in terms of increasing the investigation and at the same time strengthening its validity and reliability.

There is considerable analytical potential for the data gained during this research. It is possible, for example, to correlate all the variables listed in Table 1 with one another in order to achieve more detailed information regarding particular vocational areas. For instance it is possible to give a comprehensive profile of the job characteristics within Sports Development including location, employers, salary, qualifications required, and so on.

Importantly, too, it is intended that this research will be continued in order to provide a more substantive picture which reflects longitudinal trends in employment within the leisure industry. This of course will be contingent upon resources.

Table 1 Variables

Q1	What is the title of the post?
Q2	What is the level of responsibility of the post?
Q3	What is the maximum salary of the post?
Q4	What is the geographical location of the post?
Q5	When was the job advertised?
Q6	What is the advertised employer?
Q7	What is the job description/location?
Q8	What academic qualifications are required?
Q9	What managerial/professional qualifications are required?
Q10	Is experience required?
Q11	How many years experience are required?
Q12	Is the post suitable for a graduate?
Q13	What hard skills are required?
Q14	Is an age range specified?
Q15	What is the age range?
Q16	What 'soft skills are required?
Q17	Is the post a temporary contract?
Q18	What is the length of the contract?
Q19	To whom is the application sent?
Q20	Is the post part-time?

Research methodology

The empirical research was conducted over a four week period in June/July 1995. A research assistant was employed to analyse the ILAM job advertisements for the period September 1993 to December 1994. In total there were 742 advertisements (cases). Initially a pilot sample of fifty advertisements were analysed to test the mechanism for relating the twenty questions (variables) to the advertisements to ensure that all possible responses (codes) were covered. At this stage all the cases were double checked to ensure that correct codes had been entered for all the variables.

On completion of the pilot a template of responses was constructed. The template was then used on each advertisement to create data sheets which conformed to the inputting requirements of the software used (SNAP Professional). Significant attention was given to ensuring that the template was designed as accurately as possible to cover all the variables contained within the job advertisements. When an anomaly occurred, it was noted and contributed to the parameters of each variable.

The pilot sample proved useful in establishing the finished template particularly highlighting the need for additional codes. Once established, the translation of the job adverts into the codes and their entry onto the data sheets was commenced. To enter 742 cases took approximately fourteen days, averaging a little over fifty per day.

The potential for error was reduced as much as possible at all stages of the research process. The major difficulties appear in the translation of the job advertisements into the codes, which make up the template. Judicious 'fixing' of information was offset by listing any abnormalities. Clearly at this stage a certain amount of subjectivity creeps into the system but this was made as transparent as possible to assist future work.

Initially all the advertisements were given a case number which allowed them to be located for further inspection if necessary. Once the data were loaded into the software the potential for error is greatly reduced as the software reveals any inputting errors.

It is apparent that errors may have appeared during the inputting of data, and these were attributed to keyboard errors. For example, on some of the variables the base differed: it should always have been constant at 742 which was the total number of cases. To check this element was too costly and as the margin of error was so small it was considered negligible. (The largest error was 0.674%, which occurred once.)

Results

Q1. What is the title of the post?	
Manager	28.2%
Director	1.8%
Deputy Manager	15.8%
Supervisor	11.9%
Technical Officer	10.4%
Duty Officer	4.6%
Lecturer	4.0%
Sports Development Officer	22.4%
Other	0.7%

Clearly there are various titles for the posts advertised, but they tended to conform to many other industries in terms of Director, Manager, Supervisor distinctions. It may have been appropriate to consider Sports

Development Officer as a Technical Officer, but it was deemed appropriate to keep it separate because of the large numbers involved. The title 'Manager' appears most frequently and there is no dispute about the figures here as the advert had to mention Manager in its title.

It may, of course, be the case that some of these different titles may, in reality, have had the same responsibilities, but it is difficult to be certain of this.

Q2.	**What is the level of responsibility of the post?**	
	Managerial	31.4%
	Supervisory	34.1%
	Operative	34.4%
	Other	0.0%

The variables were reduced to three for this question in order to rationalise what may have become an over-elaborate issue. The terms Managerial, Supervisory and Operative are common terms used in industry, albeit often loosely. Here, for the vast majority of cases, they have appeared in the advertisement and therefore there is little ambiguity about the described level of responsibility.

Thankfully it redresses the imbalance shown in Q1 with respect to managers and shows that there are marginally more 'Indians' than 'chiefs'.

Q3.	**What is the maximum salary of the post?**	
	Up to £8000	1.6%
	£8,001 to £12,000	14.4%
	£12,001 to £16,000	34.0%
	£16,001 to £20,000	28.6%
	£20,001 to £24,000	10.9%
	£24,001 and above	5.8%

It has not been possible to draw comparisons with other industries but what is apparent is the marked pattern of salaries which show a normal distribution curve.

Q4.	**What is the geographical location of the post?**
Northern	2.4%
Yorkshire and Humberside	5.1%
North West	5.8%
West Midlands	8.8%
East Midlands	7.1%
Eastern	10.6%
Greater London	12.7%
Southern	9.2%
South East	9.2%
South West	9.6%
N. Ireland	0.7%
Wales	4.2%
Scotland	14.8%
Asia	0.1%
Other	0.0%

The geographical areas are consistent with the Sports Council regions. This is not entirely arbitrary, being based upon geographical size and population. Interestingly almost 15% of the jobs advertised are for Scotland which has by no means the largest population. There is a noticeable divide from the Midlands upwards with the Northern, North West and Yorkshire and Humberside regions showing markedly less job advertisements. Further evidence of a North/South divide?

Q5.	**When was the job advertised?**
October to December 1993	11.6%
January to March 1994	22.8%
April to June 1994	24.5%
July to September 1994	24.5%
October to December 1994	16.6%

Through 1994 there was a slight swell in job adverts through April to September. This is not overly significant and maybe more reflective of the major national holiday periods of Christmas and Easter.

Q6.	**What is the advertised employer?**
Local Authority — Client Side	78.2%
Local Authority — Contractor	3.8%
Commercial Sector — Client Side	10.5%
Commercial Sector — Contractor	0.4%
Voluntary Sector	2.3%
Central Government Agency	2.2%
Governing Body	2.6%
Other	0.1%

The results here confirm a known bias in this survey as Local Authorities—Client-side dominate the job adverts. With the bias in mind, it is rather meaningless to compare the various employers. However it may be appropriate to compare the Local Authority—Client side with the Local Authority—Contractor side where there is a marked difference, suggesting very limited movement in the latter. This assumes that the practice of advertising through ILAM is consistent between both sides.

Q7.	**What is the job description/type of work?**
Facility Worker — Dry side	20.4%
Facility Worker — Wet side	9.6%
Facilty Worker — Dry/Wet side	16.0%
Sports Development	24.7%
Arts Development	1.5%
Administration/Policy Unit	16.0%
Country Park	1.9%
Facility Worker — Outside	4.7%
Education	5.0%

Sports Development appears in job adverts on most occasions. The majority of the work is associated with some form of facility, either dry-side, wet-side or both. Administration/Policy units also feature to a large extent.

Q8.	**What academic qualifications are required?**
Degree/HND — Unspecified	35.6%
Degree/HND — Specified	0.8%
Degree/HND — Sports Science/Studies	6.2%
Degree/HND — Business/Admin	0.3%
Degree/HND — Leisure Mgt/Studies	11.5%
Relevant Post Grad Qualification	0.9%
Other	5.1%
Non response	39.5%

Almost 60% of job adverts mentioned some form of academic requirement. The majority were unspecified Degree/HND level. This information can contribute to debates concerning the vocational usefulness of a specified academic qualification, what it cannot tell us is whether a relevant Degree/HND would be looked upon more favourably by an employer. On this score a total of almost 18% of adverts did require a specified Degree from a sport/leisure field.

Q9.	**What Managerial/Professional qualifications are required?**
MBA	0.0%
DMS	0.3%
CMS	0.4%
NEBSS	0.4%
ILAM Diploma	0.3%
ILAM Certificate	0.1%
ILAM Dip/Cert	5.1%
Technical Qualification	2.7%
Other	0.4%
No response	90.4%

Fewer than 10% of the adverts listed this quality, but of those that did, the most sought after was an ILAM Certificate.

Q10.	**Is experience required?**	
	Yes	89.7%
	No	10.3%

The overwhelming majority, almost 90% stated that experience was required.

Q11.	**How many years experience are required?**	
	1 — 3 years	8.8%
	3 — 5 years	8.4%
	5 — 7 years	4.6%
	Other	0.3%
	No response	78.0%

Most of the adverts did not specify the actual amount of experience required. Of those that did, 1-3 years was slightly ahead of 3-5 years.

Q12.	**Is the post suitable for a graduate?**	
	Yes	1.4%
	No	98.6%

This was specially stated in only 1.4% of the advertisements.

Q13.	**What hard skills are required?**	
	First Aid	7.1%
	RLSS	0.0%
	Governing body/coaching awards	0.0%
	IT skills	0.0%
	Driving licence	0.1%
	Numeracy	0.1%
	Written	0.1%
	No response	92.6%

The base on this variable is 57 adverts, which is less than 10% of the total. Of these, the most sought after of the 'hard skills' was a First Aid qualification.

Q14.	Is an age range specified?
Yes	1.15
No	98.9%

A little over 1% specified an age range.

Q15.	What is the age range?
16 — 20	0.0%
21 — 30	0.8%
31 — 40	0.0%
Other	0.1%
No response	99.1%

Of the specified age range only 21-30 features but the frequency of this finding is negligible (less than 1%).

Q16.	What soft skills are required?
Communication	30.8%
Leadership	0.4%
Team player	0.2%
Entrepreneur/motivated/ enthusiastic	0.1%
Analytical skills	0.1%
No response	68.4%

From a base of 232 which is around 30% of the total the most sought after soft skill is communication, the remainder are negligible.

Q17.	Is the post a temporary contract?
Yes	16.9%
No	83.1%

The majority of the posts are permanent but almost 17% are advertised as temporary.

Q18.	What is the length of contract?	
	Up to 1 year	3.3%
	1 — 3 years	10.2%
	3 — 5 years	2.6%
	Other	0.1%
	No response	83.9%

Those posts that were advertised as temporary were usually for between 1 and 3 years.

Q19.	To whom is the application to be sent?	
	Personnel unit	77.7%
	Facility manager	19.8%
	Other	1.8%
	No response	0.7%

The administration of the adverts was done principally by a Personnel Unit and less frequently by a Facility Manager.

Q20.	Is the post part time?	
	Yes	5.2%
	No	94.8%

Barely 5% of the posts were advertised as part time.

Discussion of results

This discussion will take place in two parts, the first will deal with the overall picture, the second will relate the findings to the prospects for recent graduates of Higher Education.

The titles and responsibilities of the posts advertised reveal more managerial/supervisory level positions rather than operatives. This may reflect the use of this medium for advertising which may attract more 'prestigious' posts, with 'lesser' posts being advertised more locally. One clear factor to recognise is the relatively large number of Sports Development posts; and this is confirmed in the type of work which suggests that almost 25% of all adverts were recruiting for this role. It has not been possible to compare the salary spread with other services sector industries but initial impressions suggest it is rather higher than might be expected in the catering or tourism industries. This may be explained by the earlier point that this medium may attract more 'prestigious' posts.

It has not been possible to do a detailed analysis of the geographical distribution such as relations with population density. However Scotland is the highest advertiser despite not having the largest population. No explanation of this has been sought, but it is reasonable to speculate that may be related to economic activity or restructuring in local authority leisure provision.

The majority of employers' advertising is supported by the type of work i.e. facility based, the major owners of facilities who are likely to advertise through this medium are the local authorities. This is reflected in the ILAM membership which is traditionally local authority based.

In terms of qualifications Degrees/HND's are popular (but they are less likely to be specifically sport/leisure based). They are requested significantly more than any managerial/professional qualification. More importantly a level of experience is required and this is usually 1-3 years. In terms of skills required, hard skills are rarely stated although a First Aid qualification is the most desirable. The soft skill most required is the ability to communicate effectively.

Age is not really an issue as would be expected in advertisements. The vast majority of posts were on permanent contracts reflective of the type of positions advertised and the perceived relative stability of the industry. However a relatively small number of the posts were in temporary contracts the majority being between 1-3 years. This may be explained by the model often used for Sports Development posts with 3 year contracts featuring highly, usually a reflection of their funding mechanisms. The vast majority of the posts were full time again perhaps a feature of the advertising medium as it is commonly believed that a lot of the 'lower' end jobs are of a part time nature.

With respect to graduate opportunities there are two major indicators to be recognised. Firstly a large number of the adverts did stipulate that a Degree/HND was required/desirable. But large numbers required experience which is obviously a 'Catch 22' situation for new graduates. This fact is endorsed by very few of the jobs being advertised as suitable for graduate entry. It appears that the commonly held belief of 'getting your foot in the door' holds true in this survey. In terms of preparation of graduates, a few indicators are evident. Firstly it is relatively infrequent that an advert will identify a specified Degree/HND, though as many as 11.5% of adverts did request a sport/leisure degree. In terms of other qualifications there is very little stated demand for managerial/professional qualifications. This appears to be rather contradictory as it is a commonly held belief that these qualifications are increasingly sought after by employers.

There is little stated demand for 'hard' skills in this sample although it is commonly acknowledged that First Aid and Life Saving awards are essentials particularly amongst facility workers. Communication skills are often cited as desirable, this would correlate with the levels of employment which are predominantly at manager/supervisory level. It is acknowledged that requirements like 'soft' skills would not necessarily show themselves in an advert, they are more likely to show in a job description.

The type of employment is dominated by facility work and to a lesser degree sports development. This suggests two discrete groups in terms of knowledge base and skills preparation. The facility side suggests that business/managerial skills would be dominant particularly as most employers are local authority based and operating under the conditions of Compulsory Competitive Tendering. The sports development opportunities would include considerable emphasis on coaching, communication and organisation.

To summarise there is not a clear unambiguous situation regarding employment potential within the industry if we use this analysis of job advertisements as an indicator. There is also little which contradicts many established beliefs about employment trends and the potential for graduates. The picture presented suggests that relevant Degrees/HNDs are a desirable qualification for many of the posts and the data suggest that facility work and sports development are the main areas of employment.

Conclusion

The conclusion will concern itself with those parts of this research project which contribute to the position of H.E. graduates entering the leisure industry job market. Before doing so it is important to emphasise the restrictive parameters and features of this study. It is not possible to casually extrapolate information on a general basis regarding employment trends from this study, the sample is restrictive and not representative. It is also apparent thast the research is not dealing with 'new' posts, therefore any observations about employment growth and potential would be ill advised.

Where this study can contribute is to the picture emerging from the industry regarding its employment characteristics relevant to graduates in the form of job title/responsibilities, geographical locations, academic/professional qualifications required and hard/soft skills required. Perhaps less significantly it offers data on salaries, when jobs are advertised, whether experience is required and whether posts are temporary or part time.

Despite the restrictive sample it is possible to cautiously infer certain observations from this study. A major area for employment is facility work and of interest to graduates is that a large proportion of the posts are at supervisor level and above. Another major sector for employment is in sports development. There is a demand for Degree/HND holders but less requirement for professional qualifications. A large number of the posts required previous experience. It is becoming more imperative that graduates have some level of experience within the industry; but how that is achieved is another matter. Obviously having worked in the industry and then gaining an academic qualification is laudable but perhaps unrealistic for many. Part-time work or work experience placements may offer alternatives. Whichever way the message is clear, *experience is important.*

In constructing this study a major inference is made upon which the foundations of the study were laid. That is that the job advertisements were an accurate reflection of the actual posts. The results are based upon this supposition, it is highly unlikely that it does not hold true.

Finally this type of study is enhanced by adopting a long term perspective therefore allowing a longitudinal analysis to take place. It is hoped that this strategy will be adopted.

References

Baker, S. (1991) Careers in Sport and Recreation Seminar. Birmingham: Sport and Recreation Information Group (SPRIG).

Coalter, F. (1990) *Recreation management training needs — summary report.* London: Sports Council.

Department of Employment (Sept. 1994) *Employment Gazette.*

Department of Employment (Sept. 1991) *Employment Gazette.*

Eckstein, J. (1993) *Cultural Trends*: 20, employment in the cultural sector, books, libraries and reading. London: Policy Studies Institute.

Feast, A. and O'Brien J., (1995) Employment in Arts and Cultural Industries an analysis of the 1991 Census. London: Arts Council.

Feist, A. and Hutchison, R., (1989) *Cultural Trends*: 1. London: Policy Studies Institute.

Fleming, I. (1991) in Employment and Training Opportunities Careers in Sport and Recreation Seminar. Birmingham: Sport and Recreation Information Group (SPRIG).

Henley Centre for Forecasting (1991) *Leisure Futures.*

Jenkins, C. and Sherman, B. (1980) *The leisure shock.* London: Eyre Methuen.

Office of Population and Censuses Surveys, (1991) General Household Survey 1991: an inter-departmental survey carried out by OPCS. London: HMSO.

Office of Population and Censuses Surveys, (1994) General Household Survey 1992: GHS No. 23. London: HMSO.

Graduate Employment, Unemployment and Underemployment

Sharon Todd

Brunel University College

Introduction

Understanding the issues around graduate unemployment, underemployment and employability in relation to the leisure industry are of vital importance to those involved in leisure related courses in higher education. Yet the lack of accurate statistical information available on employment in the leisure industry (see Lowe, 1995; Morgan, 1995) makes comparison with other industrial sectors and national trends problematic. An overly optimistic view of employment opportunities in the leisure industry by the stakeholders in leisure education may have led to exaggerated claims about employment prospects for leisure graduates. [See also Mannerings, 1995)

The Institute of Manpower Studies (IMS) Graduate Review (1993) suggested that there was a surplus of graduates, resulting in higher graduate unemployment, a larger proportion taking further qualifications and a lower point of entry for those gaining employment. The Review concluded that:

> Even in the most optimistic climate, the expansion in higher education will mean that the supply of graduates will exceed their traditional demand in the economy. Graduates will thus become more diffuse in the workforce, taking up a wider range of jobs with different career profiles. (IMS, 1993: p. 11)

Despite a substantial increase in the number of graduates and an economic recession, the Association of Graduate Recruiters (AGR) (an association of 475 institutions in the public and private sector) claimed that one in eight of its members had unfilled graduate vacancies in 1993 (AGR, 1995), a year when one in eight graduates was unemployed (*The Independent*, 27 October, 1994). The message that the IMS and the AGR reports sent to higher education was that the question of employability required urgent consideration.

In the following year (1994) the AGR indicated that there was a 17% growth in vacancies, but again it also reported a shortage of 'good' applicants — i.e. those with the appropriate work related skills (AGR, 1995). The AGR optimism was not matched by the results of The Guardian/ Gallup survey of over a thousand graduates from forty-nine universities, which found that only 57% had secured employment six months after completing their course. The average percentage of graduates in permanent employment for 1994 was 72.1% according to the Universities Statistical Record.

The confusing statistical evidence may be related to the fact that economic growth and hence recruitment patterns vary in different industrial and service sectors. The Universities Statistical Records indicate a wide variation, up to 40%, between subject groupings, with 90.9% of education students in permanent employment compared with 59.3% of humanities students, although an additional 22% of the latter are taking further education and training compared with 3% of education students (*The Times*, 16 June 1995). There are no separate statistics relating to the leisure as distinct subject.

In 1994 the Institute of Employment Studies (IES), formerly the IMS, reported that trends in graduate employment in the United States (US) were relevant to the future patterns of the graduate labour market in the United Kingdom (UK), because the growth in the number of graduates in the UK in the last five years has been experienced in the US for two decades. There has been a threefold expansion of students in the university sector in the UK over the last ten years and despite a predicted slowing down of the rate of expansion in full-time students between 1995 and 1998 (Davies, 1995), the Government projects that one in three young people will be in higher education by the year 2000.

The US trends indicate that the proportion of graduates taking jobs where they are under-utilised has grown to 20%; graduates are taking longer to find the jobs that they want and employers are using selective employment practices, i.e. favouring those graduates with work experience and transferable skills. The Report on the US Labour Market for Graduates (1994), did conclude that the advantages of a degree are substantial compared to high school leavers because many careers have become graduate entry. Neal and Tilley (1993) speculate that this may become the future scenario in leisure, particularly as smaller companies replace the large organisations as employers of graduates.

There has been a dramatic increase in the number of undergraduates studying leisure. The number of leisure degree courses has increased from 18 in 1990 (CNAA, 1991) to over sixty (Bacon and Buswell, 1994) and the market for vocationally oriented leisure courses at all levels remains buoyant.

The Sports Council study of sport, recreation and leisure graduates of 1985 (Coalter and Potter, 1990), reported a high level of 'vocational fit' or conversion rate between the courses and the employment sectors, i.e. 79%

of graduates took their first job in sport, recreation or leisure. The majority were employed in the public sector.

However, the Sports Council study found a 'lack of articulation' between degree courses and the level of entry in the leisure industry, i.e. no recognised point of entry for graduates. This was viewed in part, as a reflection on the lack of standardisation of job titles and responsibilities and also as a reflection of the relative immaturity of the private sector. Nonetheless, it did suggest that the high turnover of employees in many organisations enabled graduates to experience more rapid career progression than non graduates.

Since 1985 there has been an economic recession and significant changes have occurred in the leisure industry, most notably in the public sector with the introduction of compulsory competitive tendering (CCT), increasing the emphasis on economic efficiency and ' leaner and fitter' organisations. In the 1990s there has been a further shift towards managerialist organisational cultures and more commercial modes of operation. Many local authorities have de-layered, making middle managers redundant and ceasing management trainee programmes.

The economic recession of the last five years has also impacted on the private sector, making it necessary for companies to keep staffing costs to a minimum in order to stay competitive. The so called "feel good" factor remains distinctly absent in many homes with consumers remaining cautious in their attitudes to spending rather than saving any spare cash (*Financial Times*, 6 June 1995). Consequently, any optimism about an upturn in the economy and the leisure industry may be slow in filtering down to impact on employment practices. Employers are taking a pragmatic view of future economic trends by opting for maximum flexibility in their workforce, preferring short-term contracts, part-time and casual appointments. Industry apparently needs an efficient, flexible and competitive labour market, yet seems reluctant to give the job security and commitment to employees that promotes the"'feel good" factor.

The interface between industry and higher education has also changed, particularly since the Further and Higher Education Act 1992. The trend is towards more partnership between employers and academics, resulting in the involvement of employers in the design, delivery and evaluation of degree courses. The Enterprise in Higher Education Initiative (EHEI) a programme funded by the Training, Enterprise and Education Directorate of the Department of Employment, was intended to assist higher education to develop 'more enterprising graduates', and in "broad terms enterprise equated to linking the curriculum more closely with the world of work" (Biggs *et al.*, 1994).

The introduction of National Vocational Qualifications (NVQs), occupational standards and the trend towards increasing professionalisation of the leisure industry have added to the pressure on academics to be sensitive to employer needs. There is however no evidence to suggest that greater professionalisation or the introduction of occupational standards has led to the emergence of a more uniform point of entry or recognised career structure for graduates. Indeed critics of occupational standards claim that they are educationally reductive and that the principle of providing a broad liberal education must be balanced against market demands for vocationalism. The CNAA Review warned that "there is a fine line between being market sensitive and market driven", particularly in an industry "that is in a state of transition" (CNAA, 1991: p. 36).

Employers demand graduates that are better prepared for employment, particularly in terms of their work related skills and experience, but also find it difficult to specify the amount of experience or the exact nature of the skills required (Fleming, 1994). On the other hand it is hardly surprising that employers in such a pressured industry as leisure, are not fully up to date with the latest trends in education (Potter, 1993). Universities are adopting a greater diversity of titles for degree courses, often for marketing purposes and also to reflect their particular specialisms or strength, but this may also confuse prospective employers who do not have the time to read the details of the qualifications of each job applicant.

Work placement

Many courses attempt not only to make learning relevant to the workplace, but also to incorporate learning *in* the workplace. Consequently an increasing number of leisure, sport and recreation undergraduate courses include some form of work placement in the programme of study. The CNAA (1991) found that the rationale for the inclusion of a work placement was a response to the increasing demand from students and employers for vocational relevance in academic courses.

According to the CNAA (1991) review, work placements have three broad purposes:

1. Experiential and developmental;
2. Integration of theory and practice;
3. Preparatory.

Work experience and the development of transferable skills are widely regarded as enhancing the employability of graduates, but well organised and supervised placements are resource intensive. Developing educationally worthwhile placements, i.e. that are appropriate and relevant, requires a contact with a network of employers and often a member of staff dedicated to employer liaison. Successful placements depend upon the development, understanding and communication of clear objectives and assessment procedures between the employer, the student and the academic institution.

Assessing the value of work placements in the relation to the additional costs and against the declared objectives may prove to be a difficult task, given the diversity of leisure organisations and the variation in the quality and length of the placement. One of the key indicators ought to be the extent to which graduates are more employable than those without formally assessed work experience.

One of the important benefits of a work placement is the opportunity to network, yet this is as difficult to measure as the value of the reputation of the academic institution. Indeed the reputation of the institution may be based on criteria other than the quality of the courses e. g. the sports performances. There is anecdotal support for the view that 'the old boy (and girl)' network of ex-students has been instrumental in helping graduates gain employment in the past. In the increasingly competitive graduate job market, systematic evaluation of student destinations and how they arrived is needed to inform career guidance and curriculum development. Advice from practitioners at the 'sharp end of the industry' may be extremely helpful and up-to-date (Bacon and Buswell, 1995), but there is also the danger that it could be narrowly focused, limited and relatively short term.

The Brunel University College Graduate Destination Survey

This paper will present a summary of the results of Graduate Destination surveys of the 1993 and the 1994 Leisure Management and Sports Studies Graduates from Brunel University College, formerly the West London Institute and Borough Road College.

Research methods

The Graduate Destination survey was conducted over a two year period, 1993 to 1995, nine months to one year after each cohort completed the course, with the first two cohorts to graduate in Leisure Management and Sports Studies. The first stage was a self complete questionnaire and the second stage consisted of follow up interviews with a selected sample of respondents. There were a total of 139 replies, i.e. a 68% response rate. 64% of the respondents were male and 36% were female, compared to 68% and 32% respectively in the population of graduates.

The gender distribution of the population reflects that of the applicants and intake of a leisure programme when combined with traditional sports studies.

Leisure Management became an admission subject within the modular Integrated Degree Scheme (IDS) in 1990, adding a new multi-disciplinary vocationally oriented programme to the long-standing Sports Studies. The IDS is characterised by flexibility and choice. With academic counselling, students may select modules from two admission subjects and vary the proportion of modules from each subject programme. The programme is structured around a core curriculum of compulsory modules, particularly at level 1 and 2, with options relating to specialisms in Leisure industry at level 3. The Work Placement and the dissertation are compulsory at level 3 for students majoring in Leisure Management. The students are responsible for finding their own placement with the support of a Placement

Officer. The placement is for a minimum of 36 days in term time, but in practice many students complete up to three months by using the summer vacation. Students have not experienced difficulty in securing an appropriate Placement, partly due to the location of Brunel University College in outer London and partly due the range of skills that they can offer employers.

Study objectives

The objectives of the survey were :

1. to identify the number of graduates employed, unemployed or continuing with full-time study;
2. to find out their first destinations and type of employment;
3. to find out the number of jobs held in the first year;
4. to ascertain their reasons for taking a particular job or jobs;
5. to determine the point of entry and starting salary;
6. to identify the most effective methods of job searching;
7. to assess the perceived value of work placements in enhancing employability.

Survey Results

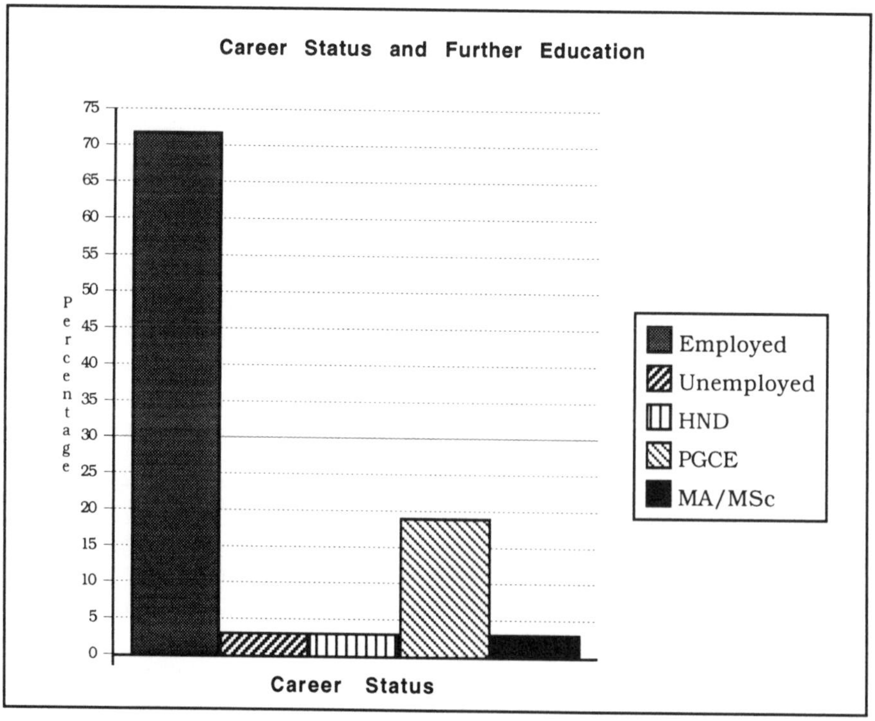

Point of entry

The majority of graduates in employment, 67% of the data set, had entered the industry at level 5 (Coalter and Potter 1990, adapted from Yates 1984), i.e. the most basic operational level.

A high proportion of the those interviewed expressed dissatisfaction and felt trapped in routine jobs. They did not believe that they were using their knowledge but realised that the market for better positions was highly competitive. They also remarked on the large number of job advertisements requiring several years experience for management posts. Most of them thought that they would do better if they were prepared to be geographically mobile, but over half had returned to the parental home to save money and pay off debts and therefore had accepted a job that was convenient.

28% of the data set had entered at level 4, i.e. supervisory /junior management. They were all mature students, i.e. over 24 years, with work experience prior to taking their degree. About half had continued to work for the same organisation whilst studying and, although they were not sponsored, had returned after graduation; 5% were on management trainee schemes with large retailers rather than with leisure organisations.

Starting salary

The IES has predicted the average national starting salary for a 1995 graduate at £14,000, an increase of 3.7% on last year (*Guardian* 23 Jan. 1995). The average declared starting salary in the Brunel University College survey was £9,500 with only 8% of the sample earning more than £15,000. This comparatively low figure may be related to the proportion (35% of the sample), working part-time or on a casual basis, usually on an hourly rate of pay. Some respondents indicated that their hourly rate of pay was relatively high, (£10–£20) particularly those coaching privately, but their hours were limited.

The 1994 Annual Remuneration Survey of the Leisure Industry found that the average salary of managers in the private sector exceeded those in the public sector. The BUC survey revealed that rates of pay at the bottom end of the ladder are comparable in the public and the private sectors.

Reason for taking current position

48% of the sample reported that they accepted their current post in order to gain experience, 43% gave financial hardship as the reason; only 9% said that the job that they had taken was their first choice. The average declared debt on graduation was £1,380, compared to the national average of £2,300 outside London and £2,800 in London (NUS, 1995).

Very few of interviewees in the Brunel University College study had unrealistic expectations about their earning capacity in the first year, and most were fully aware of the competitiveness in the job market. Only a small number had made an effort to secure employment before finishing their final examinations because they believed that job applications were very time consuming.

Number of jobs

Of the respondents, 69% had only one job since graduating; 25% had two to three jobs; 1% had no job at all.

Unemployed graduates

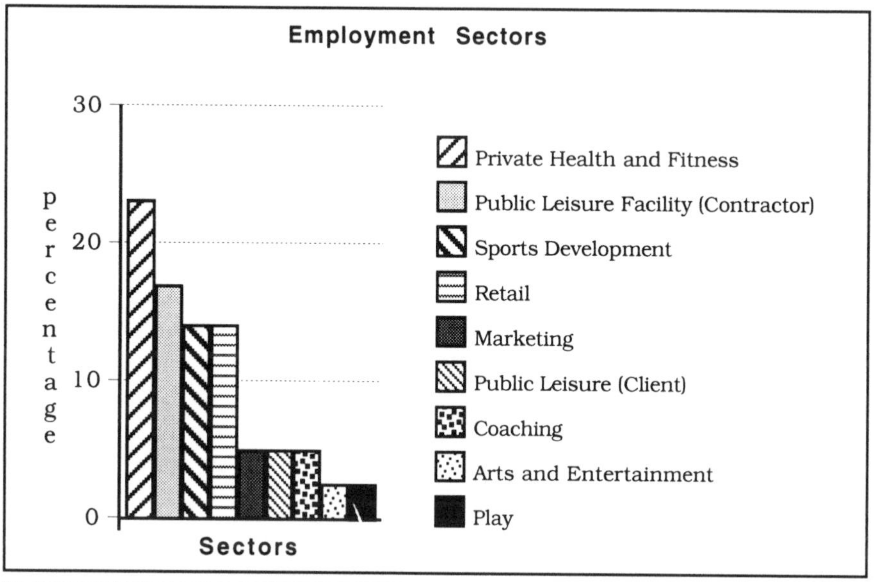

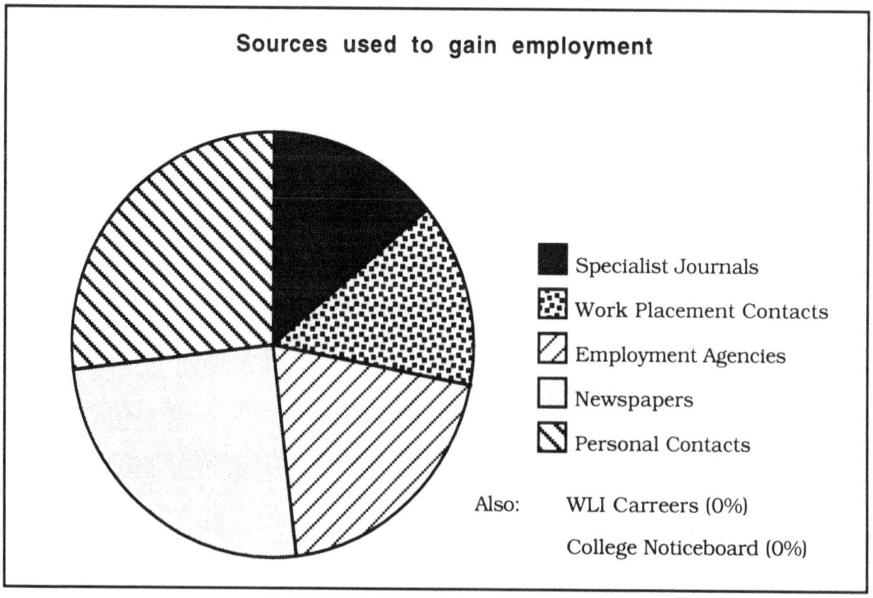

3% of the respondents were unemployed. Follow up interviews revealed that in a number of cases there were a number of factors involved other than an inability to find work. One women had recently had a baby and was a full-time carer. A male athlete was registered unemployed but was in practice a full-time athlete. Another two respondents had previously taken seasonal jobs abroad after completing their studies and had spent some time travelling and had only recently begun to look for work in the UK.

Further education

25% of the data set went on to further study compared to 31% nationally (*Guardian* 1, July 1995). 19% were taking a Post Graduate Certificate in Education (PGCE), 3% were on a taught Masters programmes and 3% on other courses including Post Graduate Diplomas and professional qualifications. The interviewees reported that they intended to enhance their career prospects and had chosen courses with a clear vocational purpose. A number of those on the PGCE reported that they thought the starting salary in teaching compared favourably with industry and would give them job security as well as job satisfaction. A further 22% of respondents reported that they were considering further study, but the fees and opportunity costs involved were prohibitive.

Key findings of BUC survey

1. Average rates of employment — 72% of graduates were employed;
2. Lower than average percentage continuing in education — 25% were studying full-time;
3. High conversion rate- 67% were employed in leisure;
4. Unwillingness to move jobs in first year — 69 % stayed in their first position;
5. Importance of networking — 43% used contacts from work placement or personal contacts to find employment;
5. Significant shift to employment in the private sector;
6. Starting salaries lower than the national average;
7. Low point of entry and no recognised point for graduate entry;
8. Work placement perceived as helping career choices and the development of work related skills;
9. No marked gender differences other than in the greater number of part-time jobs held by women whilst studying;
10. Lower than average accumulated debt on graduating.

Graduate Employability Test (GET)

Employability is increasingly viewed as an important indicator of quality in the assessment of degree courses that claim to be vocationally oriented, yet it is an ill defined concept. Is it possible to talk meaningfully about employer needs in such a fragmented and heterogeneous industry such as leisure?

There has been broad agreement about generic sets of transferable work related skills over and above the specific curricula of degree subjects in order to develop a Graduate Employability Test (GET).

A computerised assessment designed to provide a standardised measure of 'employability' is currently being developed by Drake Psychometric, a American based company, for a pilot project that has the support of the Department of Employment and Education and the Association of Graduate Employers (AGR).

The GET comprises a four part assessment of the set of criteria adopted by the steering group;

1. Basic computing skills — devised by the National Computing Centre at Manchester University;
2. Psychometric profiling — devised by Saville and Holdsworth;
3. Work Awareness;
4. Student feedback.

These elements of employability will be measured at secure test centres, situated in companies and universities, at a fee to be charged to the graduate. The graduate will receive the test result that will provide 'proof' of employability to prospective employers alongside the degree.

A prototype will be market tested with groups of 1995 graduates from the University of Humberside, some of whom will have had a sandwich year in industry.

The GET begs a number of important questions: whether it is based on a meaningful concept of employability; and if so, whether is has sufficient predictive validity to enable employers to recognise worthwhile job applicants. Furthermore it could be argued that it may undermine the credibility of degree awards and that the supposed elements are an integral part of vocationally oriented degree programmes and as such will have already been assessed. Nevertheless some graduates may welcome any additional certification that improves their chances of employment, despite the extra expense, particularly when graduating from non vocationally oriented courses.

There has been an increasing lack of confidence in the US about the quality and comparability of the degrees awarded by different universities partly due to the large numbers of undergraduates. Similarly in the UK, concerns about the 'levelling down' of standards have been raised by stakeholders in higher education.

The Committee of University Vice Chancellors and Principals recently debated national standards and the parity of awards. Their concern was to preserve academic diversity and autonomy whilst ensuring that standards in higher education are maintained. HEFC Circular (39/94, 1994) sets out Quality Assessment Methods from April 1995 and stresses the importance of assessing outcomes against the specified aims of a subject programme.

If preparation for the world of work is a stated aim of leisure courses, then the need for thorough monitoring and in-depth evaluation of graduate destinations is of vital importance.

As this paper has attempted to highlight, Statistical Indicators (SIs) of employment and further study, as well as entry profiles, progression and completion rates and student attainment are indicators of quality. SIs do however need further analysis and interpretation in order to inform the debate about graduate employment, unemployment and employability, particularly in a fast changing industry like leisure.

Acknowledgements

I would like to extend thanks to Carl Anderson, B.Sc (Hons), Research Assistant on this project.

References

Association of Graduate Recruiters (1995).

CNAA (Council for National Academic Awards) (1991) *Review of sport, recreation and leisure courses.* London: CNAA.

Coalter, F. and Potter, J. (1990) *A study of 1985 graduates from sport, recreation and leisure courses.* London: Sports Council.

Bacon, W. and Buswell, J. (1994) *Directory of UK leisure courses 1994/5.* Reading: ILAM.

Biggs C., and Brighton R. *et al.* (1994) *Thematic evaluation of EHEI.* Employment Department Research Series 38.

Davies, G. (1995) 'HEFC policies and the funding of teaching', paper presented at HCFCE Policy Conference 1995, University of Warwick.

Fleming, I. (1994) *Training needs analysis in the leisure industry.* Reading: ILAM.

Kingston, P. and Macleod, D. (1995) 'No guarantee', *The Guardian,* 1 July 1995.

Lowe, M. (1995) 'An investigation into employment levels within the leisure industry', this volume pp. 285-298.

Morgan, D. (1995) 'An investigation into employment trends in the leisure industry', this volume pp. 299-312.

Neal, L. and Tilley, C. (1993) 'Job growth', *Leisure Opportunities* ,No. 107, pp. 40-41.

O'Leary, J. (1995) 'Glut of graduates take basic jobs', *The Times*, 22 June 1995.

Potter, J. (1993) *Guide to jobs and qualifications in sport and recreation.* Reading: ILAM.

Schofield, P. (1994) 'Advantages of a degree', *The Independent*, 27 October 1994.

Ward, D. (1995) 'Job-seeking graduates find little fun at the fair', *The Guardian*, 4 July 1995.

From Theory to Practice and Back Again: An Examination of the Role and Development of Recreation Management within Higher Education

Chris Wolsey

Leeds Metropolitan University

Recreation Management

Although there are many existing definitions of both 'recreation' and 'management', their juxtaposition creates a number of tensions. For instance, by bringing the two words together, do they lose their independence or do they still retain an element of mutual exclusivity? This raises a number of interesting questions. If the two areas are regarded as disparate then it is possible to argue that management education and training should revolve around generic principles. If this is accepted, in its crudest sense, the implications are that Business Schools within Higher Education would dominate the delivery of this area. As May and Botterill (quoted in McKinney, 1984: p. 20) argue:

> Why should recreation management be different, has it got such an unusual or unique level of knowledge that general management training does not apply to it?...We are kidding ourselves if we believe that recreation management requires such a unique body of knowledge that the existing management course cannot meet the demand. In this profession we need generalists from all the fields who can adapt, not specialists.

However, if one accepts the above axiom, what about those who find it difficult to adapt? Can the profession rely on sufficiently discerning recruitment practices to differentiate between candidates in this way? Following critical reports in the mid 80s (Handy, 1987) about the state of British management it is clear is that:

> The context of management, the way managers work and the kind of managers needed in 1995 or 2001 will be different. However, the need for managers of the highest quality will remain. (Clarke, 1992)[1]

This distinction is demonstrated by Thomas (quoted in Moggridge, 1992) who charts the changing nature of management skills within the public recreation sector. He argues that a more 'commercial' outlook is a pre-requisite and that public sector managers need to be well versed in a number of areas that represent significant departures from the original routes of the service. These reflect the dynamic and changing context of public sector provision and would include the following:

- Client Relations
- Quality Standards
- Leadership
- Financial Management
- Risk Management
- Business Planning

It is clear that there is a shift in the type of skills and knowledge required by contemporary Recreation Managers. It seems appropriate, therefore, to briefly examine the nature of the recreation management profession.

The Recreation Management profession

Torkildsen (1986: p. xviii) provides a useful framework by arguing that a recreation manager is a person:

> who has evolved with a mix of education, training, inside and out-side the job situation, and some experience, into a person with motivation, ability and sufficient understanding to create and manage opportunities for people at whatever level is satisfying to them.

Clearly, the provision of appropriate training and education at different levels of the management hierarchy is a complex and dynamic process. However, it is one thing to label an individual as a recreation manager; it is another to define such terms within the context of a profession. The Yates Report (DOE, 1984)[2] viewed a 'profession' as an area that has a recognised body of theoretical knowledge:

...entry being dependant on a substantial period of systematic study, its application in practice, applied study and achievements. (p. 82)

In a consideration of the early evidence of the emergence of such a profession, however, the analysis of the non-public sector by Cousins *et al.* (1980) demonstrates that, in an area of 'management' dominated by the voluntary sector, many had no formal qualifications. Moreover, Long and Coppock (1979: p. 2) refer to a "a lack of a clearly defined career structure". Although the debate has progressed through the 80s and into the 90s there is still evidence to suggest that:

a characteristic of paid employment in sport and recreation ... is that a premium is placed on qualities such as personal effectiveness, communication skills, customer care and enthusiasm for a sport, even to the extent that the possession of more formal qualifications is disregarded". (Sport and Recreation Industry Lead Body, 1989: p. 6)

This point is echoed by more recent evidence. Potter (1994) argues that a proven track record is at least as important as a formal academic background. Moreover, he argues that the commercial sector, whose activity in this area of the economy has mushroomed during the 1980s, is even less interested in formal qualifications. The Polytechnic of North London found that 38% of those working in the area of Sport and Recreation had no formal qualifications. This is ironic as an industry that is fighting for professional status continues to marginalise the role of education in training. Paradoxically, this comes against a backdrop of a burgeoning educational and training sector. Clearly, an understanding of the dynamic that exists between the two should, at least in part, explain the apparent contradictions.

The post 16 explosion

The inexorable rise in the provision of related courses has been charted by many commentators. From its early beginnings when the Molyneux Committee (1969) reported on the provision of an appropriate Diploma in Management Studies (DMS) course for Sports Managers, there was little movement during the 70s. This perhaps explains why the majority of managers recruited into this expanding sector were ex military or police personnel. As McKinney (1984: p. 2) explains:

The large scale leisure service expansion in the 1960s and early 70s faced narrowly trained specialists with situations for which their previous experience and education were of little help.

The first two undergraduate courses were initiated during the early 1980s. Fleming (1994) estimates that there are between forty and fifty undergraduate courses and approximately 50 at postgraduate level. Potter (1994) puts the number of undergraduate courses to be in excess of sixty. Such figures are now likely to be grossly underestimated when one considers the current plethora of both degree and sub degree level qualifications in further education colleges. Despite such proliferation, there has been little work done in Britain with reference to the appropriateness of such academic courses. The majority of work has been done in the more specialised area of sports management in the United States. De Sensi *et al.* (1990: p. 41), reporting on a 'needs analysis' of American sports organisations, contradicts earlier arguments.

> Respondents expressed the view that sports management is a unique area of study and that knowledge in all aspects of sport is important. It was noted that generic management skills alone are insufficient preparation for the sports manager and that practical / internship experience is important to better understand the sports management setting.

It is clear from most of the work in this area that a balance between knowledge and application is needed. However, it is the position occupied along this continuum that engages the central discourse of this area. Potter (1994: p. i) points out that:

> Higher Education courses are interesting, varied and often good fun. They offer students the opportunity to study a fascinating and topical subject and also to gain a range of transferable skills which are vocationally relevant to their future career prospects.

Yet whilst this may be the ideal for some, there is little evidence available to either reinforce or refute such assertions. For some, the picture is one of a new area of academic development that is fighting hard to legitimise its status. Logie (cited in Glew, 1991), Chairman of the CNAA Committee for Consumer and Leisure Studies, argues that institutions should have a strong research base before they should consider offering undergraduate programs in this area. This has clear implications for the 'new' undergraduate provision provided by colleges of further education. Clearly there are those who feel that the move towards vocationalism represents a grave threat to higher education and will serve to undermine and dilute the academic credibility of this area. De Sensi *et al.* (1990: p. 51), report that 26% of the students questioned commented upon the lack of respect for their area of study. It is not surprising, therefore, as Coalter (quoted in CNAA, 1991) intimates, that vocational moves are merely accommodated by higher education establishments and do not represent the central thrust of academic and curriculum development[3]. He goes on to summarise the main issues within the academic provision of leisure related courses in Britain.

> The large number of course modifications reflects the rapidly changing nature and demands of the traditional labour markets, and the emergence of new graduate training opportunities. More generally, increased demand for 'vocational relevance' is having its effect. As in other areas of education, it is raising questions about the balance between, discipline based curricula and more subject centred approaches, and between a broad-based liberal, academic education and a more narrow vocationalism. Further pressures for change come from the increased emphasis, within educational institutions, on student centred and skills based learning and the modularisation of degree programmes. (CNAA, 1991: p. 6)

Ironically, recent attempts to define the learning needs of Britain's recreational managers have been initiated by the government promotion of vocational courses. Although the purpose of such research is not wholly congruent with an academic approach to the study of recreation and leisure, it would be foolish to disregard the work done in this area, particularly with reference to the more overtly vocational area of recreation management. Indeed, as the Government's stop-go policy towards the funding of post 16 education now turns its attention to further education, Boswell (1993)[4] asserts that between 1993 and 1996 planned government expenditure in this area is scheduled to increase by 25%. He goes on to state:

> An estimated 71% of 16 year olds and 55% of 17 year olds (1992-3) are following full time education (F.E. and schools, England), up from 42% and 27% respectively in 1979-80. But we need to increase the participation still further and to reduce the drop out from courses. (Boswell, 1993: iii)

This yields an interesting ambiguity for Post-16 education. It could be argued that increased student numbers, in tandem with increases in the incidence of student drop out, represent a cause and effect relationship that has serious implications for the teaching and learning experiences of students. Britain's teenagers have a 'Hobson's choice' when it comes to further and higher education, being unable to obtain work and being disallowed unemployment payment by recent Government changes. Glew (in CNAA, 1992b) refers to the implications of increasing student numbers, in the context of a declining unit resource. He argues that less than commensurate increases in staff numbers will inevitably lead to an increased need for pastoral care, timetabled contact time and administration. This, in turn, will result in decreases in the amount of research conducted which will, ultimately, lead to decreased teaching standards.

While this paper will examine responses to the above, it is interesting to place such discussions within a wider context. For example, while Coalter previously articulated a move toward more student centred study, he also points to the fact that such programs are often inadequately resourced. In an age dominated by increased student numbers and a declining unit resource, on a superficial level, it makes sense to adopt an approach that reduces formal student contact time. However, it could be argued that such an approach is problematic when attempting to simultaneously promote effectiveness and quality. Of course, this all takes place within approved internal and external quality control mechanisms, the most visible of which are the validating bodies.

The validating bodies

The last five years have seen major changes in the function of Britain's validating bodies. The change of the former Polytechnics to University status confers upon them the right to grant their own awards. As a result, the CNAA has lost its remit. With the majority of undergraduate courses in leiusre being dominated by the former polytechnics, this has led to a situation where no single body has an overview and accountability for the study of leisure within higher education.

Further Education is dominated by three main bodies; namely, BTEC (Business and Technical Education Council), City and Guilds, and the RSA [Royal Society pof Arts]. Since the first of October 1993, when BTEC gained independent status, all three bodies have competed for students in the same marketplace — that of vocational qualifications. However, as Preston (1993: p. xi) opines:

> Vocational education has long been the black hole of the British system, a whirlpool on the outer fringes of the education debate, sucking in a stream of ill-fated government initiatives never to be seen again.

The government response to such criticisms is the system of National Vocational Qualifications. Broadly, this has the 'potential' to address some of the recommendations of the Yates Report (1984: p. 67) which called for a systematic and co-ordinated professional career structure and argued "the merits of formal academic qualifications were rated extremely low compared with other aspects of training". Not surprisingly, this philosophy is reflected by those who deliver the management related NVQs. For example:

> NFMED[5] recognises that management education and training needs to be firmly based on what managers do in the workplace, not purely on academic study.

Such developments are mirrored by the professional, work based, qualifications offered by ILAM In addition, it is clear that those working within a general management environment, welcome the opportunity to gain qualifications that are directly related to work duties. In a pilot study conducted for the CNAA (1992a) by Klynveld-Pete Marwick Goerdeler (management consultants) into the development and use of the highest vocational management qualification, 85% of respondents cited the main advantage was its relevance to the work environment. Interestingly, however, in the same study, whilst the practical emphasis was applauded, there still appeared to be resistance to an academic approach. Not surprisingly, the review did not canvass the opinion of academics in this area but appeared to rely, exclusively, on the views of the candidates. However, the marketisation of education in this area has led to a number of problems. As a consequence, the reality has not necessarily delivered the dream.

In order to place subsequent discussions within an appropriate context, it seems necessary to consider the nature of learning and the implications for the teaching and learning strategies adopted by undergraduate programs in this area.

The relevance of learning theory

Tennant (1986: p. 121) refers to the concept of learning as an activity that is "mechanical, rational and logical". This represents quite a narrow concept of learning and appears to be oriented toward the systematic pursuit of knowledge. Whilst this may be useful in certain instances, this necessitates a deeper discussion around what constitutes knowledge. Knowledge must surely be defined relative to the individual and the environmental context in which learning takes place. Knowledge should not, therefore, be defined purely as a pursuit of what is known, but also what is not known. Education provides the focus for this wider conceptual development within the individual and takes place within the context of referent others. It is used to signify the unwritten contract between the educator and the student. It is this much maligned and misunderstood dynamic, that can inform the interpretation and thus conclusions of this paper through an analysis of appropriate teaching and learning strategies.

Although the lexicon of learning is dominated by the concept of pedagogy, I would argue that the concept of androgogy has much to contribute to the approaches adopted by recreation management courses within higher education. Knowles (1983) is regarded by many as one of the key protagonists behind such distinctions. He argues that most of the 'learning' literature is based around children who are 'educated' under conditions of 'compulsory attendance'. By implication, Knowles is making the point that there are differences in motivations between a 'child' and and 'adult'. He goes on to articulate the respective differences between dependency and that of the developing 'self concept'. In his writings Knowles implicitly draws distinctions between the differing motivations for the pursuit of knowledge. However, he does this without explicitly defining the term. Clearly, this must be regarded as a central issue. If 'knowledge' is regarded as a static concept this would be problematic in an educational context that has to provide the ability to adapt to the changing roles and quickening pace of the world in which we live.

Of all the existing definitions of androgogy, perhaps one of the clearest definitions is provided by Allman (1983: p. 117). She defines it as a:

> ...theoretically based approach to the education of adults, which derives from the emerging theory of adult development and which rests upon an identifiable set of assumptions about the nature of adult beings, the nature of learning, education, knowledge and adult development.

One of the key difficulties with theories of adult learning is the term itself. Is 'adult' to be defined in terms of chronology, or is it a legal, moral or psychological construct? Such confusion is echoed by the literature. For instance, Knowles (1983: p. 53) suggests that adulthood begins at "that point at which he perceives himself to be wholly self directing. and at that point he also experiences a deep need to be perceived by others as being self directing". He goes on to argue that this is represented b y an increasing pool of knowledge that enhances learning. Implicitly, Knowles is suggesting that the motivation to learn is perceived as a function of the utilitarian nature of knowledge. Hence, there will be a natural tendency for 'adults' to gravitate towards instrumental forms of learning that facilitate immediate solutions to problems. With continuing high unemployment levels and the competitive nature of the job market a prominent academic, interviewed as part of the research for thisd paper, argues that:

> The students are frightened...it's quite clear that these kids are more instrumental in their notions of what they need and they can't afford excursions into the esoteric and abstract that are perceived to be of less use than more vocational knowledge and skills development. (Wolsey, 1995: p. 50)

However, this short termism could be seen as contradictory to the wider notions of personal development and thus education.

Whilst Knowles offers little evidence for his assertions, it is clear that the distinction between the 'child' and the 'adult' is an arbitrary one that can be subdivided into many different periods, such as adolescence. As a consequence, the continuum that exists cannot easily be defined by discrete units of age. A reliance on chronology is therefore likely to be misguided as individuals have different potentials that may or may not be realised at different points in time.

Tennant (1988) offers a different but useful interpretation of cognitive development in adulthood. The 'stability' model assumes that cognitive processes are developed during childhood and remain relatively static thereafter. Alternatively, he argues that the intellectual qualities of the individual may reduce with age but are subject to compensation from more experiential forms of knowledge. With respect to those benefiting from higher education, this raises the critical question of where adulthood begins. If one assumes, for example, that this begins at eighteen, this has fundamental implications for teaching and learning strategies within further and higher education. This may lead to a redefinition of the objectives of such institutions as personal development would be a concept largely applicable to training and skills development.

Learning theories and recreation management

Moving from the general to the more specific application of theoretical approaches to learning, it is surprising to find a lack of information that links such theories to the specific area of recreation management. Although there is debate around the central issues of academic rigour versus the perceived dilutory affects of an approach driven by narrow vocationalism, there is little evidence to justify the opinions that are postulated. For instance, in a review of the area, Lawson (1990) argues that very little is known about the relevance of undergraduate courses with respect to progressive professional development. Conversely, without offering supporting evidence, ILAM (1994a) assert that:

> Another problem is that many managers in the leisure (and other) industries never question whether their qualifications, often obtained many years ago, are still relevant and useful. It is an alarming fact that most degrees nowadays have an 'information lifespan' of only a few years. Hence, even highly qualified people are operating on a basis of often severely outdated information — and do little or nothing to rectify the situation. The days are long gone when an initial qualification served as a relevant underpinning for a lifetime's career.

Although this paperwill seek to investigate some of the above claims, it does, perhaps, reflect a naiveté with respect to the purpose of undergraduate programs in this area. Clearly, if the central thrust of such courses related to the instrumental pursuit of relevant information, academic institutions would be doing a disservice to the student. Knowledge should be used to illustrate more general principles which can be used by students to develop their own conceptual models of reality. This contention would be supported by CNAA (1992a: p. 45):

> Many would argue that an adequate basis for knowledge and an understanding of the principles underlying competence are a necessary pre-requisite for any transferability of competence.

Whilst this leads to debates around the nature, adequacy and form of knowledge/understanding, it is interesting that ILAM seem to have a narrower conception of the purpose of higher education. This illustrates the inevitable tension between the two. Parker (in McKinney, 1984: p. 26) demonstrates this dichotomy:

> I see academic concerns as those connected with the learning process in its own right — to put it in a crude and extreme form, the pursuit of knowledge for its own sake ... professional concerns can also be expressed in a crude and extreme form: getting knowledge ... to get a qualification in order to get a job.

Although Parker simplifies the continuum somewhat and does not talk in terms of understanding and application, it does serve to highlight the clear differences that exist between the two sectors. It is interesting that both sectors have done little to articulate how their philosophy is grounded in appropriate learning theory and how this then relates to teaching and assessment strategies. Fleming (1994: p. 76) provides an example of the limited thinking around this area. He argues that learning has five associated elements:

1. Psychomotor: Manual / Practical Skills
2. Cognitive: Knowledge of Rules / Procedures etc.
3. Affective: Feelings / Opinions / Belief
4. Interpersonal: Teamwork / Working With Others / Communication
5. Self Knowledge: Knowledge of Own Behaviour

The above implies an emphasis on 'training'[6] and not the wider role of 'education'[7], as previously defined by Parker. Self Development is not represented, either implicitly or explicitly by the list. This implies a subordinate role for the learner, who is encouraged to ensure orders are understood and effectively carried out within a team environment. This narrow conception of 'training' does not promote progressive learning that encourages individual adaptation through appropriate reflection which is informed by relevant theory. As a result, far from promoting individual conceptual development, the oppositeis true. This ability is particularly important in an environment that is dominated by dynamism and volatility. It is, therefore, of critical importance to Britain's Recreation Managers.

In this context, Furnham (1994: p. 68) argues that, "Education is only a ladder to gather ripe fruit from the tree of knowledge, not the fruit itself". With this in mind, the role of higher education should be that of a conduit to higher levels of understanding. Yet this can only be achieved if the student is able to draw associations and interrelationships between the different branches of theory and practice. In this sense, it is critical that the teacher is able to illustrate the theoretical interrelationships and how these are intertwined and enhanced by relevant practical application. Of course:

> The issue of integration and academic coherence is of fundamental intellectual importance to many of the courses and academics in this area. A major concern is the need to establish the legitimacy of sports and leisure studies as coherent academic fields, rather than subject areas illuminated by, but not a central concern of, a broad range of disciplines. (Coalter, 1991: p. 29)

Although Coalter is referring to the wider area of sport and leisure studies and not management per se, the issues are still germane to this area of research. In an effort to promote an holistic and more useful understanding of related subject areas, there is an inevitable tension between a multi-disciplinary approach and the development of a cognate field of study. Hence, the distinctions between multi-disciplinary and inter-disciplinary approaches are not esoteric but of fundamental importance to the development of a more integrated and academically coherent approach to this field of study.

Curriculum development

Differences of opinion have already been touched upon and from the literature available it is apparent that commentators in this area tend to defend a position that is aligned to their own area of expertise. For example, Parker's earlier exposition (in McKinney, 1984) tends to legitimate the perceived dichotomy in this area. In this context, it is interesting that he advocates a discipline based approach to leisure studies curricula. This includes human geography, psychology and sociology as essential components and economics and a historical/philosophical component as desirable. Fred Harrison (in McKinney, 1994: pp. 40-42) adopts a wholly more pragmatic view that partially reflects the different emphasis of an undergraduate course designed to explore the issues pertinent to recreation management as opposed to the more generic approach adopted by a leisure studies program. As such, he advocates a developmental curriculum, designed to promote a progressive and holistic study of the area. This would be modular in structure and would be dominated by management based units such as marketing, finance and human resource management. This would culminate with modules designed to facilitate an appreciation of advanced management applications through the use of case studies.

The two views serve to highlight the differences in the approaches and conception of the academic community. Clearly, there is need for a balance between the esoteric and the pragmatic, between a comprehension of the social sciences and the hard-nosed pursuit of management skills. The Yates Report (1984: p. 15) recognised this and argued:

> The consequences of this gathering change in the values of society,

> its attitudes, lifestyles and interests, and of the growing dangers of unlimited demands on precious and often irreplaceable resources and of the rising concern for individual and community needs, are that there must be a greater awareness among recreation managers of the meaning and impact of their decisions, both in relation to the environment and to human development. Education and training should seek to stimulate this awareness.

This view is echoed by a number of other commentators from within this area (Kelley, *et al.*, 1994). ILAM (1994: p. 2) argue that:

> Leisure managers are not just specialist professionals, they also need to be cultivated humanists with a grounded understanding of the wider culture and problems of society, which can usefully be gained by the leisure focused study of such disciplines as history or sociology.

It is important to note, though, the apparent bias of the Yates Report towards public sector considerations. Within this context and despite the increasing importance of a societal marketing perspective within the commercial sector, the above sentiments may simply be unrealistic in the increasingly competitive environment of the 90s. In addition, one must also consider the changes imposed by the government upon the public sector in the intervening period. There is a considerable body of evidence to suggest that ever increasing levels of financial stringency and the introduction of Compulsory Competitive Tendering (CCT), has brought very real changes in the rationale of the public sector and thus the purpose of management within this area. As Coalter (1991: p. 16) argues, local government "will increasingly require a range of generic management skills and knowledge of commercially oriented subjects, such as marketing and finance". It is interesting to speculate why such subjects are automatically aligned with commercial practice. Surely, this is more an example of good practice that is equally applicable to all sectors!

Indeed, the argument outlined above merely serves to compound the complexities associated with any attempts to synthesise discernible patterns of skills and knowledge from the literature. Whilst it is true to say that the majority of research has been completed in the United States, there is a number of useful studies that have been completed in this country. The difficulty for analytical purposes is reflected by differing research rationales and methodologies. Cousins *et al.* (1980: p. 4), commenting on the situation in the non-public sector, point to the fact that "there may be no general agreement — even within a distinct part of the non public sector — upon a definite package of necessary skills".

This reflects the dichotomy between the need for general and specific elements of skills and knowledge. From the perspective of curriculum development, this would equate to a range of core modules combined with a range of specialist options that cumulatively provide an aggregated learning experience [this approach is supported by Kelley *et al.* (1994)]. While Parker (in McKinney, 1984) would advocate a curriculum of which 50% is devoted to a social science approach, Ian Fraser of ILAM concedes the value of 'philosophy' but argues that the balance should be 40% specialisms, 35% management and 25% philosophy (both opinions are cited in McKinney, 1984: pp. 49) It is useful to draw comparisons between this approach and that previously adopted by ILAM in which a social science perspective is not represented within their 'core professional disciplines'. The move towards professional accreditation based exclusively upon work practice merely serves to reinforce the changes in approach during the intervening period.

In this sense, there can be no definitive conclusions, merely informed speculation developed through the normative opinions of others. In the United States, where there is a more advanced and sophisticated, empirically based, literature, the latest review concludes that:

> Although needs assessment research studies, professional scholarly opinion, and curricula theory have addressed important issues and suggested problems that need attention, no one has dealt with creative, pragmatic and integrated curricula solutions". (Kelley *et al.*, 1994: p. 94)

The Sport and Recreation Industry Lead Body (1989) demonstrate the extent of the difficulty by identifying 380 job titles in this area alone, which they categorise into 12 functional areas. However, little explanation is given of this process and it is therefore difficult to comment upon the appropriateness of this rationalisation. Interestingly, one of the areas identified is that of sports development. This again reflects the dynamic nature of the recreation sector, as in the intervening period there has been an explosion in the number of development officers who would be excluded from this categorisation; for example in the area of leisure / community development and Health Promotions.

With this in mind, it would be counterproductive to merely provide a descriptive account of the plethora of skills which have been identified by the studies across a range of differing criteria. For instance, De Sensi *et al.* (1990: p. 31) found that the, "results...indicated major differences across settings for academic/experiential requirements, employment needs, workload distribution, and job evaluation criteria...". With this in mind, it is useful to consider the purpose of higher education curricula in this area.

The purpose of higher education

There was considerable agreement amongst the research respondents[8] *vis-à-vis* the purpose of higher education. Critical reflection and problem solving were central to this notion, together with the development of communication and social skills, the latter two being regarded by academics as implicit but not explicit within courses. This is demonstrated by a practitioner respondent, who argues:

> "...any university degree course would be of equal value after six months of experience...the course gives you the ability to think rationally, to write reports, to organise your thoughts...what you will have got through doing a job will far outweigh what you have got from doing the courses". (Wolsey, 1995: p. 46)

By implication, the respondent is making the point that it is the process, rather than the content of courses that has vocational relevance. This point is echoed by another practitioner who contends that students:

> "...come out with theory and then they have to learn how to translate it. All that university can really hope to do is to teach you to think. They need to be able to look at a situation very quickly and to decide, do I have the tools to deal with this and if I don't where do I get this information from". (Wolsey, 1995: p. 46)

Some respondents take the argument one stage further by questioning the real value of any theoretical approach to management, particularly when it is not grounded in appropriate practice. It is here that real differences begin to emerge between the practitioners and academics. For the former, the ability of students to demonstrate real experiential knowledge and achievements outweighs by far the value of theoretical understanding. This is largely perceived to be esoteric and of limited use.

The unwillingness of some practitioners to accept the educational value of academic approaches to learning was perceived by one academic to be a function of their limited experience of this area. For those working within Higher Education, the real picture was far more complex. Hardy (1987: p. 207) argues that:

> The graduate level sport management curricula must go beyond the level of providing technical competencies-it must also orient graduates to using competencies in the fulfilment of management tasks...Graduate level sport management curricula should produce managers, not entry level technicians.

It is arguable whether either outcome represents a realistic and appropriate aim for higher education. Surely higher education should not be geared towards the development of technical competencies that may become outdated as technology advances. Moreover, given an environment predominantly based in the classroom, it seems unrealistic to claim to produce students who are capable of making a quick and painless transition into the world of management. But as Lawson (1990) argues, it should be possible to provide a program designed to balance the two ideals through the development of appropriate teaching and learning strategies. Coalter *et al.* (1990) concur with this view and argue that there is a general consensus on the need for the development of generic and therefore transferable skills. This would include problem analysis, decision making, resource allocation, administration skills and staff motivation.

The vocational relevance

For those operating in this area of higher education, the real issues revolved around the extent to which courses exhibited a vocational relevance. There was a clear perception, amongst all parties, that this direction had been influenced by the pressures of government, students and, to a lesser extent, industry. There was a general level of agreement that the extent of the movement was debatable, as courses were caught up in a marketing driven competition to attract students. The point was made that changes in the titles of courses did not necessarily correlate with changes in that content. This is highlighted by the CNAA's previous reluctance to endorse courses using the term 'management' in the title. Yet there has been a significant movement in this area during recent years with a proliferation of courses substituting the word 'studies' with 'management' in the award title. Not surprisingly, given the earlier discussions, this elicits serious misgivings amongst both practitioners and academics. One academic respondent argued that a movement towards increased vocationalism has more merit if industry is able to employ the graduates that are produced. For others, this is less of a problem in a mercenary educational environment increasingly dominated by the market. This is demonstrated by the views of another prominent academic from this area:

> The branding of leisure and recreation type courses in higher education is as much, if not more, for the students sake as for potential employers. We have no longer been given the responsibility of thinking of the industry and employment...it's a competitive environment. Our responsibility is to think how we can best attract students and labelling the course leisure and recreation management is an attractive label to students. It's students who perceive it as vocational, it's students who perceive it as giving them a head start in the industry. It's students who know that the name recreation and leisure is associated with a growth industry". (Wolsey, 1995: p.48)

Paradoxically, for some the real dangers for education lie in its claim to be something that it is not. This has real implications for course content, student motivation and the delivery mechanisms that are adopted.

Course development

For academics, there are clear pressures to adopt a more vocationally-oriented approach; but there are many dangers of a move in this direction, of which the dilution of academic content is the main protagonist. This has numerous consequences, not least the decline of leisure studies' continuing struggle to legitimise itself is an area of credible academic study. In this context, one academic argued:

> There is a danger that leisure studies will be still born as a discipline because of this tension between developing theoretically and applying it vocationally. (Wolsey, 1995: p. 48)

The Leisure Studies Association is the only credible academic organisation of its type that operates in Europe and as one respondent argues, it has been unable to fulfil one of their founding aims of developing empirically through application, as well as through the development of a theoretical discourse. In some cases this may reflect an unwillingness to move away from the historical roots of this area of study. Many of the original courses were founded and developed by academics with a disciplinary base firmly focused within the social sciences. For some, this reflects the "welfare oriented, humanistic, left liberal" nature of academic thought in this area. This then feeds through to course provision and reflects the "enormous ideological problem of making money", and thus the public sector orientation of such courses. Reflecting on the differences between the academic and the vocational, one respondent argued:

> "...there is a point at which there's no difference at all...where you have applied courses that are aiming in a particular vocational direction they can reach any academic standard you like, right up to Ph.D. level and still be vocational; so there is a complete compatibility between those two words in a lot of education and the interesting thing is a lot of growth areas in education are of this exact type." (Wolsey, 1995: p. 49)

However, there was a general consensus amongst the academics interviewed that the primary influence upon course development is opportunism and academic interest and not through any real attempt to analyse the nature of the market. When the course in question is more broad in its orientation and academic pretensions, this is less problematic. However, when courses are trading on their ability to transcend theory and practice by the promotion and adoption of a more applied approach, this has real potentialities for both student and industry expectations. The difficulties are highlighted by one academic who stated:

> "...there is an attempt to make it a rational process through the various procedures that we have to negotiate. But it is a balancing act because you have to construct a course that you believe is appealing to your potential clients, useful to the marketplace, because, *unfortunately* we are in the position of training workers to some extent, and is capable of being delivered by a team with a particular set of skills and interests. (Wolsey, 1995: p.49; emphasis added)

What is interesting is the reluctance to accept the movement from academic studies towards the adoption of a more market oriented approach which increasingly demands vocational relevance. As a consequence, although there is the perception that the average student's aptitude towards the traditional academic approach is changing, there is also the recognition that the teaching and learning strategies adopted can prove significant.

Approaches to teaching and learning

The concepts of adult development reviewed above have direct linkage to this area. One respondent believed that the inte–gration of theory with relevant and meaningful practice is the key to good teaching and learning. Of course, the ability to operationalise this ideal is not only subject to the skill of teacher, but also the extent to which parti–cular areas of study are able to be placed within the student's individual frame of reference. The wider the area, the easier this is to accomplish. However, when dealing with management related issues, it is rare that 18 year old students have enough knowledge to locate theoretical approaches within a relevant experiential mindset. For most of those teaching in this area, the ability to contexualise knowledge was seen as a pre-requisite to the effectiveness of courses. Indeed one respondent contends:

> "From the point of view of students, there is no doubt in my mind that what's needed is very clear and consistent application to their focus of interest...if they didn't want that they would all be applying for business studies courses, not leisure management courses. Students want that application, they need that application for interest. It's all very well studying finance or marketing, but if you can hang it on things that they're interested in then it brings it alive". (Wolsey, 1995: p. 51)

There appears to be a general agreement, however, that this is viewed more as a means to an end, as opposed to the specific promulgation of knowledge that would be vocationally helpful outside of the educational sphere. The real focus of higher education is seen as the promotion of more generic skills such as critical reflection. Locating these skills within an area that has interest to the student is seen as a conduit to this process. Paradoxically, it could be argued that this is more difficult to accomplish at a time when higher education is being pressured to introduce higher levels of vocationalism, as this dilutes the ability of an academic education to deliver such broad and transferable skills.

The relationship between theory and practice is of critical importance in order to promote an ability to access the higher levels of conceptual development available through academic study. This tension is reflected throughout the study by academics who argue that mature and post graduate students are better able to rationalise and make sense of theory through an ability to develop meaningful associations with experiential knowledge. It is also argued that mature students are more motivated and are better able to work in a student centred environment.

Interestingly, this suggestion is given further credence, but from a different perspective, by Mel Welch, co-ordinator of the Carnegie National Sports Development Centre. With reference to the training courses he organises for those working in the area of sports development, he argues:

> The idea is that they should be very facilitative in mode...it all comes from the floor. The idea really is that you just pick little bits as they come out and help to put it together. There should be as little lecturing as possible...if you try and run theses courses with the student population, typically within F.E. you've got a problem because they've got little experience to feed in and, therefore, you've got to then deliver more yourself... in the voluntary training you wouldn't even mention the theory because they are interested in the practical application and so the line would be 'here's what you apply' not 'here's why you apply it'. Professional staff need a bit more theory because of need to be more adaptable. (Wolsey, 1995: p. 52)

This demonstrates the effectiveness of courses designed around the needs and expectancies of the learner. However, despite the adoption of an approach to learning that has clear associations with 'training' as opposed to 'education' in its wider sense, courses of this nature are being validated within an academic framework that has equivalence to both undergraduate and postgraduate standards. This effectively places the value of experiential knowledge side by side with that of a more academic nature. It is clear, that for many working in this area, this represents a grave threat to academic standards. Whilst one academic argues for a "recognition and respect for the different areas of knowledge", this is not the same as claiming comparability.

The changing nature of academic standards is also echoed in the discourse relating to disciplinary, multi-disciplinary and interdisciplinary study. Although the majority of those working within higher education accepted that the goal of interdisciplinary study was the ideal, there were clear reservations. For instance, one respondent argued:

> I have real intellectual doubts about multi-disciplinary courses. The people who developed this area largely did traditional, discipline based degrees and I'm worried about people who have a little bit of economics, a little bit of psychology, a little bit of sociology and so on. I think that only the best students will do well on such courses because it's enormously difficult to see the relevance and the links between them. (Wolsey, 1995: p.53)

Such difficulties are seen to be compounded by the claims of interdisciplinary courses and the increasing modularisation of courses. One academic argued that the inevitable by-product of interdisciplinary approaches is "an incredibly superficial scan across a range of issues without any depth of understanding" (Wolsey, 1995: p. 53).

The current picture

The provision of leisure and recreation courses is in a state of flux. The inherent tensions are seen by many to be incongruous with effective higher education and the further promotion of this area as one of legitimate academic study. The crux of such arguments centres on the perceived purpose of higher education. To both academics and practitioners, the real value of this area lies in its ability to promote a generic range of transferable skills, such as critical reflection and problem solving. This is not only viewed in terms of intellectual advancement but is seen to enhance the adaptability of the individual. Specific and more vocational forms of knowledge are seen to be of secondary importance in this regard.

This has led to a developing tension between the academic and the vocational. When placed within the context of an educational system that is increasingly driven by the market, this has led to duplicitous claims by an increasing array of 'recreation management' related courses. Given such a scenario, it is not difficult to see the possibility for a mismatch between the realities of course provision and student expectations. It is clear that courses trading under the banner of vocational relevance, have to give more consideration to the possibility that student and academic interpretations may vary in this regard. Courses must be clearer in their thinking and communication of such approaches to both existing and potential students.

Vocationally oriented courses must seek to develop a range of both personal and interpersonal aptitudes that are germane to the area of study. This is not to undermine the fundamentals of existing courses, but rather to make them more responsive and applicable to the current context by planning the development of student aptitudes within a realistic framework. This can only be achieved through effective planning and by carefully balancing a range of competing but interrelated demands.

If courses claim to be delivering an holistic and interdisciplinary approach, then it is essential that this *raison d'être* is reflected through approaches to curriculum development which would include the development of appropriate and progressively integrated teaching, learning and assessment strategies. This becomes even more important when placed within the context of increasing levels of modularisation driven by external pressures for increased access and choice.

Unfortunately, this research suggests that the contemporary approach is somewhat superficial, in a system where the pressures of time and individual interest conspire against this ultimate goal.

The academic-vocational gap

Paradoxically, neither practitioners or academics appear to value the relevance of an applied approach to this area of study. For practitioners, academic theories are deemed esoteric and lacking in the realities of work epistemologies. To academics, the increased desire to transcend the gap between theory and practice is seen to dilute the quality of the former.

However, any pretensions of vocational courses are stifled by the lack of empirical work in this area. Clearly, more integrative and applied approaches have to be driven by an adequate literature and research base. Unfortunately, although there is movement in this direction, it would be unrealistic to claim the existence of a substantive and applied literature base. This prompted one academic to argue that 'recreation management' cannot regard itself as either a profession or a legitimate academic discipline. However, with increasing moves towards more vocationally relevant forms of provision, it will be important to safeguard and develop the academic integrity of this area. He continued:

> "...we are looking to increase the quality in what we do. If you've got a whole variety of approaches and you're asking the same staff to be increasing quality as well as diversifying the nature of there qualifications, I can't see how you are going to get improved quality under these circumstances. If you concentrated on the core product and really worked hard on improving the quality of that, I think you would achieve far more than just opening up the market to this confusing degree of choice". (Wolsey, 1995: p. 63)

This relates to concerns around a number of issues, not least increasing levels of access and modularisation in tandem with the potential impact of NVQs; a development which was universally agreed to be inappropriate to higher education in their current format.

Creating a balance

With few exceptions, the perceived differences and mis-conceptions of both practitioners and academics are serving to stifle attempts to promote the integration of theory and practice. As one respondent argued:

> "Ideally there should be a meeting in the middle, but the trouble is, there very often isn't and there's also a great distrust across the two. In order to overcome that there needs to be a lot of education both ways". (Wolsey, 1995: p. 64)

The stereotypical views of both practitioners and academics can only be to the detriment of students who choose to study in this area. The ability to tolerate and understand the changing world around us, is contingent on the development of appropriate strategies for dealing with such ambiguities. The ability to reflect upon and learn from the environment should, therefore, be promoted as one of the central aims of teaching and learning strategies in this area.

Individual student differences lead to the conclusion that there is no best way to facilitate learning in this area. However, it is ironic that the academics interviewed almost universally accepted that a greater experiential knowledge of the work environment was of considerable benefit to the conceptual development of mature students. The ability to rationalise the changing world around us is contingent upon the development of appropriate strategies for dealing with such ambiguities. The ability to reflect upon and learn from the environment should, therefore, be promoted as one of the central aims of any vocationally oriented undergraduate course. Clearly, individual student differences will dictate that those with superior intellectual abilities will be disadvantaged if they are unable to draw the appropriate associations between theory and practice. In this sense, when dealing with more applied approaches to learning and development, the practitioner holds the advantage. By utilising past experience to illuminate theory, the practitioner or student is in a good position to develop conceptually. These models will be informed by theory, but more importantly, will be related to the context in which they are working. This concurs with Knowles's (1983) ideas about the nature of adult learning and the instrumentality of learning and thus the motivation to learn. It is clear that the more concepts are divorced from reality and practical application in its wider sense, the more students are likely to become disaffected.

However, this should not mean the abandonment of an academic approach to learning. Attempts should be made to reduce the gap between the level of abstraction required and the ability to locate this within examples of practical significance and thus comprehension. In this way, by using past experience to illuminate theory, the student is in a good position to develop his/her own conceptual models. These would be informed by theory and appropriate to the furtherment of knowledge that has both vocational and academic value. This is surely the key to the development of the mythical reflective and reflexive practitioner.

Future directions

Educational excellence should not be viewed as a battle between academic rigour and vocational relevance. Such areas should be viewed as symbiotic, not mutually exclusive. It is wrong to hold up such dichotomies as black or white, right or wrong. They are simply bi-polar representations of the same learning continuum. Theory should inform practice and vice-versa, on a dynamic basis. The prejudices and pre-conceptions held by those who espouse such viewpoints, have stifled a more developmental and progressive approach to both learning and knowledge. As such closer industrial links should be welcomed and more actively pursued. Future progression is best served through an integration of the two schools of thought. In this context, far from leading to a dilution of the two areas, a greater fusion would generate value by plugging the gaps of each approach, whilst still retaining the integrity and appropriateness of each.

Notes

1 Michael Clarke is the Chief Executive of the Local Government Management Board.

2 'Yates Report' is the venacular for The Recreation Management Training Committee's Final Report.

3 This point is supported by Lawson (1990) who argues that research rather than the realities of work drives many undergraduate programs in this area.

4 Tim Boswell was commenting in his capacity as the Parliamentary Under Secretary of State for Further and Higher Education. The figures are quoted from *The Times*: 'BTEC at Work Supplement', October 4, 1993.

5 NFMED [National Forum for Management Education and Development] is the Lead Body in the area of Management and Supervision

6 "Training" is defined in the Yates Report (DOE, 1984: p. v) as "any formal program of instruction in management skills, whether provided by employers and/or at an educational or other institution".

7 "Education" is defined in the Yates Report (DOE, 1984: p. v) as "generally a much broader process, where the end objective is not usually narrowly identified, and is not solely directed towards performance in a particular job".

8 The empirial research evidence repoted in this paper is taken from Wolsey (1995).

References and bibliography

Allman, P. (1983) need complete reference

Bacon, W., and Buswell, J. (1994) *Directory of U.K. Courses 1994/95 (Degree and post Graduate Level)*. ILAM/LSA/Higher Education Standing Conference on Leisure, Recreation and Sport.

Boswell, T. (1993) 'Helping Britain compete in a demanding world', *BTEC at work*, Supplement of *The Times*, 4 October: p. 111.

Clarke, M. (1991) *Standards for managers: Executive guide.* LutonL Local Government Managers Board.

CNAA (1991) *Review of sport, recreation and leisure degree courses.* London: CNAA, August.

——— (1992a) Review of management education. London: CNAA, October.

——— (1992b) *Staff development through industrial secondment: With special reference to consumer and leisure studies degree courses*, Project Report Number 40. London: CNAA.

Coalter, F., and Potter, J. (1990) *A study of 1985 graduates from sport, recreation and leisure studies.* London: Sports Council.

Coalter, F., Potter, J., and McNulty, A. (1990) *Recreation management training needs.* London: Sports Council.

Cousins, R. L., Dower, M., Roberts, S., and Verney, S. (1980) *Recreation management and training in the non-public sectors: A report to the Recreation Management Training Committee*. University of Edinburgh: Dartington Amenity Research Trust, Tourism and Recreation Research Unit.

Department of the Environment (1984) *Recreation Management Training Committee; Final Report.* London: HMSO. (The Yates Report)

De Sensi, J., Kelley, D., Dale Blanton, M. D., and Beitel, P. (1990) 'Sport management curricular evaluation and assessment: A multifaceted approach', *Journal of Sports Management*, No. 4: pp. 31-58.

Fleming, I. (1994) *Training needs analysis for the leisure industry.* Harlow: Longman.

Forman N. (1994) 'Forging ahead with skills investment', *The Times Higher Educational Supplement*,, April 1: p.11.

Furnham, A. (1994) 'Do you need management education?', *The Sunday Times*, November 6: p. 6.8.

Glew, G. (1991) *Research and scholarly activity in support of Honours Degree teaching (with special reference to consumer and leisure studies*). London, CNAA.

Hardy, S. (1987) 'Graduate curriculums in sports management: The need for a business orientation', QUEST No. 39: pp. 207-216.

Hymas, C. (1994) 'New exams face death by jargon', *The Sunday Times* October 30: p. 1.7.

ILAM (1994a) Educational Bulletin Sheet No.8.

ILAM (1994b) *ILAM guidelines for students seeking careers within the leisure industry*. Reading: ILAM.

Institute of Manpower Studies (1987) *Employment studies in tourism and leisure*. London: Institute of Manpower Studies, December.

Jamieson, L. M. (1987) 'Competency-based approaches to sport management', *Journal of Sports Management*, Vol. 1, No. 1: pp. 48-56.

Kelley, R., Beitel, A., De Sensi, J., and Dale Plantou, M. (1994) 'Undergraduate and graduate sport management curricular models: A perspective', *Journal of Sports Management*, Vol. 18, No. 2, pp. 93-101, May.

Knowles, M. (1983) 'Androgogy: An emerging technology for adult learning', in M. Tight (ed) *Adult learning and education*. London: Croom Helm/ Open University.

Lawson, H. A. (1990) 'Beyond positivism: Research practice and undergraduate professional education', QUEST No. 42: pp. 161-183.

Long, J. A., and Coppock J. T. (1979) Management Training for Leisure and Recreation: A Review of Previous Research and Existing Literature. University of Edinburgh: Tourism and Recreation Research Unit, Working Paper Series.

McKinney, G. R. (ed) (1984) *Yates and after: The management of recreation management and training* (LSA Newsletter Supplement D). Eastbourne: Leisure Studies Association.

Meizirow J. (1983) 'A critical theory of adult learning and education' in M. Tight (ed) (1983) *Adult learning and education*. (place of publication?) Croom Helm/Open University.

Moggridge, M. (1992) 'Under new management', *The Leisure Manager*, Vol. 10, No. 8: (August): pp. 11-18.

Molyneux Committee (1969) *Sports Council: Professional training for recreation management* (Molyneux Report). London: Sports Council.

National Economic Development Council (1991) Working For Pleasure, Tourism and Leisure Tomorrow. London: National Economic Development Office, Jan. 1990.

Potter, J. (1994) *A guide to jobs and qualifications in sport and recreation*. St Albans: John Potter Publications in association with ILAM.

Preston, B. (1993) 'Sowing the seeds of change', Supplement *BTEC at work*, *The Times*, October 3: pp. xi.

Sport and Recreation Lead Body (1989) *Mapping sport and recreation*, 7th June. London: A & M Training Services.

Tennant M. (1986) 'An evaluation of Knowles's theory of adult learning', *International Journal of Lifelong Learning*, Vol. 5, No. 2, pp. 113-122.

——— (1988) *Psychology and adult learning*. London: Routledge.

Tight M. (ed) (1983) *Adult learning and education*. London: Croom Helm/ Open University.

Torkildsen, G. (1986) *Leisure and recreation management* (2nd edition). London: E & FN Spon.

Wolsey, C. M. (1995) From Theory to Practice; An Investigation Into The Provision of Recreation Management Courses Within Higher Education. University of Nottingham: Unpublished M(Ed.) Dissertation.

Woodhead, C. (1994) 'Why the head must rule the heart', *The Sunday Times*, October 30: p.6.18.

Does Education Need New Leisure Courses? Does the Leisure Industry Want the Graduates?

Hugh Mannerings

Buckinghamshire College

Introduction

My interest in the subject of leisure education and industry requirements comes from my experience of recently graduating with an HND and Degree in leisure management, and seeking employment. More specifically, I am concerned with the problems currently facing many graduates now looking for jobs within the industry. Over the last five to six years the number of places available for students wishing to undertake a variety of leisure studies courses in Further and Higher Education has seen a dramatic increase, also reflected in the expansion in the number of leisure related courses now currently being offered. A directory of leisure courses on offer within the UK (Bacon and Buswell, 1995) reports that in the 54 colleges and universities that contributed to the first annual publication, 73 first degree courses were on offer with a total approximate intake of 3,500 students.

The Government White Paper 'A New Framework' (HMSO, 1991) was produced to abolish the division which existed between universities and polytechnics and colleges, and to establish a single framework for Higher Education which had in the past halted the expansion of Higher Education. This enabled colleges and universities to expand the number of people entering Higher Education. Consequently, from a position in 1979 when only 1 in 8 people went into Higher Education, this figure was increased to 1 in 7 with the 1987 Government White Paper, and today the figure is 1 in 5, with a medium-term goal of 1 in 3 18-19 year olds entering Higher Education. While this is arguably a step towards increasing the education of the population in line with the advancement within society and technology, what the 1991 white paper has effectively done is to start a process of devaluing Further and Higher Educational qualifications in terms of their currency value in the employment market. This is not to say that Further and Higher Education qualifications are easier to attain. On the contrary, it is just that their value becomes diminished because of the increasing number of people who have them.

During the 1980s the public's general perception of employment for graduates across all disciplines appeared very good, and employers seemed to regard a degree as an extremely important achievement. Thus the 1980s became a 'graduates market' where graduates were able to chose from a wide cross section of new jobs that were created. In addition, the economic climate over the last five years may have also contributed to an increase in the number of students entering Higher Education. A lack of job prospects and the ever increasing demand from industry for more educated and qualified people may also have encouraged more young people into Higher Education.

Why study leisure?

Why then such an interest in the study of Leisure Management? Is it merely due to the expanding number of new leisure facilities and attractions or is it because leisure courses are new and fashionable to study?

It seems likely that the increase in student numbers and leisure-related courses is related — at least in part — to an increase in the size and scope of the leisure industry, which now includes travel, tourism, recreation management (facility management), countryside recreation, heritage attractions and virtually any other business which can be classified as providing a leisure-related product or service. The leisure industry is now four times larger that the motor industry, employing 3 million people (13.5% of all UK employees), accounting in 1994 for £110 billion of annual consumer expenditure (ILAM factsheet 95/8). With such growth it is therefore not surprising to discover that more and more people want to study leisure, and that more and more colleges and universities are providing courses to meet this demand.

Students in the market place

From information gained from interviews with key personnel within the leisure industry, it seems that in the late 1980s young graduates were being appointed into positions normally filled by people with a number of years experience, mainly at supervisory level and sometimes higher, creating posts such as Sports Development Officer, Marketing Officer and other job titles which has previously been undertaken by the Assistant Manager or Manager.

The 1987 Compulsory Competitive Tendering (CCT) legislation has had a very dramatic effect on employment, and this began the streamlining of personnel within organisations and facilities. There are many arguments about the benefits and disadvantages of CCT, but the realisation of CCT is that leisure management is a serious occupation and for many a profession (Soucie, 1995). The introduction of CCT effectively shut the door on easy employment within the public sector of the leisure industry. Evidently employers evaluated their needs and requirements in terms of skills. This first percolated down to those who could offer many additional coaching qualifications, thus reducing the amount required to be spent on staff training. Consequently many school leavers were marginalised in their pursuit of leisure-related employment by graduates who were employed at introductory level: e.g., centre attendant/senior centre attendant.

This influx of students probably started in about 1988/89, yet preliminary research suggests that two years (BTEC, Higher National Diploma) or three years (Degree) later (graduating 1990/1) these same graduates entered the jobs market only to discover that their chances of employment were possibly at a lower entry level than they might have expected when they first started their course.

A snap-shot of the perceptions of graduates in leisure at Buckinghamshire College was compiled through the collection of data using a detailed questionnaire sent out to Leisure Management graduates from 1993 and 1994. This indicated that graduates would have wanted more practical experience or work placement incorporated with the structure of their studies. Yet Farnborough College of Technology will no longer be running its well-established sandwich course in leisure due to the prevalence of the view among students that a 'year out' is unpopular.

Interestingly, the loss of the year's placement may be offset by the part-time employment of many students in the leisure industry. Importantly too, in order for students to stand any chance of long-term, full-time employment within the leisure industry, it seems they must be currently employed in the industry in a part time capacity, so that when they graduate they might stand a better chance of gaining full time employment.

This is echoed by a spokesperson from First Leisure plc who indicated that her organisation does not consider anyone for interview who has not had practical relevant work experience within a commercial leisure organisation. First Leisure's criteria for employment within their organisation are as follows:

1) Candidates must be over 18, mobile and have a clean driving licence.
2) Academically — candidates must show evidence of competence in Maths and English to GCSE level.
3) A potential graduate must have relevant work experience.

It was further indicated that there were definite vocational qualification requirements. That is, arts and science graduates would be equal contenders alongside Leisure Management graduates. This begins to explain why there is such fierce competition amongst graduates for positions: in the case of First Leisure, an increase from the usual 40 or 50 applications for an advertised position to three or four hundred. First Leisure claim to be looking for a holistic graduate with a broad capacity to take an overview, of considerable intellect, well developed interpersonal skills, extremely focused ambition, having a realistic outlook on the leisure industry. These competencies and skills are reflected in the criteria used in the evaluation of the interviews. As the First leisure representative remarked:

> "Yes, the qualification is important ... but ... the ability to analyse, the ability to make decisions, to compare and contrast... the analytical skills are far more important, and the conceptual skills, than the piece of paper at the end."

This is, of course, only the view of one company, but First Leisure's view of most degrees was that they were aimed at the local authority sector, and that they were not commercially orientated.

Preliminary data obtained from degree graduates of the Buckinghamshire College 1993/4

Questionnaires were sent out to graduates from two years completing 1993 and 1994 of the BA in Leisure Management programme at the Buckinghamshire College the following results have been obtained. Further to those data already described, the questionnaire survey also indicated some important patterns and trends amongst BA Leisure Management graduates. Somewhat disappointingly, though not entirely surprisingly, the response rate was only 29.6%. Of these, over 80% had found full time employment leaving the remainder either unemployed, taking time out for travelling or currently in higher education undertaking postgraduate courses. Of those in full time employment, more than half had secured posts outside the leisure industry. It may be no coincidence that amongst leisure studies graduates working in leisure, the average graduate salary was in the region of £8,000 to £11,000. Outside the leisure industry, those who had studied leisure reported an average graduate salary of £10,000-11,000.

Preliminary research suggests that working in the leisure industry is not as glamorous as many graduates perceived it to be, and the comments of some respondents provide insight into their perceptions of the interface between Higher Education and employment in the leisure industry:

> "I feel that the course did not offer enough opportunities to gain practical experience.... Considering that I only did 13 hours max a week I think that the college could assist students to organise work experience during free time. I feel quite bitter that on a job specification my degree is only considered as a "desirable" skill."

> "It was very difficult trying to find a job in the travel industry as I had no practical experience and not many companies were willing to train me. It would have been useful to have been offered a work placement for perhaps 4 to 6 months as part of the course or to

have had a number of companies that were willing to train graduates to appropriate positions. My degree has helped me move up in position in the company, but I had to start from the bottom due to my lack of any practical experience."

"Since graduating I have obvious frustration with the *no job—no experience—no job* cycle. A year-out, year-in industry, I feel, would have given us some hands on experience that I think would have helped us afterwards. The careers area at college could have been a bit more helpful."

"All jobs I have applied for reply that, although I have excellent qualifications, I have no experience (even though I worked in the leisure industry for two years at UCI cinemas and many summer jobs). Perhaps a year out in employment should be incorporated into the course...."

"...more information, perhaps designated seminars/lecturers about work and careers for students when they leave college would have been most valuable. As the Tourism/Leisure industry is so vast, I also believe a more specialised course would be much more beneficial and would prepare you a lot more for a career. If I were aware of the many different jobs/careers in this industry I would have been able (and be able) to target a specific area."

"I had an excellent 3 years at Bucks college, but I do not think the course properly prepares you for the outside world. Practice is very different to theory. I believe they should incorporate some work experience."

"The HND and Top Up Degree both tended to be very reactive to the leisure industry. Whilst preaching about the need for pro-activity the courses tended to be out of touch with up to date leisure developments."

"The course did not prepare for employment, giving false expectations."

Conclusion

If an over-production of graduates is recognised, educational establishments must look at their courses in order to meet what they perceive as a demand for graduates by the leisure industry and a demand for courses by undergraduates. It is questionable whether Higher Education understands fully what the leisure industry wants from a graduate, and whether the undustry actually wants the people who have graduated in leisure-related courses. We should ask, 'what are the aims and objectives of a leisure related course?', and 'what will each student have achieved at the end of the course?'. Many students expect to be able to gain a job within the leisure industry but preliminary research shows that such expectations are often unrealistic. With only 40% securing full time employment with the leisure industry after having graduated with one to two years of experience, it may be that after having studied the subject many people find that it is simply not for them, and decide to seek alternative employment outside the industry.

References

Bacon, W. and Buswell, J. (eds) (1995) Directory of UK leisure courses 1994/5 (Degree and Postgraduate Level) Institute of Leisure and Amenity Management (ILAM).

Farnham, D. and Horton, S. (eds) (1993) 'The new public service managerialism: An Assessment', in D. Farnham and S. Horton (eds) *Managing the new public services*. London: Macmillan.

HMSO (1987) *Higher education: meeting the challenge*. HMSO: Government White Paper on Higher Education.

HMSO (1991) A new framework. HMSO: Government White Paper on Higher Education.

Leisure Consultants (1995) *Leisure Forecasts 1995-1999 Vol. 1.* Sudbury.

Soucie, D. (1995) 'But is it really a proper job?', Recreation, ISRM, March : pp. 16-22.

The Jocks, the Suits and Leisure Management: Towards a New Paradigm

Clare Brindley

Manchester Metropolitan University

Introduction

Over the last decade there has been a proliferation of leisure related courses within the UK, many of which are management orientated (Potter, 1993; UCAS, 1994). Yet, the ownership of these courses is diffuse, ranging from Hotel and Catering Departments to Sports Science Departments — leisure management is not the preserve of the business school.

Has the time now come for a new paradigm for leisure management within higher education? (Edginton, Davis and Hensley, 1994). If leisure is to strengthen its academic programmes, is it time that educationalists promoted a more consistent delivery approach ? After all if you want to study medicine it is usual to study at a medical school; therefore, it would seem to follow that if you want a management career you should study at a business school.

It is the premise of this paper that the process of developing a consistent professional focus for higher education leisure management courses is hampered by the 'territoriality' (*ibid.*) exhibited by sports and leisure departments ('The Jocks') and business and management departments ('The Suits'). If we explore the areas of expertise that we as academics and employers expect students to exhibit, perhaps it can be decided into whose domain (Chelladurai, 1994) leisure management should fall and thus ensure a stronger product identity for the discipline of leisure management.

Crewe and Alsager Faculty of Manchester Metropolitan University has recently undergone a review of its undergraduate business, leisure and sports courses and these developments are outlined in the paper to provide a platform for discussion regarding the tensions inherent in establishing a departmental focus for leisure management courses.

Industry expectations

The Institute of Leisure and Amenity Management (ILAM, 1994) has in its *Guidelines for Students Seeking Careers within the Leisure Industry* focused on the abilities graduate managers should exhibit and on how students should evaluate leisure management courses. Within the guidelines it is stated that students should not be confused when the terms, "tourism, recreation or sport" are used "since these are merely subdivisions of the overall professional discipline of Leisure Management" (ILAM, 1994: p. 1). Moreover, the guidelines recommend that leisure management courses should contain the following key areas: marketing, quality service management, operational management, law, finance and human resource management — all subject areas that are found in business departments. The need for graduates to have a knowledge of strategic issues is also highlighted, again a business area.

A review of recent job advertisements in the magazine *Leisure Opportunities* reveals that employers are looking for applicants who are knowledgeable of the key areas outlined by ILAM. For example: a knowledge of marketing to degree standard, and of financial procedures, a good understanding of quality service, commercial acumen, the ability to manage a small team etc. It would appear that business and management qualifications are a valued commodity to current recruiters.

However, as we all know, the current job market is hardly in a secure position and educationalists are responding to employer requests for multi-skilled workers who do not expect to be employed in one 'job for life'. Transferable skills, competencies and common skills are now all familiar phrases to those working in further and higher education.

It has been argued that one strength of a General National Vocational Qualification (GNVQ) "is that it recognises the future realities, the need for employees to be able to transfer their skills". (Holmes, 1995: p. 3). Employers want "people who are literate, numerate, can solve problems and who can communicate effectively" (Holmes, 1995: p. 4). If transferable skills are the way forward it could be argued that those embarking on a management career should be equipped with transferable management skills i.e. the core business areas. This view is supported by Chelladurai (1994: p. 27), who argued:

> Our responsibility to our students and community in general would require that we provide them with competencies applicable across different contexts so that they can, if necessary, find employment in other managerial fields.

Thus, the leisure management graduate should be at ease in and have the ability to cope with a career in other management sectors — a real possibility if course provision follows ILAM guidelines.

Furthermore, employers' desires for students with a business focus is not confined to the UK. The American Alliance for Health, Physical

Education, Recreation and Dance (AAHPERD) 1995 Leadership Development Conference, held in Washington DC argued that its survival depended on the organisation's membership becoming "more savvy to the techniques and tactics of the business world" (AAHPERD, July/August 1995: p. 2). This illustrates once more leisure professionals' recognition of the importance of business and management skills.

Academic expectations

According to Potter (1993: p. 5) "the expansion of qualifications has tended to mirror the ad hoc development of the industry". Hence, a quick sortie through the *Directory of Higher Education* will illustrate the diversity of curricular innovation in the area. Higher National Diplomas (HND), Higher National Certificates, Bachelor of Arts (BA) and Bachelor of Science (BSc) courses are all available. Course titles include: Leisure Studies, Leisure Management, Hospitality and Tourism Management, Heritage Management, Tourism Business Management, Leisure Policy and Administration, Recreation, Leisure Marketing. Heinz's slogan of "fifty seven varieties" could be applied to leisure higher education courses!

When departmental ownership of courses is investigated the picture becomes even more complicated. Leisure management courses "are located in a variety of institutional contexts" (ILAM, 1994: p. 3), in departments ranging from Planning, Physical Education and Geography to Management. Often, the location of courses is a the result of the institution's historical growth and development or as Harrison (1984: p. 37) argues, "too often new courses have been developed for reasons of convenience rather than for fresh vocational adequacy". The ethos of the host department will also direct course content and philosophy.

Though development of leisure courses has been rapid and from an outsiders viewpoint, ad hoc, a leaf through any course validation document should provide a more substantive rationale for the qualification's existence. Student and employer demand, research expertise and resource capability are frequently quoted as reasons for course development. It is at this development stage that tensions concerning what actually are the components of a higher education leisure management course often surface — a tension mirroring that experienced by the developers of GNVQs. Within recent editions of the ILAM Leisure Management Bulletin there has been a debate about GNVQs and the compromises that are made between for example, leisure and tourism.

What compromises are currently being made in higher education leisure courses and are these compromises made from an objective stance? As way of an exemplar of academic expectations and compromises, the recent developments at Crewe and Alsager Faculty of Manchester Metropolitan University will be discussed.

Developments at Crewe and Alsager

In 1990, the Department of Business and Management had in its portfolio of courses a large and successful HND in Business and Finance. Students undertaking the Course could follow options in Sport, Tourism, Leisure and Recreation, provided by the Department of Sports Science and the Division of Environmental Science. Due to the size of the HND and the national trend for converting HNDs to degrees a series of proposals for degree programmes was instituted. In 1991 a BA (Honours) Business, Sport and Recreation was validated and in 1992 a BA (Honours) Business, Leisure and Recreation degree was validated. Both courses were two year 'top-up' degrees for HND holders and were 'owned' by the Department of Business and Management. Typically, the new courses reflected the historical development of the institution.

Whilst the new degrees were compatible with the University's Credit Accumulation Transfer System (CATS), the HND was not, as it had been validated when the Faculty was still a college of higher education. Hence, at the end of 1994 a decision was made to review the HND to make it compatible with the CATS framework. Moving the HND from an eight unit to a six unit CATS-compatible course was a radical step. If the HND course needed to change, so did the degree courses it underpinned. Thus, the Department of Business and Management undergraduate portfolio was completely overhauled. In March 1995 the following new courses were validated (see Figure 1):

- HND Business with Sport
- HND Business with Leisure
- BA (Honours) Business with Sport (Three year)
- BA (Honours) Business with Leisure (Three year)
- BA Business with Sport (HND top up)
- BA Business with Leisure (HND top up)

The process of validating these new courses illustrated tensions that colleagues developing leisure courses in other institutions are probably all too familiar with. It appeared that most of the tensions came from 'territoriality' (Edginton, Davis and Hensley, 1994: p. 56). Whilst ownership of the new courses rested with the Department of Business and Management, input from, for instance, sports psychologists, sports scientists, environmentalists and tourism academics from outside the Department was required. Developing a course team ethos proved difficult. Even though the Department had a base of well qualified and experienced staff in the key business skills highlighted by ILAM (see above),they were viewed with suspicion by those staff who identified themselves as the 'leisure specialists'. Leisure and sports courses being organised by a business department was an anathema to many. It seemed that the ability to pole vault, tie a reef knot or run a mile was the pre-requisite for developing a leisure course.

Figure 1 New courses (boldface titles refer to leisure/sport subject specialisms

BA (Hons) Business with Leisure structure

Year 1	*Finance & Accounting+*	*Introduction to Statistics +*	*Behaviour in Organisations+*	*Economics+*	*Information Handling*	**Foundations in Leisure**
Year 2	*Cost & Management Accounting*	*Managing Organisations+*	*Marketing Strategy+*	*Business Legal Environment*	**Tourism**	**Outdoor Leisure Management**
Year 3	Quantitative Business Decision Making	Strategic Management+	Individual Project+	**Leisure Marketing**	**Leisure & Recreation Management**	**Contemporary Leisure Issues**

BA (Hons) Business with Sport structure

Year 1	*Finance & Accounting+*	*Introduction to Statistics +*	*Behaviour in Organisations+*	*Economics+*	*Information Handling*	**Effective Coaching**
Year 2	*Cost & Management Accounting*	*Managing Organisations*	*Marketing Strategy+*	*Business Legal Environment*	**Physiology of Performance**	**Progressive Coaching**
Year 3	Quantitative Business Decision Making	Strategic Management+	Individual Project+	**Leisure Marketing**	**Issues in Sport**	

A division between 'the Suits' (i.e. the business staff) and 'the Jocks' (i.e. the leisure and sports staff) became evident. Many heated debates took place before compromise solutions between the two groupings could be reached. When reached, some of these compromises were as a result of resource implications rather than a meeting of minds. Debates covered topics of balance (for example, too much business, not enough sport, and differing views on research methodologies). However, perhaps what was even more interesting was the way business skills and knowledge crept into the first drafts of syllabi for leisure and sport units. Acknowledgement by the leisure and sport specialists of the wider picture was beginning to emerge. As Chelladurai (1994: p. 26) argues:

> ... the problems of the coach can be viewed as the problems of management ... boundaries are permeable.

The new courses may not be ideal but some barriers have been broken down. For instance, leisure marketing is taught by a 'Suit' and the courses recognise that a sports or leisure graduate needs core business competencies, not as an adjunct to a specialist interest but as a foundation. Moreover, the undergraduate model delivered at Crewe and Alsager recognises pathways that put sports and leisure specialisms on par with the traditional professional routes of marketing, accounting and information technology. Such pathways reflect student opinion. Students expressed a desire for courses that gave them the opportunity to follow an area of specialist interest (for example, tourism) but that also prepared them for an uncertain lifetime career path. Transferable management skills were thus seen as important.

The Crewe and Alsager case-study is admittedly a single one, drawn from personal professional experience. The debate on what does or should constitute a leisure management course must, though, be informed by such case-studies.

The current situation

Crewe's new leisure courses may be similar to some other institution's leisure provision, but it will be very different to others. The 'territoriality' battles in other institutions may have resulted in different results and thus in different course components. Thus, the general picture of higher education leisure provision is fragmented. Such fragmentation exhibited by the plethora of course under the general banner of leisure is proving confusing to the marketplace. How can we expect a practitioner to compare one leisure graduate with another ? They would not be comparing like with like. Furthermore, as Potter (1993: p. 5) observes, "one result of the haphazard expansion is that individuals keen to work in sport and recreation have been confused as to the best route to take". Have the territorial divisions, most of which are historical in nature, caused this confusion? Confusion is a weakness and one which makes leisure courses susceptible to criticism from other academic disciplines. If the maintenance of territorial divisions is allowed to continue we may hang by our own petards. As responsive institutions we must listen to the marketplace and what is required is graduates with business skills. A job is no longer a job for life and it is only fair that students are given the opportunity to study for a varied career path.

The future

As higher education institutions, "...we should work to strengthen our academic programs in terms of their relevance and currency to societal and institutional needs" (Edginton, Davis and Hensley, 1994: p. 53). Innovative curricular development need not be stifled by a prescriptive approach to leisure management but a focus for the subject area is required. "Territoriality needs to give way to newer points of interaction" (*ibid.*). This view is supported by Chelladurai (1994: p. 26) who states that "it is not profitable ... to get into any kind of argument over territorial right". Indeed, it would be "imprudent... to cut connections with the disciplines that support the field" (*ibid.*). The confusion apparent in the market place must not be allowed to fester, for the wide distribution of a diluted product offering can generate vulnerability. What is required is a streamlined product and one which is protected from failure. In America, health, physical education and leisure studies courses have been reduced, reorganised or dissolved (Krahenbuhl, 1990) a scenario that we do not wish repeated in the United Kingdom. However, recent comments by Professor Alan Smith of Manchester University give cause for concern:

> There are some excellent vocational degrees but also bogus ones. This ...is true of engineering courses not recognised by the professional institutions. And it is true of tourism courses which I suspect do not enhance the chance of getting a job. (*The Observer*, 3 September, 1995)

Is the writing on the wall for the credibility of leisure courses ? If individual subject concerns override the need for a more consistent approach to the business and management dimensions of contexts of leisure course content, the answer may well be *yes*.

Leisure's valuable contribution to higher education must not be eroded by internal squabbles. Instead we must ensure its recognition as a valid academic discipline by developing a new paradigm that blends in expertise from what ILAM refers to as the 'sub-divisions' with business and management disciplines. Business and management departments are in an ideal position to provide the focus and direction required by our customers, prospective undergraduates and the industry practitioners. It is a tall order perhaps, but if we apply the strategic expertise practitioners are requiring from their managers and the synergy that we require from our students we may indeed provide a way forward. Let the 'Suits' and the 'Jocks' unite towards a respected future!

Business is not mounting a take-over — the Suits do not want to overpower the Jocks. But teamwork and co-operation is required to make the area of leisure a powerful discipline. The diverse nature of the industry makes consistency difficult, but medicine has many diverse fields and yet graduates at medical schools follow broadly similar courses that are nationally recognised. Specialisms are to be applauded if they exist in a more strongly developed framework.

References

AAHPERD (1995) 'President's message', *Update*, July/August: p. 2.

Chelladurai, P. (1994) 'Defining the field', *Recreation*, Vol. 53, No. 8: pp. 21-27.

Edginton, C. R., Davis, T. M. and Hensley L. D. (1994) 'Trends in higher education: implications for health, physical education, and leisure studies', *The Journal of Physical Education, Recreation and Dance*, Vol. 65, No. 7: pp. 51-57.

Harrison, F. (1984) 'A new degree in recreation management', Discussion paper. Loughborough University.

Holmes, G. (1995) 'GNVQs are the answer', *The Leisure Manager Bulletin*, July 1995: pp. 3 -4.

ILAM Education and Training (1994) *ILAM guidelines for students seeking careers within the leisure industry*. Reading: ILAM.

Krahenbuhl, G. S. (1990) 'Physical education in American higher education', *Academy Papers*, Vol. 24: pp. 89 -92.

Potter, J. (1993) *A guide to jobs and qualifications in sport and recreation*. John Potter Publications.

UCAS (University and Colleges Admissions Services (1994) 'University and College Entrance'.

Selective Index

The referencing conventions of the Leisure Studies Association comprise a variant of the Harvard, rather than Vancouver, style. This involves the citation within the text (in parentheses) of all references. Authors cited in the book can therefore be located with great ease by consulting both the main body of the text and the list of references at the end of each chapter. Details of these are not replicated in this Index.

The book is divided into thematically-led sections, with clear titles for each chapter and in most cases clear sub-headings within chapters. The information so clearly available at these levels of title is not replicated in this index.

Many contemporary Indexes are comprehensive technologically determined listings of terms. This Selective Index is the opposite of that. It prioritises some themes, concepts and interpretations (rather than topics, names and facts) which are not obviously signalled in the contents list and chapter and section headings; and which, in a few cases, recur across the different chapters.

G

H

I

K

L